HIRD EDITION

Business Accounting I

Frank Wood
B.Sc. (Econ.), F.C.A.

THIRD EDITION

Business Accounting I

Longman
London and New York

Longman Group Limited London

Associated companies, branches and representatives throughout the world

Published in the United States of America by Longman Inc., New York

First published 1967
Second Edition 1972
Sixth impression 1977
Third Edition 1979

British Library Cataloguing in Publication Data

Wood, Frank
Business accounting.
Vol. I—3rd ed.
1. Accounting
I. Title
657 HF5635 78-40835

ISBN 0-582-41560-8

Printed in Great Britain by
Richard Clay (The Chaucer Press) Ltd, Bungay, Suffolk

VOLUME ONE

Contents

Preface to the Third Edition

This textbook has been written so that a very thorough introduction to Accounting is covered in two volumes. The fact that this task has been split between two volumes is a recognition of the fact that, for many students, their grounding in the subject will not have to be as exhaustive as those who will carry on with professional examinations. Volume 1 fully covers the requirements of the General Certificate of Education at Ordinary level, as well as the first year examinations for many other examining bodies.

The questions set at the end of the relevant chapters are either from the examination papers of the above or have been specially devised. I have regarded it as a duty to ensure that all questions set can be answered by students who have worked through the text up to the chapter concerned. Questions involving needless complications have been avoided, emphasis being given to those which bring out a basic understanding of accounting.

There are some innovations for a book written at this level. First, the basic concepts and conventions of accounting are dealt with in a separate chapter, Chapter 7, as it is felt to be of paramount importance to state the assumptions on which the whole of financial accounting is based. Second, an attempt has been made in Chapter 12 to relate the accounting that a student meets in his studies with the actual modern methods of processing data.

Emphasis has been laid on the 'why' of accounting rather than merely to explain 'how'. In doing this the uses which management and others make of the accounting information are discussed. At the same time out-of-date methods have been mentioned but have not been used. These include such items as writing 'To' and 'By' in ledger accounts, charging depreciation to asset accounts, and marshalling the assets in the order of least permanence in the balance sheets of concerns other than banks.

This edition varies from the second edition in several ways. Obviously updating of the material already in the book has been made, but there have also been some important additions. The major additions are shown in the forms of Appendices, so that the chapter numbers remain unaltered. Lecturers and teachers all over the world have become used to various topics being contained in a chapter having a certain number, and I would not wish to unnecessarily confuse them by altering the chapter numbers throughout the book. Each Appendix is shown at the back of the chapter bearing the first number of the Appendix. Thus Appendix 9.1 is shown at the back of Chapter 9, and so on. A reference to the Contents page will show the reader what is contained in the various Appendices.

The demand from students and teachers for more questions seems inexhaustible. I have therefore put more questions at the back of each chapter. Some of the questions are for the students to attempt on their own, if they so wish, and the answers are to be found at the back of the book. There are also additional questions with the suffix 'A', for which answers are not shown. Such questions enable teachers and lecturers to set questions for classwork and homework, and can consequently gauge properly whether a student has thoroughly understood a particular topic or whether more work needs to be done. The fact that extra questions have been inserted has meant that a considerable number of the original questions in the second edition have been renumbered. So that teachers and lecturers can compare the questions in the two editions easily, I have shown a chart Appendix 27.2 listing the numbers of the questions in the second edition alongside the numbers given to those questions in this edition.

I would like to extend my sincere thanks to my former colleagues, Eddie Cainen, A.C.C.A., A.T.I.I., John Coy, M.Sc., A.C.C.A., A.C.I.S., and Joe Townsley, B.Com., F.C.A., for putting up with me for so many years, and for letting me pick their brains from time to time. Their help and encouragement has certainly improved the book. I also wish to acknowledge the permission to use past examination papers granted by the University of London, the Associated Examining Board, the Northern Counties Technical Examinations Council, the Royal Society of Arts, the London Chamber of Commerce, the Union of Educational Institutions, the Union of Lancashire and Cheshire Institutes, the East Midland Educational Union, the Association of Certified Accountants, the Institute of Cost and Management Accounts, the Chartered Institute of Secretaries and Administrators, and the Institute of Bankers.

Frank Wood
Stockport
Autumn 1978

1

The Accounting Equation and the Balance Sheet

Accounting is often said to be the language of business. It is used in the business world to describe the transactions entered into by all kinds of organizations. Accounting terms, concepts and conventions are therefore used by people associated with business, be they managers, owners, investors, bankers, lawyers, estate agents, stockbrokers or accountants. As it is the business language there are words and terms that mean one thing in accounting, but whose meaning is completely different in ordinary language usage. Fluency comes, as with other languages, after a certain amount of practice. When fluency has been achieved, that person will be able to survey the transactions of businesses, and will gain a greater insight into the way that business is transacted and the methods by which business decisions are taken.

The actual record-making phase of accounting is usually called book-keeping. However, accounting extends far beyond the actual making of records. Accounting is concerned with the use to which these records are put, their analysis and interpretation. An accountant should be concerned with more than the record-making phase. In particular he should be interested in the relationship between the financial results and the events which have created them. He should be studying the various alternatives open to the firm, and be using his accounting experience in order to aid the management to select the best plan of action for the firm. The owners and managers of a firm will need some accounting knowledge in order that they may understand what the accountant is telling them. Investors and others will need accounting knowledge in order that they may read and understand the financial statements issued by the firm, and adjust their relationships with the firm accordingly.

Probably there are two main questions that the managers or owners of a business want to know: first, whether or not the firm is operating at a profit; second, they will want to know whether or not the business will be able to meet its commitments as they fall due, and so not have to close down owing to lack of funds. Both these questions should be answered by the use of the accounting data of the firm.

The Accounting Equation

The whole of financial accounting is based on the accounting equation. This can be stated to be that for a firm to operate it needs resources, and that these resources have had to be supplied to the firm by someone. The resources possessed by the firm are known as Assets, and obviously some of these resources will have been supplied by the owner of the business. The total amount supplied by him is known as Capital. If in fact he was the only one who had supplied the assets then the following equation would hold true:

Capital = Assets

On the other hand, some of the assets will normally have been provided by someone other than the owner. The indebtedness of the firm for these resources is known as Liabilities. The equation can now be expressed as:

Capital + Liabilities = Assets

The two sides of the equation are therefore equal. On the one side are the resources possessed and on the other side are the sources from which these resources were obtained. The equality of the two sides will always be true no matter how many transactions are entered into. The actual assets, capital and liabilities may change, but the equality of assets with that of the total of capital and liabilities will always hold true.

Assets consist of property of all kinds, such as buildings, machinery, stocks of goods and motor vehicles, also benefits such as debts owing by customers and the amount of money in the bank account.

Liabilities consist of money owing for goods supplied to the firm, and for expenses, also for loans made to the firm.

Capital is often called the owner's equity or net worth.

The Balance Sheet and the Effects of Business Transactions

The accounting equation is expressed in a financial position statement called the Balance Sheet. It is not the first accounting record to be made, but it is a convenient place to start to consider accounting.

The Introduction of Capital

On 1 May 19–7 B. Blake started in business and deposited £5,000 in a bank account. The balance sheet would appear:

B. Blake

Balance Sheet as at 1 May 19–7

	£	*Assets*	£
Capital	5,000	Cash at bank	5,000
	5,000		5,000

The Purchase of an Asset by Cheque

On 3 May 19–7 Blake buys a building for £3,000. The effect of this transaction is that the cash at bank is decreased and a new asset, buildings, appears.

B. Blake

Balance Sheet as at 3 May 19–7

	£	*Assets*	£
Capital	5,000	Buildings	3,000
		Cash at bank	2,000
	5,000		5,000

The Purchase of an Asset and the Incurring of a Liability

On 6 May 19–7 Blake buys some goods for £500 from D. Smith, and agrees to pay for them some time within the next two weeks. The effect of this is that a new asset, stock of goods, is acquired, and a liability for the goods is created. A person to whom money is owed for goods is known in accounting language as a creditor.

B. Blake

Balance Sheet as at 6 May 19–7

Capital and Liabilities	£	*Assets*	£
Capital	5,000	Buildings	3,000
Creditor	500	Stock of goods	500
		Cash at bank	2,000
	5,500		5,500

Sale of an Asset on Credit

On 10 May 19–7 goods which had cost £100 were sold to J. Brown for the same amount, the money to be paid later. The effect is a reduction in the stock of goods and the creation of a new asset. A person who owes the firm money is known in accounting language as a debtor. The balance sheet now appears as:

B. Blake

Balance Sheet as at 10 May 19–7

Capital and Liabilities	£	*Assets*	£
Capital	5,000	Buildings	3,000
Creditor	500	Stock of goods	400
		Debtor	100
		Cash at bank	2,000
	5,500		5,500

Sale of an Asset for Immediate Payment

On 13 May 19–7 goods which had cost £50 were sold to D. Daley for the same amount, Daley paying for them immediately by cheque. Here one asset, stock of goods, is reduced, while another asset, bank, is increased. The balance sheet now appears:

B. Blake

Balance Sheet as at 13 May 19–7

Capital and Liabilities	£	*Assets*	£
Capital	5,000	Buildings	3,000
Creditor	500	Stock of goods	350
		Debtor	100
		Cash at bank	2,050
	5,500		5,500

The Payment of a Liability

On 15 May 19–7 Blake pays a cheque for £200 to D. Smith in part payment of the amount owing. The asset of bank is therefore reduced, and the liability of the creditor is also reduced. The balance sheet now appears:

B. Blake
Balance Sheet as at 15 May 19–7

Capital and Liabilities	£	*Assets*	£
Capital	5,000	Buildings	3,000
Creditor	300	Stock of goods	350
		Debtor	100
		Cash at bank	1,850
	5,300		5,300

Collection of an Asset

J. Brown, who owed Blake £100, makes a part payment of £75 by cheque on 31 May 19–7. The effect is to reduce one asset, debtor, and to increase another asset, bank. This results in a balance sheet as follows:

B. Blake
Balance Sheet as at 31 May 19–7

Capital and Liabilities	£	*Assets*	£
Capital	5,000	Buildings	3,000
Creditor	300	Stock of goods	350
		Debtor	25
		Cash at bank	1,925
	5,300		5,300

It can be seen that every transaction has affected two items. Sometimes it has changed two assets by reducing one and increasing the other. Other times it has reacted differently. A summary of the effect of transactions upon assets, liabilities and capital is shown below.

Example of Transaction

1.	Buy goods on credit.	Increase Asset (Stock of Goods)	Increase Liability (Creditors)
2.	Buy goods by cheque.	Increase Asset (Stock of Goods)	Decrease Asset (Bank)
3.	Pay creditor by cheque.	Decrease Asset (Bank)	Decrease Liability (Creditors)

4. Owner pays more capital into the bank.	Increase Asset (Bank)	Increase Capital
5. Owner takes money out of the business bank for his own use.	Decrease Asset (Bank)	Decrease Capital
6. Owner pays creditor from private money outside the firm.	Decrease Liability (Creditors)	Increase Capital

Each transaction has therefore maintained the equality of the total of assets with that of capital and liabilities. This can be shown:

Number of transaction as above	*Asset*	*Liabilities and Capital*	*Effect on balance sheet totals*
1	+	+	Each side added to equally.
2	+ −		A plus and a minus both on the assets side cancelling out each other.
3	−	−	Each side has equal deductions.
4	+	+	Each side has equal additions.
5	−	−	Each side has equal deductions.
6		− +	A plus and a minus both on the liabilities side cancelling out each other.

Exercises

Note: **Questions without the suffix 'A' have answers shown at the back of this book. These questions are normally the first ones listed. Questions with the suffix 'A' are set without answers in this book so that teachers/lecturers can set the questions for classwork or homework.**

All of the questions set in the second edition of Business Accounting 1 are also contained in this edition. There have been some extra questions added, which has meant that various questions have had to be renumbered. On the last page of Appendix 27.2 a chart is shown which lists the numbers of the questions in the second edition alongside the numbers given to the questions in this, the third edition.

1.1. You are to complete the gaps in the following table:

	Assets	*Liabilities*	*Capital*
	£	£	£
(*a*)	12,500	1,800	?
(*b*)	28,000	4,900	?
(*c*)	16,800	?	12,500
(*d*)	19,600	?	16,450
(*e*)	?	6,300	19,200
(*f*)	?	11,650	39,750

1.2. Complete the columns to show the effects of the following transactions:

	Effect upon Assets	Effect upon Liabilities
(*a*) We pay a creditor £70 in cash		
(*b*) Bought fixtures £200 paying by cheque		
(*c*) Bought goods on credit £275		
(*d*) The proprietor introduces another £500 cash into the firm		
(*e*) J. Walker lends the firm £200 in cash		
(*f*) A debtor pays us £50 by cheque		
(*g*) We return goods costing £60 to a supplier whose bill we had not paid		
(*h*) Bought additional shop premises paying £5,000 by cheque.		

1.3. Distinguish from the following list the items that are liabilities from those that are assets:

Office machinery
Loan from C. Shore
Fixtures and fittings
Motor vehicles
We owe rent to the landlord
Bank balance

1.4. State which of the following are shown under the wrong classification for J. Jordan's business:

Assets	*Liabilities*
Loan from C. Smith	Stock of goods
Cash in hand	Debtors
Machinery	Bank overdraft
Creditors	
Premises	
Motor vehicles	

1.5. A. Smart sets up a new business. Before he actually sells anything he has bought Motor Vehicles £2,000, Premises £5,000, Stock of goods £1,000. He did not pay in full for his stock of goods and still owes £400 in respect of them. He had borrowed £3,000 from D. Bevan. After the events just described, and before trading starts, he has £100 Cash in Hand and £700 Cash at Bank. You are required to calculate the amount of his Capital.

1.6. B. Blake has the following items in his Balance Sheet as at 31 May 19–7:

Capital £5,000; Creditor £300; Buildings £3,000; Stock of goods £350: Debtor £25; Cash at Bank £1,925

During the first week of June he then

(i) Buys a motor van £1,800, paying for it by cheque.
(ii) Borrows £1,000 from D. Kelly and pays this sum into the bank.
(iii) Pays a cheque of £140 to the creditor.
(iv) Receives a cheque of £25 from the debtor. This is paid into the bank.

You are to draw up the Balance Sheet on 7 June 19–7 after the above transactions have been completed.

1.7A. You are to complete the gaps in the following table:

	Assets	*Liabilities*	*Capital*
	£	£	£
(*a*)	55,000	16,900	?
(*b*)	?	17,200	34,400
(*c*)	36,100	?	28,500
(*d*)	119,500	15,400	?
(*e*)	88,000	?	62,000
(*f*)	?	49,000	110,000

1.8A. Complete the columns to show the effects of the following transactions:

		Assets	*Liabilities*	*Capital*
(*a*)	Bought a motor van on credit £500			
(*b*)	Repaid by cash a loan owed to P. Smith £1,000			
(*c*)	Bought goods for £150 paying by cheque			
(*d*)	The owner puts a further £5,000 cash into the business			
(*e*)	A debtor returns to us £80 goods. We agree to make an allowance for them.			
(*f*)	Bought goods on credit £220			
(*g*)	The owner takes out £100 cash for his personal use			
(*h*)	We pay a creditor £190 by cheque.			

1.9A. Classify the following items into liabilities and assets:

Motor vehicles
Premises
Creditors for goods
Stock of goods
Debtors
Bank overdraft
Cash in hand
Loan from D. Jones
Machinery

1.10A. Draw up Jordan's Balance Sheet as at 30 June 19–2 from the following items:

	£
Capital	13,000
Office machinery	9,000
Creditors	900
Stock of goods	1,550
Debtors	275
Cash at bank	5,075
Loan from C. Smith	2,000

1.11A. Draw up Evett's Balance Sheet as at 31 December 19–4 from the following items:

	£
Motor van	3,600
Premises	5,000
Loan from D. Deedes	1,000
Cash at bank	1,650
Stock of goods	4,800
Creditors	2,560
Cash in hand	250
Debtors	6,910

You will have to deduce the figure of Capital.

1.12A. C. Farley has the following items in his Balance Sheet as at 30 June 19–2:

Capital £7,000; Creditor £600; Loan from D. Pilling £1,000; Shop Fittings £2,000; Stock of Goods £1,900; Debtors £1,800; Cash at Bank £2,900.

During the first week of July 19–2 he then:

(i) Bought some goods on credit for £700
(ii) Repaid D. Pilling £1,000
(iii) One of the debtors paid a cheque for £400
(iv) Bought some Shop Fittings £600 paying for them by cheque
(v) Paid a creditor £200 by cheque

You are to draw up the Balance Sheet on 7 July 19–2 after the above transactions have been completed.

1.13A. C. Shaw has the following Balance Sheet as at 31 March 19–5

Balance Sheet as at 31 March 19–5

Capital and Liabilities	£	*Assets*	£
Capital	14,400	Buildings	6,000
Loan from L. Moran	2,000	Motor Vehicle	4,000
Creditors	1,600	Stock of Goods	2,000
		Debtors	2,800
		Cash at Bank	3,200
	18,000		18,000

The following transactions occur:

2 April Paid a cheque of £500 to a creditor.
4 April Bought some goods, to be paid for later, for £900.
5 April Bought Fixtures for £800 paying by cheque immediately.
8 April A debtor paid C. Shaw £300 by cheque.
10 April L. Moran is repaid £1,000 by cheque.

Draw up a Balance Sheet on 10 April 19–5 after the transactions have been completed.

2

The Double Entry System for Assets and Liabilities

It has been seen that each transaction affects two items. To show the full effect of each transaction, accounting must therefore show its effect on each of the two items, be they assets, capital or liabilities. From this need arose the double entry system where to show this twofold effect each transaction is entered twice, once to show the effect upon one item, and a second entry to show the effect upon the other item.

It may be thought that drawing up a new balance sheet after each transaction would provide all the information required. However, a balance sheet does not give enough information about the business. It does not, for instance, tell who the debtors are and how much each one of them owes the firm, nor who the creditors are and the details of money owing to each of them. Also, the task of drawing up a new balance sheet after each transaction becomes an impossibility when there are many hundreds of transactions each day, as this would mean drawing up hundreds of balance sheets daily. Because of the work involved, balance sheets are in fact only drawn up periodically, at least annually, but sometimes half-yearly, quarterly, or monthly.

The double entry system divides the pages into two halves. The left-hand side of each page is called the debit side, while the right-hand side is called the credit side. The words debit and credit are accounting terms for the left-hand side and right-hand side respectively, they must not be confused with the normal language usage of the word credit, as that is often completely at variance with the kinds of entries made on the credit side of the books. For every asset and every liability an account (meaning 'a history of') is opened. Thus there is to be a Motor Van Account (being the history of the motor van), a Shop Premises Account (being the history of the shop premises) and so on for every asset and liability. There should be a separate page for each account.

The title of the account is written across the top of the account at the centre.

The two sides of the page in fact represent the two sides of the accounting equation. The debit side is taken for assets and the credit side for capital and liabilities. There was no rational reason in the way in which the sides were chosen to represent the different items, and the credit side could have easily been the left-hand side and the debit the right-hand side. The Venetian merchants who were the first known business men to use double entry just happened to select the left-hand or debit side for the assets and the opposite side to represent capital and liabilities, and so it has remained ever since.

It will be noticed that assets in a balance sheet appear on the right-hand side, while in the accounts an asset appears on the left-hand side. Similarly, a liability appears in the balance sheet on the left-hand side, while in the accounts it is on the right-hand side. This is due to a long-standing, if illogical, custom of English accounting in which items appear in the balance sheet on the opposite sides to which they are found in the accounts.

The problem of showing a decrease, i.e. a negative effect, to one of the items in the accounting equation is solved by making an entry in the requisite account, but on the opposite side to where positive entries are made. This is merely a different arithmetical way of showing subtractions. Instead of showing a subtraction as a deduction on the line underneath on the same side of the page, it is shown as an item on the opposite side of the page. Thus an increase to an asset, i.e. a positive item, is shown by a debit entry in an asset account, but a decrease or negative item is shown by an entry on the credit side of that account. Likewise, an increase in the Capital or Liability Account, i.e. a positive item, is shown by an entry on the credit side of the requisite account, while a decrease is shown by an entry on the debit side of the account.

This can be summarized:

	Entry in the account
To increase an asset	Debit the asset account
To increase a liability	Credit the liability account
To increase the capital	Credit the capital account
To decrease an asset	Credit the asset account
To decrease a liability	Debit the liability account
To decrease the capital	Debit the capital account

Looking at the accounts the rules will appear as:

Any asset account		*Any liability Account*		*Capital account*	
Increases	Decreases	Decreases	Increases	Decreases	Increases
+	−	−	+	−	+

The entry of a few transactions can now be attempted:

1. The proprietor starts the firm with £1,000 in cash on 1 August 19–6.

Effect	*Action*
(*a*) Increases the asset of cash in the firm	Debit the cash account
(*b*) Increases the capital	Credit the capital account

These are entered:

Cash

19–6		£			
Aug 1		1,000			

Capital

			19–6		£
			Aug 1		1,000

The date of the transaction has already been entered. Now there remains the description which is to be entered alongside the amount. This is completed by a cross reference to the title of the other account in which double entry is completed. The double entry to the item in the cash account is completed by an entry in the capital account, therefore the word 'Capital' will appear in the cash account. Similarly, the double entry to the item in the capital account is completed by an entry in the cash account, therefore the word 'Cash' will appear in the capital account.

It always used to be the custom to prefix the description on the debit side of the books with the word 'To', and to prefix the description on the credit side of the books with the word 'By'. These have now fallen into disuse in modern firms, and as they serve no useful purpose they will not be used in this book.

The finally completed accounts are therefore:

Cash

19–6		£			
Aug 1	Capital	1,000			

Capital

			19–6		£
			Aug 1	Cash	1,000

2. A motor van is bought for £275 cash on 2 August 19–6.

Effect	*Action*
(*a*) Decreases the asset of cash	Credit the cash account
(*b*) Increases the asset of motor van	Debit the motor van account

Cash

		19–6	£
		Aug 2 Motor van	275

Motor Van

19–6	£		
Aug 2 Cash	275		

3. Fixtures bought on credit from Shop Fitters Ltd £115 on 3 August 19–6.

Effect	*Action*
(*a*) Increase in the asset of fixtures	Debit fixtures account
(*b*) Increase in the liability of the firm to Shop Fitters Ltd	Credit Shop Fitters Ltd account

Fixtures

19–6	£		
Aug 3 Shop Fitters Ltd	115		

Shop Fitters Ltd

		19–6	£
		Aug 3 Fixtures	115

4. Paid the amount owing in cash to Shop Fitters Ltd on 17 August 19–6.

Effect	*Action*
(*a*) Decrease in the asset of cash	Credit the cash account
(*b*) Decrease in the liability of the firm to Shop Fitters Ltd	Debit Shop Fitters Ltd account

Cash

		19–6	£
		Aug 17 Shop Fitters Ltd	115

Shop Fitters Ltd

19–6	£		
Aug 17 Cash	115		

Transactions to date

Taking the transactions numbered 1 to 4 above, the records will now appear:

Cash

19–6		£	19–6		£
Aug 1	Capital	1,000	Aug 2	Motor van	275
			,, 17	Shop Fitters Ltd	115

Motor Van

19–6		£			
Aug 2	Cash	275			

Shop Fitters Ltd

19–6		£	19–6		£
Aug 17	Cash	115	Aug 3	Fixtures	115

Fixtures

19–6		£			
Aug 3	Shop Fitters Ltd	115			

Capital

			19–6		£
			Aug 1	Cash	1,000

A Further Worked Example

	Transactions	*Effect*	*Action*
May 1	Started an engineering business putting £1,000 into a business bank account.	Increases asset of bank.	Debit bank account.
		Increases capital of proprietor.	Credit capital account.
,, 3	Brought works machinery on credit from Unique Machines Ltd £275.	Increases asset of machinery.	Debit machinery account.
		Increases liability to Unique Machines Ltd.	Credit Unique Machines Ltd account.
,, 4	Withdrew £200 cash from the bank and placed it in the cash till.	Decreases asset of bank.	Credit bank account.
		Increases asset of cash.	Debit cash account.
,, 7	Bought motor van paying in cash £180	Decreases asset of cash.	Credit cash account.
		Increases asset of motor van.	Debit motor van account.
,, 10	Sold some of machinery for £15 on credit to B. Barnes.	Decreases asset of machinery.	Credit machinery account.
		Increases asset of money owing from B. Barnes.	Debit B. Barnes account.

„ 21	Returned some of machinery value £27 to Unique Machines Ltd.	Decreases asset of machinery.	Credit machinery account.
		Decreases liability to Unique Machines Ltd.	Debit Unique Machines Ltd.
„ 28	B. Barnes pays the firm the amount owing, £15, by cheque.	Increases asset of bank.	Debit bank account.
		Decreases asset of money owing by B. Barnes.	Credit B. Barnes account.
„ 30	Bought another motor van paying by cheque £420.	Decreases asset of bank.	Credit bank account.
		Increases asset of motor vans.	Debit motor van account.
„ 31	Paid the amount of £248 to Unique Machines Ltd by cheque.	Decreases asset of bank.	Credit bank account.
		Decreases liability to Unique Machines Ltd.	Debit Unique Machines Ltd.

In account form this is shown:

Bank

		£			£
May 1	Capital	1,000	May 4	Cash	200
„ 28	B. Barnes	15	„ 30	Motor van	420
			„ 31	Unique Machines Ltd	248

Cash

		£			£
May 4	Bank	200	May 7	Motor van	180

Capital

					£
			May 1	Bank	1,000

Machinery

		£			£
May 3	Unique Machines Ltd	275	May 10	B. Barnes	15
			„ 21	Unique Machines Ltd	27

Motor Van

		£
May 7	Cash	180
„ 30	Bank	420

Unique Machines Ltd

		£			£
May 21	Machinery	27	May 3	Machinery	275
„ 31	Bank	248			

B. Barnes

		£			£
May 10	Machinery	15	May 28	Bank	15

Exercises

Note: **Questions without the suffix 'A' have answers shown at the back of this book. These questions are normally the first ones listed. Questions with the suffix 'A' are set without answers in this book so that teachers/lecturers can set the questions for classwork or homework.**

All of the questions set in the second edition of Business Accounting 1 are also contained in this edition. There have been some extra questions added, which has meant that various questions have had to be renumbered. On the last page of Appendix 27.2 a chart is shown which lists the numbers of the questions in the second edition alongside the numbers given to the questions in this, the third edition.

2.1. Complete the following table showing which accounts are to be credited and which to be debited:

	Account to be debited	*Account to be credited*
(*a*) Bought motor van for cash		
(*b*) Bought office machinery on credit from J. Sumner & Son		
(*c*) Introduced capital in cash		
(*d*) A debtor, J. Crawshaw, pays us by cheque		
(*e*) Paid a creditor, U. Cope, in cash.		

2.2. The following table is also to be completed, showing the accounts to be debited and credited:

	Account to be debited	*Account to be credited*
(*a*) Bought machinery on credit from A. Loft & Son		
(*b*) Returned machinery to A. Loft & Son		
(*c*) A debtor pays us in cash		
(*d*) J. Smith lends us money, giving it to us by cheque		
(*e*) Sold office machinery for cash.		

2.3. Write up the asset and liability accounts in the records of D. Coy to record these transactions:

19–2
May 1 Started business with £1,000 cash
„ 3 Bought a motor lorry on credit from Speed & Sons for £698

„ 14 Brought office machinery by cash from Duplicators Ltd for £60
„ 31 Paid Speed & Sons the amount owing to them, £698, in cash.

2.4. Write up the asset and liability accounts to record the following transactions in the records of G. Brew.

19–3
July 1 Started business with £2,500 in the bank
„ 2 Bought office furniture by cheque £150
„ 3 Bought machinery £750 on credit from Planers Ltd
„ 5 Bought a motor van paying by cheque £600
„ 8 Sold some of the office furniture—not suitable for the firm—for £60 on credit to J. Walker & Sons
„ 15 Paid the amount owing to Planers Ltd £750 by cheque
„ 23 Received the amount due from J. Walker £60 in cash
„ 31 Bought more machinery by cheque £280.

2.5. You are required to open the asset and liability accounts and record the following transactions for June 19— in the records of C. Shore.

19–4
June 1 Started business with £2,000 in cash
„ 2 Paid £1,800 of the opening cash into a bank account for the business
„ 5 Bought office furniture on credit from Betta-Built Ltd for £120
„ 8 Bought a motor van paying by cheque £950
„ 12 Bought works machinery from Evans & Sons on credit £560
„ 18 Returned faulty office furniture costing £62 to Betta-Built Ltd
„ 25 Sold some of the works machinery for £75 cash
„ 26 Paid amount owing to Betta-Built Ltd £58 by cheque
„ 28 Took £100 out of the bank and put it in the cash till
„ 30 J. Smith lent us £500—giving us the money by cheque.

2.6. Write up the various accounts needed in the books of S. Lange to record the following transactions:

19–4
April 1 Opened business with £10,000 in the bank
„ 3 Bought office equipment £700 on credit from J. Davidson Ltd
„ 6 Bought motor van paying by cheque £3,000
„ 8 Borrowed £1,000 from H. Townsley—he gave us the money by cheque
„ 11 S. Lange put further capital into the firm in the form of cash £500
„ 12 Paid £350 of the cash in hand into the bank account
„ 15 Returned some of the office equipment costing £200—it was faulty—to J. Davidson Ltd
„ 17 Bought more office equipment, paying by cash £50
„ 19 Sold the motor van, as it had proved unsuitable, to R. Jones for £3,000. R. Jones will settle for this by three payments later this month
„ 21 Received a loan in cash from J. Hawkins £400
„ 22 R. Jones paid us a cheque for £1,000
„ 23 Bought a suitable motor van £3,600 on credit from Manchester Garages Ltd
„ 26 R. Jones paid us a cheque for £1,800
„ 28 Paid £2,000 by cheque to Manchester Garages Ltd
„ 30 R. Jones paid us cash £200.

2.7A. Complete the following table showing which accounts are to be debited and which to be credited:

	Account to be debited	*Account to be credited*
(*a*) Bought motor lorry for cash		
(*b*) Paid a creditor by cheque		
(*c*) Repaid P. Pearce's loan by cash		
(*d*) Sold motor lorry for cash		
(*e*) Bought office machinery on credit from Ultra Ltd		
(*f*) A debtor pays us by cash		
(*g*) A debtor pays us by cheque		
(*h*) Proprietor puts a further amount into the business by cheque		
(*i*) A loan of £200 in cash is received from L. Lowe		
(*j*) Paid a creditor by cash.		

2.8A. Write up the asset, capital and liability accounts in the books of C. Peers to record the following transactions:

19–5
June 1 Started business with £5,000 in the bank
,, 2 Bought motor van paying by cheque £1,200
,, 5 Bought office fixtures £400 on credit from Harbern Ltd
,, 8 Bought motor van on credit from Super Motors £800
,, 12 Took £100 out of the bank and put it into the cash till
,, 15 Bought office fixtures paying by cash £60
,, 19 Paid Super Motors a cheque for £800.
,, 21 A loan of £1,000 cash is received from J. Jarvis
,, 25 Paid £800 of the cash in hand into the bank account
,, 30 Bought more office fixtures paying by cheque £300.

2.9A. Write up the accounts to record the following transactions:

19–3
March 1 Started business with £1,000 cash
,, 2 Received a loan of £5,000 from M. Percy by cheque, a bank account being opened and the cheque paid into it
,, 3 Bought machinery for cash £60
,, 5 Bought display equipment on credit from Better-View Ltd £550
,, 8 Took £300 out of the bank and put it into the cash till
,, 15 Repaid part of Percy's loan by cheque £800
,, 17 Paid amount owing to Better-View £550 by cheque
,, 24 Repaid part of Percy's loan by cash £100
,, 31 Bought additional machinery, this time on credit from D. Smith for £500.

2.10A. Write up the asset, capital and liability accounts in the books of N. Marsland to record the following transactions:

19–3
May 1 Started business with £14,000 cash
,, 2 Paid £13,600 of the opening cash into a bank account for the business
,, 3 Bought shop fittings on credit from Mottershead Ltd for £600

„ 4 Bought a motor van paying by cheque £4,000
„ 6 A. Mason lent us £500 by cheque
„ 7 Bought another motor van on credit from Pear Tree Garage £2,800
„ 10 Bought shop fittings for cash £350
„ 14 Returned some of shop fittings costing £150 to Mottershead Ltd as they were unsuitable
„ 16 Took £300 out of the bank and put it into the cash till
„ 18 Bought machinery for cash £280
„ 21 Paid Mottershead Ltd the amount owing to them by cheque
„ 23 Repaid part of Mason's loan by cheque £200
„ 28 Bought machinery on credit from Better Built Ltd £1,300
„ 31 Paid Pear Tree Garage by cheque £2,800.

3

The Asset of Stock

Goods are sometimes sold at the same price at which they are bought, but this is not usually the case. Normally they are sold above cost price, the difference being profit; sometimes however they are sold at less than cost price, the difference being loss.

If all sales were at cost price, it would be possible to have a stock account, the goods sold being shown as a decrease of an asset, i.e. on the credit side. The purchase of stock could be shown on the debit side as it would be an increase of an asset. The difference between the two sides would then represent the cost of the goods unsold at that date, if wastages and losses of stock are ignored. However, most sales are not at cost price, and therefore the sales figures include elements of profit or loss. Because of this, the difference between the two sides would not represent the stock of goods. Such a stock account would therefore serve no useful purpose.

The Stock Account is accordingly divided into several accounts, each one showing a movement of stock. These can be said to be:

1. Increases in the stock. This can be due to one of two causes.
(*a*) By the purchase of additional goods.
(*b*) By the return in to the firm of goods previously sold. The reasons for this are numerous. The goods may have been the wrong type, they may have been surplus to requirements, have been faulty and so on.

To distinguish the two aspects of the increase of stocks of goods two accounts are opened. These are:
(i) Purchases Account—in which purchases of goods are entered.
(ii) Returns Inwards Account—in which goods being returned in to the firm are entered. The alternative name for this account is the Sales Returns Account.

2. Decreases in the stock of goods. This can be due to one of two causes if wastages and losses of stock are ignored.
(*a*) By the sale of goods.
(*b*) Goods previously bought by the firm now being returned out of the firm to the supplier.

To distinguish the two aspects of the decrease of stocks of goods

two accounts are opened. These are:
(i) Sales Account—in which sales of goods are entered.
(ii) Returns Outwards Account—in which goods being returned out to a supplier are entered. The alternative name for this is the Purchases Returns Account.

Some illustrations can now be shown.

Purchases of Stock on Credit

1 August. Goods costing £165 are bought on credit from D. Fine.

First, the twofold effect of the transactions must be considered in order that the book-keeping entries can be ascertained.

1. The asset of stock is increased. An increase in an asset needs a debit entry in an account. Here the account concerned is a stock account showing the particular movement of stock, in this case it is the 'Purchases' movement so that the account concerned must be the purchases account.

2. An increase in a liability. This is the liability of the firm to D. Fine in respect of the goods bought which have not yet been paid for. An increase in a liability needs a credit entry, so that to enter this aspect of the transaction a credit entry is made in D. Fine's account.

Purchases

	£		
Aug 1 D Fine	165		

D. Fine

			£
		Aug 1 Purchases	165

Purchases of Stock for Cash

2 August. Goods costing £22 are bought, cash being paid for them immediately.

1. The asset of stock is increased, necessitating a debit entry. The movement of stock is that of a purchase, so that the purchases account needs debiting.

2. The asset of cash is decreased. To reduce an asset a credit entry is called for, and the asset is that of cash so that the cash account needs crediting.

Cash

			£
		Aug 2 Purchases	22

Purchases

	£		
Aug 2 Cash	22		

Sales of Stock on Credit

3 August. Sold goods on credit for £250 to J. Lee.

1. The asset of stock is decreased. For this a credit entry to reduce an asset is needed. The movement of stock is that of a 'Sale' so the account credited is the sales account.

2. An asset account is increased. This is the account showing that J. Lee is a debtor for the goods. The increase in the assets of debtors requires a debit and the debtor is J. Lee, so that the account concerned is that of J. Lee.

Sales

			£
		Aug 3 J. Lee	250

J. Lee

	£		
Aug 3 Sales	250		

Sales of Stock for Cash

4 August. Goods are sold for £55, cash being received immediately upon sale.

1. The asset of cash is increased. This needs a debit in the cash account to show this.

2. The asset of stock is reduced. The reduction of an asset requires a credit and the movement of stock is represented by 'Sales'. Thus the entry needed is a credit in the sales account.

Sales

			£
		Aug 4 Cash	55

Cash

	£		
Aug 4 Sales	55		

Returns Inwards

5 August. Goods which had been previously sold to F. Lowe for £29 are now returned by him.

1. The asset of stock is increased by the goods returned. Thus a debit representing an increase of an asset is needed, and this time the movement of stock is that of 'Returns Inwards'. The entry therefore required is a debit in the returns inwards account.

2. A decrease in an asset. The debt of F. Lowe to the firm is now reduced, and to record this a credit is needed in F. Lowe's account.

Returns Inwards

	£		
Aug 5 F. Lowe	29		

F. Lowe

			£
		Aug 5 Returns inwards	29

Returns Outwards

6 August. Goods previously bought for £96 are returned by the firm to K. Shore.

1. The asset of stock is decreased by the goods sent out. Thus a credit representing a reduction in an asset is needed, and the movement of stock is that of 'Returns Outwards' so that the entry will be a credit in the returns outwards account.

2. The liability of the firm to K. Shore is decreased by the value of the goods returned to him. The decrease in a liability needs a debit, this time in K. Shore's account.

Returns Outwards

			£
		Aug 6 K. Shore	96

K. Shore

	£		
Aug 6 Returns outwards	96		

A Worked Example

May 1 Bought goods on credit £68 from D. Slater Ltd
„ 2 Bought goods on credit £77 from A. Lyon & Son
„ 5 Sold goods on credit to D. Hughes for £60
„ 6 Sold goods on credit to M. Rider for £45
„ 10 Returned goods £15 to D. Slater Ltd
„ 12 Goods bought for cash £100
„ 19 M. Rider returned £16 goods to the firm
„ 21 Goods sold for cash £150
„ 22 Paid cash to D. Slater Ltd £53
„ 30 D. Hughes paid the amount owing by him £60 in cash
„ 31 Bought goods on credit £64 from A. Lyon & Son.

Purchases

		£			£
May 1	D. Slater Ltd	68			
„ 2	A. Lyon & Son	77			
„ 12	Cash	100			
„ 31	A. Lyon & Son	64			

Sales

					£
			May 5	D. Hughes	60
			„ 6	M. Rider	45
			„ 21	Cash	150

Returns Outwards

			May 10	D. Slater Ltd	15

Returns Inwards

		£			
May 19	M. Rider	16			

D. Slater Ltd

		£			£
May 10	Returns outwards	15	May 1	Purchases	68
„ 22	Cash	53			

A. Lyon & Son

					£
			May 2	Purchases	77
			„ 31	Purchases	64

D. Hughes

		£			£
May 5	Sales	60	May 30	Cash	60

M. Rider

		£			£
May	6 Sales	45	May 19	Returns inwards	16

Cash

		£			£
May 21	Sales	150	May 12	Purchases	100
,, 30	D. Hughes	60	,, 22	D. Slater Ltd	53

Restricted Meaning of 'Sales' and 'Purchases'

It must be emphasized that 'Sales' and 'Purchases' have a restricted meaning in accounting when compared to ordinary language usage.

'Purchases' in accounting means the purchase of those goods which the firm buys with the prime intention of selling. Obviously, sometimes the goods are altered, added to, or used in the manufacture of something else, but it is the element of resale that is important. To a firm that deals in typewriters for instance, typewriters constitute purchases. If something else is bought, such as a motor van, such an item cannot be called purchases, even though in ordinary language it may be said that a motor van has been purchased. The prime intention of buying the motor van is for usage and not for resale.

Similarly, 'Sales' means the sale of those goods in which the firm normally deals and were bought with the prime intention of resale. The word 'Sales' must never be given to the disposal of other items.

Failure to keep to these meanings would result in the different forms of stock account containing something other than goods sold or for resale.

Comparison of Cash and Credit Transactions for Purchases and Sales

The difference between the records needed for cash and credit transaction can now be seen.

The complete cycle for purchases of goods where they are paid for immediately needs entries:

1. Credit the cash account.
2. Debit the purchases account.

On the other hand the complete cycle for the purchase of goods on credit can be broken down into two stages. First, the purchase of the goods and second, the payment for them.

The first part is:

1. Debit the purchases account.
2. Credit the supplier's account.

While the second part is:

1. Credit the cash account.
2. Debit the supplier's account.

The difference can now be seen in that with the cash purchase no record is kept of the supplier's account. This is because cash passes immediately and therefore there is no need to keep a check of indebtedness to a supplier. On the other hand, in the credit purchase the records should reveal the identity of the supplier to whom the firm is indebted until payment is made.

A study of cash sales and credit sales will reveal a similar difference.

Exercises

Note: **Questions without the suffix 'A' have answers shown at the back of this book. These questions are normally the first ones listed. Questions with the suffix 'A' are set without answers in this book so that teachers/lecturers can set the questions for classwork or homework.**

All of the questions set in the second edition of Business Accounting 1 are also contained in this edition. There have been some extra questions added, which has meant that various questions have had to be renumbered. On the last page of Appendix 27.2. a chart is shown which lists the numbers of the questions in the second edition alongside the numbers given to the questions in this, the third edition.

3.1. Complete the following table showing which accounts are to be credited and which are to be debited:

	Account to be debited	*Account to be credited*
(*a*) Goods bought, cash being paid immediately		
(*b*) Goods bought on credit from E. Flynn		
(*c*) Goods sold on credit to C. Grant		
(*d*) A motor van sold for cash		
(*e*) Goods sold for cash.		

3.2. Similarly, complete this next table:

	Account to be debited	*Account to be credited*
(*a*) Goods returned to H. Poirot		
(*b*) Goods bought on credit from P. Wimsey		
(*c*) Goods sold on credit to S. Templar		
(*d*) M. Spillane returns goods to us		
(*e*) Goods bought being paid for by cheque immediately.		

3.3. Enter up the following transactions in the requisite accounts:

19—
June 1 Bought goods on credit £72 from C. Breeze
„ 3 Bought goods on credit £90 from C. Farr
„ 5 Returned goods to C. Breeze £15
„ 19 Sold goods for cash £25
„ 21 Sold goods on credit £64 to E. Rase
„ 30 Bought goods on credit from A. Price £145.

3.4. You are to write up the following in the books:

19—
July 1 Started business with £500 cash
„ 3 Bought goods for cash £85
„ 7 Bought goods on credit £116 from E. Mitting
„ 10 Sold goods for cash £42
„ 14 Returned goods to E. Mitting £28
„ 18 Bought goods on credit £98 from A. Loft
„ 21 Returned goods to A. Loft £19
„ 24 Sold goods to A. Knight £55 on credit
„ 25 Paid E. Mitting's account by cash £88
„ 31 A. Knight paid his account in cash £55.

3.5. You are to enter the following in the accounts needed:

19—
Aug 1 Started business with £1,000 cash
„ 2 Paid £900 of the opening cash into the bank
„ 4 Bought goods on credit £78 from S. Holmes
„ 5 Bought a motor van by cheque £500
„ 7 Bought goods for cash £55
„ 10 Sold goods on credit £98 to P. Moriarty
„ 12 Returned goods to S. Holmes £18
„ 19 Sold goods for cash £28
„ 22 Bought fixtures on credit from Manchester Equipment Co £150
„ 24 D. Watson lent us £100 paying us the money by cheque
„ 29 We paid S. Holmes his account by cheque £60
„ 31 We paid Manchester Equipment Co by cheque £150.

3.6. Enter up the following transactions in the records of E. Schofield:
July 1 Started business with £10,000 in the bank
„ 2 T. Cooper lent us £400 in cash
„ 3 Bought goods on credit from F. Jones £840 and S. Chipchase £3,600
„ 4 Sold goods for cash £200
„ 6 Took £250 of the cash and paid it into the bank
„ 8 Sold goods on credit to C. Percy £180
„ 10 Sold goods on credit to J. Noel £220
„ 11 Bought goods on credit from F. Jones £370
„ 12 C. Percy returned goods to us £40
„ 14 Sold goods on credit to H. Morgan £190 and J. Peat £320
„ 15 We returned goods to F. Jones £140
„ 17 Bought motor van on credit from Stockport Motors £2,600
„ 18 Bought office furniture on credit from Faster Supplies Ltd £600

„ 19 We returned goods to S. Chipchase £110
„ 20 Bought goods for cash £220
„ 24 Goods sold for cash £70
„ 25 Paid money owing to F. Jones by cheque
„ 26 Goods returned to us by H. Morgan £30
„ 27 Returned some of office furniture costing £160 to Faster Supplies Ltd
„ 28 E. Schofield put a further £500 into the business in the form of cash
„ 29 Paid Stockport Motors £2,600 by cheque
„ 31 Bought office furniture for cash £100.

3.7A. Complete the following table showing which accounts are to be credited and which are to be debited:

	Account to be debited	*Account to be credited*
(*a*) Goods bought on credit from J. Rhodes		
(*b*) Goods sold on credit to B. Perkins		
(*c*) Motor van bought on credit from H. Quick		
(*d*) Goods sold, a cheque being received immediately		
(*e*) Goods sold for cash		
(*f*) Goods we returned to H. Hardy		
(*g*) Machinery sold for cash		
(*h*) Goods returned to us by J. Nelson		
(*i*) Goods bought on credit from D. Sprake		
(*j*) Goods we returned to H. Frobisher.		

3.8A. Complete the table showing the accounts to be debited and those which are to be credited:

	Account to be debited	*Account to be credited*
(*a*) Goods we returned to A. Palmer		
(*b*) Office fixtures sold for cash		
(*c*) Goods bought on credit from G. Player		
(*d*) Goods sold on credit to J. Nicklaus		
(*e*) Shop fittings bought on credit from T. Watson Ltd		
(*f*) Goods returned to us by B. Hogan		
(*g*) Repaid part of loan owing to N. Faldo		
(*h*) Goods sold for cash		
(*i*) Settled loan owing to J. Miller by giving him some office fixtures		
(*j*) Goods bought on credit from H. Clark		
(*k*) Goods returned by us to S. Ballesteros		

3.9A. Enter up the following transactions in the records:

19–5
May 1 Started business with £2,000 in the bank
„ 2 Bought goods on credit from C. Spartan £900
„ 3 Bought goods on credit from F. Hughes £250
„ 5 Sold goods for cash £180
„ 6 We returned goods to C. Spartan £40
„ 8 Bought goods on credit from F. Hughes £190
„ 10 Sold goods on credit to G. Hood £390

„ 12 Sold goods for cash £210
„ 18 Took £300 of the cash and paid it into the bank
„ 21 Bought machinery by cheque £550
„ 22 Sold goods on credit to L. Moore £220
„ 23 G. Hood returned goods to us £140
„ 25 L. Moore returned goods to us £10
„ 28 We returned goods to F. Hughes £30
„ 29 We paid Spartan by cheque £860
„ 31 Bought machinery on credit from D. Loftus £270

3.10A. You are to enter the following in the accounts needed:

June 1 Started business with £1,000 cash
„ 2 Paid £800 of the opening cash into a bank account for the firm
„ 3 Bought goods on credit from H. Garner £330
„ 4 Bought goods on credit from D. Clark £140
„ 8 Sold goods on credit to B. Miller £90
„ 8 Bought office furniture on credit from Barringtons Ltd £400
„ 10 Sold goods for cash £120
„ 13 Bought goods for credit from H. Garner £200
„ 14 Bought goods for cash £60
„ 15 Sold goods on credit to H. Sharples £180
„ 16 We returned goods £50 to H. Garner
„ 17 We returned some of the office furniture £30 to Barringtons Ltd
„ 18 Sold goods on credit to B. Miller £400
„ 21 Paid H. Garner's account by cheque £480
„ 23 B. Miller paid us the amount owing in cash £490
„ 24 Sharples returned to us £50 goods
„ 25 Goods sold for cash £150
„ 28 Bought goods for cash £370
„ 30 Bought motor van on credit from J. Kilshaw £600

3.11A. The following transactions are to be entered up in the records of C. Willis:

19–6
Aug 1 Started business with £7,500 in cash
„ 2 Paid £6,800 of the opening cash into a bank account
„ 2 Bought goods on credit from E. Mills £880, D. Tiler £540, C. Orton £300
„ 3 Bought office equipment on credit from Hamilton & Co, £188
„ 4 Sold goods for cash £120
„ 5 Sold goods on credit to Marshall Ltd £144, Gordon & Co £57, Carne Ltd £680
„ 6 Bought motor van paying by cheque £2,400
„ 7 Sold goods on credit to Marshall Ltd £76, H. Wragg £150
„ 8 We returned goods to D. Tiler £40
„ 10 Bought office equipment, paying by cheque £70
„ 11 Goods returned to us by Carne Ltd £60, Gordon & Co £7
„ 13 We paid by cheque D. Tiler £500, C. Orton £300
„ 15 We paid by cheque Hamilton & Co £188
„ 18 Marshall Ltd paid us by cash £144
„ 21 D. Goodman lent us £1,000 giving us the money by cheque
„ 22 Bought goods on credit from C. Orton £296
„ 23 Sold goods for cash £145

„ 25 Some of office equipment £28 returned to Hamilton & Co as it was faulty
„ 26 Goods returned to us by H. Wragg £16
„ 27 Hamilton & Co paid us £28
„ 28 C. Willis put another £1,000 into the business bank account from his private monies outside the business
„ 31 Repaid part of D. Goodman's loan by cheque £300.

4

The Double Entry System for Expenses and Revenues. The Effect of Profit or Loss on Capital

Up to now this book has been concerned with the accounting need to record changes in assets and liabilities, but this is subject to one exception, the change in the capital caused by the profit earned in the business. By profit is meant the excess of revenues over expenses for a particular period. Revenues consist of the monetary value of goods and services that have been delivered to customers. Expenses consist of the monetary value of the assets used up in obtaining these revenues. Particularly in American accounting language the word 'income' is used instead of 'profit'.

It is possible to see the effect of profit upon capital by means of an example:

On 1 January the assets and liabilities of a firm are:

Assets: Motor van £500, Fixtures £200, Stock £700, Debtors £300, Cash at Bank £200.

Liabilities: Creditors £600.

The capital is therefore found by the formula Assets−Liabilities = Capital.

£500+£200+£700+£300+£200−£600 = £1,300.

During January the whole of the £700 stock is sold for £1,100 cash. On the 31 January the assets and liabilities have become:

Assets: Motor van £500, Fixtures £200, Stock—, Debtors £300, Cash at Bank £1,300.

Liabilities: Creditors £600.

Assets−Liabilities = Capital

£500+£200+£300+£1,300−£600 = £1,700.

Profit therefore affects the capital thus:

Old Capital+Profit = New Capital

£1,300 +£400 = £1,700

On the other hand a loss would have reduced the capital so that it would become:

Old Capital − Loss = New Capital.

To alter the capital account it will therefore have to be possible to calculate profits and losses. They are, however, calculated only at intervals, usually annually but sometimes more often. This means that accounts will be needed to collect together the expenses and revenues pending the periodical calculation of profits. All the expenses could be charged to an omnibus 'Expenses Account', but obviously it is far more informative if full details of different expenses are shown in Profit and Loss Calculations. The same applies to revenues also. Therefore a separate account is opened for every type of expense and revenue. For instance there may be accounts as follows:

Rent Account	Postages Account
Rates Account	Stationery Account
Wages Account	Insurance Account
Salaries Account	Motor Expenses Account
Telephone Account	General Expenses Account
Rent Receivable Account	Lighting and Heating Expenses Account

It is purely a matter of choice in a firm as to the title of each expense or revenue account. For example, an account for postage stamps could be called 'Postage Stamps Account', 'Postages Account', 'Communication Expenses Account' and so on. Also different firms amalgamate expenses, some having a 'Rent and Rates Account', others a 'Rent, Rates and Insurance Account', a 'Postages, Telephone and Telegrams Account', etc. Infrequent or small items of expense are usually put into a 'Sundry Expenses Account' or a 'General Expenses Account'.

Debit or Credit

It must now be decided as to which side of the records revenues and expenses are to be recorded. Assets involve expenditure by the firm and are shown as debit entries. Expenses also involve expenditure by the firm and are therefore also recorded on the debit side of the books. In fact assets may be seen to be expenditure of money for which something still remains, while expenses involve expenditure of money which has been used up in the running of the business and for which there is no benefit remaining at the date of the balance sheet.

Revenue is the opposite of expenses and therefore appears on the opposite side to expenses, that is revenue accounts appear on the credit side of the books. Revenue also increases profit, which in turn increases capital. Pending the periodical calculation of profit therefore, revenue is collected together in appropriately named accounts, and until it is transferred to the profit calculations it will therefore need to be shown as a credit.

An alternative explanation may also be used for expenses. Every expense results in a decrease in an asset or an increase in a liability, and because of the accounting equation this means that the capital is reduced by each expense. The decrease of capital needs a debit entry and therefore expense accounts contain debit entries for expenses.

Consider too that expenditure of money pays for expenses, which are used up in the short term, or assets, which are used up in the long term, both for the purpose of winning revenue. Both of these are shown on the debit side of the pages, while the revenue which has been won is shown in the credit side of the pages.

Effect of Transactions

A few illustrations will demonstrate the double entry required.

1. The rent of £20 is paid in cash.

Here the twofold effect is:

(*a*) The asset of cash is decreased. This means crediting the cash account to show the decrease of the asset.

(*b*) The total of the expenses of rent is increased. As expense entries are shown as debits, and the expense is rent, so the action required is the debiting of the rent account.

Summary: Credit the cash account with £20.
Debit the rent account with £20.

2. Motor expenses are paid by cheque £55.

The twofold effect is:

(*a*) The asset of money in the bank is decreased. This means crediting the bank account to show the decrease of the asset.

(*b*) The total of the motor expenses paid is increased. To increase an expenses account needs a debit, so the action required is to debit the motor expenses account.

Summary: Credit the bank account with £55
Debit the motor expenses account with £55.

3. £60 cash is received for commission earned by the firm.

(*a*) The asset of cash is increased. This needs a debit in the cash account to increase the asset.

(*b*) The revenue of commissions received is increased. Revenue is shown by a credit entry, therefore to increase the revenue account in question the Commissions Received Account is credited.

Summary: Debit the cash account
Credit the commissions received account

It is now possible to study the effects of some more transactions showing the results in the form of a table:

		Increase	Action	Decrease	Action
June 1	Paid for postage stamps by cash £5	Expense of postages	Debit postages account	Asset of cash	Credit cash account
,, 2	Paid for advertising by cheque £29	Expense of advertising	Debit advertis-ing account	Asset of bank	Credit bank account
,, 3	Received rent in cash £38	Asset of cash	Debit cash account		
		Revenue of rent	Credit rent received account		
,, 4	Paid insurance by cheque £42	Expense of insurance	Debit insurance account	Asset of bank	Credit bank account

The above four examples can now be shown in account form:

Cash

		£			£
June 3	Rent received	38	June 1	Postages	5

Bank

					£
			June 2	Advertising	29
			,, 4	Insurance	42

Advertising

		£			
June 2	Bank	29			

Insurance

		£			
June 4	Bank	42			

Postages

		£			
June 1	Cash	5			

Rent Received

					£
			June 3	Cash	38

It is clear that from time to time the proprietor will want to take cash out of the business for his private use. In fact he will sometimes take goods, this will be dealt with later. However, whether the withdrawals are cash or goods they are known as 'Drawings'. Drawings in fact decrease the claim of the proprietor against the resources of the business, in other words they reduce the amount of capital. According to the way in which the accounting formula is represented by debits and credits the decrease of capital needs a debit entry in the capital account. However, the accounting custom has grown up of debiting a 'Drawings Account' as an interim measure.

An example will demonstrate the twofold effect of cash withdrawals from the business.

Example: 25 August. Proprietor takes £50 cash out of the business for his own use.

	Effect	*Action*
1.	Capital is decreased by £50	Debit the drawings account £50
2.	Cash is decreased by £50	Credit the cash account £50

Cash

			£
		Aug 25 Drawings	50

Drawings

	£		
Aug 25 Cash	50		

Divisions of Accounts

Traditionally, accounts were divided between Personal and Impersonal Accounts. Personal accounts were those of debtors and creditors. Impersonal accounts were further sub-divided between Real and Nominal Accounts. Real accounts referred to accounts in which property was recorded, such as buildings, machinery or stock. Nominal accounts were those that referred to revenue and expenses.

Exercises

4.1. You are to complete the following table, showing the accounts to be debited and those to be credited:

	Account to be debited	*Account to be credited*
(*a*) Paid rates by cheque		
(*b*) Paid wages by cash		
(*c*) Rent received by cheque		
(*d*) Received by cheque rebate of insurance previously paid		
(*e*) Paid general expenses by cash		

4.2. Enter the following transactions in the necessary accounts in double entry:

19–8
January 1 Started business with £200 in the bank
,, 2 U. Surer lent us £1,000 giving us the money by cheque
,, 3 Bought goods on credit £296 from X. Press & Co
,, 5 Bought motor van by cheque £250
,, 6 Cash sales £105
,, 7 Paid motor expenses in cash £15
,, 8 Paid wages in cash £18
,, 10 Bought goods on credit from C. Moore £85
,, 12 Paid insurance by cheque £22
,, 25 Received commission in cash £15
,, 31 Paid electricity bill by cheque £17.

4.3. You are to enter the following transactions, completing double entry in the books for the month of May 19—:

19–7
May 1 Started business with £2,000 in the bank
,, 2 Purchases goods £175 on credit from M. Micawber
,, 3 Bought fixtures and fittings £150 paying by cheque
,, 5 Sold goods for cash £275
,, 6 Bought goods on credit £114 from S. Weller
,, 10 Paid rent by cash £15
,, 12 Bought stationery £27, paying by cash
,, 18 Goods returned to M. Micawber £23
,, 21 Let off part of the premises receiving rent by cheque £5
,, 23 Sold goods on credit to U. Heap for £77
,, 24 Bought a motor van paying by cheque £300
,, 30 Paid the month's wages by cash £117
,, 31 The proprietor took cash for himself £44.

4.4. Write up the following transactions in the books of L. Tolstoy:

19–8
March 1 Started business with cash £1,500
,, 2 Bought goods on credit from A. Christie £296
,, 3 Paid rent by cash £28
,, 4 Paid £1,000 of the cash of the firm into a bank account
,, 5 Sold goods on credit to E. Linklater £54
,, 7 Bought stationery £15 paying by cheque
,, 11 Cash sales £49
,, 14 Goods returned by us to A. Christie £17
,, 17 Sold goods on credit to S. Maugham £29
,, 20 Paid for repairs to the building by cash £18
,, 22 E. Linklater returned goods to Tolstoy £14
,, 27 Paid Christie by cheque £279
,, 28 Cash purchases £125
,, 29 Bought a motor van paying by cheque £395
,, 30 Paid motor expenses in cash £15
,, 31 Bought fixtures £120 on credit from A. Waugh.

4.5A. Complete the following table, showing the accounts to be debited and those to be credited:

	Accounts to be debited	*Accounts to be credited*
(*a*) Paid insurance by cheque		
(*b*) Paid motor expenses by cash		
(*c*) Rent received in cash		
(*d*) Paid rates by cheque		
(*e*) Received refund of rates by cheque		
(*f*) Paid for stationery expenses by cash		
(*g*) Paid wages by cash		
(*h*) Sold surplus stationery receiving proceeds by cheque		
(*i*) Received sales commission by cheque		
(*j*) Bought motor van by cheque.		

4.6A. Enter the following transactions in double entry:

July 1 Started business with £8,000 in the bank
„ 2 Bought stationery by cheque £30
„ 3 Bought goods on credit from I. Walsh £900
„ 4 Sold goods for cash £180
„ 5 Paid insurance by cash £40
„ 7 Bought machinery on credit from H. Morgan £500
„ 8 Paid for machinery expenses by cheque £50
„ 10 Sold goods on credit to D. Small £320
„ 11 Returned goods to I. Walsh £70
„ 14 Paid wages by cash £70
„ 17 Paid rent by cheque £100
„ 20 Received cheque £200 from D. Small
„ 21 Paid H. Morgan by cheque £500
„ 23 Bought stationery on credit from Express Ltd £80
„ 25 Sold goods on credit to N. Townsley £230
„ 28 Received rent £20 in cash for part of premises sub-let
„ 31 Paid Express Ltd by cheque £80.

4.7A. Write up the following transactions in the records of D. Deronde:

Feb 1 Started business with £3,000 in the bank and £500 cash
„ 2 Bought goods on credit from: T. Small £250; C. Todd £190; V. Ryan £180
„ 3 Bought goods for cash £230
„ 4 Paid rent in cash £10
„ 5 Bought stationery paying by cheque £49
„ 6 Sold goods on credit to: C. Crosby £140; R. Rogers £100; B. Grant £240
„ 7 Paid wages in cash £80
„ 10 We returned goods to C. Todd £60
„ 11 Paid rent in cash £10
„ 13 R. Rogers returns goods to us £20
„ 15 Sold goods on credit to: J. Burns £90; J. Sellers £130; N. Thorn £170
„ 16 Paid rates by cheque £130
„ 18 Paid insurance in cash £40
„ 19 Paid rent by cheque £10

„ 20 Bought motor van on credit from C. White £600
„ 21 Paid motor expenses in cash £6
„ 23 Paid wages in cash £90
„ 24 Received part of amount owing from B. Grant by cheque £200
„ 28 Received refund of rates £10 by cheque
„ 28 Paid following by cheque: T. Small £250; C. Todd £130; C. White £600.

4.8A. You are to enter the following transactions, completing double entry in the records of J. Collins for the month of June 19–5:

June 1 Started business with £10,000 in the bank and £300 cash
„ 1 Bought goods on credit from: J. Caplan £400; F. McIntyre £1,188; C. Morrison £1,344
„ 2 Bought shop fittings by cheque £240
„ 3 Bought shop fittings on credit from M. Jayes Ltd £575
„ 5 Paid insurance by cash £88
„ 6 Bought motor van paying by cheque £3,200
„ 7 Sold goods for cash £140
„ 7 Sold goods on credit to: W. Greer & Co £450; F. Padstow Ltd £246; D. R. Edwards £80
„ 8 Bought office stationery £180 on credit from D. Ball & Co
„ 9 Paid rent by cheque £75
„ 10 Paid rates by cheque £250
„ 11 We returned goods to F. McIntyre £168
„ 12 Paid D. Ball & Co £180 by cheque
„ 13 Sold goods on credit to K. P. Priest & Co £220; F. Padstow Ltd £154; Kay & Edwards Ltd £270
„ 14 Goods returned to us by W. Greer & Co £40
„ 15 Paid wages by cash £120
„ 16 Loan from D. Clayton by cheque £500
„ 17 W. Greer & Co paid us the amount owing by cheque
„ 18 Some of office stationery was bought unwisely. We sell it for cash £15
„ 20 We had overpaid insurance. A refund of £8 received by cheque
„ 21 Paid motor expenses by cash £55
„ 23 Paid wages by cash £120
„ 25 Cheques received from K. P. Priest & Co £220; F. Padstow Ltd £100 (as part payment).
„ 26 Some of shop fittings were unsuitable and were returned to M. Jayes Ltd £25
„ 28 Paid F. McIntyre £1,188 by cheque
„ 29 Paid rent by cheque £75
„ 30 J. Collins took drawings by cheque £200.

4.9A. Enter the following transactions in double entry in the records of C. Mayall for the month of July 19–4:

July 1 Started business putting £5,000 of own money into a bank account plus £2,000 borrowed from G. Andrews
„ 2 Bought goods on credit: B. Gould Ltd £550; C. Girling £210; I. Sinclair & Co £1,800
„ 3 Bought office equipment paying by cheque £330
„ 4 Paid rent by cheque £120
„ 5 Took £200 cash from the bank account and put it into the cash till
„ 6 Paid wages in cash £96

„ 7 Sold goods on credit: S. Keen Ltd £142; T. Howard & Co £300; R. Gregory & Son £100
„ 8 We returned goods to: B. Gould Ltd £20; I. Sinclair & Co £150
„ 10 Bought goods paying in cash £40
„ 11 Bought office equipment on credit from Baverstock Ltd £370
„ 12 Goods returned to us by S. Keen Ltd £12
„ 13 C. Mayall introduced more capital in the form of cash £500
„ 14 Bought goods on credit: C. Girling £340; J. Gallagher £160
„ 15 Bought shop fitting paying by cheque £700
„ 16 Goods returned to us by T. Howard & Co £50
„ 18 Bought motor van by cheque £1,800
„ 19 Paid wages in cash £110
„ 20 Goods sold for cash £180
„ 22 Repaid the whole of the loan from G. Andrews by cheque
„ 23 T. Howard & Co, also R. Gregory & Son paid us what they owed by cheque
„ 24 Paid motor expenses by cash £33
„ 25 We paid B. Gould Ltd the amount owing by cheque
„ 26 Paid for insurance by cheque £77
„ 28 Paid sundry expenses by cash £15
„ 31 C. Mayall took £50 cash as drawings.

5

Balancing off Accounts and the Trial Balance

Up to now only the actual making of debit and credit entries in the accounts has been considered. Periodically, however, it will be necessary to ascertain the cumulative effect of entries on the accounts. This is done by finding the 'Balance' on each account. The balance is the accounting term meaning the difference between the two sides of an account.

If the total of the debit entries exceeds the total of the credit entries, the account is said to have a Debit Balance.

If the total of the credit entries exceeds the total of the debit entries, the account is said to have a Credit Balance.

The actual balancing process at a month end can now be seen:

Accounts prior to balancing on 31 August

D. Knight

	£		£
Aug 1 Sales	158	Aug 28 Cash	158
,, 15 ,,	206		
,, 30 ,,	118		

E. Williamson

Aug 21 Bank	100	Aug 2 Purchases	248
		,, 18 ,,	116

These are now balanced off, i.e. the difference found, by first adding up the side of the account which will have the greatest total and then inserting the difference (the balance) on the opposite side so as to make the totals of both sides equal. When doing this ensure that the two totals are written on a level with one another.

Once found and entered, the balance must be entered on the opposite side of the books to preserve double entry. This is done by making the opposite entry on the next line under the totals. In the details column the words 'balance carried down' are inserted above the

the totals, and the balance shown below the totals is described as 'balance brought down'.

D. Knight

	£		£
Aug 1 Sales	158	Aug 28 Cash	158
„ 15 „	206	„ 31 Balance carried down	324
„ 30 „	118		
	482		482
Sept 1 Balance brought down	324		

Notes:

1. The words balance carried down may be abbreviated to balance c/d, and balance brought down may be written as balance b/d.
2. Theoretically the balance is calculated at the end of the day, and is carried down as the opening balance of the following day. Thus the date at which the balance is carried down is 31 August, and the date it is brought down is shown as 1 September. It is the same as saying that the closing balance for one period is the opening balance of the next period.
3. As the total of the debit side originally exceeded the total of the credit side, the balance is said to be a debit balance. This being a personal account (for a person), the person concerned is said to be a debtor—the accounting term for anyone who owes money to the firm. The use of the term debtor for a person whose account has a debit balance can again thus be seen.

E. Williamson

	£		£
Aug 21 Bank	100	Aug 2 Purchases	248
„ 31 Balance	c/d 264	„ 18 „	116
	364		364
		Sept 1 Balance	b/d 264

As the total of the credit side exceeded the total of the debit side, the balance is said to be a credit balance. As this is a personal account, the person concerned is said to be a creditor—the accounting term for anyone to whom money is owed. The use of the term creditor for a person whose account has a credit balance can thus be seen.

If accounts contain only one entry it is unnecessary to enter the total. A double line ruled under the entry will mean that the entry is its own total. For example:

B. Wareham

		£			£
Aug 18 Sales		51	Aug 31 Balance	c/d	51
Sept 1 Balance	b/d	51			

If an account contains one entry only on each side which are equal to one another totals are again unnecessary. For example:

D. Flatley

	£		£
Aug 19 Cash	14	Aug 12 Purchases	14

Accounting Machinery and Three Column Ledger Accounts

Throughout the main part of this book the type of account used shows the left-hand side of the account as the debit side, and the right-hand side is shown as the credit side. However, when most accounting machinery is used the style of the ledger account is different. It appears as three columns of figures, being one column for debit entries, another column for credit entries, and the last column for the balance.

The accounts used in this chapter will now be redrafted to show the typical machine ledger account.

D. Knight

	Debit	*Credit*	*Balance (and whether debit or credit)*
	£	£	£
Aug 1 Sales	158		158 Dr
,, 15 ,,	206		364 Dr
,, 28 Cash		158	206 Dr
,, 31 Sales	118		324 Dr

E. Williamson

	Debit	*Credit*	*Balance*
	£	£	£
Aug 2 Purchases		248	248 Cr
,, 18 ,,		116	364 Cr
,, 21 Bank	100		264 Cr

B. Wareham

	Debit	*Credit*	*Balance*
	£	£	£
Aug 18 Sales	51		51 Dr

D. Flatley

	Debit	*Credit*	*Balance*
	£	£	£
Aug 12 Purchases		14	14 Cr
„ 19 Cash	14		0

It will be noticed that the balance is calculated afresh after every entry. This is effected quite simply when using accounting machinery, because it is the machine which automatically calculates the new balance. However, when manual methods are in use it is often too laborious to have to calculate a new balance after each entry, and it also means that the greater the number of calculations the greater the possible number of errors. For these reasons it is usual for students to use two-sided accounts. However, it is important to note that there is no difference in principle, the final balances are the same using either method.

The Trial Balance

It has already been stated that the method of book-keeping in use is that of the double entry method, every debit entry needing a corresponding credit entry, and every credit entry needing a corresponding debit entry. From this it is obvious that the total amount of all the debit entries made in the books should equal the total of all the credit entries. To see if the two totals are equal, or in accounting terminology to see if the two sides of the books 'balance', a Trial Balance may be drawn up periodically.

A form of a trial balance could be drawn up by listing all the accounts and adding together all the debit entries, at the same time adding together all the credit entries. Using the worked exercise on pages 23 and 24 such a trial balance would appear as follows, bearing in mind that it could not be drawn up until after all the entries had been made, and will therefore be dated as on 31 May 19—.

Trial Balance as on 31 May 19—

	Dr	*Cr*
	£	£
Purchases	309	
Sales		255
Returns outwards		15
Returns inwards	16	
D. Slater	68	68
A. Lyon and Son		141
D. Hughes	60	60
M. Rider	45	16
Cash	210	153
	708	708

However, this is not the normal method of drawing up a trial balance, but it is the easiest to understand in the first instance. Usually, a trial balance is a list of balances only, arranged as to whether they are debit balances or credit balances. If the above trial balance had been drawn up using the conventional balances method it would have appeared as follows:

Trial Balance as on 31 May 19–

	Dr	*Cr*
	£	£
Purchases	309	
Sales		255
Return outwards		15
Returns inwards	16	
A. Lyon and Son		141
M. Rider	29	
Cash	57	
	411	411

Here the two sides also 'balance'. The sums of £68 in D. Slater's account, £60 in D. Hughes' account, £16 in M. Rider's account and £153 in the cash account have however been cancelled out from each side of these accounts by virtue of taking only the balances instead of totals. As equal amounts have been cancelled from each side, £297 in all, the new totals should still equal one another, as in fact they do at £411.

This latter form of trial balance is the easiest to extract when there are more than a few transactions during the period, also the balances are either used later when the profits are being calculated or else appear in a balance sheet, so that it is not just for ascertaining whether or not errors have been made that trial balances are extracted.

Trial Balances and Errors

It may at first sight appear that the balancing of a trial balance proves that the books are correct. This is however quite wrong. It means that certain types of errors have not been made, but there are several types of errors that will not affect the balancing of a trial balance. Examples of the errors which would be revealed, provided there are no compensating errors which cancel them out, are errors in additions, using one figure for the debit entry and another figure for the credit entry, entering only one aspect of a transaction and so on.

As mentioned, there are several types of errors which a trial balance does not reveal. These are:

1. Errors of omission—where a transaction is completely omitted from the books.

2. Errors of commission—this type is where the correct amount is entered but in the wrong person's account, e.g. where a sale of £11 to C. Green is entered in the account of P. Green. It will be noted that the correct class of account was used, both the accounts concerned being personal accounts.

3. Errors of principle—where an item is entered in the wrong class of account, e.g. if an asset such as a motor van is debited to an expenses account such as motor expenses account.

4. Compensating errors—where errors cancel out each other. If the sales account was added up to be £10 too much and the purchases account also added up to be £10 too much, then these two errors would cancel out in the trial balance.

5. Errors of original entry—where the original figure entered is incorrect, yet double entry is still observed using this incorrect figure. An example of this would be if a credit sale of £98 was entered in both the sales account and the personal account as £89.

6. Complete reversal of entries—where the correct accounts are used but each item is shown on the wrong side of the account, e.g. sales account debited and personal account credited instead of vice versa.

Exercises

5.1. You are to enter up the necessary accounts for the month of May from the following details, and then balance off the accounts and extract a trial balance as at 31 May:

19—

May	1	Started firm with capital in cash of £250
,,	2	Bought goods on credit from the following persons: D. Eaton £54; C. Males £87; K. Gibson £25; D. Booth £76; L. Lowe £64
,,	4	Sold goods on credit to: C. Bailey £43; B. Hughes £62; H. Spencer £176
,,	6	Paid rent by cash £12
,,	9	Bailey paid us his account by cheque £43
,,	10	H. Spencer paid us £150 by cheque
,,	12	We paid the following by cheque: K. Gibson £25; D. Eaton £54
,,	15	Paid carriage by cash £23
,,	18	Bought goods on credit from: C. Males £43; D. Booth £110
,,	21	Sold goods on credit to B. Hughes £67
,,	31	Paid rent by cheque £18.

5.2. Enter up the books from the following details for the month of March, and extract a trial balance as at 31 March:

19—
March 1 Started firm with £800 in the bank
„ 2 Bought goods on credit from the following persons: K. Heyworth £76; M. Hill £27; T. Buckley £56
„ 5 Cash sales £87
„ 6 Paid wages in cash £14
„ 7 Sold goods on credit to: H. Elliot £35; L. Lane £42; J. Coy £72
„ 9 Bought goods for cash £46
„ 10 Bought goods on credit from: M. Hill £57; T. Buckley £98
„ 12 Paid wages in cash £14
„ 13 Sold goods on credit to: L. Lane £32; J. Coy £23
„ 15 Bought shop fixtures on credit from Betta Ltd £50
„ 17 Paid M. Hill by cheque £84
„ 18 We returned goods to T. Buckley £20
„ 21 Paid Betta Ltd a cheque for £50
„ 24 J. Coy paid us his account by cheque £95
„ 27 We returned goods to K. Heyworth £24
„ 30 J. King lent us £60 by cash
„ 31 Bought a motor van paying by cheque £400.

5.3. The following transactions are to be entered up in the books for June, and accounts balanced off and a trial balance extracted as at 30 June:

19—
June 1 Started business with £600 in the bank and £50 cash in hand
„ 2 Bought £500 goods on credit from C. Jones
„ 3 Credit sales: H. Heaton £66; N. Norris £25; P. Potter £43
„ 4 Goods bought for cash £23
„ 5 Bought motor van paying by cheque £256
„ 7 Paid motor expenses by cheque £12
„ 9 Credit sales: B. Barnes £24; K. Liston £26; M. Moores £65
„ 11 Goods bought on credit: C. Jones £240; N. Moss £62; O. Huggins £46
„ 13 Goods returned by us to C. Jones £25
„ 15 Paid motor expenses by cash £5
„ 19 Goods returned to us by N. Norris £11
„ 20 Cash taken for own use (drawings) £10
„ 21 We paid the following by cheque: N. Moss £62; O. Huggins £46
„ 23 H. Heaton paid us in cash £66
„ 25 P. Potter paid us by cheque £43
„ 26 Cash sales £34
„ 27 Cash taken for own use £24
„ 28 Goods returned by us to C. Jones £42
„ 29 Paid for postage stamps by cash £4
„ 30 Credit sales: N. Norris £43; M. Edgar £67; K. Liston £45.

5.4. Record the following transactions of D. Clancy for the month of May 19–6, balance off all the accounts, and then extract a trial balance as on 31 May 19–6:

19–6
May 1 D. Clancy started business with £8,000 cash
„ 2 Put £7,500 of the cash into a bank account

„ 2 Bought goods on credit from: Bateman Brothers £180; Leah & Co £560; P. McDonald £380; K. Beverley Ltd £410
„ 3 Bought office fixtures by cheque £185
„ 4 Bought goods for cash £190
„ 5 Cash Sales £110
„ 6 Goods sold on credit: J. Garner & Son £190; P. Gould £340; T. Sutherland £110; T. Bourne Ltd £300
„ 7 Paid rent by cheque £100
„ 8 Paid wages by cash £70
„ 10 Bought goods on credit from Leah & Co £340; C. Rose £160
„ 11 Goods returned to us by J. Garner & Son £60
„ 13 Goods sold on credit to: N. Melvyn £44; J. Garner & Son £300
„ 14 Bought office fixtures on credit from Tru-kits Ltd £178
„ 15 Bought office stationery for cash £90
„ 16 Paid cheques to the following: Tru-kits Ltd £178; Bateman Brothers £180
„ 17 Paid wages by cash £90
„ 18 D. Clancy takes £100 drawings in cash
„ 20 We returned goods to P. McDonald £60; K. Beverley Ltd £44
„ 22 Bought office stationery £220 on credit from E.P. & Co
„ 24 Received cheques from N. Melvyn £44; T. Bourne Ltd £180
„ 26 Cash Sales £140
„ 29 D. Clancy took cash drawings £150
„ 31 Paid sundry expenses by cash £5.

5.5A. Record the following details for the month of November 19–3 and extract a trial balance as at 30 November:

Nov 1 Started firm with £5,000 in the bank
„ 3 Bought goods on credit from: T. Heywood £160; J. Smithers £230; W. Rogers £400; P. Bailey £310
„ 5 Cash sales £240
„ 6 Paid rent by cheque £20
„ 7 Paid rates by cheque £190
„ 11 Sold goods on credit to: L. Meadows £48; K. Ashley £32; R. Hall £1,170
„ 17 Paid wages by cash £40
„ 18 We returned goods to: T. Heywood £14; P. Bailey £20
„ 19 Bought goods on credit from: P. Bailey £80; W. Rogers £270; D. Dent £130
„ 20 Goods were returned to us: K. Ashley £2; L. Meadows £4
„ 21 Bought motor van on credit from U.Z. Motors £500
„ 23 We paid the following by cheque: T. Heywood £146; J. Smithers £230; W. Rogers £300
„ 25 Bought another motor van, paying by cheque immediately £700
„ 26 Received a loan of £400 cash from A. Whittam
„ 28 Received cheques from: L. Meadows £44; L. Ashley £30
„ 30 Proprietor brings a further £300 into the business, by a payment into the business bank account.

5.6A. Record the following for the month of January, balance off all the accounts, and then extract a trial balance as at 31 January 19–4:

19–4
Jan 1 Started business with £3,500 cash
„ 2 Put £2,800 of the cash into a bank account
„ 3 Bought goods for cash £150
„ 4 Bought goods on credit from: L. Clothier £360; M. Burton £490; T. Hill £110; C. Small £340
„ 5 Bought stationery on credit from Swift Ltd £170
„ 6 Sold goods on credit to: S. Willis £90; T. Beeley £150; C. Howard £190; P. Pearson £160
„ 8 Paid rent by cheque £55
„ 10 Bought fixtures on credit from Mallik Ltd £480
„ 11 Paid salaries in cash £120
„ 14 Returned goods to: M. Burton £40; T. Hill £60
„ 15 Bought motor van by cheque £700
„ 16 Received loan from J. Hawks by cheque £600
„ 18 Goods returned to us by: S. Willis £20; C. Howard £40
„ 21 Cash sales £90
„ 24 Sold goods on credit to: T. Beeley £100; P. Pearson £340; J. Smart £115
„ 26 We paid the following by cheque: M. Burton £450; T. Hill £50
„ 29 Received cheques from: J. Smart £115; T. Beeley £250
„ 30 Received a further loan from J. Hawks by cash £200
„ 30 Received £500 cash from P. Pearson

5.7A. You are required to enter up the following transactions for May 19–5. The accounts are then to be balanced off and a trial balance extracted as at 31 May 19–5:

19–5
May 1 R. Groves started firm by depositing £15,000 into a bank account
„ 2 Bought motor van on credit from K. Fryer & Son £3,400
„ 2 Bought shop fittings by cheque £600
„ 3 Bought goods on credit from: K. Heslop Ltd £1,350; C. Dewey £810; P. Truman £180; C. Ross Ltd £440
„ 4 Paid rent by cheque £80
„ 5 Received loan of £300 in cash from D. Kerr
„ 5 Sold goods on credit to: H. Twidale & Partners £500; P. Nelmes £373; D. Price £140; P. Waterhouse Ltd £390
„ 6 Bought office equipment on credit from Arthur Young & Co £740
„ 7 Cash Sales £260
„ 8 Paid wages in cash £90
„ 9 Bought office stationery for cash £28
„ 11 Sold goods on credit to: D. Price £80; L. Grant & Son £115
„ 12 We returned goods to: C. Dewey £54; C. Ross Ltd £60
„ 13 Paid K. Fryer & Son £3,400
„ 14 Bought office stationery on credit from Rowland Supplies £150
„ 15 Bought goods on credit from: P. Truman £310; R. Gibson & Daughter £770
„ 16 Goods returned to us by P. Nelmes £11; P. Waterhouse Ltd £45
„ 17 We paid K. Heslop Ltd £1,350 by cheque
„ 18 Paid wages in cash £95
„ 19 Repaid part of D. Kerr's loan by cheque £120.

„ 20 Cheques received from D. Price £80; P. Waterhouse Ltd £345
„ 21 R. Groves took £100 drawings in cash
„ 22 Some of shop fittings were unsuitable and were sold for £60 cash
„ 24 Bought another motor van paying by cheque immediately £3,700
„ 26 Paid wages in cash £110
„ 28 Bought goods for cash £90
„ 31 Paid P. Truman by cheque £490

6

Trading and Profit and Loss Accounts and Balance Sheets

Probably the main objective of the accounting function is the calculation of the profits earned by a business or the losses incurred by it. The earning of profit is after all usually the main reason why the business was set up in the first place, and the proprietor will want to know for various reasons how much profit has been made. First he will want to know how the actual profits compare with the profits he had hoped to make. He may also want to know his profits for such diverse reasons as: to assist him to plan ahead, to help him obtain a loan from a bank or from a private individual, to show to a prospective partner or to a person to whom he hopes to sell the business, or maybe he will need to know his profits for income tax purposes.

Chapter 4 was concerned with the grouping of revenue and expenses prior to bringing them together to compute profit. In the case of a trader, meaning by this someone who is mainly concerned with buying and selling, the profits are calculated by drawing up a special account called a Trading and Profit and Loss Account. For a manufacturer it is also useful to prepare Manufacturing Accounts, but this will be dealt with in a later chapter.

Undoubtedly one of the most important uses of the trading and profit and loss account is comparing the results obtained with the results expected. Many businesses attach a great deal of importance to their gross profit percentage. This is the amount of Profit made, before deducting expenses, for every £100 of sales. In order that this may easily be deduced from the profit calculations, the account in which profit is computed is split into two sections—one in which the Gross Profit is found, and the next section in which the Net Profit is calculated. The gross profit, found by the use of the Trading Account, is the excess of sales over the cost of goods sold. The net profit, found when the Profit and Loss Account is prepared, consists of the gross profit plus any revenue other than that from sales, such as discounts received or commissions earned, less the total costs used up during the period. Where the cost of goods sold is greater than the sales the result would be a Gross Loss, but this is a relatively rare occurrence. Where the costs used up exceed the gross profit plus other revenue then the result is said to be a Net Loss. By taking the figure of sales less the cost of goods sold, it can be seen that the accounting custom is to calculate a trader's profits only when the goods have been disposed of and not before.

As was seen in Chapter 4, profit increases the capital of the proprietor, profit in this context meaning the net profit. The fact that an interim figure of profit, known as the gross profit is calculated, is due to the two figures of profit being more useful for purposes of comparison with both these profits of previous periods, than by just comparing net profits only. Were it not for this accounting custom it would not be necessary to calculate gross profit at all.

The trial balance of B. Swift, Exhibit 6.1, drawn up as on 31 December 19–5 after the completion of his first year in business can now be looked at.

Exhibit 6.1

B. Swift

Trial Balance as on 31 December 19–5

	Dr	*Cr*
	£	£
Sales		3,850
Purchases	2,900	
Rent	240	
Lighting and heating	150	
General expenses	60	
Fixtures and fittings	500	
Debtors	680	
Creditors		910
Bank	1,510	
Cash	20	
Drawings	700	
Capital		2,000
	6,760	6,760

The first task is to draw up the trading account using the above information. Immediately there is a problem. Sales less the cost of goods sold is the definition of gross profit, but purchases will only equal cost of goods sold if in fact all the goods purchased had been sold leaving no stock of goods on 31 December 19–5. It would be normal to find that a trader always keeps a stock of goods for resale, as the stock of goods is constantly being replenished. However, there is no record in the books of the value of the stock of unsold goods, and the only way that Swift can find this out is by a stock-taking on 31 December 19–5 after the business of that day. By stocktaking is meant that he would make a list of all the unsold goods and then find out their value. The value he would normally place on them would be the cost price of the goods. Assume that this was £300. Then the cost of purchases less the cost of unsold goods would equal the cost of goods sold, ignoring losses by theft or wastage. This figure would then be deducted from the figure of sales to find the gross profit.

Swift could perform this calculation arithmetically:

Sales—Cost of goods sold = Gross Profit
(Purchases—unsold stock)
£3,850—(£2,900–£300) = £1,250

This however is not performing the task by using double entry accounts. In double entry the balance of the sales account is transferred to the trading account by debiting the sales account (thus closing it) and crediting the trading account. The balance of the purchases account would then be transferred by crediting the purchases account (thus closing it) and debiting the trading account. Now the accounts connected with stock movements have been closed, and accounts are being drawn up to a point in time, in this case 31 December 19–5. At this point of time Swift has an asset, namely stock (of unsold goods), for which no account exists. This must be rectified by opening a stock account and debiting the amount of the asset to it. Now as already stated, the closing stock needs to be brought into the calculation of the gross profit, and the calculation of the gross profit is effected in the trading account. Therefore the credit for the closing stock should be in the trading account thus completing the double entry.

It is now usual for the trading and profit and loss accounts to be shown under one combined heading, the trading account being the top section and the profit and loss account being the lower section of this combined account.

B. Swift

Trading and Profit and Loss Account for the year ended 31 December 19–5

	£		£
Purchases	2,900	Sales	3,850
Gross profit c/d	1,250	Closing stock	300
	4,150		4,150
		Gross profit b/d	1,250

The balance shown on the trading account is shown as gross profit rather than being described as a balance. When found the gross profit is carried down to the profit and loss section of the account.

The accounts so far used appear as follows:

Sales

19–5	£	19–5	£
Dec 31 Trading A/c	3,850	Dec 31 Balance b/d	3,850

Purchases

19–5	£	19–5	£
Dec 31 Balance b/d	2,900	Dec 31 Trading A/c	2,900

Stock

19–5	£		
Dec 31 Trading A/c	300		

The entry of the Closing Stock on the credit side of the trading and profit and loss account is in effect a deduction from the purchases on the debit side. In present-day accounting it is usual to find the closing stock actually shown as a deduction from the purchases on the debit side, and the figure then disclosed being described as 'cost of goods sold'. This is illustrated in Exhibit 6.2.

The profit and loss account can now be drawn up. Any revenue accounts, other than sales which have already been dealt with, would be transferred to the credit of the profit and loss account. Typical examples are commissions received and rent received. In the case of B. Swift there are no such revenue accounts.

The costs used up in the year, in other words the expenses of the year, are transferred to the debit of the profit and loss account. It may also be thought, quite rightly so, that as the fixtures and fittings have been used during the year with the subsequent deterioration of the asset, that something should be charged for this use. The methods for doing this are left until Chapter 10.

The revised trading account with the addition of the profit and loss account will now appear as follows:

Exhibit 6.2

B. Swift

Trading and Profit and Loss Account for the year ended 31 December 19–5

	£		£
Purchases	2,900	Sales	3,850
Less Closing stock	300		
Cost of goods sold	2,600		
Gross Profit c/d	1,250		
	3,850		3,850
Rent	240	Gross profit b/d	1,250
Lighting and heating	150		
General expenses	60		
Net profit	800		
	1,250		1,250

Net profit increases the capital of the proprietor. The credit entry for the net profit is therefore in the capital account. The trading and profit and loss accounts, and indeed all the revenue and expense accounts can thus be seen to be devices whereby the capital account is saved from being concerned with unnecessary detail. Every sale of a good at a profit increases the capital of the proprietor as does each item of revenue such as rent received. On the other hand each sale of a good at a loss, or each item of expense decreases the capital of the proprietor. Instead of altering the capital afresh after each transaction the respective items of profit and loss and of revenue and expense are collected together using suitably described accounts. Then the whole of the details are brought together in one set of accounts, the trading and profit and loss account and the increase to the capital, i.e. the net profit is determined. Alternatively, the decrease in the capital as represented by a Net Loss is ascertained.

The fact that a separate drawings account has been in use can now also be seen to have been in keeping with the policy of avoiding unnecessary detail in the capital account. There will thus be one figure for drawings which will be the total of the drawings for the whole of the period, and will be transferred to the debit of the capital account.

The accounts closed off and the capital account will now appear:

Rent

	£		£
19–5		19–5	
Dec 31 Balance b/d	240	Dec 31 Profit and Loss A/c	240

Lighting and Heating

	£		£
19–5		19–5	
Dec 31 Balance b/d	150	Dec 31 Profit and Loss A/c	150

General Expenses

	£		£
19–5		19–5	
Dec 31 Balance b/d	60	Dec 31 Profit and Loss A/c	60

Capital

	£		£
19–5		19–5	
Dec 31 Drawings	700	Jan 1 Cash	2,000
„ 31 Balance c/d	2,100	Dec 31 Net Profit from Profit and Loss A/c	800
	2,800		2,800
		19–6	
		Jan 1 Balance b/d	2,100

The Balance Sheet

After the trading and profit and loss accounts have been completed a statement is drawn up in which the remaining balances in the books are arranged according to whether they are asset balances or liability or capital balances. This statement is called a balance sheet, and it may be recalled that chapter 1 contained examples. The assets are shown on the right-hand side and the liabilities on the left-hand side. The balance sheet is not part of the double entry system of book-keeping, so that no entry is made in the actual asset and liability accounts. This is in direct contrast to the trading and profit and loss accounts. The word 'account' means in fact that it is part of the double entry system, so that anything which is not an account is outside the double entry system.

It may be thought peculiar that assets should be on the right-hand side of the balance sheet as an asset is a debit balance, being a balance on the left-hand side of the books. A liability is on the right-hand side of the books, while it is shown on the left-hand side of the balance sheet. As the balance sheet is not part of the double entry system, it does not have to comply with the system, and the allocation of the sides is purely due to a long-established custom in Great Britain. In certain other parts of the world the opposite arrangement is used, and from a logical point of view it has much to commend it.

It should be pointed out that there is no legal significance in this, a firm would not have done anything unlawful by putting the assets on the right-hand side of the balance sheet and liabilities and capital on the left-hand side instead of the other way around. In fact, as will be demonstrated in Volume 2, most large companies do not show them in either of these two ways. They list them one under the other, so that possibly assets may be shown at the top and then capital and liabilities shown underneath instead of side by side. It is probably true to say that at this stage of your studies it is easier for you to envisage a balance sheet shown with two sides to it, and so this method will be adhered to in the rest of this volume. Most examining bodies for their first examinations in particular would prefer this method.

Although it is not necessary to redraft the trial balance after the trading and profit and loss accounts have been prepared, it will be useful to do so in order to establish which balances still remain in the books.

The first thing to notice is that the stock account, not originally in the trial balance, is in the redrafted trial balance, as the item was not created as a balance in the books until the trading account was prepared.

B. Swift
Trial Balance as on 31 December 19–5
(after Trading and Profit and Loss Accounts completed)

	Dr	*Cr*
	£	£
Fixtures and fittings	500	
Debtors	680	
Creditors		910
Stock	300	
Bank	1,510	
Cash	20	
Capital		2,100
	3,010	3,010

Marshalling the Assets and Liabilities in the Balance Sheet

Assets are called Fixed Assets when they are of long life, are material items, held to be used in the business and are not primarily for resale or for conversion into cash. Examples are buildings, machinery, motor vehicles and fixtures and fittings.

On the other hand, assets are called Current Assets when they represent cash or are primarily for conversion into cash or have a short life. An example of a short-lived asset is that of the stock of oil held to power the boilers in a factory, as this will be used up in the near future. Other examples of current assets are cash itself, stocks of goods, debtors and bank balances.

In the balance sheet the two groups of assets are best shown under the separate headings of fixed assets and current assets. There is a choice of two methods of listing the assets under their respective headings. The first, being the most preferable since it helps standardize the form of sole traders' accounts with those of limited companies, is that the assets are listed starting with the most permanent asset, or to put it another way the most difficult to turn into cash progressing to the asset which is least permanent or easiest to turn into cash. The fixed assets will thus appear under that heading followed by the current assets under their heading. The other method, used by banks but fast falling into disuse in most other kinds of organizations, is the complete opposite. In this method it is the least permanent asset that appears first and the most permanent asset which appears last.

The object of establishing a set order for assets is that standardization enables balance sheet items to be found more quickly. In addition it greatly assists the comparison of the balance sheets of two or more firms if similar items are shown in similar places in the different balance sheets.

Using the first method an illustration may now be seen of the order in which assets are displayed:

Fixed Assets
Land and buildings
Fixtures and fittings
Machinery
Motor vehicles

Current Assets
Stock
Debtors
Bank
Cash

The order with which most students would disagree is that stock has appeared before debtors. On first sight stock would appear to be more easily realizable than debtors. In fact, however, debtors could normally be more quickly turned into cash by factorizing them, i.e. selling the rights to the amounts owing to a finance company for a specified amount. On the other hand, to dispose of all the stock of a business is often a long and difficult task. Another advantage is that the method follows the order in which full realization of the asset takes place. First before any sale takes place there must be a stock of goods, which when sold on credit becomes translated into debtors, and when payment is made by the debtors it turns into cash.

The order of the liabilities is preferably that of starting with capital, progressing via Long-Term Liabilities such as loans not requiring repayment within the near future, and finishing with Current liabilities, being liabilities such as debts for goods which will have to be discharged in the near future. This then comprises the order in which the claims against the assets would be discharged. The other method of listing the liabilities is the complete reversal of this, starting with current liabilities and finishing at the bottom with capital. This method also conflicts with most company accounts and is best avoided if the benefits of standardization are to be attained.

When the balance sheet of B. Swift is drawn up in accordance with the above it will appear as in Exhibit 6.3 overleaf:

Notes to Exhibit 6.3

1. A total for capital and for each class of assets and liabilities should be shown, e.g. the £2,510 total of current assets. For this purpose the individual figures of current assets are inset and the resultant total extended into the end column.

2. It is not necessary to write the word 'account' after each item.

3. The proprietor will obviously be most interested in his capital. To have merely shown the balance would invariably invite his request to show how the final balance of the capital account had been arrived at.

To overcome this, accounting custom always shows the full details of the capital account. Compare this with the other items above where only the closing balance is shown.

4. Compare the date on the balance sheet with that on the trading and profit and loss account. You can see from these that the essential natures of these two statements are revealed. A trading and profit and loss account is a period statement, because it covers a specified lapse of time, in this case the whole of 19–5. On the other hand a balance sheet is a position statement, it is drawn up at a particular point in time, in this case at the precise end of 19–5.

B. Swift
Balance Sheet as at 31 December 19–5

	£	£		£	£
Capital			*Fixed Assets*		
Cash introduced	2,000		Furniture and fittings		500
Add Net profit for the year	800				
	2,800		*Current Assets*		
Less Drawings	700				
		2,100	Stock	300	
			Debtors	680	
			Bank	1,510	
Current Liabilities			Cash	20	
Creditors		910			2,510
		3,010			3,010

Capital Expenditure and Revenue Expenditure

Capital expenditure is either that incurred in the purchase of fixed assets or that which adds to the value of fixed assets. Examples of this form of expenditure are improvements to buildings, the purchase of additional machinery, legal costs incurred in the purchase of a building, and of course the purchase price of the building.

Revenue expenditure is that which does not add to the value of fixed assets, but is merely the costs incurred in running the business during a particular period.

The distinction is important because it is the revenue expenditure which is chargeable to the trading and profit and loss accounts, while the capital expenditure will merely reflect itself in increased figures of fixed assets in the balance sheet. If capital expenditure is inadvertently treated as revenue expenditure then too much will be charged as expenses, thus the net profit will be understated. If the reverse applies the net profit will be overstated. The calculation of the net profit thus depends on the allocation of expenditure between that which is revenue expenditure and that which is capital expenditure. Capital expenditure treated as revenue expenditure will cause understatement of assets and therefore of capital.

Some items of expenditure will be both part capital and part revenue expenditure. For instance, a factory building may have work done on it which is partly repair work (revenue expenditure) and partly improvements (capital expenditure). In such cases the expenditure will have to be split, the repairs portion being entered in a Building Repairs Account later to be charged to the profit and loss account, and the improvement portion to be entered in the Buildings Account which will show as an increased amount in the balance sheet.

B. Swift's Second Year

At the end of his second year of trading, on 31 December 19–6, B. Swift extracts another trial balance. It will be noticed that there are accounts now in existence for kinds of transactions which did not occur in the first year.

B. Swift

Trial Balance as on 31 December 19–6

	Dr	*Cr*
	£	£
Sales		6,620
Purchases	4,050	
Returns inwards	120	
Returns outwards		80
Lighting and heating	190	
Rent	240	
Wages	520	
General expenses	70	
Carriage inwards	90	
Carriage outwards	110	
Shop premises	2,000	
Fixtures and fittings	750	
Debtors	1,200	
Creditors		900
Bank	120	
Cash	40	
Loan from I. Twist		1,000
Drawings	900	
Capital		2,100
Stock	300	
	10,700	10,700

Notes:

1. Carriage (cost of transport) into a firm is called Carriage Inwards, and carriage out of the firm, i.e. to customers, is called Carriage Outwards.

Some goods are bought carriage paid and this means that the price is that of the goods delivered to the buyer's place of business. Other goods are bought carriage forward and this is where the buyer himself has to pay separately for the carriage. The purchases account therefore contains goods bought at two different price levels, some including the cost of carriage and some not. To ensure that the figure for goods bought is comparable one period to the next, carriage inwards is added to the purchase figure in the trading account to make the resultant figure the cost of goods as delivered to the business.

Failing this, the volume of goods bought carriage paid might vary between one year and the next and in this case the figures between the first year and the second year would not be properly comparable as they would be figures built up on a different basis.

Carriage outwards, however, is charged to the profit and loss account as an expense.

It is important to note that both are expenses of B. Swift.

2. The stock shown in the trial balance is that brought forward from the previous year, it is therefore the opening stock of 19–6. The closing stock at 31 December 19–6 can only be found by stocktaking. Assume it amounts at cost to be £550.

3. For the gross profit calculations the figure of sales required is that of the Net Sales, as some of the goods sold by Swift were later returned to him. Similarly, the figure of purchases required is that of the Net Purchases as he in turn also returned goods to his suppliers. To obtain these figures the returns inwards should be deducted from the sales and the returns outwards should be deducted from the purchases.

The gross profit, if calculated arithmetically, becomes:

	£	£	£
Sales = Total Sales		6,620	
Less Returns inwards		120	6,500
Stock 1 January 19–5		300	
Add Total purchases	4,050		
Less Returns outwards	80	3,970	
Add Carriage inwards		90	
Cost of total goods available for sale		4,360	
Less still in stock 31 December 19–5		550	
Cost of goods sold			3,810
Gross profit			2,690

The trading account should also show as expenses any productive wages or any other expenses concerned with putting the product into a saleable condition. Let us assume here that the wages are merely those of a sales assistant, and are therefore non-productive in character. The wages in this case will be chargeable to the profit and loss account.

Now the trading and profit and loss accounts can be drawn up using double entry.

Trading and Profit and Loss Account for the year ended 31 December 19–6

	£	£		£	£
Opening stock		300	Sales	6,620	
Add Purchases	4,050		*Less* Returns inwards	120	
Less Returns outwards	80	3,970			6,500
Carriage inwards		90			
		4,360			
Less Closing stock		550			
Cost of goods sold		3,810			
Gross profit c/d		2,690			
		6,500			6,500
Wages		520	Gross profit b/d		2,690
Lighting and heating		190			
Rent		240			
General expenses		70			
Carriage outwards		110			
Net profit		1,560			
		2,690			2,690

The balances now remaining in the books, including the new balance on the stock account, are now drawn up in the form of a balance sheet. See Exhibit 6.4 overleaf.

Final Accounts

The term 'Final Accounts' is often used to mean collectively the trading and profit and loss accounts and the balance sheet. The term is misleading as the balance sheet is not an account.

Exhibit 6.4

Balance Sheet as at 31 December 19–6

	£	£		£	£
Capital			*Fixed Assets*		
Balance 1 Jan 19–6	2,100		Shop premises		2,000
Add Net profit for year	1,560		Fixtures and fittings		750
	3,660				2,750
Less Drawings	900				
		2,760	*Current Assets*		
Long-term liability			Stock	550	
Loan from I. Twist		1,000	Debtors	1,200	
Current Liabilities			Bank	120	
Creditors		900	Cash	40	
					1,910
		4,660			4,660

Stock Account

It is perhaps helpful if the stock account covering both years can now be seen:

Stock

	£		£
19–5		19–6	
Dec 31 Trading A/c	300	Jan 1 Trading A/c	300
19–6			
Dec 31 Trading A/c	550		

Adjustments in the Final Accounts. Distinction Between Different Forms of Capital

It has been seen that the trading and profit and loss accounts are concerned with taking the revenue for a period and deducting from it the expenses for that period, the result being the net profit or net loss. Up to this point it has been assumed that the revenue expenditure in the expense accounts was exactly used up during the period of the trading and profit and loss accounts. However, this is not always the case, as the amount in an expense account may cover a greater period or may in fact be only part of the costs used up.

The expense accounts normally contain the amount actually paid by cash or cheque during the period. If all of the costs used up during a period are also paid during that period then the balance of the account can be charged as an expense in the trading or profit and loss account. Where on the other hand the costs used up and the amount paid are not equal to one another, then an adjustment will be required in respect of the overpayment or underpayment of the costs used up during the period.

In all of the following examples the trading and profit and loss accounts being drawn up are for the year ended 31 December 19–5.

Underpayment of Expenses

Consider the case of rent being charged at the rate of £100 per year. It is payable at the end of each quarter of the year for the three months tenancy that has just expired. It can be assumed that the tenancy commenced on 1 January 19–5. The rent was paid for 19–5 on 31 March, 2 July and 4 October of 19–5 and on 5 January 19–6.

During the year ended 31 December 19–5 the rent account will appear:

Rent

19–5			
Mar 31 Cash	25		
Jul 2 ,,	25		
Oct 4 ,,	25		

The rent paid in 19–6 will appear in the books of that year as part of the double entry.

The costs used up during 19–5 are obviously £100 as that is the year's rent, and this is the amount needing to be transferred to the profit and loss account. To make the account balance the £25 rent owing for 19–5 but paid in 19–6 must be carried down to 19–6 as a credit balance because it is a liability on 31 December 19–5. Instead of Rent Owing it could be called Rent Accrued or just simply as an accrual. The completed account can now be shown.

Rent

19–5	£	19–5	£
Mar 31 Cash	25	Dec 31 Profit and Loss A/c	100
Jul 2 ,,	25		
Oct 4 ,,	25		
Dec 31 Accrued c/d	25		
	100		00
		19–6	
		Jan 1 Accrued b/d	25

Expenses Prepaid

A property is occupied on 1 January 19–5. Rates are paid as follows:

Feb 28 19–5 £21 for period of three months to 31 March 19–5
Aug 31 19–5 £42 for period of six months to 30 September 19–5
Nov 18 19–5 £42 for period of six months to 31 March 19–6

The rates account will be shown in the books:

Rates

19–5	£		
Feb 28 Cash	21		
Aug 31 ,,	42		
Nov 18 ,,	42		

Now the last payment of £42 is not just for 19–5, it can be split as to £21 for the three months to 31 December 19–5 and £21 for the three months ended 31 March 19–6. Rates are therefore running at the amount of £84 for 12 months and this is therefore the figure needing to be transferred to the profit and loss account. The amount needed to balance the account will therefore be £21, and at 31 December 19–5 this is a benefit paid for but not used up, it is an asset and needs carrying forward as such to 19–6, i.e. as a debit balance.

The account can now be completed.

Rates

19–5	£	19–5	£
Feb 28 Cash	21	Dec 31 Profit and Loss A/c	84
Aug 31 ,,	42	,, ,, Prepaid c/d	21
Nov 18 ,,	42		
	105		105
19–6			
Jan 1 Prepaid b/d	21		

Prepayment also occurs when goods other than purchases are bought for use in the business, and these have not been fully used up in the period. For instance, stationery is normally not entirely used up over the period in which it is bought, there being a stock of stationery in hand at the end of the period. This stock is therefore a form of prepayment and needs carrying down to the following period in which it will be used.

This can be seen in the following example:

Year ended 31 December 19–6:
Stationery bought in the year £220
Stock of stationery in hand as at 31 December 19–6 £40

Stationery

19–6	£	19–6	£
Dec 31 Cash	220	Dec 31 Profit and Loss A/c	180
		„ „ Stock c/d	40
	220		220
19–7			
Jan 1 Stock b/d	40		

The stock of stationery is not added to the stock of purchases in hand in the balance sheet, but is added to the other prepayments of expenses.

Outstanding Revenue other than Sales

Sales revenue outstanding is already shown in the books as debit balances on the customers' personal accounts. It is the other kinds of revenue such as rent receivable, commissions receivable, etc. which need to be considered. The revenue to be brought into the profit and loss account is that which has been earned during the period. Should all the revenue earned actually be received during the period, then revenue received and revenue earned will be the same amount and no adjustment would be needed in the revenue account. Where the revenue has been earned but the full amount has not been received the revenue due to the business must be brought into the accounts, the amount receivable is after all the revenue used when calculating profit.

Example:

Commission is earned and payment is made on a quarterly basis. Earnings for the year 19–5 and the dates and the amounts received were:

19–5. Apl 4.	For three months to 31 March 19–5, £85
19–5 Jul 6.	For three months to 30 June 19–5, £110
19–5 Oct 9.	For three months to 30 September 19–5, £92 and on Jan 7 19–6 the firm received £100 for the three months to 31 December 19–5.

The account for 19–5 appeared:

Commissions Receivable

		19–5	£
		Apl 4 Cash	85
		Jul 6 „	110
		Oct 9 „	92

The amount to be transferred to the profit and loss account is however the amount earned in 19–5, i.e. £85+£110+£92+£100 = £387. The commission account is completed by carrying down the balance owing as a debit balance to 19–6. The amount owing is after all an asset on 31 December 19–5.

The Commissions Receivable Account can now be completed:

Commissions Receivable

19–5	£	19–5	£
Dec 31 Profit and Loss A/c	387	Apl 4 Cash	85
		Jul 6 ,,	110
		Oct 9 ,,	92
		Dec 31 Accrued c/d	100
	387		387
19–6			
Jan 1 Accrued b/d	100		

Expense and Revenue Account Balances and the Balance Sheet

In all the cases listed dealing with adjustments in the final accounts, there will still be a balance on each account after the preparation of the trading and profit and loss accounts. All such balances remaining should appear in the balance sheet. The only question left is to where and how they shall be shown.

The amounts owing for expenses are usually added together and shown as one figure. These could be called Expense Creditors, Expenses Owing, or Accrued Expenses. The item would appear under current liabilities as they are expenses which have to be discharged in the near future.

The items prepaid are also added together and called Prepayments, Prepaid Expenses, or Payments in Advance. Often they are added to the debtors in the balance sheet, otherwise they are shown next under the debtors.

Amounts owing for commissions receivable or rents receivable are usually added to debtors.

The balance sheet in respect of the accounts so far seen in this chapter would appear:

Balance Sheet as at 31 December 19–5

Current Liabilities	£	*Current Assets*	£
Trade creditors		Stock	
Accrued expenses	50	Debtors	100
		Prepayments	21
		Bank	
		Cash	

Distinctions Between Various Kinds of Capital

The capital account represents the claim of the proprietor against the assets of the business at a point in time. The word 'Capital' is, however, often used in a specific sense. The main meanings are listed below:

1. Capital invested. This means the actual amount of money, or money's worth, brought into the business by the proprietor from his outside interests. The amount of capital invested is not disturbed by the amount of profits made by the business or losses incurred.

2. Capital employed. Candidates at an early stage in their studies are often asked to define this term. In fact, for those who progress to a more advanced stage, it will be seen in Volume 2 that it could have several meanings as the term is often used quite loosely. At an elementary level it is taken to mean the effective amount of money that is being used in the business. Thus, if all the assets were added together and the liabilities of the business deducted the answer would be that the difference is the amount of money employed in the business. You will by now realize that this is the same as the balance of the capital account. It is also sometimes called Net Assets.

3. Working capital is a term for the excess of the current assets over the current liabilities of a business.

Now look at a balance sheet and calculate from it the amounts of the different kinds of capital.

N. Crank
Balance Sheet as at 31 December 19–5

Capital	£	£	*Fixed Assets*	£	£
Cash introduced on			Land and buildings		5,000
1 Jan 19–5	11,300		Machinery		2,000
Add Net profit for			Motor vehicles		1,000
the year	1,800				
					8,000
	13,100		*Current Assets*		
Less Drawings	1,200		Stock	3,500	
		11,900	Debtors	1,300	
Current Liabilities			Bank	700	
Trade creditors	1,550		Cash	100	
Accrued expenses	150				5,600
		1,700			
		13,600			13,600

Capital invested £11,300
Capital employed £11,900

	£
Working Capital, Current Assets	5,600
Less Current Liabilities	1,700
	3,900

Display of Working Capital in the Balance Sheet

Quite frequently firms show the amount of Working Capital as a figure in their balance sheets. This is achieved by deducting the Current Liabilities from the Current Assets, the result being the Working Capital. The balance sheet of N. Crank just considered will now be redrafted to illustrate this method.

N. Crank
Balance Sheet as at 31 December 19–5

Capital	£	£	*Fixed assets*	£	£	£
Cash introduced on 1 Jan 19–5	11,300		Land and buildings			5,000
Add net profit for the year	1,800		Machinery			2,000
	13,100		Motor vehicles			1,000
Less drawings	1,200	11,900				8,000
			Current Assets			
			Stock		3,500	
			Debtors		1,300	
			Bank		700	
			Cash		100	
					5,600	
			Less Current Liabilities			
			Trade Creditors	1,550		
			Accrued expenses	150		
					1,700	3,900
		11,900				11,900

Adequacy of Working Capital

It cannot be stressed too strongly that the Working Capital should be adequate to finance the running of the business without undue strain. A shortage of working capital can mean that creditors cannot be paid on time, thus losing valuable Cash Discounts; that creditors may take legal action to enforce the payment of debts which may cause the firm to close down if it is unable to meet such commitments; or that the business is unable to take part in certain profitable activities that may occur, for instance a bulk purchase of goods at a very low price may have to be missed.

The question of the adequacy of working capital is dealt with in greater detail in Volume 2.

Goods for Own Use

Proprietors of businesses very often take goods for their own use without making payment for them. There is nothing illegal about this as long as entries are made to record the action. This is brought about quite simply by crediting the purchases account and debiting the drawings account.

It should be noted that, for tax purposes in the U.K., any goods taken by the proprietor(s) should be charged to him at selling price. There is the choice between showing the transfer at selling price in the accounts, or else the transfer may be made at cost, leaving the profit difference to be adjusted by the Inland Revenue when the tax liability is being calculated. In examination questions the transfer should be made at the figure as given.

The Valuation of Stock

For the sake of simplicity this volume assumes that the valuation of stock is something that is easily done, and is the 'cost' of goods unsold at the end of the accounting period. However, on reflection you may start to wonder what is meant by 'cost'. It could mean the average cost, the cost of the first goods bought or the cost of the last goods bought. Different firms use each of these different concepts of cost.

Also, when the 'market value' of unsold goods is less than the cost then 'market value' is the figure that is taken. However, different firms also use different concepts of market value. This leads to the valuation of stock being quite complex. It has therefore been left until Volume 2 where a fuller investigation into the valuation of stock is carried out.

Vertical Presentation of Accounting Statements

Chapter 42, in the second volume of this book, considers this method of display in greater detail, but it is perhaps pertinent to give a brief introduction in this volume.

Throughout this book the two-sided presentation is used. For many reasons this is easier to use from a teaching and learning point of view. It does not however mean that in practice it would have to be adhered to strictly. It should be pointed out that what really matters is whether or not the presentation still results in the right answer being shown.

Final accounts could therefore be presented in a vertical fashion rather than use a two-sided presentation.

Exhibits 6.3 and 6.4 can be redrafted to disclose exactly the same information in a vertical fashion.

B. Swift

Trading and Profit and Loss Account for the year ended 31 December 19–5

	£	£
Sales		3,850
Less Cost of Goods Sold:		
Purchases	2,900	
Less Closing stock	300	2,600
Gross Profit		1,250
Less Expenses:		
Rent	240	
Lighting and heating	150	
General expenses	60	450
Net profit		800

B. Swift

Balance Sheet as at 31 December 19–5

	£	£
Capital		
Cash Introduced		2,000
Add Net Profit for the year		800
		2,800
Less Drawings		700
		2,100
Represented by:		
Fixed assets		
Furniture and Fittings		500
Current assets		
Stock	300	
Debtors	680	
Bank	1,510	
Cash	20	
	2,510	
less: Current liabilities		
Creditors	910	
Net Working Capital		1,600
		2,100

This simply shows one way of presenting the final accounts in a vertical fashion. This is only one way of arranging the items vertically; it can be done in a variety of ways. Those who will be proceeding to Volume 2 will examine this in greater detail. What can be stipulated here is that the information presented is exactly the same whether the vertical or the two-sided presentation is used, the only difference being in the manner in which it is displayed.

Balance Sheets and Missing Figures

It is quite common in examinations to find that the examiner has given all of the balances which would be found in a trial balance, or in a balance sheet, with the exception of one item. That item is usually the figure of Capital. A student is entitled to assume that the missing figure needed to allow both sides of the trial balance or balance sheet to agree is in fact the correct figure for Capital. Of course, if a student draws up a Trial Balance, knowing full well that the figure of Capital is missing, but then puts one of the other items in the Trial Balance on the wrong side, then, (barring a compensating error) the difference on the Trial Balance will not be the figure of Capital. You will find examples of this type of question at the end of the chapter, in particular Questions 6.8 and 6.15A.

The Next Step

Before attempting any of the questions at the end of this chapter the reader should turn to Appendix 27.1, which is shown at the end of Chapter 27. Part of the way through the Appendix, at the chapter which starts off 'This is probably the first examination you will have taken in book-keeping and Accounting', there is a line of asterisks down the side of the page. Start to read that part of the Appendix and finish at the point where the asterisks finish, which is at the end of the sentence 'Always therefore put in the headings properly, don't wait until your examination to start this correct practice.'

The reason for this instruction should be obvious to the reader after going through that part of the Appendix. If effort is needed to bring work to the required standard, it is more likely that the effort will be made if the reader can understand why the author should make such a request.

Exercises

6.1. From the following trial balance of B. Webb extract a trading and profit and loss account for the year ended 31 December 19–6 and a balance sheet as at that date.

Trial Balance as at 31 December 19–6

	Dr	*Cr*
	£	£
Stock 1 January 19–6	3,249	
Sales		18,462
Purchases	11,380	
Salaries	2,150	
Motor expenses	520	
Rent and rates	670	
Insurance	111	
General expenses	105	
Premises	1,500	
Motor vehicles	1,200	
Debtors	1,950	
Creditors		1,538
Cash at bank	1,654	
Cash in hand	40	
Drawings	895	
Capital		5,424
	25,424	25,424

Stock at 31 December 19–6 was £2,548.

6.2. From the following trial balance of C. Worth you are required to draw up a trading and profit and loss account for the year ended 30 June 19–4 and a balance sheet as at that date.

Trial Balance as at 30 June 19–4

	Dr	*Cr*
	£	£
Sales		28,794
Purchases	21,428	
Rent and rates	854	
Lighting and heating expenses	422	
Stock 1 July 19–3	2,375	
Salaries and wages	3,164	
Insurance	105	
Shop buildings	50,000	
Shop fixtures	1,000	
Debtors	3,166	

Trade expenses	506	
Creditors		1,206
Cash at bank	3,847	
Drawings	2,400	
Motor vans	5,500	
Motor running expenses	1,133	
Capital		65,900
	95,900	95,900

Stock at 30 June 19–4 was £4,166.

6.3. The final accounts of Lonsdale and Co are made up to 30 April in each year.

Harry Towne and William Briggs occupied buildings which were the property of Lonsdale and Co. On 30 April 19–2 Towne paid to Lonsdale and Co £75, representing rent for the month of May 19–2. At the same date Briggs owed to Lonsdale and Co £90 for rent for the month of April 19–2.

During the year to 30 April 19–3, Lonsdale and Co received from Towne £750, representing rent for the ten months to 31 March 19–3, and from Briggs £1,260, representing rent for the fourteen months to 31 May 19–3. The rent due from Towne for April 19–3, was not paid until May 19–3.

Show the rent receivable account in the Ledger of Lonsdale and Co for the year to 30 April 19–3. There are no personal accounts for Towne and Briggs in the books of Lonsdale and Co.

Note.
The buildings were first let as follows:
(i) To Briggs from 1 April 19–2.
(ii) To Towne from 1 May 19–2.
(Union of Educational Institutions)

6.4. L. Gorse rents premises at a rental of £1,000 per annum.

He sublets part of the premises to S. Hill at £300 per annum and another part to A. Pine at £200 per annum.

On 1 January 19–4 Gorse had paid his own rent up to date: Hill's rent was 3 months in arrear and Pine had paid his rent to 31 March 19–4.

During the year 19–4.

(i) Gorse paid his rent at the end of each quarter except the amount due at 31 December 19–4 which was outstanding.
(ii) Gorse received the following amounts from Hill: 31 January £150; 1 April £75; 5 July £75; 4 December £150.
(iii) Gorse received the following amount from Pine. 10 October £100.

Show the accounts for (*a*) rent payable and (*b*) rent receivable in Gorse's ledger for the year ended 31 December 19–4.

Note.
No personal accounts are kept for Hill and Pine.
(Associated Examining Board 'A' Level)

6.5. N. Reeves is a wholesaler who heats his premises by oil-fired central heating. On 1 January 19–5 the Stock of Oil in hand was £35 and £50 was in hand on 31 December 19–5. Reeves owed £60 to the Oil Suppliers on 1 January 19–5 and there was an invoice for oil supplied during 19–5, unpaid on 31 December 19–5 of £145. During the year 19–5 payments made to the Oil Suppliers amounted to £260.

Write up Reeves' Fuel Account for the year ending 31 December 19–5 showing the appropriate transfer to Profit and Loss Account and bringing down any remaining balances.
(Royal Society of Arts)

6.6. From the following trial balance of K. Mellish draw up a trading and profit and loss account for the year ended 30 September 19–6, and a balance sheet as at that date.

	Dr	*Cr*
	£	£
Stock 1 October 19–5	2,368	
Purchases	12,389	
Sales		18,922
Salaries and wages	3,862	
Rent and rates	504	
Insurance	78	
Motor expenses	664	
Office expenses	216	
Lighting and heating expenses	166	
General expenses	314	
Premises	5,000	
Motor vehicles	1,800	
Fixtures and fittings	350	
Debtors	3,896	
Creditors		1,731
Cash at bank	482	
Drawings	1,200	
Capital		12,636
	33,289	33,289

Notes at 30 September 19–6:
1. Stock £2,946
2. Rates owing £60
3. Insurance prepaid £12
4. Lighting and heating expenses owing £32
5. Ignore depreciation of fixed assets.

6.7. The following trial balance was extracted from the books of N. Lomas on 30 April 19–7. From it, and the notes, prepare his trading and profit and loss account for the year ended 30 April 19–7, and a balance sheet as at that date.

	Dr	Cr
	£	£
Sales		18,955
Purchases	12,556	
Stock 1 May 19–6	3,776	
Salaries and wages	2,447	
Motor expenses	664	
Rent	456	
Rates	120	
Insurances	146	
Packing expenses	276	
Lighting and heating expenses	665	
Sundry expenses	115	
Motor vehicles	2,400	
Fixtures and fittings	600	
Debtors	4,577	
Creditors		3,045
Cash at bank	3,876	
Cash in hand	120	
Drawings	2,050	
Capital		12,844
	34,844	34,844

Notes at 30 April 19–7:

1. Expenses which have been prepaid—Rates £20; Insurances £35.
2. Expenses which are owing—motor expenses £56; Rent £24; Sundry expenses £26.
3. Stock £4,998.
4. Ignore depreciation of fixed assets.

6.8. You are to draw up a Trial Balance as on 31 December 19–5 from the following list of balances.

	£
Rent	609
Sales	25,500
Carriage inwards	207
Carriage outwards	300
Machinery	2,000
Cash at Bank	150
Stock at 1 January 19–5	3,200
Drawings	1,750
Debtors	8,800
Purchases	18,670
General expenses	770
Creditors	5,680
Motor van	2,400
Loan from M. Lewis	1,000
Capital	?

6.9A. From the following trial balance of L. Austin draw up a trading and profit and loss account for the year ended 31 December 19–3, and a balance sheet as at that date.

	Dr	*Cr*
	£	£
Salaries and wages	4,800	
Rent and rates	300	
Sales		25,600
Purchases	16,700	
Stock 1 January 19–3	4,350	
Insurance	150	
Motor expenses	420	
General expenses	280	
Premises	15,000	
Motor vehicles	2,000	
Debtors	4,320	
Creditors		3,140
Bank	840	
Capital		23,320
Drawings	2,900	
	52,060	52,060

Notes at 31 December 19–3:

1. Stock £4,590.
2. Rates prepaid £40.
3. General expenses owing £30.
4. Insurance prepaid £40.
5. Ignore the depreciation of fixed assets.

6.10A. The following is the trial balance of J. Jamieson as on 31 October 19–4. You are to draw up a Trading and Profit and Loss Account for the year ended 31 October 19–4 and a Balance Sheet as at that date.

	Dr	*Cr*
	£	£
Purchases	16,950	
Sales		23,240
Stock in hand 31 October 19–3	4,135	
Postages and telephone	228	
Motor expenses	399	
Salaries	4,364	
Sundry expenses	83	
Rent	390	
Rates	155	
Debtors	4,698	
Creditors		3,174
Premises	10,000	
Motor vehicles	2,350	

Fixtures and fittings	1,120	
Bank overdraft		1,458
Drawings	3,850	
Capital		20,850
	48,722	48,722

Notes at 31 October 19–4:
1. Stock on hand was £2,859.
2. Expenses owing: Sundry expenses £22; Motor expenses £58.
3. Expenses prepaid: Rates £23; Telephone £11.
4. Ignore depreciation of fixed assets.

6.11A. From the following trial balance of D. Morris as on 30 June 19–5 draw up a Trading and Profit and Loss Account for the year ended 30 June 19–5 and a Balance Sheet as at that date.

	Dr	*Cr*
	£	£
Sales		50,000
Rent	560	
Insurance	290	
Purchases	35,600	
Salaries and wages	3,400	
Packing and postage	560	
Rates	210	
Sundry expenses	390	
Carriage inwards	110	
Carriage outwards	205	
Stock at 30 June 19–4	7,800	
Debtors	8,400	
Creditors		3,900
Cash at bank	896	
Cash in hand	80	
Buildings	20,000	
Machinery	6,000	
Motor vehicles	3,980	
Drawings	4,500	
Capital		39,081
	92,981	92,981

Notes at 30 June 19–5:
1. Stock £9,665.
2. Expenses owing: Carriage inwards £33.
3. Expenses prepaid: Insurance £14; Rent £40; Packing and post £28.
4. Ignore depreciation of fixed assets.

6.12A. At 31 March 19–3, the stock of stationery held by J. W., a trader, was valued at £54 and £21 was owing to suppliers of stationery.

During the year to 31 March, 19–4, payments to suppliers of stationery amounted to £463. This total included a payment of £80 on 31 March 19–4, to one supplier, for stationery to be delivered in April 19–4. On 31 March 19–4, J.W. owed £38 to other suppliers of stationery, and the stock of stationery on J.W.'s premises was valued at £18.

During the year to 31 March 19–4, stationery which had cost £6 was taken by J.W., from his business supplies, for private purposes not connected with the business.

You are required to show the stationery account, in J.W.'s ledger, for the year to 31 March 19–4, making suitable entries for all the matters mentioned above, and showing the transfer to the profit and loss account at 31 March 19–4. No personal accounts for suppliers of stationery are kept in J.W.'s books.

6.13A. G. Hunt is a sewing machine manufacturer.

On 1 January 19–3 the insurance prepaid from the previous year was £180.

On 1 April 19–3 he pays by cheque employers liability insurance £240 for the year to 31 March 19–4.

On 1 August 19–3 fire insurance of £276 for the following 12 months is paid by cheque.

At 31 December 19–3 Hunt realises that the burglary insurance of £300 per annum, due on 1 December 19–3, has not been paid. He pays this by cheque on 15 January 19–4.

Write up Hunt's Insurance Account for the year ended 31 December 19–3, showing the appropriate transfer to Profit and Loss Account and bringing down any remaining balances.

6.14A. R. Funseth, Solicitor, keeps an account in which both Rent and Rates are entered. His financial year end is 31 October.

On 1 November 19–5 he still owed £60 rent for one month of the previous year, but had the benefit yet to come of £100 prepaid rates.

He makes the following payments by cheque:

1 December 19–5	Rent for 3 months £180
1 April 19–6	Rent for 6 months £360
1 June 19–6	In respect of the rates bill for the year to 31 March 19–7 of £300 he pays £150 on account
21 October 19–6	Rent for 4 months £240

Write up Funseth's Rent and Rates Account for the year ended 31 October 19–6. Show the appropriate transfer to the Profit and Loss Account and carry forward any necessary balances.

6.15A. From the following list of balances construct a Trial Balance at 31 March 19–4, showing the Capital Account balance at that date:

	£
Fixtures and fittings	425
Delivery vans	3,250
Administration expenses	2,345
Cash at bank	423
Creditors	612
Debtors	1,952

	£
Purchases	15,242
Sales	27,283
Returns inwards	154
Returns outwards	173
Stock at 1 April 1973	4,275
Wages	3,872
Carriage inwards	547
Carriage outwards	276

7

Accounting, Concepts and Conventions

The book so far has, in the main, been concerned with the recording of transactions in the books. Much of the rest of the book is about the classifying, summarizing and interpreting of the records that have been made. Before this second stage is reached it would be beneficial to the reader to examine the basic concepts and conventions of accounting.

It does not follow that you will necessarily agree with the concepts and conventions. They are often attacked by accountants and others, and are constantly undergoing changes as better methods of accounting are found. Accounting is not a static subject, it is constantly undergoing change. However, according to many people, both inside and outside the accountancy profession, it does not change quickly enough. The consideration of this last point is outside the scope of this book.

The Trading and Profit and Loss Accounts and Balance Sheets shown in the previous chapter were drawn up so as to be of benefit to the owner of the business. Of course, as is shown later in the book, businesses are often owned by more than just one person and these accounting statements are for the benefit of them all. Now in the case of a sole trader he may well also use copies of the Final Accounts for the purpose of showing them as evidence when his income tax on his profits is worked out, or when he wants to obtain a loan from a bank or from some other person. He may well also show a copy to someone who is interested in buying his business from him, or if he wants to have extended credit for a large amount from a supplier as proof of his financial stability. In the case of partners and shareholders for businesses owned by more than one person the final accounts will be used for similar purposes.

Now of course if it had always been the custom to draft different kinds of final accounts for different purposes, so that one type was given to a banker, another type to someone wishing to buy the business, etc., then Accounting would be different than it is today. However, as yet it is deemed appropriate to give copies of the same set of final accounts to all the various parties, so that the banker, the prospective buyer of the business, the owner, the income tax inspector and the other people involved see the same Trading and Profit and Loss Account and Balance Sheet. This is not really an ideal situation as the interests of each party are different and really demand different kinds of information from that possessed by the others. For instance the bank manager would really like to know how much the assets would fetch if the firm ceased trading, so that he could judge in that case what the possibility would be of the bank obtaining repayment of its loan. Other parties would also like to see the information expressed in terms of values which were relevant to them. Yet in fact normally only one sort of final accounts is available for these different parties.

This means that Trading and Profit and Loss Accounts are multi-purpose documents, and to be of any use the various parties have to agree to the way in which they are drawn up. Assume that you are in a class of students and that you are faced with the problem of valuing your assets, which consists of 10 text-books. The first value you decide to assess is that of how much you could sell them for. Your own assessment is £9, but the other members of the class may give figures ranging from (say) £3 to £15. Suppose that you now decide to put a value on their use to you. You may well think that the use of these books will enable you to pass your examinations and so you will get a good job. Another person may well have completely the opposite idea concerning the use of the books to him. The use values placed on the books by individuals will therefore tend to vary widely. Finally you decide to value them by reference to cost. You take out of your pocket the bills for the books which show that you paid a total of £25 for the books. Assuming that the rest of the class do not think that you have altered the bills in any way, then they also can all agree that the value expressed as cost is £25. As this is the only value that you can all agree to then each of you decides to use the idea of showing the value of his asset of books at the cost price.

The use of a measure which gains consensus of opinion, rather than to use one's own measure which might conflict with other people's, is said to be objective. Thus the use of cost for asset valuation is an attempt to be objective. On the other hand the use of your own measure irrespective of whether people agree with it or not is said to be subjective. The desire to provide the same set of accounts for many different parties, and thus to provide a measure that gains their concensus of opinion, means that objectivity is sought for in financial accounting. If you are able to understand this desire for objectivity, then many of the apparent contradictions can be understood because it is often at the heart of the financial accounting methods in use at the present time.

Financial Accounting seeks objectivity, and of course it must have rules which lay down the way in which the activities of the business are recorded. These rules are generally known as concepts.

Basic Concepts

1. The Cost Concept

The need for this has already been described. It means that assets are normally shown at cost price, and that this is the basis for assessing the future usage of the asset.

2. The Money Measurement Concept

Accounting is only concerned with those facts that can be measured in monetary terms with a fair degree of objectivity. This means that Accounting can never show the whole of the information needed to give you a full picture of the state of the business or how well it is being conducted. Accounting does not record that the firm has a good, or a bad, management team. It does not show that the poor morale prevalent among the staff is about to lead to a serious strike, or that various managers will not co-operate with one another. Nor would it reveal that a rival product is about to take over a large part of the market occupied at present by the firm's own goods.

This means quite simply that just looking at a set of accounting figures does not tell you all that you would like to know about a business. Some people imagine that Accounting gives you a full picture, but from what has been said they are quite obviously deluding themselves. Others would maintain that really Accounting ought to put monetary values on these other factors as yet ignored in Accounting. Those who object to this state that this would mean a considerable loss of objectivity. Imagine trying to place a value of the future services to be given to the firm by one of its managers. Different people would tend to give different figures, and so, at present, as the final accounts are of a multi-purpose nature, which figures would be acceptable to the many parties who use the accounts? As the answer is that no one set of acceptable figures could be agreed in this case by all parties, then in Accounting as it stands the task is just not undertaken at all. It would seem likely that, eventually, the vital factor of placing a value on labour and management, usually known as 'Human Asset' accounting, will play a full part in the construction of balance sheets.

3. The Going Concern Concept

Unless the opposite is known, Accounting always assumes that the business will continue to operate for an indefinitely long period of time. Only if the business was going to be sold would it be necessary to show how much the assets would fetch. In the accounting records normally this is assumed to be of no interest to the firm. This is obviously connected with the cost concept, as if firms were not assumed to be going concerns the cost concept could not really be used, e.g. if firms were always to be treated as though they were going to be sold immediately after the accounting records were drafted, then the saleable value of the assets would be more relevant than cost.

4. The Business Entity Concept

The transactions recorded in a firm's books are the transactions that affect the firm. The only attempt to show how the transaction affects the owners of a business is limited to showing how their capital in the firm is affected. For instance, a proprietor puts £1,000 more cash into the firm as capital. The books will then show that the firm has £1.000 more cash and that his capital has increased by £1,000. They do not show that he has £1,000 less cash in his private resources. The accounting records are therefore limited to the firm and do not extend to the personal resources of the proprietors.

5. The Realization Concept

In accounting, profit is normally regarded as being earned at the time when the goods or services are passed to the customer and he incurs liability for them, i.e. this is the point at which the profit is treated as being realized. Note that it is not when the order is received, nor the contract signed, neither is it dependent on waiting until the customer pays for the goods or services. It can mean that profit is brought into account in one period, and it is found to have been incorrectly taken as such when the goods are returned in later period because of some deficiency. Also the services can turn out to be subject to an allowance being given in a later period owing to poor performance. If the allowances or returns can be reasonably estimated an adjustment may be made to the calculated profit in the period when they passed to the customer.

6. The Dual Aspect Concept

This states that there are two aspects of Accounting, one represented by the assets of the business and the other by the claims against them. The concept states that these two aspects are always equal to each other. In other words:

Assets = Liabilities + Capital.

Double entry is the name given to the method of recording the transactions so that the dual aspect concept is upheld.

7. The Accrual Concept

The fact that net profit is said to be the difference between revenues and expenses rather than between cash receipts and expenditures is known as the Accrual Concept. A great deal of attention is therefore paid to this which, when the mechanics needed to bring about the Accrual Concept are being performed, is known as 'matching' expenses against revenues.

This concept is particularly misunderstood by people not well versed in Accounting. To many of them the actual payment of an item in a period is taken as being matched against the revenue of the period when the net profit is calculated. The fact that expenses consist of the assets used up in a particular period in obtaining the revenues of that period, and that cash paid in a period and expenses of a period are usually different, comes as a surprise to a great number of them.

The Assumption of the Stability of Currency

One does not have to be very old to remember that a few years ago many goods could be bought with less money than today. If one listens to one's parents or grandparents then many stories will be heard of how little this item or the other could be bought for *x* years ago. The currencies of the countries of the world are not stable in terms of what each unit of currency can buy over the years.

Accounting, however, uses the cost concept, this stating that the asset is normally shown at its cost price. This means that accounting statements will be distorted because assets will be bought at different points in time at the price then ruling, and the figures totalled up to show the value of the assets in cost terms. As an instance, suppose that you had bought a building 20 years ago for £20,000. You now decide to buy an identical additional building, but the price has now risen to £40,000. You buy it, and the buildings account now shows buildings at a figure of £60,000. One building is measured cost-wise in terms of the currency of 20 years ago, whilst the other is taken at today's currency value. The figure of a total of £60,000 is historically correct, but, other than that, the total figure cannot be said to be particularly valid for any other use.

This means that to make a correct assessment of accounting statements one must bear in mind the distorting effects of changing price levels upon the accounting entries as recorded. There are techniques of adjusting accounts so as to try and eliminate these distortions, but these are outside the scope of this volume.

The Conventions of Accounting

The concepts of Accounting have become accepted in the business world, their assimilation having taken place over many years. The concepts, however, are capable of being interpreted in many ways. What has therefore grown up in Accounting are generally accepted approaches to the application of the concepts. These approaches are known as the conventions of Accounting. The main conventions may be said to be: 1. Materiality, 2. Conservatism, 3. Consistency.

1. Materiality

Accounting does not serve a useful purpose if the effort of recording a transaction in a certain way is not worthwhile. Thus, if a bottle of ink was bought it would be used up over a period of time, and this cost is used up every time someone dips his pen into the ink. It is possible to record this as an expense every time it happens, but obviously the price of a bottle of ink is so little that it is not worth recording it in this fashion. The bottle of ink is not a material item, and therefore would be charged as an expense in the period it was bought, irrespective of the fact that it could last for more than one accounting period. In other words do not waste your time in the elaborate recording of trivial items.

Similarly, the purchase of a cheap metal ashtray would also be charged as an expense in the period it was bought because it is not a material item, even though it may in fact last for twenty years. A motor lorry would however be deemed to be a material item, and so, as will be seen in the chapter on depreciation, an attempt is made to charge each period with the cost consumed in each period of its use.

Firms fix all sorts of arbitrary rules to determine what is material and what is not. There is no law that lays down what these should be, the decision as to what is material and what is not is dependent upon judgment. A firm may well decide that all items under £100 should be treated as expenses in the period which they were bought even though they may well be in use in the firm for the following ten years. Another firm, especially a large one, may fix the limit of £1,000. Different limits may be set for different types of items.

It can be seen that the size and the type of firm will affect the decisions as to which items are material. With individuals, an amount of £1,000 may well be more than you, as a student, possess. For a multimillionaire this is an insignificant amount. The decisions of you and the millionaire as to what is a material item and what is not will almost certainly not be comparable. Just as individuals vary then so do firms. Some firms have a great deal of machinery and may well treat all items of machinery costing less than £1,000 as not being material, whereas another firm which makes about the same amount of profits, but has very little machinery, may well treat a £600 machine as being a material item as they have fixed their limit at £100.

2. *Conservatism*

Very often an accountant has to make a choice as to which figure he will take for a given item. The convention of conservatism means that normally he will take the figure which will understate rather than overstate the profit. Alternatively, this could be expressed as choosing the figure which will cause the capital of the firm to be shown at a lower amount rather than at a higher one. This could also be said to be to make sure that all losses are recorded in the books, but that profits should not be anticipated by recording them prematurely.

It was probably this convention that led to accountants being portrayed as being rather miserable by nature; they were used to favouring looking on the black side of things and ignoring the bright side. However, the convention has seen considerable changes in the last few decades, and there has been a shift along the scale away from the gloomy view and more towards the desire to paint a brighter picture when it is warranted.

3. Consistency

The concepts and conventions already listed are so broad that in fact there are many different ways in which items may be recorded in the accounts. Each firm should, within these limits, select the methods which give the most equitable picture of the activities of the business. However, this cannot be done if one method is used in one year and another method in the next year and so on. Constantly changing the methods would lead to a distortion of the profits calculated from the accounting records. Therefore the convention of consistency comes into play. This convention is that when a firm has once fixed a method of the accounting treatment of an item it will enter all similar items that follow in exactly the same way.

However, it does not bind the firm to following the method until the firm closes down. A firm can change the method used, but such a change is not affected without the deepest consideration. When such a change occurs and the profits calculated in that year are affected by a material amount, then either in the profit and loss account itself or in one of the reports accompanying it, the effect of the change should be stated.

Accounting Terminology

Unfortunately many of the terms used in the description of Accounting theory mean quite different things to different people. Things described as concepts and conventions in this book may well be called principles by someone else, or alternatively they will all be called concepts without any attempt to divide them between concepts and conventions. Provided that the reader realises this then no harm will result.

Probably the most recent attempt to change a term is the use of the word 'Prudence' instead of 'Conservatism'. As most accounting literature uses the word 'Conservatism' then this is the one used in this book. Both of these words can be taken to mean the same for the purposes of this text-book.

8

The Division of the Ledger: Two- and Three-Column Cash Books and Discount Accounts

While the firm has an extremely small number of transactions all the double entry accounts could be maintained in one book called the ledger. With the growth in the number of transactions it would become obvious that one ledger would be too bulky for convenient use. As more than one book would now be needed the problem could be resolved in several ways. One method would be to have two or more ledgers with the accounts contained in them being chosen at random. However, it would be difficult to remember exactly which accounts were in each ledger, and constantly referring to the wrong ledger is time-wasting.

The usual solution is to divide the ledger up into its different functions. Thus for the personal accounts we could have two ledgers, one for the customers' personal accounts which would be called a Sales Ledger, and another for the suppliers' personal accounts which would be called the Purchases Ledger or Bought Ledger. Another function requiring a considerable number of entries is that of receiving and paying out money. To cover this function the cash account and the bank account are taken out of the ledger and combined in one book called the Cash Book. The remaining accounts, which are the expense and revenue accounts and the other asset and liability accounts, could be retained in the ledger which could now be called by one of the alternative names of a General Ledger or Nominal Ledger. All the ledgers and the cash book contain accounts, in other words they are all part of the double entry system.

If more than one person becomes engaged in book-keeping the division of the ledger into different books will greatly aid their task. The book-keeping to be done could be allocated by functions, each book-keeper taking over the book or books for one or more functions.

The general ledger, in its present state, would still need to be constantly used, for it would contain the sales account, purchases account, and the returns inwards and outwards accounts besides all the other accounts for income, expenses, assets other than cash and debtors, and liabilities other than creditors. In order that the general ledger would not constantly be used by more than one person a technique is used to save the sales, purchases, and returns accounts from being cluttered up with unnecessary detail. To this end four new books are opened for credit transactions only, one book being used for Credit Sales, one for Credit Purchases and one each for Returns Inwards and Returns Outwards. They are dealt with in detail in Chapter 9. The basic idea is that when for instance a credit sale is made, an entry is made in the customer's personal account but no entry is made in the sales account. Instead, the item is listed in the sales book and the total of the sales book is transferred at regular intervals to the credit of the sales account. It will only be at the time of transfer of the total from the sales book to the sales account that the general ledger would need the collaboration of two people, the person whose job it is to look after the general ledger together with the person who looks after the sales book. A similar process would happen with the purchases and the returns.

With the growth of the firm then, each book-keeper will tend to specialize in different functions recorded in the books. How far this will proceed depends largely on the size that the firm eventually attains. As the number of transactions needing recording continues to grow the work will have to be sub-divided. For instance, the growth in the number of accounts in the sales ledger would eventually outstrip the ability of that particular book-keeper to keep the sales ledger accounts up to date. The sales ledger would therefore have to be divided so that two persons could each look after a part of it. The method of division should be that which is most suitable from the firm's point of view and this may differ as between one firm and another. It might be an alphabetical division, for instance one sales ledger containing all those customers' personal accounts whose business names begin with the letters A to M and another sales ledger for those with letters N to Z. Should it be preferred the sales ledger could be split into geographical divisions, one sales ledger for Great Britain and another for Overseas. Any other convenient method could be used. Similarly, the cash book could be divided into a Cash Payments Book and a Cash Receipts Book.

The main concern at this point is with the first basic divisions of the ledger rather than the later sub-divisions. These are:

Sales Ledger Purchases Ledger Cash Book General Ledger	All contain accounts and are therefore part of the double entry system.
Sales Book Purchases Book Returns Inwards Book Returns Outwards Book	Mere listing devices to save the relevant accounts from unnecessary detail.

The Cash Book

The Two-column Cash Book

The cash book is merely the cash account and the bank account brought together in one book. Previously these two accounts would have been shown on two separate pages of the ledger. Now it is more convenient to place the account columns together so that the recording of all money received and of all money paid out on a particular date can be found on the same page. The cash book is ruled so that the debit column of the cash account is placed alongside the debit column of the bank account, and the credit columns of the cash and the bank accounts are also placed alongside each other.

A cash account and a bank account can now be looked at as they would have been if they had been kept separately, and then as they would be shown if the transactions had instead been kept in a cash book.

The bank column contains details of the payments made by cheque and of the money received and paid into the bank account. The bank which is handling the firm's money will of course have copy of the account in its own books. The bank will periodically send a copy of the account in the bank's books to the firm, this copy usually being known as the Bank Statement. When the firm receives the bank statement it will check it against the bank column in its own cash book to ensure that there are no discrepancies.

Cash

19–5		£	19–5		£
Aug	1 Balance b/d	33	Aug	8 Rent	20
,,	5 G. Brew	25	,,	12 M. Player	19
,,	15 B. Hooley	37	,,	28 Wages	25
,,	30 H. Hawk	18	,,	31 Balance c/d	49
		113			113
Sept	1 Balance b/d	49			

Bank

19–5		£	19–5		£
Aug	1 Balance b/d	949	Aug	7 Rates	105
,,	3 I. Pell Ltd	295	,,	12 D. Sayers Ltd	95
,,	16 G. Peck	408	,,	26 N. Foulkes	268
,,	30 B. Smailes	20	,,	31 Balance c/d	1,204
		1,672			1,672
Sept	1 Balance b/d	1,204			

Cash Book

	Cash	Bank		Cash	Bank
19–5	£	£	19–5	£	£
Aug 1 Balances b/d	33	949	Aug 7 Rates		105
„ 3 I. Pell Ltd		295	„ 8 Rent	20	
„ 5 G. Brew	25		„ 12 M. Player	19	
„ 15 B. Hooley	37		„ „ D. Sayers Ltd		95
„ 16 G. Peck		408	„ 26 N. Foulkes		268
„ 30 B. Smailes		20	„ 28 Wages	25	
„ „ H. Hawk	18		„ 31 Balance c/d	49	1,204
	113	1,672		113	1,672
Sept 1 Balances b/d	49	1,204			

Cash Paid into the Bank

In the illustration already seen, the payments into the bank have consisted of cheques received by the firm which have been banked immediately. There is, however, the case to be considered of cash being paid into the bank.

Now look at the position when a customer pays his account in cash, and later a part of this cash is paid into the bank. The receipt of the cash is debited to the cash column on the date received, the credit entry being in the customer's personal account. Now the cash banked has the following effect needing action as shown:

Effect	*Action*
1. Asset of cash is decreased.	Credit the asset account, i.e. the cash account which is represented by the cash column in the cash book.
2. Asset of bank is increased.	Debit the asset account, i.e. the bank account which is represented by the bank column in the cash book.

A receipt of £100 from Dobson and Hawkes on 1 August 19–5, later followed by the banking on 3 August of £80 of this amount would appear in the cash book thus:

	Cash	Bank		Cash	Bank
19–5	£	£	19–5	£	£
Aug 1 Dobson and	100		Aug 3 Bank	80	
„ 1 Hawkes					
„ 3 Cash		80			

The details column shows entries against each item stating the name of the account in which the completion of double entry had taken place. Against the cash payment of £80 appears the word 'bank' meaning that the debit of £80 is to be found in the bank column, and the converse applies.

Where the whole of the cash received is banked immediately the receipt can be treated in exactly the same manner as a cheque received, i.e. it can be entered directly in the bank column.

Sometimes, when the firm requires cash for future payments and it has not got a sufficient amount of cash in hand for the purpose, it may withdraw cash from the bank. This is done by making out a cheque to pay itself a certain amount of cash. The proprietor, or an authorized person, visits the bank where he is given cash in exchange for the cheque. This is sometimes known as 'cashing' a cheque for business use.

The twofold effect and the action required may be summarized:

Effect	*Action*
1. Asset of bank is decreased.	Credit the asset account, i.e. the bank column in the cash book.
2. Asset of cash is increased.	Debit the asset account, i.e. the cash column in the cash book.

A withdrawal of £75 cash on 1 June 19–5 from the bank would appear in the cash book thus:

	Cash	*Bank*		*Cash*	*Bank*
19–5	£		19–5		£
June 1 Bank	75		June 1 Cash		75

Where an item does not need entering in another book as double entry has already taken place within the cash book, then this item is known as a 'contra' being the Latin word for against. Thus cash paid into the bank and cash withdrawn from the bank are both contra items. As there is a debit item and a credit item for the same amount double entry has already been completed, so that no account exists elsewhere for contra items.

The Use of Folio Columns

As already seen, the details column in an account contains the name of the other account in which double entry has been completed. Anyone looking through the books for any purpose would thus be assisted to find where the other half of the double entry was situated. However, with the growth in the number of books in use the mere mention of the name of the other account would not be sufficient to give quick reference to the other account. An extra aid is therefore needed and this is brought about by the use of a 'folio' column. In each account and in each book in use an extra column is added, this always being shown on the immediate left of the money columns. In this column the name of the other book, in abbreviated form, and the number of the page in the other book where double entry is completed is stated against each and every entry in the books.

Thus an entry of receipt of cash from C. Shelley whose account was on page 45 of the sales ledger, and the cash recorded on page 37 of the cash book, would use the folio columns thus:

In the cash book. In the folio column alongside the entry of the amount would appear SL 45.

In the sales ledger. In the folio column alongside the entry of the amount would appear CB 37.

By this means full cross reference would be given. Each of the contra items, being shown on the same page of the cash book, would use the letter 'C' in the folio column.

The folio column is only filled in when double entry for the item has been completed. The act of using one book as a medium for entering the items to the relevant account so as to complete double entry is known as 'posting' the items. Where the folio column has not been filled it will be seen at a glance that double entry has not been completed, thus the error made when only one-half of the double entry is complete is made less frequently and can often be detected easily.

A Worked Example

The following transactions are written up in the form of a cash book. The folio columns are also filled in as though double entry had been completed to the other ledgers.

19–5		£
September	1 Balances brought forward from last month:	
	Cash	20
	Bank	940
,,	2 Received cheque from M. Black	115
,,	4 Cash sales	82
,,	6 Paid rent by cash	35
,,	7 Banked £50 of the cash held by the firm	50
,,	15 Cash sales paid direct into the bank	40
,,	23 Paid cheque to M. Bell	277
,,	29 Withdrew cash from the bank	120
,,	30 Paid wages in cash	118

Cash Book

	Folio	Cash	Bank		Folio	Cash	Bank
19–5		£	£	19–5		£	£
Sept 1 Balances	b/d	20	940	Sept 6 Rent	GL 65	35	
„ 2 M. Black	SL 98		115	„ 7 Bank	C	50	
„ 4 Sales	GL 87	82		„ 23 M. Bell	PL 23		277
„ 7 Cash	C		50	„ 29 Cash	C		120
„ 15 Sales	GL 87		40	„ 30 Wages	GL 39	118	
„ 29 Bank	C	120		„ 30 Balances	c/d	19	748
		222	1,145			222	1,145
Oct 1 Balances	b/d	19	748				

The Three-Column Cash Book

Cash Discounts

To encourage customers to pay their accounts promptly a firm may offer to accept a lesser sum in full settlement providing payment is made within a specified period of time. The amount of the reduction of the sum to be paid is known as a cash discount. The term 'cash discount' thus refers to the allowance given for speedy payment, it is still called cash discount, even though the account was paid by cheque.

The rate of cash discount is usually quoted as a percentage, and full details of the percentage allowed and the period within which payment is to be made are quoted on all sales documents by the selling company. A typical period during which discount may be allowed is one month from the date of the original transaction.

A firm will thus encounter cash discounts from two different angles. First, it may allow cash discounts to firms to whom it sells goods, and second it may receive cash discounts from firms from whom it buys goods. To be able to distinguish easily between the two, the first kind are known as Discounts Allowed, the second kind are known as Discounts Received.

The effect of discounts can now be seen by looking at two examples.

Example 1

F. Cope owed £100. He pays on 2 September 19–5 by cash within the time limit laid down, and the firm allows him 5 per cent cash discount. Thus he will pay £100−£5 = £95 in full settlement of his account.

Effect	*Action*
1. Of cash:	
Cash is increased by £95.	Debit cash account, i.e. entered £95 in debit column of cash book.
Asset of debtors is decreased by £95.	Credit F. Cope £95.

Effect	*Action*
2. Of discounts:	
Asset of debtors is decreased by £5. (After the cash was paid the balance still appeared of £5. As the account is deemed to be settled this asset must now be cancelled.)	Credit F. Cope £5.
Expenses of discounts allowed increased by £5.	Debit discounts allowed account £5.

Example 2

The firm owed W. Smith £400. It pays him on 3 September 19–5 by cheque within the time limit laid down by him and he allows $2\frac{1}{2}$ per cent cash discount. Thus the firm will pay £400−£10 = £390 in full settlement of the account.

Effect	*Action*
1. Of cheque:	
Asset of bank is reduced by £390.	Credit bank, i.e. enter in credit bank column, £390.
Liability of creditors is reduced by £390.	Debit W. Smith's account £390.
2. Of discounts:	
Liability of creditors is reduced by £10. (After the cheque was paid the balance of £10 remained. As the account is deemed to be settled the liability must now be cancelled.)	Debit W. Smith's account £10.
Revenue of discounts received increased by £10.	Credit discounts received account £10.

The accounts in the firm's books would appear:

Cash Book (Page 32)

		Cash	*Bank*			*Cash*	*Bank*
19–5		£	£	19–5		£	£
Sept 2 F. Cope	SL 12	95		Sept 3 W. Smith	PL 75		390

Discounts Received (General Ledger page 18)

			19–5		
			Sept 2 W. Smith	PL 75	10

Discounts Allowed (General Ledger page 17)

19–5					
Sept 2 F. Cope	CB 12	5			

F. Cope (Sales Ledger page 12)

19–5			19–5		
Sept 1 Balance b/d		100	Sept 2 Cash	CB 32	95
			„ 2 Discount	GL 17	5
		100			100

Cash Book (Page 32)

W. Smith (Purchases Ledger page 75)

		Cash	Bank		Cash	Bank
19–5		£	£	19–5	£	£
Sept 3 Bank	CB 32		390	Sept 1 Balance b/d		400
„ 3 Discounts	GL 18		10			
			400			400

It is the accounting custom merely to enter the word 'Discount' in the personal account, not distinguishing as to whether it is a discount received or a discount allowed. This is obviously to save time as the full description against each discount would be unnecessary. After all, the sales ledger accounts will only contain discounts allowed, and the purchases ledger accounts will only contain discounts received.

The discounts allowed account and the discounts received account are contained in the general ledger along with all the other revenue and expense accounts. It has already been stated that every effort should be made to avoid constant reference to the general ledger. In the case of discounts this is achieved quite simply by adding an extra column on each side of the cash book in which the amounts of discounts are entered. Discounts received are entered in the discounts column on the credit side of the cash book, and discounts allowed in the discounts column on the debit side of the cash book.

The cash book, if completed for the two examples so far dealt with, would appear:

Cash Book

		Discount	Cash	Bank			Discount	Cash	Bank
19–5		£	£	£	19–5		£	£	£
Sept 2					Sept 3				
F. Cope	SL 12	5	95		W. Smith	PL 75	10		390

There is no alteration to the method of showing discounts in the personal accounts.

The entry of discounts in the cash book in such a fashion can be seen to be a time-saving technique. First, the amount to be entered as a discount must obviously be calculated at the same time as the payment is made or the money received. The cash book has therefore to be used in any case. The amount of discount is entered in the relevant discount column and no additional entry is required in the details column. It therefore saves the discount accounts being referred to for every entry of discount and also saves a separate entry of the details and date of each discount.

The discounts columns in the cash book are not however part of the double entry system, because they are not accounts as are the cash and bank columns. They are merely listing devices or collection points for discounts. Half of the double entry has already been made in the personal accounts. What is now required is the entry in the discounts accounts. The way that it is done in this case is by transferring the total of the discounts received column to the credit of a discounts received account, and the total of the discounts allowed account is transferred to the debit of a discounts allowed account.

This at first sight appears to be incorrect. How can a debit total be transferred to the debit of an account? Here one must look at the entries for discounts in the personal accounts. Discounts allowed have been entered on the credit sides of the individual personal accounts. The entry of the total in the expense account of discounts allowed must therefore be on the debit side to preserve double entry balancing. The converse applies to discounts received.

The sides on which the two types of discounts are entered in the discounts accounts in the general ledger can be easily reconciled if discounts allowed are seen as an expense of attracting money. As an expense they will be found as a debit in the discounts allowed account. Similarly discounts received may be seen as income received for prompt payment of accounts, and as revenue will therefore appear on the credit side in the discounts received account.

The following is a worked example of a three-column cash book for the whole of a month, showing the ultimate transfer of the totals of the discount columns to the discount accounts.

19–5			£
May	1	Balances brought down from April:	
		Cash Balance	29
		Bank Balance	654
		Debtors accounts:	
		B. Knott	120
		N. Campbell	280
		D. Strong	40
		Creditors accounts:	
		U. Barrow	60
		A. Ayres	440
		R. Long	100
,,	2	B. Knott pays us by cheque, having deducted 2½ per cent cash discount £3	117
,,	8	We pay R. Long his account by cheque, deducting 5 per cent cash discount £5	95
,,	11	We withdrew £100 cash from the bank for business use	100
,,	16	N. Campbell pays us his account by cheque, deducting 2½ per cent discount £7	273
,,	25	We paid wages in cash	92
,,	28	D. Strong pays us in cash after having deducted 2½ per cent cash discount	38
,,	29	We pay U. Barrow by cheque less 5 per cent cash discount £3	57
,,	30	We pay A. Ayres by cheque less 2½ per cent cash discount £11	429

Cash Book Page 64

	Folio	Discount	Cash	Bank		Folio	Discount	Cash	Bank
19–5		£	£	£	19–5		£	£	£
May 1 Balances	b/d		29	654	May 8 R. Long	PL 58	5		95
May 2 B. Knott	SL 13	3		117	May 11 Cash	C			100
May 11 Bank	C		100		May 25 Wages	GL 77		92	
May 16 N. Campbell	SL 84	7		273	May 29 U. Barrow	PL 15	3		57
May 28 D. Strong	SL 91	2	38		May 30 A. Ayres	PL 98	11		429
					May 31 Balances	c/d		75	363
		12	167	1,044			19	167	1,044
Jun 1 Balances	b/d		75	363					

Sales Ledger

B. Knott Page 13

		£			£
19–5			19–5		
May 1 Balance b/d		120	May 2 Bank	CB 64	117
			„ 2 Discount	CB 64	3
		120			120

N. Campbell Page 84

		£			£
19–5			19–5		
May 1 Balance b/d		280	May 16 Bank	CB 64	273
			„ 16 Discount	CB 64	7
		280			280

D. Strong Page 91

		£			£
19–5			19–5		
May 1 Balance b/d		40	May 28 Cash	CB 64	38
			„ 28 Discount	CB 64	2
		40			40

Purchases Ledger

U. Barrow Page 15

		£			£
19–5			19–5		
May 29 Bank	CB 64	57	May 1 Balance b/d		60
„ 29 Discount	CB 64	3			
		60			60

R. Long Page 58

19–5			£	19–5		£
May	8 Bank	CB 64	95	May	1 Balance b/d	100
,,	8 Discount	CB 64	5			
			100			100

A. Ayres Page 89

19–5			£	19–5		£
May	30 Bank	CB 64	429	May	1 Balance b/d	440
,,	30 Discount	CB 64	11			
			440			440

General Ledger

Wages Page 77

19–5		£			
May 25 Cash	CB 64	92			

Discounts Received

			19–5		£
			May 31 Total for the month	CB 64	19

Discounts Allowed

19–5		£			
May 31 Total for the month	CB 64	12			

As can now be checked, the total of the discounts received entered in the purchases ledger accounts amounts to £19 on the debit side, the total entered in the discounts received account on the credit side amounts also to £19. Thus double entry principles are upheld. A check on the discounts allowed will reveal a debit of £12 in the discounts allowed account and a total of £12 on the credit side of the accounts in the sales ledger.

Bank Overdrafts

A firm may borrow money from a bank by means of a bank overdraft. This means that the firm is allowed to pay more out of the bank account, by paying out cheques, for a total amount greater than that which it has placed in the account.

Up to this point the bank balances have all represented money at the bank, thus they have all been assets, i.e. debit balances. When the account is overdrawn the firm owes money to the bank, the account is a liability and the balance becomes a credit one.

Taking the cash book last illustrated, suppose that the amount payable to A. Ayres was £1,429 instead of £429. Thus the amount placed in the account, £1,044, is exceeded by the amount withdrawn. The cash book would appear as follows:

Cash Book

	Discount	*Cash*	*Bank*		*Discount*	*Cash*	*Bank*
19–5	£	£	£	19–5	£	£	£
May 1 Balances b/d		29	654	May 8 R. Long	5		95
„ 2 B. Knott	3		117	„ 11 Cash			100
„ 11 Bank		100		„ 25 Wages		92	
„ 16 N. Campbell	7		273	„ 29 U. Barrow	3		57
„ 28 D. Strong	2	38		„ 30 A. Ayres	11		1,429
„ 31 Balance c/d			637	„ 31 Balance c/d		75	
	12	167	1,681		19	167	1,681
Jun 1 Balance b/d		75		Jun 1 Balance b/d			637

Exercises

8.1. Write up a two-column cash book from the following details, and balance off as at the end of the month:

19–5
May 1 Started business with capital in cash £100
„ 2 Paid rent by cash £10
„ 3 F. Lean lent us £500, paying by cheque
„ 4 We paid B. Minter by cheque £65
„ 5 Cash sales £98
„ 7 N. Merton paid us by cheque £62
„ 9 We paid B. Burton in cash £22
„ 11 Cash sales paid direct into the bank £53
„ 15 G. Morton paid us in cash £65
„ 16 We took £50 out of the cash till and paid it into the bank account
„ 19 We repaid F. Lean £100 by cheque
„ 22 Cash sales paid direct into the bank £66
„ 26 Paid motor expenses by cheque £12
„ 30 Withdrew £100 cash from the bank for business use
„ 31 Paid wages in cash £97.

8.2. Write up a two-column cash book from the following details, and balance off as at the end of the month:

19–6
Mar 1 Balances brought down from last month:
Cash in hand £56
Cash in bank £2,356
„ 2 Paid rates by cheque £156
„ 3 Paid for postage stamps in cash £5
„ 5 Cash sales £74
„ 7 Cash paid into bank £60

„ 8 We paid T. Lipton by cheque £75
„ 10 We paid C. Brookes in cash £2
„ 12 J. Moores pays us £150, £50 being in cash and £100 by cheque
„ 17 Cash drawings by proprietor £20
„ 20 P. Jones pays us by cheque £79
„ 22 Withdrew £200 from the bank for business use
„ 24 Bought a motor van for £195 cash
„ 28 Paid rent by cheque £40
„ 31 Cash sales paid direct into the bank £105.

8.3. Write up a three-column cash book from the following details, balance off at the end of the month, and show the relevant discount accounts as they would appear in the general ledger:

19–6
Apl 1 Started business with £500 in the bank
„ 2 Bought goods paying by cheque £345
„ 4 Cash sales £135
„ 5 Received loan from B. Luckham in the form of a cheque £100
„ 6 Paid J. Jordan £50 owing to him by means of a cheque £47, he allowing us £3 discount
„ 7 K. Smithson paid us his account of £75 by means of a cheque for £71, we allowed him £4 discount
„ 8 Paid H. Hodges a cheque for £156, discount received £6
„ 9 We received a cheque for £234 from N. Nixon, discount allowed £8
„ 10 We paid each of the following accounts by cheque, in each case we first deducted a cash discount of 5 per cent: L. Higgs £60; B. Franks £100; J. Moxon £140
„ 11 We paid H. Statham a cheque for £56
„ 12 P. Peters pays us a cheque for £76
„ 16 The following persons pay us their accounts by cheque, in each case deducting a cash discount of $2\frac{1}{2}$ per cent: B. Hollies £240; C. Herman £160; D. Hill £40
„ 15 Paid J. Jukes his account of £40 by cash £38, having deducted £2 cash discount
„ 19 Paid motor expenses by cheque £24
„ 25 Cash Drawings £50
„ 26 Cash sales paid direct into the bank £76
„ 29 P. Terry pays us a cheque for £78, having deducted £2 cash discount.
„ 30 We pay G. Godson his account of £240 by cheque £230, £10 being deducted for cash discount.

8.4. Write up a three-column cash book from the following details, balance off at the end of the month, and show the relevant discount accounts as they would appear in the general ledger:

19–7
May 1 Balances brought forward:
Cash in hand £78
Cash at bank £1,256
„ 2 The following persons paid us their accounts by cheque, in each case they deducted 5 per cent cash discount:
Accounts: P. Kirk £80; M. Miller £60; L. Luxion £20; H. Hare £120
„ 3 We paid rent by cash £12

„ 4 We paid T. Holly his account of £67 by cheque, no discount being deducted
„ 6 Cash sales paid direct into the bank £75
„ 8 We paid the following accounts by cheque, in each case deducting a 5 per cent discount: G. Hughes £20; L. Ball £60; M. Midgeley £360; P. Peers £80
„ 10 Cash Drawings £40
„ 11 K. Kilvert pays us his account of £89 by cheque £85, deducting £4 cash discount
„ 17 Cash withdrawn from the bank £100 for business use
„ 19 Salaries paid in cash £80
„ 21 The following persons paid us their accounts by cheque, in each case they deducted a 5 per cent cash discount:
Accounts: J. Braddock £140; M. Wild £1,500; D. Sheldon £380
„ 27 Paid postage stamps by cash £10
„ 29 Proprietor pays a further £1,000 capital into the bank from his private moneys
„ 31 H. Moon paid us £76 in cash.

8.5A. Write up a two-column cash book for J. McGee from the following details. Balance off at the end of the month.

19–4
Jan 1 Started business with £500 in cash
„ 2 Paid rent in cash £140
„ 3 We took £200 out of the cash till and paid it into the bank
„ 5 Bought office fixtures, paying by cheque £127
„ 6 Cash sales paid direct into the bank £696
„ 7 C. Coody paid us by cheque £110
„ 14 Paid wages in cash £77
„ 18 G. Burns paid us in cash £29
„ 22 We paid H. Twitty by cheque £95
„ 24 Cash sales £66
„ 30 Paid motor expenses by cheque £169
„ 31 L. Wadkins paid us by cheque £188.

8.6A. From the following details write up a two-column cash book for N. Lopez, and balance off at the end of the month.

19–7
July 1 Balances brought forward from last month:
Cash in hand £48
Cash at bank £806
„ 2 We paid each of the following by cheque: S. Post £49; S. Little £106; D. Young £59
„ 3 D. Massey paid us in cash £72
„ 5 We paid rent in cash £49
„ 7 J. Stephenson paid us by cheque £204
„ 8 Cash Sales £190
„ 10 Paid wages in cash £188
„ 12 We paid D. Austin in cash £19
„ 18 Drawings by cheque £100
„ 21 Cash Sales direct into the bank £210
„ 24 Withdrew £200 from the bank for business use

„ 27 Paid carriage inwards by cheque £12
„ 28 Paid carriage outwards in cash £15
„ 30 Paid rent in cash £49
„ 31 J. Blalock paid us by cheque £124.

8.7A. From the following details write up a three-column cash book, balance off at the end of the month, and show the relevant discount accounts as they would appear in the general ledger:

19–3
Mar 1 Balances brought forward:
Cash in hand £211
Cash at bank £3,984
„ 2 We paid each of the following accounts by cheque, in each case we deducted a 5 per cent discount: T. Adams £80; C. Bibby £260; D. Clarke £440
„ 4 C. Potts pays us a cheque for £98
„ 6 Cash Sales paid direct into the bank £49
„ 7 Paid insurance by cash £65
„ 9 The following persons pay us their accounts by cheque, in each case they deducted a discount of 2½ per cent: R. Smiley £160; J. Turner £640; R. Pimlott £520
„ 12 Paid motor expenses by cash £100
„ 18 Cash Sales £98
„ 21 Paid salaries by cheque £120
„ 23 Paid rent by cash £60
„ 28 Received a cheque for £500 being a loan from R. Godfrey
„ 31 Paid for stationery by cheque £27.

8.8A. Write up a three-column cash book from the following details, balance off at the end of the month, and show the relevant discount accounts as they would appear in the general ledger:

19–2
Oct 1 Started business with £6,000 in the bank
„ 2 Received a cash loan of £500 from D. Gillert
„ 3 Bought motor van paying by cheque £1,100
„ 4 Bought goods for cash £460
„ 5 Cash withdrawn from the bank £300
„ 7 Paid rent in cash £70
„ 8 Cash drawings £100
„ 10 We paid the following accounts by cheque less 5 per cent discount in each case: T. Sprite £100; T. Thomas £260; R. Lomas £60; A. Hardacre £340
„ 12 We paid J. Jackson his account of £80, no cash discount being allowed
„ 15 The following persons paid us their accounts, in each case deducting a 2½ per cent discount: L. Hart £200; R. Mellings £360; A. Reid £160
„ 17 Received a further loan of £500 from D. Gillert by cheque
„ 20 Cash sales paid direct into the bank £98
„ 22 Paid for motor expenses in cash £18
„ 24 Received rent for sub-lease by cheque £20
„ 25 The following persons paid us their accounts by cheque, in each case deducting a 2½ per cent discount: R. Stannard £560; L. Vernon £120; T. Sutton £440

„ 26 We paid the following accounts by cheque, in each case deducting a 5 per cent discount: M. Percy £80; T. Constable £500; R. Bain £220

„ 28 Paid insurance by cash £70

„ 30 Drawings by cheque £80.

8.9A. You are to write up a three-column cash book for M. Pinero from the details which follow. Then balance off at the end of the month and show the discount accounts in the general ledger.

19–6

May 1 Balances brought forward:

Cash in hand	£58
Bank overdraft	£1,470

„ 2 M. Pinero pays further Capital into the bank £1,000

„ 3 Bought office fixtures by cheque £780

4 4 Cash Sales £220

„ 5 Banked cash £200

„ 6 We paid the following by cheque, in each case deducting $2\frac{1}{2}$ per cent cash discount: B. Barnes £80; T. Horton £240; T. Jacklin £400

„ 8 Cash Sales £500

„ 10 We paid the following accounts less 5 per cent discount in each case: By cheque: S. Torrance £500; M. Bembridge £260. By cash: B. Huggett £60; S. Lyle £320.

„ 12 Paid motor expenses in cash £77

„ 15 Cash withdrawn from the bank £400

„ 16 Cash Drawings £120

„ 18 The following firms paid us their accounts by cheque, in each case deducting a 5 per cent discount: L. Graham £80; B. Crenshaw £140; H. Green £220

„ 20 Salaries paid in cash £210

„ 22 T. Weiskopf paid us his account in cash £204

„ 24 The following firms paid their accounts in cash, in each case deducting a 5 per cent discount: T. Kite £40; A. North £60

„ 26 Paid insurance by cheque £150

„ 28 We banked all the cash in our possession except for £20 in the cash till

„ 31 Bought motor van, paying by cheque £4,920.

9

Sales, Purchases, Returns Inwards and Returns Outwards Books

It has already been stated in the last chapter that the recording of transactions has been divided up into the various functions of the business. Mention has been made on page 88 of the fact that, in order to keep the general ledger free from unnecessary detail, separate books are kept for credit transactions concerning sales, purchases, returns inwards and returns outwards. These books can now be examined in detail.

The Sales Book

In many businesses a considerable proportion of sales will be made on credit rather than for immediate cash. In fact, the sales of some businesses will consist entirely of credit sales. For each credit sale the selling firm will send a document to the buyer showing full details of the goods sold and the prices of the goods. This document is known as an Invoice, and to the seller it is known as a Sales Invoice. The seller will keep one or more copies of each sales invoice for his own use. Exhibit 9.1 is an example of an invoice. The invoice shown is concerned with goods on which Value Added Tax, abbreviated as VAT, is not chargeable. Value Added Tax will be examined later in the chapter.

It is from the copy sales invoices that the seller enters up his sales book. This book is merely a list, in date order, of each sales invoice, showing the date, the name of the firm to whom the goods have been sold, the number of the invoice for reference purposes, and the net amount of the invoice. There is no need to show in the sales book a description of the goods sold, as this information can be found by referring to the copy of the sales invoice which will have been filed after recording it in the sales book.

Reference to the specimen invoice will disclose an item of £140 for trade discount. This illustrates one of the two methods of the pricing out of goods sold. Each invoice may just show the customer the actual amount that he is being charged for the goods. On the other

Exhibit 9.1

			UXY Ltd
Invoice No. 9/158			Over Warehouse
Your Purchase Order 10/A/980			Lower End
Terms: $1\frac{1}{4}$% cash discount			Manchester
if paid within one month			1 September 19–5
INVOICE			
Messrs D. Picton & Sons			
45 Charles Street			
Worthing			
	£	£	
20 cases McBrand Pears × £21	420		
16 cartons Kay's Flour × £10	160		
6 cases Joy's Vinegar × £20	120		
	700		
Less 20% trade discount	140		
		560	

hand, the goods may be shown at one figure less an amount for trade discount, the net figure being the amount actually charged for the goods. Trade discount is allowed for one of the following reasons:

(*a*) Traders are often charged for goods at the retail price by manufacturers and wholesalers, but a trade discount is deducted equalling the difference between the manufacturer's or wholesaler's price and the retail price. The net figure is therefore the price payable by the retailer, and the trade discount will be the gross profit he will make if he later sells the goods at the full retail price. Thus the invoice will also act as information of the expected retail selling price of the goods. It also greatly simplifies matters where a firm sells both to the general public and to traders. All sales are priced out at the same figure to both kinds of customers, but in the case of traders a deduction of the percentage trade discount is made. Thus the sales personnel will only have to consult one set of prices for both sets of customers, the adjustment of the prices as between the two kinds of customers being made by deduction of the trade discount for traders.

(*b*) As a special discount to a trader buying goods in large quantities.

There will be no entry for trade discount anywhere in the books as it is merely a means of calculating the net selling price of the goods, and it is this latter figure that the firm is concerned with in the accounts. Contrast this with the use of cash discounts which are a vital feature of the double entry system.

An example of a sales book, starting with the record of the sales invoice already illustrated can now be shown:

Sales Book

		Invoice No.	*Folio*	Page 26
19–5				£
Sept 1	D. Picton & Sons	9/158	SL 12	560
„ 8	T. Cadiz	9/159	SL 39	1,640
„ 28	C. Cook	9/160	SL 125	220
„ 30	D. Seton & Co	9/161	SL 249	1,100
	Transferred to Sales Account		GL 44	3,520

The entry of these credit sales in the customers' accounts in the sales ledger adheres to the principles of personal accounts as described in earlier chapters. Apart from the fact that the customers' accounts are now contained in a separate book known as the sales ledger, and that the reference numbers in the folio columns will be different, each individual personal account retains its original characteristics. The act of using the sales book entries as the basis for entering up the customers' accounts is known as 'posting' the sales book.

Sales Ledger

D. Picton & Sons — Page 12

19–5			£
Sept 1	Sales	SB 26	560

T. Cadiz — Page 39

19–5			£
Sept 8	Sales	SB 26	1,640

C. Cook — Page 125

19–5			£
Sept 28	Sales	SB 26	220

D. Seton & Co — Page 249

19–5			£
Sept 30	Sales	SB 26	1,100

The personal accounts have therefore been debited with a total of £3,520 for credit sales. However, as yet no credit entry has been made for these items. The sales book itself, being merely a list, is not an account and therefore does not of itself form part of the double entry system. Double entry is therefore completed by taking the total of the sales book for the period and entering it on the credit side of the sales account in the general ledger. This is usually done at least once a month, but it could be effected weekly or for some other period of time.

General Ledger

			Sales		Page 44
	19–5				£
	Sept 30	Credit Sales for the month		SB 26	3,520

If this is now compared with the entries that would have been made when all the accounts were kept in one ledger, the overall picture should become clearer. The eventual answer is the same, personal accounts would have been debited with credit sales amounting in total to £3,520 and the sales account would have been credited with sales amounting in total to £3,520. The differences are now that first, the personal accounts are contained in a separate sales ledger, and second, the individual items of credit sales have been listed in the sales book, merely the total being credited to the sales account. The different books in use also mean a change in the reference numbers in the folio columns.

Alternative names for the Sales Book are Sales Journal and Sales Day Book.

The Purchases Book

Obviously, if a large proportion of sales are credit sales it follows that a large proportion of the purchase of goods by firms will be credit purchases. The sales invoice sent by the selling firm to its customer will become a purchases invoice in the eyes of that customer.

Much unnecessary confusion is caused to students in that the credit sale of one firm is the credit purchase of another. The fact to be borne in mind is that the invoice must be identified from the viewpoint of the firm whose books are being written up. When the firm is selling, the invoice concerned is a sales invoice and when the firm is buying, the invoice concerned is a purchases invoice.

The entry of credit purchases in the books follows a similar plan to that of credit sales. The net amount of the invoice, i.e. after deduction of trade discount, is listed in the purchases book and the items are then posted to the credit of the personal accounts in the purchases ledger. The invoice is then filed away for future reference. At the end of the period the total of the purchases book is transferred to the debit of the purchases account in the general ledger. An example of a purchase book and the posting of the entries to the purchases ledger and the total to the purchases account is now shown:

Purchases Book

		Invoice No.	Folio	Page 49
19–5				£
Sept 2	R. Sharples	9/101	PL 16	670
,, 8	B. Hives & Son	9/102	PL 29	1,380
,, 19	C. Brown	9/103	PL 55	120
,, 30	K. Gee	9/104	PL 89	510
	Transferred to Purchases Account		GL 63	2,680

Purchases Ledger

R. Sharples — Page 16

			19–5			£
			Sept 2	Purchases	PB 49	670

B. Hives & Son — Page 29

			19–5			£
			Sept 8	Purchases	PB 49	1,380

C. Brown — Page 55

			19–5			£
			Sept 19	Purchases	PB 49	120

K. Gee — Page 89

			19–5			£
			Sept 30	Purchases	PB 49	510

General Ledger

Purchases — Page 63

19–5			£				
Sept 30	Credit purchases for the month	PB 49	2,680				

The Purchases Book is often known also as the Purchases Journal or as the Purchases Day Book.

The Returns Inwards Book

When goods are returned by customers, or there is a dispute concerning goods, and an allowance is made by the firm, a document known as a credit note is sent to the customer. The term 'credit note' takes its name from the fact that the customer's account will be credited by the amount of the allowance to show the decrease in his indebtedness to the firm, in other words an asset account is reduced. Very often credit notes are printed in red so that they are easily distinguishable from invoices.

Imagine that the firm of D. Picton & Sons to whom goods were sold on 1 September 19–5 as per the sales invoice on page 105 returned some of the goods on 8 September 19–5, the credit note might appear as shown in Exhibit 9.2.

Exhibit 9.2

U.X.Y. Ltd
Over Warehouse
Lower End
Manchester
8 September 19–5

Note No. 9/37

Messrs D. Picton & Sons
45 Charles Street
Worthing

CREDIT NOTE

	£	£
5 Cartons Kay's Flour × £10	50	
Less 20 % Trade Discount	10	
	—	40

The credit notes are listed in a Returns Inwards Book which is then used to post the items to the credit of the personal accounts in the sales ledger. To complete the double entry the total of the returns inwards book for the period is transferred to the debit of the Returns Inwards Account in the general ledger.

An example of a returns inwards book showing the items posted to the sales ledger and the general ledger is now shown:

Returns Inwards Book

		Note No.	*Folio*	Page 10
19–5				£
Sept 8	D. Picton & Sons	9/37	SL 12	40
„ 17	A. Bowser	9/38	SL 58	120
„ 19	C. Vickers	9/39	SL 99	290
„ 29	M. Noone	9/40	SL 112	160
	Transferred to Returns Inwards Account		GL 114	610

Sales Ledger

D. Picton & Sons Page 12

			£
19–5			
Sept 8	Returns Inwards	RI 10	40

		A. Bowser			Page 58
		19–5			£
		Sept 17	Returns Inwards	RI 10	120

		C. Vickers			Page 99
		19–5			£
		Sept 19	Returns Inwards	RI 10	290

		M. Noone			Page 112
		19–5			£
		Sept 29	Returns Inwards	RI 10	160

General Ledger

		Returns Inwards			Page 114
19–5			£		
Sept 30	Returns for the month	RI 10	610		

Alternative names in use for the returns inwards book are Returns Inwards Journal or Sales Returns Book, the latter name arising from the fact that it is the sales which are returned at a later date.

The Returns Outwards Book

Conversely, when goods are returned to a supplier a document called a debit note is sent to him stating the amount of allowance to which the firm is entitled. The debit note could also cover allowances due because the goods bought were deficient in some way. The term 'debit note' stems from the fact that as the liability to the supplier is accordingly reduced his personal account must be debited to record this. The debit note is the evidence that this has been done.

The debit notes are listed in a Returns Outwards Book and the items then posted to the debit of the personal accounts in the purchases ledger. To complete double entry the total of the returns outwards book for the period is transferred to the credit of the Returns Outwards Account in the general ledger. An example of a returns outwards book followed by the subsequent postings to the purchases ledger and the general ledger is shown below:

Returns Outwards Book

		Note No.	*Folio*	Page 7
19–5				£
Sept 11	B. Hives & Son	9/34	PL 29	180
„ 16	B. Rose	9/35	PL 46	100
„ 28	C. Blake	9/36	PL 55	30
„ 30	S. Sayers	9/37	PL 87	360
	Transferred to Returns Outwards Account		GL 116	670

Purchases Ledger

B. Hives & Son Page 29

			£
19–5			
Sept 11	Returns Outwards	RO 7	180

B. Rose Page 46

			£
19–5			
Sept 16	Returns Outwards	RO 7	100

C. Blake Page 55

			£
19–5			
Sept 28	Returns Outwards	RO 7	30

S. Sayers Page 87

			£
19–5			
Sept 30	Returns Outwards	RO 7	360

General Ledger

Returns Outwards Page 116

			£
19–5			
Sept 30	Returns for the month	RO 7	670

Alternative names in use for the returns outwards book are Returns Outwards Journal or Purchases Returns Book, the latter name arising from the fact that it consists of the purchases which are returned to the supplier at a later date.

Books as Collection Points

The Sales, Purchases, Returns Inwards and Returns Outwards Books are in fact collection points for data concerned with these particular activities. They save the Sales, Purchases, Returns Inwards and Returns Outwards accounts from containing too much detail and of course they make possible the division of labour in the accounting office by having different clerks handling different parts of the whole system.

It must not be thought that in a real firm there actually have to be books as described in this chapter. It was described in that way to make it easier for you to grasp. The main thing is that there has to be a collection point for the data for each of these different types of activity. Now it could well be that, instead of having a Sales Book, the amount from the sales invoice is posted direct to the personal account of the customer, no entry being made in a Sales Book. The sales invoices could then be collected in, say, a box file, so that at the end of a period, say a month, all the customers' accounts would have been debited with the amount of goods sold to them, and the box file would contain the relevant copies of all of these sales invoices. If then the whole of the invoice totals were added up, the grand total of the sales invoices in the box file would represent the total sales for the month. This grand total would be the same figure that would have been obtained if a Sales Book had been used and then totalled up at the end of the month. This total would then be entered on the credit side of the Sales Account. Thus double entry could be made to work even though a Sales Book as such did not exist. Exactly the same sort of thing could be done for Purchases, Returns Inwards and Returns Outwards, so that these books are not a necessary part of double entry, but the idea of having collection points for data certainly is a part.

Different firms will take different kinds of short-cuts, or may even take a longer way around the problem of collecting together this sort of data. The answers will be exactly the same; it is just the way that the mechanics are performed to find the answers that will be different.

Internal Check

When sales invoices are being made out they should be scrutinized very carefully. A system is usually set up so that each stage of the preparation of the invoice is checked by someone other than the person whose job it is to send out the invoice. If this was not done then it would be possible for someone inside a firm to send out an invoice, as an instance, at a price less than the true price. Any difference could then be split between that person and the outside firm. If an invoice should have been sent to Ivor Twister & Co for £2,000, but the invoice clerk made it out deliberately for £200, then, if there was no cross-check, the difference of £1,800 could be split between the invoice clerk and the proprietor of Ivor Twister & Co.

Similarly outside firms could send invoices for goods which were never received by the firm. This might be in collaboration with an employee within the firm, but there are firms sending false invoices which rely on the firms receiving them being inefficient and paying for items never received. There have been firms sending invoices for such items as advertisements which have never been published. The cashier of the firm receiving the invoice, if the firm is an inefficient one, might possibly think that someone in the firm had authorized the advertisements and would pay the bill.

Besides these there are of course genuine errors, and these should also be detected. A system is therefore set up whereby the invoices have to be subject to scrutiny, at each stage, by someone other than the person who sends out the invoices or is responsible for paying them. Incoming invoices will be stamped with a rubber stamp, with spaces for each stage of the check. For instance, one person will have authority to certify that the goods were properly ordered, another that the goods were delivered in good order, another that the prices are correct, that the calculations are correct, and so on. Naturally in a small firm, simply because the office staff might be quite small, this cross-check may be in the hands of only one person other than the person who will pay it. A similar sort of check will be made in respect of sales invoices being sent out.

Exercises

9.1. You are to enter up the sales journal from the following details, post the items to the relevant accounts in the sales ledger and then show the transfer to the sales account in the general ledger.

19–6			
Mar	1	Credit sales to J. Gordon	£187
,,	3	Credit sales to G. Allenby	£166
,,	6	Credit sales to V. Wavell	£12
,,	10	Credit sales to J. Gordon	£55
,,	17	Credit sales to F. Woolfenden	£289
,,	19	Credit sales to U. Radcliffe	£66
,,	27	Credit sales to V. Wavell	£28
,,	31	Credit sales to L. Shaw	£78

9.2. You are to enter up the purchases journal and the returns outwards journal from the following details, then to post the items to the relevant accounts in the purchases ledger and to show the transfers to the general ledger at the end of the month.

19–7
May 1 Credit purchase from H. Lloyd £119
,, 4 Credit purchases from the following:
D. Scott £98; A. Simpson £114; A. Whiteley £25; S. Woodson £56
,, 7 Goods returned by us to the following: H. Lloyd £16; D. Scott £14
,, 10 Credit purchase from A. Simpson £59
,, 18 Credit purchases from the following:
M. Wallworth £89; J. Wild £67; H. Mellor £196; H. Leah £119
,, 25 Goods returned by us to the following: J. Wild £5; A. Simpson £11
,, 31 Credit purchases from: A. Whiteley £56; C. Clapham £98.

9.3. You are to enter up the sales, purchases and the returns inwards and returns outwards journals from the following details, then to post the items to the relevant accounts in the sales and purchase ledgers. The total of the journals are then to be transferred to the accounts in the general ledger.

19–6
May 1 Credit sales: T. Terry £56; L. Ramsden £148; K. Barton £145
„ 3 Credit purchases: P. Potter £144; H. Hacker £25; B. Spencer £76
„ 7 Credit sales: K. Kelly £89; N. Moynihan £78; N. Lee £257
„ 9 Credit purchases: B. Perkins £24; H. Hacker £58; H. Miles £123
„ 11 Goods returned by us to: P. Potter £12; B. Spencer £22
„ 14 Goods returned to us by: T. Terry £5; K. Barton £11; K. Kelly £14
„ 17 Credit purchases: H. Hacker £54; B. Perkins £65; L. Nixon £75
„ 20 Goods returned by us to B. Spencer £14
„ 24 Credit sales: K. Moxon £57; K. Kelly £65; O. Green £112
„ 28 Goods returned to us by N. Moynihan £24
„ 31 Credit sales: N. Lee £55.

9.4A. Enter up the sales, purchases and returns journals from the following details. Then post the individual items to the relevant accounts in the sales and purchases ledger, and transfer the totals of the various journals to the accounts in the general ledger.

19–2
Mar 1 Credit purchases: R. Dunning £115; C. Walton £144; E. Schofield £205; P. Burton £44
„ 5 Credit sales: A. Davies £290; N. Thorn £105; B. Downing £67; C. Sherman £78
„ 9 Credit purchases: A. Thomas £88; B. Shepherd £95; P. Burton £99
„ 12 Goods returned by us to: R. Downing £25; E. Schofield £16
„ 15 Credit sales: N. Thorn £108; C. Sherman £222; F. Thwaite £66
„ 18 Goods returned to us by: A. Davies £40; C. Sherman £17
„ 31 Credit sales: K. Mountain £49.

9.5A. After entering the following in the various journals write up the personal accounts, then transfer the journal totals to the relevant ledger accounts.

19–3
July 1 Credit sales: F. Jackson £238; P. Isaacs £116; F. Oswald £69; J. Simpson £84
„ 5 Credit purchases: D. Duncan £122; E. Varney £204; K. Patrick £78
„ 10 Credit sales: J. Simpson £92; M. Blake £160; T. Oakes £15
„ 15 Credit purchases: E. Varney £67; J. Cartwright £41; N. Wendell £123
„ 21 Goods returned to us by: J. Simpson £62; M. Blake £14
„ 30 Goods returned by us to: K. Patrick £3; N. Wendell £65.

9.6A. Enter up the relevant journals and personal accounts, and then transfer the journal totals to the relevant ledger accounts:

19–7
May 1 Credit purchases: F. White & Co £104; G. Hulley £89; D. Gosling £197; A. Jones Ltd £200
„ 5 Credit sales: A. Mayall & Son £188; G. Cheadle £70; R. Willis Ltd £400
„ 8 Credit purchases: E. Darbyshire £105; D. Gosling £210

„ 10 Credit Sales: G. Cheadle £145; J. Hayes & Co £66
„ 15 Goods returned to us by A. Mayall & Son £18; R. Willis Ltd £23
„ 22 Goods returned by us to: G. Hulley £19; A. Jones Ltd £18; D. Gosling £22
„ 31 Credit sales: I. Wager £294.

APPENDICES—GENERAL NOTES

Throughout the book there will be various items shown as appendices. For instance, immediately following this is APPENDIX 9.1. These are sometimes shown as appendices because they may not necessarily be relevant to the needs of a particular student. In the case of APPENDIX 9.1 the student reading this book may be taking examinations set in his own country, not the United Kingdom, and such an examination may not have Value Added Tax in the syllabus. There would not be much point in such a student bothering to read all of the details of that topic if it is completely of no use to him.

Other appendices may have been classified to be an appendix because they are not strictly part of a chapter. Throughout the book there are various appendices concerned with guides to students sitting examinations. Rather than disturb the system of numbering chapters, and giving such an appendix a chapter number, they are called appendices.

APPENDIX 9.1

Students overseas should ensure whether or not this appendix is relevant to their examination needs.

Value Added Tax

Value Added Tax, which will be shown hereafter in its abbreviated form as VAT, is charged in the United Kingdom on both the supply of goods and of services by persons and firms who are taxable. Some goods and services are not liable to VAT. Examples of this are food and postal charges. The rates at which VAT is levied have changed from time to time. Some goods will also attract a different rate of VAT from the normal rate. Instances of this in the past have been motor-cars and electrical goods which have varied from the rates levied on most other goods. In this book the examples shown will all be at a VAT rate of 10 per cent. This does not mean that this is the rate applicable at the time when you are reading this book. It is, however, an easy figure to work out in an examination room, and most examining bodies have set questions assuming that the VAT rate was 10 per cent.

The Government department which deals with VAT in the United Kingdom is the Customs and Excise department.

Taxable Firms

Imagine that firm A takes raw materials that it has grown and processes them and then wants to sell them. If VAT did not exist it would sell them for £100, but VAT of 10 per cent must be added, so it sells them to firm B for £100+VAT £10 = £110. Firm A must now pay the figure of £10 VAT to the tax authorities. Firm B having bought for £110 alters the product slightly and then resells to firm C for £140+10 per cent VAT £14 = £154. Firm B now gives the tax authorities a cheque for the amount added less the amount it had paid to firm A for VAT £10, so that the cheque payable to the tax authorities by firm B is £4. Firm C is a retailer who then sells the goods for £200 to which he must add VAT 10 per cent £20 = £220 selling price to the customer. Firm C then remits £20−£14 = £6 to the tax authorities.

It can be seen that the full amount of VAT tax has fallen on the ultimate customer who bought the goods from the retail shop, and that he suffered a tax of £20. The machinery of collection was however geared to the value added at each stage of the progress of the goods from manufacture to retailing, i.e. Firm A handed over £10, Firm B £4 and Firm C £6, making £20 in all.

Exempted Firms

If a firm is exempted then this means that it does not have to add the VAT tax on to the price at which it sells its products or services. On the other hand it will not get a refund of the amount it has paid itself on the goods and services which it has bought and on which it has paid VAT tax. Thus such a firm may buy goods for £100+VAT tax £10 = £110. When it sells them it may sell at £130, there being no need to add VAT tax at all. It will not however get a refund of the £10 VAT tax it had itself paid on those goods.

Instances of firms being exempted are insurance companies, which do not charge VAT on the amount of insurance premiums payable by its customers, and banks, which do not add VAT on to their bank charges. Small firms with a turnover of less than a certain amount (the limit is changed upwards from time to time and so is not given here) do not have to register for VAT if they don't want to, and they would not therefore charge VAT on their goods and services. On the other hand many of these small firms could register if they wished, but they would then have to keep full VAT records in addition to charging out VAT. It is simply an attempt by the UK Government to avoid crippling very small businesses with unnecessary record-keeping that gives most small businesses this right to opt out of charging VAT.

Zero Rated Firms

These do not add VAT tax to the final selling price of their products or services. They do however obtain a refund of all VAT tax paid by them on goods and services. This means that if one of the firms buys goods for £200+VAT tax £20 = £220, and later sells them for £300 it will not have to add VAT on to the selling price of £300. It will however be able to claim a refund of the £20 VAT tax paid when the goods were purchased. It is this latter element that distinguishes it from an exempted firm. A zero rated firm is therefore in a better position than an exempted firm. Illustrations of these firms are food, publishing and the new construction of buildings.

Partly Exempt Traders

Some traders will find that they are selling some goods which are exempt and some which are zero rated and others which are standard rated. These traders will have to apportion their turnover accordingly, and follow the rules already described for each separate part of their turnover.

Accounting for VAT

It can be seen that, except for firms that are exempted from VAT, firms do not suffer VAT as one expense. They either get a refund of whatever VAT they have paid, in the case of zero-rated businesses, or else additionally collect VAT from their customers and merely therefore act as tax collectors in the case of taxable firms. Only the exempted firms actually suffer VAT as they pay it and are not allowed a refund and cannot specifically pass it on to their customers. The following discussion will therefore be split between those two sorts of firms who do not suffer VAT expense, compared with the exempted firms who do suffer VAT.

Firms Which Can Recover VAT Paid

1. Taxable Firms

Value Added Tax and Sales Invoices A taxable firm will have to add VAT to the value of the Sales invoices. It must be pointed out that this is based on the amount of the invoice *after* any trade discount has been deducted.

Exhibit 9.3 is an invoice drawn up from the following details:

On 2 March 19–2, W. Frank & Co, Hayburn Road, Stockport, sold the following goods to R. Bainbridge Ltd, 267 Star Road, Colchester: Bainbridge's order No was A/4/559, for the following items:

200 Rolls T56 Black Tape at £6 per 10 rolls
600 Sheets R64 Polythene at £10 per 100 sheets
7,000 Blank Perspex B49 Markers at £20 per 1,000

All of these goods are subject to VAT at the rate of 10 per cent.

A trade discount of 25 per cent is given by Frank & Co. The sales invoice is numbered 8851.

Exhibit 9.3

W. Frank & Co,
Hayburn Road,
Stockport

INVOICE No. 8851 Date: 2 March 19–2

To: R. Bainbridge Ltd Your order no. A/4/559
267 Star Road
Colchester

	£
200 Rolls T56 Black Tape @ £6 per 10 rolls	120
600 Sheets R64 Polythene @ £10 per 100 sheets	60
7,000 Blank Perspex B49 Markers @ £20 per 1,000	140
	320
Less Trade Discount 25%	80
	240
Add VAT 10%	24
	264

Where a cash discount is offered for speedy payment, VAT is calculated on an amount represented by the value of the invoice less such a discount. Even if the cash discount is lost because of late payment, the VAT will not change.

The Sales Book will normally have an extra column for the VAT content of the Sales Invoices. This is needed to facilitate accounting for VAT. The entry of several sales invoices in the Sales Book and in the ledger accounts can now be examined:

W. Frank & Co sold the following goods during the month of March 19–2:

			Total of Invoice, after trade discount deducted but before VAT added	*VAT 10%*
19–2			£	£
March	2	R. Bainbridge Ltd (see Exhibit 9–3)	240	24
,,	10	S. Lange & Son	300	30
,,	17	K. Bishop	160	16
,,	31	R. Andrews & Associates	100	10

Sales Book Page 58

		Invoice No.	*Folio*	*Net*	*VAT*
19–2				£	£
March 2	R. Bainbridge Ltd	8851	SL 77	240	24
,, 10	S. Lange & Son	8852	SL 119	300	30
,, 17	K. Bishop	8853	SL 185	160	16
,, 31	R. Andrews & Associates	8854	SL 221	100	10
Transferred to General Ledger				GL 76 800	GL 90 80

The Sales Book having been written up, the first task is then to enter the invoices in the individual customer's accounts in the Sales Ledger. The customer's accounts are simply charged with the full amounts of the invoices including VAT. For instance, K. Bishop will owe £176 which he will have to pay to W. Frank & Co. He does not remit the VAT £16 to the Customs and Excise, instead he is going to pay the £16 to W. Frank & Co who will thereafter ensure that the £16 is included in the total cheque payable to the Customs and Excise.

Sales Ledger

R. Bainbridge Ltd Page 77

19–2			£
March 2	Sales	SB 58	264

S. Lange & Son Page 119

19–2			£
March 10	Sales	SB 58	330

K. Bishop Page 185

19–2			£
March 17	Sales	SB 58	176

R. Andrews & Associates Page 221

19–2			£
March 31	Sales	SB 58	110

In total therefore the personal accounts have been debited with £880, this being the total of the amounts which the customers will have to pay. The actual sales of the firm are not £880, the amount which is actually sales is £800, the other £80 being simply the VAT that W. Frank & Co are collecting on behalf of the Government. The credit transfer to the Sales Account in the General Ledger is restricted to the Sales content, i.e. £800. The other £80, being VAT, is transferred to a VAT account.

General Ledger

Sales Page 76

19–2				£
March 31	Credit Sales for the month		SB 58	800

Value Added Tax Page 90

19–2				£
March 31	Sales Book: VAT content		SB 58	80

Value Added Tax and Purchases In the case of a taxable firm, the firm will have to add VAT to its sales invoices, but it will also be able to claim a refund of the VAT which it pays on its purchases. What will happen is that the total of the amount of VAT paid on Purchases will be deducted from the total of the VAT collected by the additions to the Sales Invoices. Normally the VAT on Sales will be greater than that on Purchases, and therefore periodically the net difference will be paid to the Customs and Excise. It can happen sometimes that more VAT has been suffered on Purchases than has been charged on Sales, and in this case it would be the Customs and Excise which would refund the difference to the firm. These payments or receipts via the Customs and Excise will be either monthly or quarterly depending on the arrangement which the particular firm has made.

The recording of Purchases in the Purchases Book and Purchases Ledger is similar to that of Sales, naturally with items being shown in a reverse fashion. These can now be illustrated by continuing the month of March 19–2 in the books of the firm already considered, W. Frank & Co, this time for Purchases.

W. Frank & Co made the following purchases during the month of March 19–2:

			Total of Invoice after trade discount deducted but before VAT added	*VAT 10%*
19–2			£	£
March	1	E. Lyal Ltd (see Exhibit 9–3)	180	18
,,	11	P. Portsmouth & Co	120	12
,,	24	J. Davidson	40	4
,,	29	B. Cofie & Son Ltd	70	7

Before looking at the recording of these in the Purchases Records, compare the first entry for E. Lyal Ltd with Exhibit 9-4, to ensure that the correct amounts have been shown.

Exhibit 9.4

E. Lyal Ltd
College Avenue
St Albans
Hertfordshire

INVOICE No. K453/A

Date: 1/3/19–2
Your order No. BB/667

To: W. Frank & Co
Hayburn Road
Stockport

Terms: Strictly net 30 days

50 metres of BYC plastic 1 metre wide × £3 per metre	150
1,200 metal tags 500 mm × 10p each	120
	270
Less Trade Discount at 33⅓%	90
	180
Add VAT 10%	18
	198

It can be seen that the purchases invoice from E. Lyal Ltd differs slightly in its layout to that of W. Frank & Co per Exhibit 9-3. This is to illustrate that in fact each firm designs its own invoices, and there will be wide variations. The basic information shown will be similar, but they may have such information displayed in quite different ways.

Purchases Book Page 38

			Folio		Net		VAT
19–2					£		£
March	1	E. Lyal Ltd	PL 15		180		18
,,	11	P. Portsmouth & Co	PL 70		120		12
,,	24	J. Davidson	PL 114		40		4
,,	29	B. Cofie & Son Ltd	PL 166		70		7
Transferred to General Ledger				GL 54	410	GL 90	41

These are entered in the Purchases Ledger. Once again there is no need for the VAT to be shown as separate amounts in the accounts of the suppliers.

Purchases Ledger

E. Lyal Ltd Page 15

				19–2			£
				March 1	Purchases	PB 38	198

P. Portsmouth & Co Page 70

				19–2			£
				March 11	Purchases	PB 38	132

J. Davidson Page 114

				19–2			£
				March 24	Purchases	PB 38	44

B. Cofie & Son Ltd Page 166

				19–2			£
				March 29	Purchases	PB 38	77

The personal accounts have accordingly been credited with a total of £451, this being the total of the amounts which Frank & Co will have to pay to them. The actual purchases are not however, £451; the correct amount is £410 and the other £41 is the VAT which the various firms are collecting for the Customs & Excise, and which amount is reclaimable from the Customs & Excise by Frank & Co. The debit transfer to the Purchases Account is therefore restricted to the figure of £410, for this is the true amount that the goods are costing the firm. The other £41 is transferred to the debit of the VAT account. It will be noticed that in this account there is already a credit of £80 in respect of VAT on Sales for the month.

General Ledger

Purchases Page 54

19–2		£				
March 31	Credit Purchases for the month	410				

Value Added Tax Page 90

19–2		£	19–2			£
March 31	Purchase Book: VAT content PB 38	41	March 31	Sales Book: VAT content SB 58		80
,, 31	Balance c/d	39				
		80				80
			April 1	Balance b/d		39

Assuming that a Trading and Profit and Loss Account was being drawn up for the month, the Trading Account would be debited with

£410 as a transfer from the Purchases Account, whilst the £800 in the Sales Account would be transferred to the credit side of the Trading Account. The Value Added Tax would simply appear as a creditor of £39 in the Balance Sheet as at 31 March 19–2.

2. *Zero Rated Firms*

It has been already stated that these firms do not have to add VAT on to their sales invoices, as their rate of VAT is zero or nil. On the other hand any VAT that they pay on Purchases can be reclaimed from the Customs and Excise. Such firms, which include publishers, are therefore in a rather fortunate position. There will accordingly be no need at all to enter VAT in the Sales Book as VAT simply does not apply to Sales in such a firm. The Purchases Book and the Purchases Ledger will appear exactly as has been seen in the case of W. Frank & Co. The VAT account will only have debits in it, representing the VAT on Purchases. This balance will be shown on the Balance Sheet as a debtor until it is settled by the Customs and Excise.

Firms Which Cannot Recover VAT Paid

These firms do not have to add VAT on to the value of their Sales Invoices. On the other hand they do not get a refund of VAT paid on Purchases. All that happens in this type of firm is that there is no Value Added Tax Account, the VAT paid is simply included as part of the cost of the goods. If therefore a firm receives an invoice from a supplier for Purchases of £80, with VAT added of £8, then £88 will have to be paid for these goods and the firm will not receive a refund from the Customs and Excise. In the Purchases Book the item of Purchases will be shown as £88, and the supplier's account will be credited with £88. As VAT is not added to Sales Invoices then there cannot be any entries for VAT in the Sales Book.

Perhaps a comparison of two firms with identical Purchases from the same supplier, one a zero rated firm, and one a firm which cannot recover VAT paid, would not come amiss here. On the assumption that for each firm the only item of Purchases for the month was that of goods £120 plus VAT £12 from D. Oswald Ltd, the entries for the month of May 19–4 would be as follows:

(a) Firm which cannot recover VAT:

Purchases Book

19–4		£
May 16	D. Oswald Ltd	132

Purchases Ledger

D. Oswald Ltd

					£
			19–4		£
			May 16	Purchases	132

General Ledger

Purchases

19–4		£	19–4		£
May 31	Credit Purchases for the month	132	May 31	Transfer to Trading Account	132

Trading Account for the month ended 31 May 19–4 (extract)

	£
Purchases	132

(b) Firm which can recover VAT (e.g. zero rated firm):

Purchases Book

		Net	*VAT*
19–4		£	£
May 16	D. Oswald Ltd	120	12

Purchases Ledger

D. Oswald Ltd

					£
			19–4		£
			May 16	Purchases	132

General Ledger

Purchases

19–4		£	19–4		£
May 31	Credit Purchases for the month	120	May 31	Transfer to Trading Account	120

Value Added Tax

19–4		£
May 31	Purchases Book	12

Trading Account for the month ended 31 May 19–4 (extract)

	£
Purchases	120

Balance Sheet as at 31 May 19–4 (extract)

	£
Debtor	12

VAT on Items Other Than Sales and Purchases

Value Added Tax is not just paid on purchases, it is also payable on many items of expense and on the purchase of fixed assets. In fact it would not be possible for this to be otherwise, as an item which is a Purchase for one firm would be a Fixed Asset in another. For instance, if a firm which dealt in shop fittings buys a display counter for resale then that item would be classified as Purchases. A retail shop which bought it for use in the shop would classify such a shop counter as a fixed asset. The firm which sells goods on which VAT is added does not concern itself whether or not the firm buying it is doing so for resale, or whether it is for use. The VAT will therefore be added to all of its Sales Invoices. The treatment of VAT in the accounts of the firm buying the item will depend on whether or not that firm can reclaim VAT paid or not. The general rule is that if the VAT can be reclaimed then the item should be shown net, i.e. VAT should be excluded from the expenses or fixed asset account. When VAT cannot be reclaimed then VAT should be included in the expense or fixed asset account as part of the cost of the item. For example, two businesses buying similar items, would treat the following items as shown:

	Firm which can reclaim VAT		*Firm which cannot reclaim VAT*	
Buys Machinery £200+VAT £20	Debit Machinery	£200	Debit Machinery	£220
	Debit VAT Account	£20		
Buys Stationery £150+VAT £15	Debit Stationery	£150	Debit Stationery	£165
	Debit VAT Account	£15		

VAT Owing

VAT owing by or to the firm can be included with debtors or creditors, as the case may be. There is no need to show the amount(s) owing as separate items.

Exercises to Appendix 9.1

9.7. On 1 May 19–7, D. Wilson Ltd, 1 Hawk Green Road, Stockport, sold the following goods on credit to G. Christie & Son, The Golf Shop, Hole-in-One Lane, Marple, Cheshire:
Order No. A/496

3 sets of 'Boy Michael' golf clubs at £270 per set.
150 Watson golf balls at £8 per 10 balls.
4 Faldo golf bags at £30 per bag.
Trade discount is given at the rate of $33\frac{1}{3}\%$.
All goods are subject to VAT at 10%.

(i) Prepare the Sales Invoice to be sent to G. Christie & Son. The invoice number will be 10586.
(ii) Show the entries in the Personal Ledgers of D. Wilson Ltd and G. Christie & Son.

9.8. The following sales have been made by S. Thompson Ltd during the month of June 19–5. All the figures are shown net after deducting trade discount, but before adding VAT at the rate of 10 per cent.

19–5			
August	1	to M. Sinclair & Co	£150
,,	8	to M. Brown & Associates	£260
,,	19	to A. Axton Ltd	£80
,,	31	to T. Christie	£30

You are required to enter up the Sales Book. Sales Ledger and General Ledger in respect of the above items for the month.

9.9. The following sales and purchases were made by R. Colman Ltd during the month of May 19–6.

			Net	*VAT added*
19–6			£	£
May	1	Sold goods on credit to B. Davies & Co	150	15
,,	4	Sold goods on credit to C. Grant Ltd	220	22
,,	10	Bought goods on credit from:		
		G. Cooper & Son	400	40
		J. Wayne Ltd	190	19
,,	14	Bought goods on credit from B. Lugosi	50	5
,,	16	Sold goods on credit to C. Grant Ltd	140	14
,,	23	Bought goods on credit from S. Hayward	60	6
,,	31	Sold goods on credit to B. Karloff	80	8

Enter up the Sales and Purchases Books, Sales and Purchases Ledgers and the General Ledger for the month of May 19–6. Carry the balance down on the VAT account.

9.10A. On 1 March 19–6, A. Bembridge & Son, Maldon Way, Swansea, sold the following goods on credit to James Foster, 26 Broad Street, Birmingham, 4:

Order No. 162.
10,000 Coils Sealing Tape @ £4.46 per 1,000 coils
20,000 Sheets Bank A5 @ £4.50 per 1,000 sheets
12,000 Sheets Bank A4 @ £4.20 per 1,000 sheets

All goods are subject to VAT at 10%.

(a) Prepare the Sales Invoice to be sent to James Foster.
(b) Show the entries in the Personal Ledgers of James Foster, and A. Bembridge & Son.

(Royal Society of Arts)

9.11A. The following Sales are made by L. Macari Ltd during the month of October 19–8. All of the items are shown at the net prices, after deducting the trade discount, but before adding Value Added Tax. The rate of VAT should be taken to be 10 per cent.

19–8	
October 5 to S. McQueen & Co	£90
October 14 to S. Coppell Ltd	£350
October 21 to A. Grimes	£10
October 31 to J. Jordan Ltd	£160

You are required to enter up the Sales Book, Sales Ledger and General Ledger for the month.

9.12A. The credit sales and purchases for the month of December 19–3 in respect of C. Dennis & Son Ltd were:

			Net, after trade discount	*VAT 10%*
19–3			£	£
December	1	Sales to M. Morris	140	14
,,	4	Sales to G. Ford Ltd	290	29
,,	5	Purchases from P. Hillman & Son	70	7
,,	8	Purchases from J. Lancia	110	11
,,	14	Sales to R. Volvo Ltd	180	18
,,	18	Purchases from T. Leyland & Co	160	16
,,	28	Sales to G. Ford Ltd	100	10
,,	30	Purchases from J. Lancia	90	9

Write up all of the relevant books and ledger accounts for the month.

APPENDIX 9.2

Purchases Analysis Books

Provided firms finish up with the items needed for display in their final accounts, the actual manner in which they do it is completely up to them. Some firms use one book to record all items got on credit. These consist not only of the Purchases, but also of items such as Motor Expenses, Stationery, Fixed Assets, Carriage Inwards and so on. The idea is that all invoices for items which will not be paid for on the day that the item is received will be entered in this book. However, all of the various types of items are not simply lumped together, as the firm needs to know how much of the items were for Purchases, how much for Stationery, how much for Motor Expenses, etc., so that the relevant expense accounts can have the correct amount of expenses entered in them. This is achieved by having a set of analysis columns in the book, all of the items are entered in a Total Column, but then they are analysed as between the different sorts of expenses, etc.

Exhibit 9-5 shows such a Purchases Analysis book drawn up for a month from the following list of items (VAT is ignored here) got on credit:

19–5		£
May	1 Bought goods from D. Watson Ltd on credit	296
„	3 Bought goods on credit from W. Donachie & Son	76
„	5 Motor van repaired, received invoice from Barnes Motors Ltd	112
„	6 Bought stationery from J. Corrigan & Co	65
„	8 Bought goods on credit from C. Bell Ltd	212
„	10 Motor lorry serviced, received invoice from Barnes Motors Ltd	39
„	13 Bought Stationery on credit from A. Hartford & Co	35
„	16 Bought goods on credit from M. Doyle Ltd	243
„	20 Received invoice for carriage inwards on goods from G. Owen	58
„	21 Bought goods on credit from B. Kidd & Son	135
„	24 Bought goods on credit from K. Clements	122
„	24 Received invoice for carriage inwards from Channon Haulage	37
„	26 Bought goods on credit from C. Bell Ltd	111
„	28 Bought stationery on credit from A. Hartford & Co	49
„	29 Bought goods on credit from B. Kidd & Son	249
„	31 Received invoice for petrol for the month, to be paid for in June, from Barnes Motors Ltd	280

Exhibit 9.5

Purchases Analysis Book page 105

Date	*Name of Firm*	*PL Folio*	*Total*	*Purchases*	*Stationery*	*Motor Expenses*	*Carriage Inwards*
19–5			£	£	£	£	£
May 1	D. Watson Ltd	129	296	296			
„ 3	W. Donachie & Son	27	76	76			
„ 5	Barnes Motors Ltd	55	112			112	
„ 6	J. Corrigan & Co	88	65		65		
„ 8	C. Bell Ltd	99	212	212			
„ 10	Barnes Motors Ltd	55	39			39	
„ 13	A. Hartford & Co	298	35		35		
„ 16	M. Doyle Ltd	187	243	243			
„ 20	G. Owen	222	58				58
„ 21	B. Kidd & Son	188	135	135			
„ 24	K. Clements	211	122	122			
„ 24	Channon Haulage	305	37				37
„ 26	C. Bell Ltd	99	111	111			
„ 28	A. Hartford & Co	298	49		49		
„ 29	B. Kidd & Son	188	249	249			
„ 31	Barnes Motors Ltd	55	280			280	
			2,119	1,444	149	431	95
				GL 77	GL 97	GL 156	GL 198

Exhibit 9–5 shows that the figure for each item is entered in the Total column, and is then also entered in the column for the particular type of expense. At the end of the month the arithmetical accuracy of the additions can be checked by comparing the total of the Total column with the sum of the totals of all of the other columns. These two grand total figures should equal each other. In this case 1,444+149+431+95 = 2,119. The total column will also be useful for Control Accounts; these will be examined in Chapter 17.

It can be seen that the total of Purchases for the month of May was £1,444 and therefore this can be debited to the Purchases Account in the General Ledger; similarly the total of Stationery bought on credit in the month can be debited to the Stationery Account in the General

Ledger and so on. The folio number of the page to which the relevant total has been debited is shown immediately under the total figure for each column, e.g. under the column for Purchases is GL 77, meaning that the item has been entered in the General Ledger page 77. The entries can now be shown:

General Ledger

Purchases Account — Page 77

		£
19–5		
May 31	Purchases Analysis 105	1,444

Stationery — Page 97

		£
19–5		
May 31	Purchases Analysis 105	149

Motor Expenses — Page 156

		£
19–5		
May 31	Purchases Analysis 105	431

Carriage Inwards — Page 198

		£
19–5		
May 31	Purchase Analysis 105	95

The individual accounts of the creditors, whether they be for goods or for expenses such as Stationery or Motor Expenses, can be kept together in a single Purchases Ledger. There is no need for the Purchases Ledger simply to have accounts only for creditors for Purchases. Perhaps there is a slight misuse of the name Purchases Ledger where this happens, but it is common practice amongst a lot of firms.

To carry through the double entry involved with Exhibit 9–5 the Purchases Ledger is now shown.

Purchases Ledger

W. Donachie & Son — Page 27

			£
19–5			
May 3	Purchases	PB 105	76

Barnes Motors Ltd — Page 55

			£
19–5			
May 5	Purchases	PB 105	112
„ 10	„	PB 105	39
„ 31	„	PB 105	280

Purchases Ledger

J. Corrigan & Co Page 88

19–5			£
May 6	Purchases	PB 105	65

C. Bell Ltd Page 99

19–5			£
May 8	Purchases	PB 105	212
„ 26	„	PB 105	111

D. Watson Ltd Page 129

19–5			£
May 1	Purchases	PB 105	296

M. Doyle Ltd Page 187

19–5			£
May 16	Purchases	PB 105	243

B. Kidd & Son Page 188

19–5			£
May 21	Purchases	PB 105	135
„ 29	„	PB 105	249

K. Clements Page 211

19–5			£
May 24	Purchases	PB 105	122

G. Owen Page 222

19–5			£
May 20	Purchases	PB 105	58

A. Hartford & Co Page 298

19–5			£
May 13	Purchases	PB 105	35
„ 28	„	PB 105	49

Channon Haulage Page 305

19–5			£
May 24	Purchases	PB 105	37

Purchases Analysis Books and VAT

Where a firm can recover VAT paid on items bought, and a Purchases Analysis Book is in use, an extra column is inserted for the VAT content of each item. The total of the VAT column is then transferred to the debit of the Value Added Tax account at the end of the month,

Sales Analysis Books

Although the reader may have expected to find these described here, it should be pointed out that they are for a different purpose than Purchases Analysis Books. A full description of them will be found in Chapter 25 of *Business Accounting*.

Exercises to Appendix No. 9.2

9.13. Enter up a Purchases Analysis Book with columns for the various expenses for M. Winter Ltd for the month from the following information on credit items. VAT is ignored.

19–6			£
July	1	Bought goods from L. Gladstone Ltd	220
,,	3	Bought goods from E. Heath & Co	390
,,	4	Received electricity bill (lighting & heating) from Northern Electricity Board	88
,,	5	Bought goods from H. Wilson & Son	110
,,	6	Motor lorry repaired, received bill from Disraeli Motors	136
,,	8	Bought stationery from W. Pitt Ltd	77
,,	10	Motor van serviced, bill from Disraeli Motors	55
,,	12	Gas bill received from North Gas Board (lighting and heating)	134
,,	15	Bought goods from A. Palmerston	200
,,	17	Bought light bulbs (lighting & heating) from O. Cromwell Ltd	24
,,	18	Goods bought from H. Macmillan	310
,,	19	Invoice for carriage inwards from R. MacDonald	85
,,	21	Bought stationery from J. Callaghan Ltd	60
,,	23	Goods bought from H. Wilson & Son	116
,,	27	Received invoice for carriage inwards from D. Melbourne Ltd	62
,,	31	Invoice for petrol supplied during the month received from Disraeli Motors	185

9.14. Enter up the relevant accounts in the Purchases and General Ledgers from the Purchases Analysis Book you have completed for question 9.13.

9.15A. The following items for the firm of M. Peters Ltd are to be entered in an appropriate manner in a Purchases Analysis Book. The relevant ledger accounts are then to be completed.

19–5			£
May	1	Bought goods on credit from T. Barker Ltd	180
,,	2	Stationery bought from M. Julian & Son	120
,,	4	Bought books (Research Expenses) from Haigh & Co	96
,,	5	Bought test-tubes (Research Expenses) from Lowe Ltd	179
,,	6	Goods bought on credit from T. Johnson	280
,,	8	Motor vehicle repaired: bill from J. Woolley Ltd	158
,,	10	Bought stationery from M. Julian & Son	84
,,	11	Bought goods on credit from A. Sinclair Ltd	109
,,	12	Motor van serviced by J. Woolley Ltd: bill for	78
,,	14	Motor Tyres bought from Top Ten Tyres	250
,,	16	Bought books (Research Expenses) from Haigh & Co	60

19–5		£
„	19 Carriage Inwards: invoice from Express Carriers	70
„	21 Goods bought on credit from T. Barker Ltd	114
„	24 Invoice for Carriage Inwards from Speedsteers Ltd	80
„	27 Bill for petrol from Wiley & Co	214
„	31 Received bill from Hauliers Ltd for carriage inwards	70

10

Depreciation of Fixed Assets

Fixed Assets have already been stated to be those assets of material value that are of long-life, are held to be used in the business, and are not primarily for resale or for conversion into cash.

Usually, with the exception of land, fixed assets have a limited number of years of useful life. Motor vans, machines, buildings and fixtures, for instance, do not last for ever. Even land itself may have all or part of its usefulness exhausted after a few years. Some types of land used for quarries, mines, or land of another sort of wasting nature would be examples. When a fixed asset is bought, then later put out of use by the firm, that part of the cost that is not recovered on disposal is called depreciation.

It is obvious that the only time that depreciation can be calculated accurately is when the fixed asset is disposed of, and the difference between the cost to its owner and the amount received on disposal is then ascertained. If a motor van was bought for £1,000 and sold five years later for £20, then the amount of depreciation is £1,000−£20 = £980.

Depreciation is thus the part of the cost of the fixed asset consumed during its period of use by the firm. Therefore, it has been a cost for services consumed in the same way as costs for such items as wages, rent, lighting and heating, etc. Depreciation is, therefore, an expense and will need charging to the profit and loss account before ascertaining net profit or loss. Provision for depreciation suffered will therefore have to be made in the books in order that the net profits may be profits remaining after charging all the expenses of the period.

Causes of Depreciation

These may be divided into the main classes of physical deterioration, economic factors, the time factor, and depletion.

Physical deterioration is caused mainly from wear and tear when the asset is in use, but also from erosion, rust, rot, and decay from being exposed to wind, rain, sun and other elements of nature.

Economic factors may be said to be those that cause the asset to be put out of use even though it is in good physical condition. These are largely obsolescence and inadequacy.

Obsolescence means the process of becoming obsolete or out of date. A prime example of this were the steam railway locomotives, some of them in good physical condition, which were rendered obsolete by the introduction of diesel and electric locomotives. The steam locomotives were put out of use by British Rail when they still had many more miles of potential use, because the newer locomotives were more efficient and economical to run.

Inadequacy refers to the termination of the use of an asset because of the growth and changes in the size of a firm. For instance, a small ferryboat that is operated by a firm at a seaside resort is entirely inadequate when the resort becomes more popular. It is found that it would be more efficient and economical to operate a larger ferry-boat, and so the smaller boat is put out of use by the firm.

Both obsolescence and inadequacy do not necessarily mean that the asset is scrapped. It is merely put out of use by the firm. Another firm will often buy it. For example, many of the computers put out of use by large companies are bought by smaller firms.

The time factor is obviously associated with all the causes mentioned already. However, there are fixed assets to which the time factor is connected in another way. These are assets with a fixed period of legal life such as leases, patents and copyrights. For instance a lease can be entered into for any period, while a patent's legal life is sixteen years, but there are certain grounds on which this can be extended. Provision for the consumption of these assets is called amortisation rather than depreciation.

Other assets are of a wasting character, perhaps due to the extraction of raw materials from them. These materials are then either used by the firm to make something else, or are sold in their raw state to other firms. Natural resources such as mines, quarries and oil wells come under this heading. To provide for the consumption of an asset of a wasting character is called provision for depletion.

Appreciation

At this stage of the chapter the reader may well begin to ask himself about the assets that increase (appreciate) in value. The answer to this is that normal accounting procedure would be to ignore any such appreciation, as to bring appreciation into account would be to contravene both the cost concept and the convention of conservatism as discussed in Chapter 7. Nevertheless, in certain circumstances appreciation is taken into account in partnership and limited company accounts, but this is left until partnerships and limited companies are considered.

Provisions for Depreciation as Allocation of Cost

Depreciation in total over the life of an asset can be calculated quite simply as cost less amount receivable when the asset is put out of use by the firm. If the item is bought and sold within the one accounting period then the depreciation for that period is charged as a revenue expense in arriving at that period's Net Profit. The difficulties start when the asset is used for more than one accounting period, and an attempt has to be made to charge each period with the depreciation for that period.

For well over one hundred years, accountants have tried to find a 'true' depreciation provision method which would charge the 'true' amount of depreciation in each year's profit and loss account. At first depreciation was regarded as a fall in value, but which 'value' was to be taken? It could be exchange value, use value, market value, replacement value, and so on. At the present time, depreciation is looked at from the viewpoint that costs of fixed assets are used up over a period of time, and the task is to determine how these costs should be apportioned to each accounting period that the asset is in use. Thus, fluctuations in 'value' of a fixed asset are ignored in depreciation provision calculations.

Even though depreciation provisions are now regarded as allocating cost to each accounting period, it does not follow that there is any 'true' method of performing even this task. All that can be said is that the cost should be allocated over the life of the asset in such a way as to charge it as equitably as possible to the periods in which the asset is used. The difficulties involved are considerable and some of them are now listed.

1. Apart from a few assets, such as a lease, how accurately can a firm assess an assets useful life? Even a lease may be put out of use if the premises leased have become inadequate.

2. How does one measure use? A car owned by a firm for three years may have been driven one year by a very careful driver, one year by an average driver and another year by a reckless driver. The standard of driving will affect the motor car and also the amount of cash receivable on its disposal. How should such a firm apportion the car's depreciation costs?

3. There are other expenses besides depreciation such as repairs and maintenance of the fixed asset. As both of these affect the rate and amount of depreciation should they not also affect the depreciation provision calculations?

4. How can a firm possibly know the amount receivable in x years time when the asset is put out of use?

These are only some of the difficulties. Therefore, the methods of calculating provisions for depreciation are mainly accounting customs.

The Main Methods of Calculating Provisions for Depreciation

The two main methods in use are the Straight Line Method and the Reducing Balance Method. The straight line method is used by nearly all firms in the United States of America and in Canada, and is being increasingly used in Great Britain. In fact it has now become regarded in Great Britain that though other methods may be more applicable in certain cases, the straight line method is the one that is generally most suitable.

1. Straight Line Method

This allows an equal amount to be charged as depreciation for each year of expected use of the asset.

The basic formula is:

$$\frac{\text{Cost} - \text{Estimated Residual Value}}{\text{Number of years of expected use}} = \begin{array}{l}\text{Depreciation provision}\\ \text{per annum.}\end{array}$$

The reason for this method being called the straight line method is that if the charge for depreciation was plotted annually on a graph and the points joined together, then the graph would reveal a straight line.

For example, a machine costs £10,000, it has an expected life of four years, and has an estimated residual value of £256. The depreciation provision per annum will be

$$\frac{£10{,}000 - £256}{4} = £2{,}436.$$

In practice, the residual value is often ignored where it would be a relatively small amount.

2. Reducing Balancing Method

To calculate the depreciation provision annually, a fixed percentage is applied to the balance of costs not yet allocated as an expense at the end of the previous accounting period. The balance of unallocated costs will therefore decrease each year, and as a fixed percentage is being used the depreciation provision will therefore be less with each passing year. Theoretically, the balance of unallocated costs at the end of the expected life should equal the estimated residual value.

The basic formula used to find the requisite percentage to apply with this method is:

$$r = 1 - \sqrt[n]{\frac{s}{c}}$$

where n = the number of years

s = the net residual value (this must be a significant amount or the answers will be absurd, since the depreciation rate would amount to nearly one)

c = the cost of the asset

r = the rate of depreciation to be applied.

Using, as an example, the figures used for the machine for which depreciation provisions were calculated on the straight line method, the calculations would appear as:

$$r = 1 - \sqrt[4]{\frac{£256}{£10{,}000}} = 1 - \frac{4}{10} = 0{\cdot}6 \text{ or } 60 \text{ per cent}$$

The depreciation calculation applied to each of the four years of use would be:

	£
Cost	10,000
Year 1. Depreciation provision 60 per cent of £10,000	6,000
Cost not yet apportioned, end of year 1.	4,000
Year 2. Depreciation provision 60 per cent of £4,000	2,400
Cost not yet apportioned, end of year 2.	1,600
Year 3. Depreciation provision 60 per cent of £1,600	960
Cost not yet apportioned, end of year 3.	640
Year 4. Depreciation provision 60 per cent of £640	384
Cost not yet apportioned, end of year 4.	256

In this case the percentage to be applied worked out conveniently to a round figure. However, the answer will often come out to several places of decimals. In this case it would be usual to take the nearest whole figure as a percentage to be applied.

The percentage to be applied, assuming a significant amount for residual value, is usually between two to three times greater for the reducing balance method than for the straight line method.

The advocates of this method usually argue that it helps to even out the total charged as expenses for the use of the asset each year. They state that provisions for depreciation are not the only costs charged, there are the running costs in addition and that the repairs and maintenance element of running costs usually increase with age. Therefore, to equate total usage costs for each year of use the depreciation provisions should fall as the repairs and maintenance element increases. However, as can be seen from the figures of the example already given, the repairs and maintenance element would have to be comparatively large to bring about an equal total charge for each year of use.

The use of this method has declined considerably in recent years being often superseded by the straight line method. Many small firms use it because it is the usual method that is used as an allowance for the depreciation of fixed assets when calculating Income Tax and Corporation Tax. It is contended by many accountants, however, that using a method in accounting purely because it is used for tax purposes can be very misleading as the aims of accounting and the aims of taxation often conflict with one another. On the other hand, it must be borne in mind that many small businesses would not bother to have trading and profit and loss accounts and balance sheets drawn up but for the fact that tax laws make them necessary.

The Amendment of Incorrect Estimates of Depreciation Provisions

Of course, it may well happen that the asset lasts longer than the expected life. In this case the total provisions for depreciation should not exceed the expected total depreciation. With reference to the machine used in the two examples already given, once £9,744 has been charged as depreciation provisions for the machine then further provisions are not required irrespective of how many more years the asset is in use. This is because the objective of allocating the total depreciation as provisions for depreciation has already been achieved. What has happened however, is not that the total provisions are wrong, but that the amounts allocated to each period have been overstated because the expected life has been exceeded by the actual life of the asset.

What happens when the actual period of use of the asset is less than the expected period of use? Here the problem is that the provisions charged are less than the depreciation actually suffered. Corrective action is applied via the Assets Disposals Account, mentioned later, by which the years profit and loss account during which the asset is put out of use is charged not only with the basic amount of the provision but also with the amount by which the total provisions for depreciation have fallen short of the depreciation suffered.

Corrective action is also made via the assets disposals account when the actual amount received on disposal varies from the estimated residual value, but the expected life and actual life are the same. If the amount received on disposal is less than the estimated amount then a further charge needs to be made to the profit and loss account. Conversely, if the cash received is greater than the estimated residual value too much will have been charged over the years for depreciation provisions and the corrective action needed is a credit in the profit and loss account.

The Adjustment of Depreciation Provision Rates

It will often become obvious well before the asset is put out of use that the percentage rates of depreciation provision in use are excessive or inadequate. Revision of depreciation provision percentages will have to be made, but the way in which this is done is outside the scope of this volume.

Depreciation Provisions and Assets Bought or Sold

There are two main methods of calculating depreciation provisions for assets bought or sold during an accounting period.

1. To ignore the dates during the year that the assets were bought or sold, merely calculating a full period's depreciation on the assets in use at the end of the period. Thus, assets sold during the accounting period will have had no provision for depreciation made for that last period irrespective of how many months they were in use. Conversely, assets bought during the period will have a full period of depreciation provision calculated even though they may not have been owned throughout the whole of the period.

2. Provision for depreciation made on the basis of one month's ownership, one month's provision for depreciation. Fractions of months are usually ignored. This is obviously a more scientific method than that already described.

For examination purposes, where the dates on which assets are bought and sold are shown then method No. 2 is the method expected by the examiner. If no such dates are given then obviously method No. 1 will have to be used.

The Recording of Depreciation Provisions

Once the arithmetic of calculating the depreciation provision is completed there still remains the task of recording the provision in the books. Prior to 1948 it was usual to find depreciation provisions being entered in the asset accounts, this method will be described as the old method. Since 1948, to help comply with the provisions of the Companies Act of that year many companies have kept Depreciation Provisions in separate accounts away from the asset accounts. Partnerships and sole traders have also shown a tendency to transfer to this method which will be called hereinafter the modern method.

These methods can now be illustrated. In a business with financial years ended 31 December a machine is bought for £2,000 on 1 January 19–5. It is to be depreciated at the rate of 20 per cent using the reducing balance method. The records for the first three years showing each method are as follows:

Old method

Machinery

	£		£
19–5		19–5	
Jan 1 Cash	2,000	Dec 31 31 Depreciation	400
		„ „ Balance c/d	1,600
	2,000		2,000
19–6		19–6	
Jan 1 Balance b/d	1,600	Dec 31 Depreciation	320
		„ „ Balance c/d	1,280
	1,600		1,600
19–7		19–7	
Jan 1 Balance b/d	1,280	Dec 31 Depreciation	256
		„ „ Balance c/d	1,024
	1,280		1,280
19–8			
Jan 1 Balance b/d	1,024		

Depreciation

	£		£
19–5		19–5	
Dec 31 Machinery	400	Dec 31 Profit and Loss	400
19–6		19–6	
Dec 31 Machinery	320	Dec 31 Profit and Loss	320
19–7		19–7	
Dec 31 Machinery	256	Dec 31 Profit and Loss	256

Profit and Loss Account for the year ended 31 December

19–5 Depreciation	400
19–6 Depreciation	320
19–7 Depreciation	256

Usually shown on the balance sheet as follows:

Balance Sheets

	£	£
As at 31 December 19–5		
Machinery at cost	2,000	
Less Depreciation for the year	400	
		1,600

Balance Sheets

	£	£
As at 31 December 19–6		
Machinery as at 1 January 19–6	1,600	
Less Depreciation for the year	320	
		1,280
As at 31 December 19–7		
Machinery as at 1 January 19–7	1,280	
Less Depreciation for the year	256	
		1,024

Modern Method

Machinery

	£		
19–5			
Jan 1 Cash	2,000		

Provision for Depreciation—Machinery

	£		£
19–5		19–5	
Dec 31 Balance c/d	400	Dec 31 Profit and Loss	400
19–6		19–6	
Dec 31 Balance c/d	720	Jan 1 Balance b/d	400
		Dec 31 Profit and Loss	320
	720		720
19–7		19–7	
Dec 31 Balance c/d	976	Jan 1 Balance b/d	720
		Dec 31 Profit and Loss	256
	976		976
		19–8	
		Jan 1 Balance b/d	976

Profit and Loss Account for the year ended 31 December

19–5 Depreciation	400
19–6 Depreciation	320
19–7 Depreciation	256

Now the balance on the Machinery Account is shown on the balance sheet at the end of each year less the balance on the Provision for Depreciation Account.

Balance Sheets

	£	£
As at 31 December 19–5		
Machinery at cost	2,000	
Less Depreciation to date	400	
		1,600
As at 31 December 19–6		
Machinery at cost	2,000	
Less Depreciation to date	720	
		1,280
As at 31 December 19–7		
Machinery at cost	2,000	
Less Depreciation to date	976	
		1,024

The modern method is much more revealing as far as the balance sheet is concerned. By comparing the depreciation to date with the cost of the asset, a good indication as to the relative age of the asset can be obtained. In the second and third balance sheets using the old method no such indication is available. For instance an item in a balance sheet as follows:

Motor Car as at 1 January 19–5	500	
Less Depreciation for the year	100	
		400

might turn out to be using the new method as either of the following:

Motor Car at cost	6,000	
Less Depreciation to date	5,600	
		400
Motor Car at cost	600	
Less Depreciation to date	200	
		400

The modern method is therefore more revealing and is far preferable from the viewpoint of more meaningful accounting reports. From this point in this book, the recording of depreciation provisions are all made by the modern method.

Disposal of an Asset

When an asset is put out of use, the cost of the asset is transferred to the debit of an Assets Disposal Account, while the amount of depreciation provided on the asset from the date bought to the date of disposal is transferred from the provision for depreciation account to the assets disposal account. By this method the balance on the asset account represents the cost of the assets retained, while the balance on the provision for depreciation account is also concerned only with the retained assets. Any cash received is credited to the disposal account.

If there is a shortage on the credit side of the disposal account then the account will be balanced off by a transfer of this amount to the debit side of the profit and loss account. It will represent the amount by which actual depreciation has exceeded depreciation provisions on the asset. Any shortage on the debit side of the disposals account will mean that the account is to be balanced off by a transfer to the credit side of the profit and loss account. This will represent the amount by which depreciation provisions have exceeded depreciation.

Exhibit 10.1 is an example of the accounts needed when assets are disposed of, including the profit and loss account and balance sheet extracts.

Exhibit 10.1

A machine is bought on 1 January 19–5 for £1,000 and another one on 1 October 19–6 for £1,200. The first machine is sold on 30 June 19–7 for £720. The firm's financial year ends on 31 December. The machinery is to be depreciated at ten per cent, using the straight line method and based on assets in existence at the end of each year ignoring items sold during the year.

Machinery

	£		£
19–5			
Jan 1 Cash	1,000		
19–6		19–6	
Oct 1 Cash	1,200	Dec 31 Balance c/d	2,200
	2,200		2,200
19–7		19–7	
Jan 1 Balance b/d	2,200	Dec 31 Disposals	1,000
		" " Balance c/d	1,200
	2,200		2,200
19–8			
Jan 1 Balance b/d	1,200		

Provision for Depreciation—Machinery

	£		£
		19–5	
		Dec 31 Profit and Loss	100
19–6		19–6	
Dec 31 Balance c/d	320	Dec 31 Profit and Loss	220
	320		320

19–7		£	19–7		£
Dec 31	Disposals (2 years × 10 per cent × £1,000)	200	Jan 1	Balance b/d	320
,, 31	Balance c/d	240	Dec 31	Profit and Loss	120
		440			440
			19–8		
			Jan 1	Balance b/d	240

Disposals of Machinery

19–7			19–7		
Dec 31	Machinery	1,000	Jun 30	Cash	720
			Dec 31	Provision for Depreciation	200
			,, 31	Profit and Loss	80
		1,000			1,000

Profit and Loss Account for the year ended 31 December

19–5	Provision for Depreciation	100
19–6	Provision for Depreciation	220
19–7	Provision for Depreciation	120
	Previous under provision for Depreciation on machinery sold	80

Balance Sheet (Extracts) as at 31 December

		£	£
	Machinery at cost	1,000	
	Less Depreciation to date	100	
			900
19–6	Machinery at cost	2,200	
	Less Depreciation to date	320	
			1,880

Balance Sheet (Extracts) as at 41 December

		£	£
19–7	Machinery at cost	1,200	
	Less Depreciation to date	240	
			960

Another example can now be given. This is somewhat more complicated owing first to a greater number of items, and secondly because the depreciation provisions are calculated on a proportionate basis, i.e. one month's depreciation for every one month's ownership.

Exhibit 10.2

A business with its financial year end being 31 December buys two motor vans, No. 1 for £800 and No. 2 for £500, both on 1 January 19–1. It also buys another motor van, No. 3, on 1 July 19–3 for £900 and another, No. 4, on 1 October 19–3 for £720. The first two motor vans are sold, No. 1 for £229 on 30 September 19–4, and the other, No. 2, was sold for scrap £5 on 30 June 19–5.

Depreciation is on the straight line basis, 20 per cent per annum, ignoring scrap value in this particular case when calculating depreciation per annum. Show the extracts from the assets account, provision for depreciation account, disposal account, profit and loss account for the years ended 31 December 19–1, 19–2, 19–3, 19–4, and 19–5, and the balance sheets as at those dates.

Motor Vans

		£			£
19–1					
Jan 1	Cash	1,300			
19–3					
July 1	Cash	900	19–3		
Oct 1	Cash	720	Dec 31	Balance c/d	2,920
		2,920			2,920
19–4			19–4		
Jan 1	Balance b/d	2,920	Sept 30	Disposals	800
			Dec 31	Balance c/d	2,120
		2,920			2,920
19–5			19–5		
Jan 1	Balance b/d	2,120	June 30	Disposals	500
			Dec 31	Balance c/d	1,620
		2,120			2,120

19–6					
Jan 1	Balance b/d	1,620			

Provision for Depreciation—Motor Vans

		£			£
			19–1		
			Dec 31	Profit and Loss	260
19–2			19–2		
Dec 31	Balance c/d	520	Dec 31	Profit and Loss	260
		520			520
19–3			19–3		
			Jan 1	Balance b/d	520
Dec 31	Balance c/d	906	Dec 31	Profit and Loss	386
		906			906
19–4			19–4		
Sept 30	Disposals	600	Jan 1	Balance b/d	906
Dec 31	Balance c/d	850	Dec 31	Profit and Loss	544
		1,450			1,450
19–5			19–5		
June 30	Disposals	450	Jan 1	Balance b/d	850
Dec 31	Balance c/d	774	Dec 31	Profit and Loss	374
		1,224			1,224
			19–6		
			Jan 1	Balance b/d	774

Workings—Depreciation Provisions

		£	£
19–1	20% of £1,300		260
19–2	20% of £1,300		260
19–3	20% of £1,300 × 12 months	260	
	20% of £900 × 6 months	90	
	20% of £720 × 3 months	36	
			386
19–4	20% of £2,120 × 12 months	424	
	20% of £800 × 9 months	120	
			544
19–5	20% of £1,620 × 12 months	324	
	20% of £500 × 6 months	50	
			374

Workings—Transfers of Depreciation Provisions to Disposal Accounts

Van 1 Bought Jan 1 19–1 Cost £800
Sold Sept 30 19–4
Period of ownership $3\frac{3}{4}$ years
Depreciation provisions $3\frac{3}{4} \times 20\% \times £800 = £600$

Van 2 Bought Jan 1 19–1 Cost £500
Sold June 30 19–5
Period of ownership $4\frac{1}{2}$ years
Depreciation provisions $4\frac{1}{2} \times 20\% \times £500 = £450$

Disposals of Motor Vans

		£			£
19–4			19–4		
Sept 30	Motor Van	800	Sept 30	Provision for Depreciation	600
Dec 31	Profit and Loss	29	,, ,,	Cash	229
		829			829
19–5			19–5		
June 30	Motor Van	500	June 30	Provision for Depreciation	450
			,, ,,	Cash	5
			Dec 31	Profit and Loss	45
		500			500

Profit and Loss Account for the year ended 31 December (extracts)

		£			£
19–1	Provision for Depreciation	260			
19–2	Provision for Depreciation	260			
19–3	Provision for Depreciation	386			
19–4	Provision for Depreciation	544	19–4	Previous over-provision for Depreciation on motor van sold	29
19–5	Provision for Depreciation	374			
	Previous under provision for Depreciation on motor van sold	45			

Balance Sheets (Extracts) as at 31 December

		£	£
19–1	Motor Vans at cost	1,300	
	Less Depreciation to date	260	
			1,040
19–2	Motor Vans at cost	1,300	
	Less Depreciation to date	520	
			780
19–3	Motor Vans at cost	2,920	
	Less Depreciation to date	906	
			2,014
19–4	Motor Vans at cost	2,120	
	Less Depreciation to date	850	
			1,270
19–5	Motor Vans at cost	1,620	
	Less Depreciation to date	774	
			846

Depreciation Provisions and the Replacement of Assets

The purpose of making provision for depreciation is to ensure that the cost of an asset is charged as an expense in an equitable fashion over its useful life in the firm. Parts of the cost are allocated to different years until the whole of the asset's cost has been expensed. This does not mean that depreciation provisions of the type described already provide funds with which to replace the asset when it is put out of use. Such provisions might affect the owner's actions so that funds were available to pay for the replacement of the asset, but this is not necessarily true in all cases.

Imagine a case when a machine is bought for £1,000 and it is expected to last for 5 years, at the end of which time it will be put out of use and will not fetch any money from its being scrapped. If the machine has provisions for depreciation calculated on the straight line basis then £200 per year will be charged as an expense for 5 years. This means that the recorded net profit will be decreased £200 for each of the 5 years because of the depreciation provisions. Now the owner may well, as a consequence, because his profits are £200 less also reduce his drawings by £200 per annum. If the action of charging £200 each year for depreciation also does reduce his annual drawings by £200 then that amount will increase his bank balance (or reduce his bank overdraft), so that at the end of 5 years he may have the cash available to buy a new machine for £1,000 to replace the one that has been put out of use. In fact this is not necessarily true at all, the owner may still take the same amount of drawings for each of the 5 years whether or not a provision for depreciation is charged. In this case nothing has been deliberately held back to provide the cash with which to buy the replacement machine.

There is nothing by law that says that if your recorded profits are £x then the drawings must not exceed £y. For instance a man may make £5,000 profit for his first year in business whilst his drawings were £1,000 in that year, whilst in the second year his profit might be £2,000 and his drawings are £4,000. In the long run an owner may go out of business if his drawings are too high, but in the short term his drawings may well bear no relationship to profits whatsoever. This means that the amounts charged for depreciation provisions thus affecting the profits recorded may not affect the drawings at all in the short term.

Exercises

10.1. A company starts in business on 1 January 19–1. You are to write up the motor vans account and the provision for depreciation account for the year ended 31 December 19–1 from the information given below. Depreciation is at the rate of 20 per cent per annum, using the basis of 1 month's ownership needs one month's depreciation.

19–1 Bought two motor vans for £1,200 each on 1 January
Bought one motor van for £1,400 on 1 July

10.2. A company starts in business on 1 January 19–3, the financial year end being 31 December. You are to show:

(*a*) The machinery account
(*b*) The provision for depreciation account
(*c*) The balance sheet extracts

for each of the years 19–3, 19–4, 19–5, 19–6.
The machinery bought was:

19–3	1 January	1 machine costing £800
19–4	1 July	2 machines costing £500 each
	1 October	1 machine costing £600
19–6	1 April	1 machine costing £200

Depreciation is at the rate of 10 per cent per annum, using the straight line method, machines being depreciated for each proportion of a year.

10.3. A company maintains its fixed assets at cost. Depreciation provision accounts, one for each type of asset, are in use. Machinery is to be depreciated at the rate of $12\frac{1}{2}$ per cent per annum, and fixtures at the rate of 10 per cent per annum, using the reducing balance method. Depreciation is to be calculated on assets in existence at the end of each year, giving a full year's depreciation even though the asset was bought part of the way through the year.

The following transactions in assets have taken place:

19–5	1 January	Bought machinery £640, Fixtures £100
	1 July	Bought fixtures £200
19–6	1 October	Bought machinery £720
	1 December	Bought fixtures £50

The financial year end of the business is 31 December.

You are to show:

(*a*) The machinery account
(*b*) The fixtures account
(*c*) The two separate provision for depreciation accounts

(*d*) The fixed assets section of the balance sheet at the end of each year, for the years ended 31 December 19–5 and 19–6.

10.4. A company depreciates its plant at the rate of 20 per cent per annum, straight line method, for each month of ownership. From the following details draw up the Plant Account and the provision for depreciation account for each of the years 19–4, 19–5, 19–6, and 19–7.

19–4 Bought plant costing £900 on 1 January
Bought plant costing £600 on 1 October
19–6 Bought plant costing £550 on 1 July
19–7 Sold plant which had been bought on 1 January 19–4 for £900 for the sum of £275 on 30 September 19–7.

You are also required to draw up the plant disposal account and the extracts from the balance sheet as at the end of each year.

10.5. A company maintains its fixed assets at cost. Depreciation provision accounts for each asset are kept.

At 31 December 19–8 the position was as follows:

	Total cost to date	*Total depreciation to date*
Machinery	52,590	25,670
Office Furniture	2,860	1,490

The following additions were made during the financial year ended 31 December 19–9:

Machinery £2,480, office furniture £320

Some old machines bought in 19–5 for £2,800 were sold for £800 during the year.

The rates of depreciation are:

Machinery 10 per cent, office furniture 5 per cent,

using the straight line basis, calculated on the assets in existence at the end of each financial year irrespective of date of purchase.

You are required to show the asset and depreciation accounts for the year ended 31 December 19–9 and the balance sheet entries at that date.

10.6. The vehicles and plant register of Hexagon Transport Ltd shows the following vehicles in service at 30 September 19–3:

Registration No.	ABC 242	DEF 108	GHI 832	KLM 23	NOP 666
Purchased during the year ended 30 September	19–9	19–0	19–1	19–2	19–3
Original cost	£800	£860	£840	£950	£980

Up to 30 September 19–3, the company had depreciated its motor vehicles by 20 per cent per annum on the diminishing balance system, but as from 1 October 19–3, it is decided to adopt the straight line method of depreciation, and to write all the vehicles down to an estimated residual value of £20 each over an estimated life of five years. The company wishes to adjust the accrued depreciation provisions on the existing vehicles in line with this policy.

During the year ended 30 September 19–4, the company has purchased vehicle QRS 913 for £960 and sold DEF 108 for £60.

A whole year's depreciation is provided for every vehicle on hand at the end of any accounting period.

You are required to:

(*a*) reconstruct the entries for each vehicle in the register, as it appeared on 30 September 19–3

(*b*) calculate the necessary adjustments to be made in respect of the depreciation provisions on 1 October 19–3.

(*c*) complete the entries in the register for the year to 30 September 19–4, showing clearly how you calculate any adjustment necessary in respect of the sale of DEF 108.

Calculations should be made to the nearest £1.

(Institute of Cost and Management Accountants)

10.7A. On 1 January, 19–5 John Smith purchased 6 machines for £1,500 each. His accounting year ends on 31 December. Depreciation at the rate of 10 per cent per annum on cost has been charged against income each year and credited to a provision for depreciation account.

On 1 January, 19–6 one machine was sold for £1,250 and on 1 January, 19–7 a second machine was sold for £1,150. An improved model which cost £2,800 was purchased on 1 July, 19–6. Depreciation was charged on this new machine at the same rate as that on earlier purchases.

Required:

(*a*) the machinery account and the provision for depreciation account for 19–5, 19–6 and 19–7; and

(*b*) the entry for machines in the balance sheet at 31 December, 19–7.

(Institute of Bankers)

10.8A. The balance sheet of T. Ltd, as at 31 December, 19–7, contains the following item:

	£	£
Motor vehicles		
Balance, 1 January, 19–7, at cost		297,000
Add: Purchases during 19–7, at cost		17,000
		314,000
Less: Sales during 19–7 (cost price)	11,000	
Depreciation provision as at 31 December, 19–7	71,000	
		82,000
		232,000

Depreciation is charged at 20 per cent per annum on cost over five years. A full year's depreciation is charged in the year of acquisition but none in the year of disposal.

During 19–8 the following motor vehicle transactions took place:

Purchases

		£
March 31	Lorry	6,500
April 30	Lorry	8,400
Aug 31	Saloon	1,650
Dec 31	Lorry	4,200

Sales

		Purchased	*Cost*	*Proceeds*
			£	£
April 30	Lorry	31.1.–6	3,500	450
June 30	Saloon	30.6.–4	950	75
Sept 30	Lorry	31.12.–1	4,000	250
Nov 30	Lorry	1.1.–7	3,500	800

Required:
Write up the motor vehicles, motor vehicles depreciation provision and motor vehicles disposal accounts for 19–8 in the company's ledger. Also show the relevant entries in the company's profit and loss account and balance sheet at the end of 19–8.
(Chartered Institute of Secretaries and Administrators)

10.9A. Haulage Ltd, which makes up its accounts to June 30 in each year, has a fleet of motor lorries. Annual depreciation on motor lorries is calculated at a rate of 25 per cent on the reducing balances, with a full year's charge being made in the year in which a lorry is purchased, but no charge in the year of sale.

An extract from the company's Balance Sheet as on 30 June, 19–6, showed the following:

	£
Motor lorries at cost	82,450
Less provision for depreciation	46,691
	35,759

During the year ended 30 June 19–7 purchases and sales of motor lorries were:

Purchases

		£
19–6		
July 30	HLV 496D	4,250
Oct 14	HLV 997D	3,500
19–7		
Feb 25	DLV 509E	4,500
June 24	DLV 507E	2,950

Sales

		Purchased	*Cost*	*Proceeds*
19–6			£	£
July 30	NBG 12	14 May, 19–2	796	150
Oct 1	VBG 616A	10 July, 19–3	1,280	425
19–7				
Mar 1	ALV 696C	9 Mar, 19–5	4,000	2,300
June 25	UMA 992C	21 Sept 19–5	1,824	1,350

You are required to write up the following accounts in the company's books for the year ended 30 June 19–7:

(*a*) Motor Lorries Account;

(*b*) Motor Lorries Depreciation Provision Account; and
(*c*) Motor Lorries Disposal Account.
(Institute of Chartered Accountants)

10.10A. Carrier owned three lorries at 1 April 19–6, viz.:

A	Purchased	21 May 19–2	Cost £1,560
B	,,	20 June 19–4	,, £980
C	,,	1 January 19–6	,, £2,440

Depreciation is taken at 20 per cent of cost per annum, ignoring fractions of a year.

During the year to 31 March 19–7, the following transactions occurred:

(*a*)	1 June 19–6	B	was involved in an accident and considered a write-off by the Insurance Company, who paid £525 compensation.
(*b*)	7 June 19–6	D	was purchased for £1,640.
(*c*)	21 August 19–6	A	was sold for £350.
(*d*)	30 October 19–6	E	was purchased for £1,950.
(*e*)	6 March 19–7	E	was not considered suitable for carrying the type of goods required and was exchanged for F. The value of F was considered to be £1,880.

You are required to show the accounts to record these transactions, including the depreciation charge for the year to 31 March, 19–7, in Carrier's books.
(Association of Certified Accountants)

10.11A. The net profits of Abel, Baker and Co for 19–5, 19–6 and 19–7 were £2,960, £3,155 and £3,187 respectively. It has now been found that the wrong method was used for depreciation of machinery and fixtures and fittings when calculating these profit figures.

All the assets in question were acquired on 1 January 19–5 for £12,800 (machinery) and £2,560 (fixtures and fittings).

The method used was the straight line (or equal instalment) method, assuming for the machinery a working life of 8 years and scrap value £1,000, and for the fixtures and fittings a working life of 12 years and scrap value £400. The method which should have been used was the reducing balance method (machinery 25 per cent per annum, fixtures and fittings 12½ per cent per annum).

You are asked to re-calculate the net profits for 19–5, 19–6 and 19–7.
(Oxford Local Examination, 'O' Level)

11

Bad Debts, Provisions for Bad Debts, Provisions for Discounts on Debtors

With many businesses a large proportion, if not all, of the sales are on a credit basis. The business is therefore taking the risk that some of the customers may never pay for the goods sold to them on credit. This is a normal business risk, and therefore bad debts as they are called are a normal business expense and must be charged as such when calculating the profit or loss for the period.

When a debt is found to be bad, the asset as shown by the debtor's account is worthless, and must accordingly be eliminated as an asset account. This is done by crediting the debtor's account to cancel the asset and increasing the expenses account of bad debts by debiting it there. Sometimes the debtor will have paid part of the debt, leaving the remainder to be written off as a bad debt. The total of the bad debts account is later transferred to the profit and loss account.

An example of debts being written off as bad can now be shown:

Exhibit 11.1

C. Bloom

19–5	£	19–5	£
Jan 8 Sales	50	Dec 31 Bad Debts	50

R. Shaw

19–5	£	19–5	£
Feb 16 Sales	240	Aug 17 Cash	200
		Dec 31 Bad Debts	40
	240		240

Bad Debts

19–5	£	19–5	£
Dec 31 C. Bloom	50	Dec 31 Profit and Loss	90
,, ,, R. Shaw	40		
	90		90

Profit and Loss Account for the year ended 31 December 19–5

	£
Bad Debts	90

Provision for Bad Debts

The ideal situation from the accounting point of view of measuring net income, i.e. calculating net profit, is for the expenses of the period to be matched against the revenue of that period which the expenses have helped to create. Where an expense such as bad debt is matched in the same period with the revenue from the sale, then all is in order for the purposes of net profit calculation. However, it is very often the case that it is not until a period later than that in which the sale took place is it realized that the debt is a bad debt.

Therefore, to try to bring into the period in which the sale was made a charge for the bad debts resulting from such sales, the accountant brings in the concept of an estimated expense. Such an item of expense for an expense that has taken place, but which cannot be calculated with substantial accuracy is known as a Provision. The item of estimated expense for bad debts is therefore known as a Provision for Bad Debts.

The estimate is arrived at on the basis of experience, a knowledge of the customers and of the state of the country's economy at that point in time with its likely effect on customers' debt paying capacity. Sometimes the schedules of debtors are scrutinized and a list of the likely bad debts made. Other firms work on an overall percentage basis to cover possible bad debts. Sometimes a provision is based on specified debtors.

Ageing Schedule for Estimated Bad Debts

Period debt owing	*Amount*	*Estimated percentage bad*	*Provision for bad debts*
	£		£
Less than one month	5,000	1	50
1 month to 2 months	3,000	3	90
2 months to 3 months	800	4	32
3 months to 1 year	200	5	10
Over 1 year	160	20	32
	9,160		214

Another method is that of preparing an ageing schedule and taking different percentages for debts owing for different lengths of time. This is somewhat more scientific than the overall percentage basis, as in most trades and industries the longer a debt is owed the more chance there is of it turning out to be a bad debt. The schedule might appear as on page 156.

There are in fact two different methods of recording the provisions for bad debts. An adjustment may be made in the Bad Debts Account, or alternatively a completely separate account can be opened catering for the bad debts provision only. The net amount shown as bad debt expenses will be the same using the two methods, also the balance sheet will look exactly the same whichever method is used. The two methods are best illustrated in the following example, Exhibit 11–2.

It should be pointed out that, in practice, the more likely method will be that shown in Method A where the adjustment is shown in the Bad Debts Account. Examiners have however very often tended to choose a style having a completely separate account for the provision, this is shown as Method B. Either way is perfectly correct, and if the reader finds that he/she has difficulty with one method, but finds the other method simpler to follow, then obviously the simpler method will be the choice for that person.

Exhibit 11.2

A business starts on 1 January 19–2 and its financial year end is 31 December annually. A table of the debtors, the bad debts written off and the estimated bad debts at the end of each year is now given.

Year to 31 December	*Debtors at end of year (after bad debts written off)*	*Bad Debts written off during year*	*Debts thought at end of year to be impossible to collect*
	£	£	£
19–2	6,000	423	120
19–3	7,000	510	140
19–4	8,000	604	155
19–5	6,400	610	130

Method A—using a Bad Debts Account only with adjustments being used for provisions for bad debts.

Profit and Loss Account for the year ended 31 December (extracts)

	£		£
19–2 Bad Debts	543		
19–3 Bad Debts	530		
19–4 Bad Debts	619		
19–5 Bad Debts	585		

Bad Debts

	£		£
19–2		19–2	
Dec 31 Sundries	423		
„ „ Provision c/d	120	Dec 31 Profit and Loss	543
	543		543
19–3		19–3	
Dec 31 Sundries	510	Jan 1 Provision b/d	120
„ „ Provision c/d	140	Dec 31 Profit and Loss	530
	650		650
19–4		19–4	
Dec 31 Sundries	604	Jan 1 Provision b/d	140
„ „ Provision c/d	155	Dec 31 Profit and Loss	619
	759		759
19–5		19–5	
Dec 31 Sundries	610	Jan 1 Provision b/d	155
„ „ Provision c/d	130	Dec 31 Profit and Loss	585
	740		740
		19–6	
		Jan 1 Provision b/d	130

Balance Sheets as at 31 December (extracts)

	£	£
19–2 Debtors	6,000	
Less Provision for Bad Debts	120	
		5,880
19–3 Debtors	7,000	
Less Provision for Bad Debts	140	
		6,860
19–4 Debtors	8,000	
Less Provision for Bad Debts	155	
		7,845

Balance Sheets as at 31 December (extracts)

	£	£
19–5 Debtors	6,400	
Less Provision for Bad Debts	130	
		6,270

Method B—using a separate Bad Debts Account and a provision for Bad Debts Account.

The Bad Debts Account is charged with the debts found to be bad during the accounting period, while the provision for Bad Debts Account shows the provision as at the end of each period. Once the provision account is created it stays open until the end of the next accounting period, and all that it then requires is the amount needed to increase it or reduce it to the newly estimated figure. In the balance sheet at the end of each period the provision for bad debts is shown as a deduction from debtors, so that the net amount is the expected amount of collectable debts.

Profit and Loss Accounts for the year ended 31 December (extracts)

	£		£
19–2 Bad Debts	423		
Provision for Bad Debts	120		
19–3 Bad Debts	510		
Increase in provision for Bad Debts	20		
19–4 Bad Debts	604		
Increase in provision for Bad Debts	15		
19–5 Bad Debts	610	19–5 Reduction in provision for Bad Debts	25

Provision for Bad Debts

	£		£
		19–2	
		Dec 31 Profit and Loss	120
19–3		19–3	
Dec 31 Balance c/d	140	Dec 31 Profit and Loss	20
	140		140
		19–4	
19–4		Jan 1 Balance b/d	140
Dec 31 Balance c/d	155	Dec 31 Profit and Loss	15
	155		155

Provision for Bad Debts

19–5		£	19–5		£
Dec 31	Profit and Loss	25	Jan 1	Balance b/d	155
„ „	Balance c/d	130			
		155			155
			19–6		
			Jan 1	Balance b/d	130

Bad Debts

		£			£
19–2			19–2		
Dec 31	Sundries	423	Dec 31	Profit and Loss	423
19–3			19–3		
Dec 31	Sundries	510	Dec 31	Profit and Loss	510
19–4			19–4		
Dec 31	Sundries	604	Dec 31	Profit and Loss	604
19–5			19–5		
Dec 31	Sundries	610	Dec 31	Profit and Loss	610

The balance sheet for Method B will be exactly the same as the balance sheet in Method A.

Comparing the amounts charged as expense to the Profit and Loss Account it can be seen that:

	Method A	*Method B*
19–2	543	423+120 = total 543
19–3	530	510+ 20 = total 530
19–4	619	604+ 15 = total 619
19–5	585	610− 25 = net 585

At first sight it might appear that the provisions were far short of reality. For instance at the end of the first year the provision was £120 yet bad debts in the second year amounted to £510. This, however, is not a fair comparison if the amount of debtors at each year end equalled in amount approximately three months of sales, this being the average time in which debtors pay their accounts. In this case the provision is related to three months of sales, while the bad debts written off are those relating to twelve months of sales.

Provisions for Discounts on Debtors

Some firms create provisions for Discounts to be allowed on the debtors outstanding at the balance sheet date. This, they maintain, is quite legitimate, as the amount of debtors less any bad debt provision is not the best estimate of collectable debts, owing to cash discounts which will be given to debtors if they pay within a given time. The cost of discounts, it is argued, should be charged in the period when the sales were made.

To do this the procedure is similar to the bad debts provision. It must be borne in mind that the estimate of discounts to be allowed should be based on the net figure of debtors less bad debts provision, as it is obvious that discounts are not allowed on bad debts!

Example:

Year ended 31 December	*Debtors*	*Provision for Bad Debts*	*Provision for discounts allowed*
	£	£	%
19–3	4,000	200	2
19–4	5,000	350	2
19–5	4,750	250	2

Profit and Loss Account for the year ended 31 December (extracts)

	£		£
19–3 Provision for discounts on debtors (2 per cent of £3,800)	76		
19–4 Increase in Provision for discounts on debtors (to 2 per cent of £4,650)	17		
		19–5 Reduction in provision for discounts on debtors (to 2 per cent of £4,500)	3

Provision for Discounts on Debtors

			£
		19–3	
		Dec 31 Profit and Loss	76
19–4		19–4	
Dec 31 Balance c/d	93	Dec 31 Profit and Loss	17
	93		93
19–5		19–5	
Dec 31 Profit and Loss	3	Jan 1 Balance b/d	93
,, ,, Balance c/d	90		
	93		93
		19–6	
		Jan 1 Balance b/d	90

Balance Sheets as at 31 December (extracts)

	£	£	£
19–3 Debtors		4,000	
Less Provision for Bad Debts	200		
„ Provision for discounts on debtors	76		
	—	276	
		——	3,724
19–4 Debtors		5,000	
Less Provision for Bad Debts	350		
„ Provision for discounts on debtors	93		
	—	443	
		——	4,557
19–5 Debtors		4,750	
Less Provision for Bad Debts	250		
„ Provision for discounts on debtors	90		
	—	340	
		——	4,410

Discounts on Creditors

It is also the practice of some firms to take into account the fact that the amount of creditors at the balance sheet date does not represent the amount which will be paid. This is because where advantage is taken of cash discount arrangements, a smaller sum will be payable to discharge the debts.

This is anticipating income, and therefore contravenes the accounting convention of conservatism. However, it is perhaps felt that if a firm creates a provision for discounts on debtors, it should also take into account discounts on creditors.

Example:

Year ended 31 December	*Creditors*	*Discounts receivable*
	£	%
19–4	5,000	2
19–5	5,600	2
19–6	4,800	2

Profit and Loss Account for the year ended 31 December (extracts)

	£		£
		19–4 Discounts on creditors	100
		19–5 Discounts on creditors	12
19–6 Reduction in discounts on creditors	16		

Allowance for Discounts on Creditors

		£			£
19–4					
Dec 31	Profit and Loss	100			
19–5			19–5		
Dec 31	Profit and Loss	12	Dec 31	Balance c/d	112
		112			112
19–6			19–6		
Jan 1	Balance b/d	112	Dec 31	Profit and Loss	16
			,, ,,	Balance c/d	96
		112			112
19–7					
Jan 1	Balance b/d	96			

Balance Sheets as at 31 December (extracts)

	£	£
19–4 Creditors	5,000	
Less Allowance for discounts	100	
		4,900
19–5 Creditors	5,600	
Less Allowance for discounts	112	
		5,488
19–6 Creditors	4,800	
Less Allowance for discounts	96	
		4,704

Exercises

11.1. In a new business during the year ended 31 December 19–4 the following debts are found to be bad, and are written off on the dates shown:

30 April	H. Gordon	£110
31 August	D. Bellamy Ltd	£ 64
31 October	J. Alderton	£ 12

On 31 December 19–4 the schedule of remaining debtors, amounting in total to £6,850, is examined, and it is decided to make a provision, for bad debts of £220.

You are required to show:

(i) The bad debts account, with the provision to be a part of it.
(ii) The change to the Profit and Loss Account.
(iii) The relevant extracts from the Balance Sheet as at 31 December 19–4.

11.2. A business started trading on 1 January 19–6. During the two years ended 31 December 19–6 and 19–7 the following debts were written off to bad debts account on the dates stated:

31 August 19–6	W. Sykes & Son	£ 85
30 September 19–6	S. D. Kidd Ltd	£140
28 February 19–7	L. J. Silver & Co	£180
31 August 19–7	N. Kelly	£ 60
30 November 19–7	A. Capone Associates	£250

On 31 December 19–6 there had been a total of debtors remaining of £40,500. It was decided to make a provision for bad debts of £550.

On 31 December 19–7 there had been a total of debtors remaining of £47,300. It was decided to make a provision for bad debts of £600.

You are required to show:

(i) The Bad Debts Account for each of the two years, with the provisions included in this account.
(ii) The charges to the Profit and Loss Account for each of the two years.
(iii) The relevant extracts from the balance sheets as at 31 December 19–6 and 19–7.

11.3. A business had always made a provision for doubtful debts at the rate of 5 per cent of debtors. On 1 January 19–3 the provision for this, brought forward from the previous year, was £260.

During the year to 31 December 19–3 the bad debts written off amounted to £540.

On 31 December 19–3 the remaining debtors totalled £6,200 and the usual provision for bad debts is to be made.

You are to show:

(i) The Bad Debts Account for the year ended 31 December 19–3.
(ii) Extract from the Profit and Loss Account for the year.
(iii) The relevant extract from the balance sheet as at 31 December 19–3.

11.4. A business, which started trading on 1 January 19–5, adjusted its bad debt provisions at the end of each year on a percentage basis, but each year the percentage rate is adjusted in accordance with the current 'economic climate'. The following details are available for the three years ended 31 December 19–5, 19–6 and 19–7.

	Bad Debts written off year to 31 December	*Debtors at 31 December*	*Per cent provision for Bad Debts*
	£	£	
19-5	656	22,000	5
19–6	1,805	40,000	7
19–7	3,847	60,000	6

Using the method shown as Method A in Chapter 11, you are required to show the following:

(i) Bad Debts Accounts for each of the three years, showing provisions carried forward.
(ii) Balance Sheet extracts as at 31 December 19–5, 19–6 and 19–7.

11.5. For students sitting examinations where separate Provision for Bad Debt account questions are asked, attempt questions 11.4. using Method B as stated in Chapter 11.

11.6. A company makes a provision for doubtful debts of 5 per cent on debtors and a provision at the rate of 2½ per cent for discount on debtors.

On 1 January 19–4 the balances standing in the relevant accounts were provision for doubtful debts £672 and provision for discount on debtors £319.
(*a*) Enter the balances in the appropriate accounts.
(*b*) During 19–4 the company incurred bad debts £1,480 and allowed discounts £3,289. On 31 December 19–4 debtors amounted to £12,800. Show the entries in the appropriate accounts for the year 19–4, assuming that the company's accounting year ends on 31 December 19–4.
(Associated Examining Board 'A' Level)

11.7. From the following figures calculate the
(*a*) provision for bad debts,
(*b*) provision for discounts allowed
and state clearly the amounts to be charged to the profit and loss account:

	£
Debtors—before adjustment for any bad debts therein	41,000
Provision for Bad Debts	3,900
Proportion of Debtors which are bad	1,000

Provisions for bad debts is to be 10 per cent on debtors and a provision for discounts allowed to be 5 per cent on debtors. Clearly state in answer the separate provisions and the charge to profit and loss account.
(East Midland Educational Union)

11.8. The following trial balance was extracted from the books of Fletcher, a trader, as at 31 December 19–4:

	£	£
Capital account		20,500
Purchases	46,500	
Sales		60,900
Repairs to buildings	848	
Motor car	950	
Car expenses	318	
Freehold land and buildings	10,000	
Balance at bank	540	
Furniture and fittings	1,460	
Wages and salaries	8,606	
Discounts allowed	1,061	
Discounts received		814
Drawings	2,400	
Rates and insurances	248	
Bad Debts	359	
Provision for bad debts, 1 January 19–4		140
Trade debtors	5,213	
Trade creditors		4,035
General expenses	1,586	
Stock-in-trade, 1 January 19–4	6,300	
	86,389	86,389

The following matters are to be taken into account:

1. Stock-in-trade, 31 December 19–4, £8,800.
2. Wages and salaries outstanding at 31 December 19–4, £318.
3. Rates and insurances paid in advance at 31 December 19–4, £45.
4. The provision for bad debts is to be reduced to £100.

5. During 19–4, Fletcher withdrew goods, valued at £200, for his own use. No entry has been made in the books for the withdrawal of these goods.
6. The item 'Repairs to buildings, £848' includes £650 in respect of alterations and improvements to the buildings.
7. One third of the car expenses represents the cost of Fletcher's motoring for private, as distinct from business, purposes.

You are required to prepare a trading and profit and loss account for the year 19–4, and a balance sheet as on 31 December 19–4.

Ignore depreciation of fixed assets.
(Institute of Bankers)

11.9. The following trial balance was extracted from the books of Henry Clifton, a trader, as at 31 December 19–3:

	£	£
Capital account		15,000
Freehold land and building	7,000	
Furniture and fittings	1,400	
Stock-in-trade, 1 January 19–3	6,100	
Purchases	58,700	
Sales		69,300
Trade debtors	5,850	
Trade creditors		4,345
Rents received		275
Loan from Crawford at 5 per cent per annum		1,200
Interest on Crawford's loan outstanding at 1 January 19–3		30
Discounts allowed	1,320	
Discounts received		925
Provision for bad debts, 1 January 19–3		110
Bad debts	325	
Wages and salaries	7,045	
Drawings	1,600	
General expenses	865	
Balance at bank	680	
Rates and insurances	300	
	91,185	91,185

The following matters are to be taken into account:

1. Stock-in-trade, 31 December 19–3, £8,500.
2. Wages and salaries outstanding at 31 December 19–3, £415.
3. Rates paid in advance at 31 December 19–3, £50.
4. The provisions for bad debts is to be increased to £170.
5. Clifton did not pay the interest on Crawford's loan during 19–3.
6. Part of the freehold building was let to a tenant who owed £25 for rent at 31 December 19–3.

You are required to prepare a trading and profit and loss account for the year 19–3 and a balance sheet as at 31 December 19–3.

Note:
Ignore depreciation of fixed assets.
(Institute of Bankers)

11.10A. The following trial balance was extracted from the books of Lancaster, a trader, at 31 December 19–7:

	£	£
Capital account		19,364
Freehold land and building	12,500	
Furniture and fittings	840	
Motor car (cost 1 January 19–5: £950)	650	
Purchases	46,982	
Sales		66,649
Rent received		360
Drawings	3,230	
Car expenses	396	
Stock-in-trade, 1 January 19–7	4,988	
Bad debts	422	
Provision for bad debts, 1 January 19–7		226
General expenses	827	
Rent and rates	1,162	
Trade debtors	7,921	
Trade creditors		6,933
Wages and salaries	8,983	
Discounts allowed	2,164	
Balance at bank	2,467	
	93,532	93,532

The following matters are to be taken into account:

1. Stock-in-trade, 31 December 19–7, £5,429.
2. Wages and salaries accrued, 31 December 19–7, £198.
3. Rates paid in advance, 31 December 19–7, £48.
4. The provision for bad debts is to be increased by £32.
5. Provide for depreciation on the motor car on the basis that it will be in service for four years and will then be traded in for £350.
6. Part of the building was let to a tenant who owed £120 at 31 December 19–7.
7. Lancaster rents a postal franking machine. Unused stamps at 31 December 19–7 were worth £47. Postages are included in general expenses.

Required:

Lancaster's trading and profit and loss account for 19–7 and a balance sheet as at 31 December 19–7.

(Institute of Bankers)

11.11A. The following trial balance was extracted from the books of Rodney, a trader, at 31 December 19–7:

	£	£
Capital		20,271
Drawings	2,148	
Debtors and creditors	7,689	5,462
Sales		81,742
Purchases	62,101	
Rent and rates	880	
Lighting and heating	246	
Salaries and wages	8,268	
Bad debts	247	
Provision for doubtful debts at 31 December 19–6		326
Stock-in-trade, 31 December 19–6	9,274	
Insurances	172	

	£	£
General expenses	933	
Bank balance	1,582	
Motor vans at cost	8,000	
Provision for depreciation of motor vans at 31 December 19–6		3,600
Proceeds of sale of van		250
Motor expenses	861	
Freehold premises at cost	10,000	
Rent received		750
	112,401	112,401

The following matters are to be taken into account:

1. Stock-in-trade 31 December 19–7, £9,884.
2. Rates paid in advance 31 December 19–7, £40.
3. Rent receivable, due at 31 December 19–7, £250.
4. Lighting and heating due at 31 December 19–7, £85.
5. Provision for doubtful debts to be increased to £388.
6. Included in the amount for insurances, £172, is an item for £82 for motor insurances and this amount should be transferred to motor expenses.
7. Depreciation has been and is to be charged on vans at the annual rate of 20 per cent of cost.
8. On 1 January 19–7 a van which had been purchased for £1,000 on 1 January 19–4 was sold for £250. The only record of the matter is the credit of £250 to proceeds of sale of van account.

Required:

A trading and profit and loss account for 19–7 and a balance sheet at 31 December 19–7.

(Institute of Bankers)

11.12A. On 31 December 19–7, a trader decided to raise a provision for bad debts based on 5 per cent of debtors and to maintain the provision at that percentage at the end of each financial year. Any bad debts were to be written off against the provision.

After bad debts had been written off, the debtors' balances totalled:

		£
31 December	19–7	72,500
	19–8	79,500
	19–9	66,000
	19–0	55,500

Bad debts written off were:

		£
Year ending 31 December	19–7	2,500
	19–8	1,200
	19–9	1,750
	19–0	1,250

A bad debt of £50, which had been written off in 19–8, was recovered in 19–0. Prepare the provision for bad debts account for the years ended 31 December 19–7 to 19–0.

(East Midland Educational Union)

11.13A. After examination of the Sales Ledger it was decided to make specific provision in the accounts for the year ended 31 May, 19–9, for the following doubtful debts.

Customer A £38
Customer B £7
Customer C £48
Customer D £204

It was also decided to make a general provision of 5 per cent on the *other* debtors who at the 31 May 19–9, amounted to £18,000.

No further business transactions were entered into with any of these debtors but the liquidators of A and D sent final dividends of £11 and £78 respectively and C paid his debt in full.

On 31 May, 19–0, it was decided to maintain the provision against B's debt and to make further provisions for the following debts considered doubtful:

X £29
Y £48
Z £11

The *other* debtors amounted to £21,000 and it was required to make the general provision for doubtful debts equal to 5 per cent of these debts.

You are required to show the entries for both years in the firm's Nominal ledger to give effect to the above.

(Royal Society of Arts and London Chamber of Commerce Joint Scheme)

12

Modern Methods of Processing Data

So far this book has been dealing mainly with the principles of double entry, and the book-keeping records have been in the form of the basic conventional system. However, it must not be thought that all the book-keeping methods in use are necessarily the same as the one described in this book. What is important is that the main ends which the financial book-keeping records purport to serve remain the same, but it is the means by which the actual records are effected that can be altered. Just because a mechanized or streamlined system is used does not mean that the answers will change. The question 'What is the total of debtors?' should receive the same answer whether the firm uses bound books, loose-leaf ledgers, keyboard accounting machines, punched card equipment, or a computer. The final accounts should remain the same whatever system is in use. The change takes place in the means by which the information or data is gathered together and processed so as to give the answers, and the speed with which this is accomplished.

It would, however, be a mistake to think that a more advanced system would only give, more quickly, exactly the same answers as before and nothing else. The system should be designed so that besides the essential answers which must be given by any book-keeping system further desirable information is obtainable as a by-product. Any such information must stand up to the criticism of whether or not it is worth obtaining. If the cost of obtaining it is greater than the benefits which flow to the firm from having it, then clearly it is not worthwhile information. The system should therefore be designed so as to give worthwhile information and exclude information which fails to stand up to the test.

You may well ask why it is that so far you have been studying mainly the basic conventional double entry book-keeping system. Has it not all been a waste of time? The answer to that must be that all of the more modern methods have developed from the conventional system. The basic information obtainable from any other book-keeping method remains the same. This consists of the changes in assets and liabilities, and convenient collection points are established to aggregate expenses and revenue so that the changes in the capital can be calculated. Thus the double entry system is capable of being used by any type of firm. When a person first learns book-keeping, he does not know exactly which systems will be in use at firms that he will be in contact with during his working life. In five years' time from now a firm employing keyboard accounting machinery may rely entirely on computers, another now using a conventional system may be using punched cards, another may still retain the conventional system or a relatively slight adaptation of it. By understanding the ends towards which the double entry system is aimed, the student will therefore appreciate the ends towards which the other methods are aimed.

There is also another very simple answer. Book-keeping, like other mathematical subjects, needs a certain amount of practice if one is to be fluent in its use. The cost of equipping each student with accounting machinery on which the exercises are to be done would be prohibitive. It would also obviously preclude exercises being done at any other but fixed places where machinery was situated.

Probably one of the best ways to introduce modern methods is to trace their development from the conventional double entry system. The firm at which you are employed, or will be employed, would then be at some stage along this span of development. You should then be able to relate the firms book-keeping methods to what used to be done, and also to what may be done in your firm in the future.

It must always be borne in mind that, barring the legal needs which accounts fulfil, the costs of running the system should not exceed the benefits. To take an exaggerated example, a local grocer's shop could hardly be expected to use an expensive computer, as the costs of running it would far exceed any benefits which the firm might receive. Before advocating a more advanced system of book-keeping this test should always be applied.

The Development of Modern Methods

1. Bound Books

Up to the advent of the typewriter in 1866, bound volumes were universally used for book-keeping records. The accounts took the basic double entry form described in this book, but there was much manual copying of items that have now been eliminated from the present basic system. As carbon paper had not been invented, the sales invoices, debit and credit notes were copied into the sales and returns books before they were dispatched to customers and suppliers. Now, of course, copy sales invoices and debit and credit notes obtained by the use of carbon paper obviate any need for a copy to be made in the books. It is rather interesting to note that the purchases invoices were also usually copied into the purchases book, even though reference could easily be made to the purchases invoice received by the firm.

2. *Loose-Leaf Ledgers and Carbon Paper*

The typewriter and the consequent development of carbon paper led to the transition away from bound books to loose-leaf ledgers.

Typewriters could obviously be used more easily with loose sheets of paper, and with the use of carbon paper could give several copies of such things as invoices and debit and credit notes. Typed ledger accounts were also neater than hand-written records.

At first, the loose-leaf ledgers were kept in covers which could be opened and closed by operating a key. The loose sheets therefore had to be extracted and placed into the typewriter, then removed from the typewriter and replaced in the covers. Soon it was seen that continually extracting them and replacing them in the covers was a waste of time. The loose leaves, especially if they were somewhat sturdier and in the form of cards, could easily be kept in trays.

Experiments then began as to how one operation could produce several different records. This was done by designing special stationery with interleaved carbon or with a carbon backing on the sheets. This stationery was in the form of sets. For instance, one typing operation with a sales set might produce the following records:

Two sales invoices—one to be retained as a copy and the other sent to the customer.

An advice note for the customer

Instructions to the warehouse to send the goods.

3. *The Typewriter and the Adding Machine to the Accounting Machine*

Adding machines were in existence in the latter part of the nineteenth century. In 1901, an accounting machine was constructed in the United States which was a combination of the adding machine and the typewriter. Other machines were developed, some primarily being based on the adding machine while others were developed from the typewriter.

These machines were used eventually in combination with multi-copy carbon stationery much more sophisticated than the sales set already described. Different coloured paper for forms so that it was easy to distinguish between various records came more into use. One operation produced not only several records but also automatically calculated the new balance on the account after the entry was made, and also totalled up the amount of each type of entry made for control purposes. These machines are used not only for financial accounting records but for costing records as well. Very often they are specially designed for use by particular firms.

4. *Punched Card Accounting Machines*

A class of accounting machine which works in an entirely different way was also developed. This was the punched card machine developed in the United States by Dr Hollerith in 1884.

This method of accounting is based on information which has been recorded by the means of holes being punched into cards. The whole system can be summarized into:

1. Punching holes into cards to represent the information that is being dealt with.

2. Sorting the cards out into a required order.

3. Getting the machines to tabulate the information in printed form in a way desired by the firm.

To do this the firm needs three basic kinds of machines:

1. A punch
2. A sorter
3. A tabulator

However, the most important part of the system is the actual punched cards. These are all the same size with one corner cut off so that in a pile of cards it is easy to see if one is facing the wrong way. The card consists of a number of columns across with ten positions running down the card.

Each set of columns across will be put to a different use. For instance the date would take up six columns. The reason is obvious if the date 14.12.72 is studied, as there are six numbers, so one number is required for each part of the date. The next set of columns might be taken up with the account number. Suppose there are about 4,000 accounts then the next four columns will be needed, one for each possible digit. If the amount comes next a decision will have to be made as to the highest figure expected to be shown in the accounts. A column will then be reserved for each possible digit. Each group of columns used for a particular purpose are known as a 'field'.

The remaining columns can be used for other purposes such as identification of the salesman, the type of goods sold, the geographical area in which the customer's business is located, and so on. By the judicious use of the columns desirable management information can be found as a by-product of the accounting system. This represents a considerable step forward from the conventional accounting system which confines itself to book-keeping entries.

After the cards have been punched they are run through a sorter, this puts the cards into any desired groupings. They are then stored away until such time as they are needed to produce printed records.

When the time arrives for printed records to be made the cards are then put through the tabulator. This reads them and prints the information they contain on to stationery held within the tabulator. If sales invoice cards are put through a sales journal could be printed together with an output of statistical information.

If besides the sales invoice cards there are also placed opening balance cards, payments and returns, and discounts cards then a sales ledger can also be produced along with statements for the customers.

Similarly a programme is arranged for purchases and for other sections of the book-keeping work. To repeat what has been said earlier the system is basically one of punching, sorting and tabulating.

Electronic Computers

As far as accounting work is concerned computer techniques follow on logically from punched cards. Digital computers are the kind that are used for commercial purposes, while analogue computers are used mainly for scientific purposes. Computers were not used for business purposes until around the year 1952.

The main advantages of an electronic computer over a punched card installation from the book-keeping point of view are: first that more operations are possible in one machine, obviously meaning less handling of the media on which the records are kept, be they punched cards or tapes. Second, the computer can be programmed so that it makes various decisions automatically. Third, a computer is much faster than punched card machinery.

A computer may be said to have five basic components:

1. The input unit
2. A store or 'memory' unit
3. An arithmetic unit
4. An output unit
5. A control unit

At the input end information is normally fed into the computer by means of punched cards or punched paper tape. The information fed in is converted into electronic impulses, these being transmitted to the storage unit where they wait until the information is needed for further action. The storage unit can be of various types, the type chosen depending on the length of time for which the information is to be kept.

When the next step is taken, the control unit transmits a signal to the store and the information is then passed on to the arithmetic unit. This unit performs the tasks of division, subtraction, addition, or multiplication. When this is done the information duly processed emerges via the output unit. The form in which it emerges depends on the use that the firm is going to make of it. It may be in the form of magnetic tape, punched paper tape, punched cards, or as ordinary printed data.

The control unit's function is to accept instructions which are programmed into it, and to see that the instructions are carried out by the other parts of the computer.

Computers are however more than just machines which can handle book-keeping. Many management problems can be solved, some as automatic by-products of the book-keeping system. An instance of this is stock control.

Three-in-One Systems

It has already been described, under the heading of 'Loose-Leaf Ledgers and Carbon Paper', that specially designed stationery with sensitized paper for producing copies, has been developed quite extensively. The main benefit was that one operation, using this special stationery, could produce several records. Syllabuses have started to mention as a specific item 'Three-in-One Systems'. These are basically systems which have been specially designed to take advantage of such special stationery to make book-keeping, when performed manually, as efficient as possible. It is outside the scope of this book to examine any one of the 'Three-in-One Systems' book-keeping packages being sold by various firms. The details of the various forms, and the exact use of them, would take up far too much space in a book such as this, which is concerned with basic principles rather than the actual operation of the many types of accounting systems in use.

The main point which needs to be made here is that a 'Three-in-One System' is still a double-entry book-keeping system. The term 'double entry' does not necessarily relate only to an item being written twice in a set of records, it means instead that the two-fold aspect of a transaction is fully recorded. If by manipulating the use of sensitized or carbon paper the writing of the item can be undertaken once only on a top sheet with the carbon copy, etc., coming through in a space on a form tucked underneath the top sheet, the system in use is still a double-entry book-keeping system, for such a single writing has recorded both aspects of the transaction rather than simply one aspect.

Such systems also can provide control accounts—these will be examined later in Chapter 17—on a continuing basis instead of waiting until the end of each month to do them. This is very often of considerable advantage. They are also very useful for small firms in dealing with Value Added Tax.

The stationery and equipment needed normally has two clear characteristics. The stationery has holes punched along its sides. There will also be a board with pegs along one side. This board will be called the peg board, billing board or writing board. Now the whole idea is that when the stationery is placed on the board, with the pegs projecting through the holes in the stationery, each piece can be placed with the pegs through the relevant punched holes so that the copy of the writing on the top sheet will appear in the correct spaces on the lower copies.

Where particular examining boards ask for a specific knowledge of the working of the three-in-one systems, your teachers/lecturers/ correspondence courses will have to demonstrate the use of the various forms, billing boards, etc.

13

Bank Reconciliation Statements

Before examining bank reconciliation statements, it will be useful to look at the way in which the banking system operates. A firm or an individual can open an account which is either a current account or a deposit account. A current account is one which is used for the regular banking and withdrawal of money. With this type of account a cheque book will be given by the bank to the customer for him to make payments to people to whom he owes money. He will also be given a paying-in book for him to pay money into the account. A deposit account, on the other hand, is an account which will be concerned normally with putting money into the bank and not withdrawing it for some time. The usual object of having a deposit account is that interest is given on the balance held in the account, whilst interest is not given on balances in current accounts. Obviously therefore there is no point in keeping unnecessarily large balances in current accounts at banks; customers are far better off transferring excess amounts to somewhere where they could get interest on their money.

With a current account the customer of the bank has a cheque book which he can use to make payments. Normally he can only make payments to the extent that he has money in his account. If he wishes to pay out more money than he has in his account then he will have to see his bank manager and get his permission to 'overdraw' his account, this being known as an 'overdraft'. If he does not get this permission, and then pays out more than his balance in cheques, he will normally find that, unless it is a very small amount, the bank will refuse to let the cheques pass through his account. They will refuse to honour them; the cheques are therefore known as 'dishonoured' cheques. These cheques will be returned to the person(s) to whom the cheques had been paid, and the bank will make a note on the cheque to the fact that the cheque had been dishonoured. So that the reader does not jump to the conclusion that all cheques returned are because of insufficient funds on the part of the payer of the cheque, it should be pointed out that a cheque would also be returned for other reasons such as it being made out incorrectly. For instance, the payer of the cheque might have written in words 'Thirty Pounds' on the cheque, but in the space for the sum in figures he may have written 'Thirty Three Pounds'. Such a cheque will be returned for amendment, and the person to whom the cheque has been paid will then have the task of getting the payer either to make out a new cheque or else to amend properly the old cheque. Quite a lot of cheques are returned simply because the payer has forgotten to sign them, and this was not noticed by the recipient.

Now the payer of the cheque will enter the payment in the bank column of his cash book on the day that he makes out the cheque and gives or sends it to the person to whom he owes money. The recipient may in fact receive it by post two or three days later and will then bank it. By the time the cheque has passed through the banking system in the U.K., and been charged up to the account of the payer, another two or three days may have passed. There is therefore a gap of several days between the payer entering the payment in his books, and the bank entering into his account at the bank that in fact the payment has been made.

When banking money in the United Kingdom, a person can in fact bank the money for the benefit of his account by paying it into a bank some distance from his own. He does not necessarily have to go to his own bank to pay money into his account. Special paying-in slips are used for this purpose. He can thus go, say, into Barclays Bank in Liverpool and pay money into the bank there, which is in fact for the benefit of his own bank account at the National Westminster Bank in Southampton. He will enter the banking in his bank column of the cash book on the day that he actually banked the money. His bank, the National Westminster, will show the banking as being made as on the day that they receive the money through the banking system, and this will be a day or two later.

All of this means that the records of money paid into and out of the firm's bank account are entered in the firm's cash book at one point in time, but the bank will enter the same items in the account in their books at a different point of time. Therefore, the bank balance at a given date according to the firm's books will normally be different from that according to the bank's books. Some items will have been entered in the firm's books but not in the bank's books and vice versa.

The bank will give a copy of the bank account as it appears in the bank's books to the firm from time to time. If it takes the form of loose sheets it will be known as a bank statement or as bank pass sheets. Bound books, known as bank pass books, are now very rarely used for current accounts. On the receipt of the bank statement it must not be thought that no action is necessary by the firm. There may be discrepancies in either the books of the firm or of the bank. In order to ensure that the difference between the two balances is due merely to the time difference in entering items, a bank reconciliation statement is drawn up. This statement is an arithmetical proof which commences with one of the balances and adjustments are then made for the items which are properly at that time not entered in both sets of books. The figure then arrived at should be the balance according to the other set of books. If the figure is different from the balance an error or errors will have been made. The cash book and the bank statement will then be checked in detail to find the discrepancy.

Before progressing to the construction of bank reconciliation statements the reasons for the time difference in entering items can now be looked at in more detail.

1. Items in the payments side of the cash book not on the bank statement. These are usually cheques paid out by the firm which are passing through the bank clearing system, and have not yet been presented to the bank where the account is maintained. They have already been described as unpresented cheques.

2. Items on the receipts side of the cash book not on the bank statement. This consists of bankings made at other banks by the proprietor for the benefit of the firm, as already described, or cheques received which have not yet been banked. It could also be money banked on the same day as the copy of the bank statement was sent to the firm, and at the time of the day the bank's accounting system had not entered the item in the firm's account.

3. Payments on the bank statement not in the cash book. This can be a variety of payments such as bank charges taken out of the account by the bank but not yet notified to the firm. A firm can also instruct its bank to make regular payments of fixed amount at stated dates to certain persons or firms. These are standing orders. An instance of this could be the payment of rates to a local authority in the U.K., whereby a rates bill of, say, £900 might be paid by £90 per month for the next 10 months. These payments would be automatically effected by the bank without the firm having to make out cheques or doing anything else once the instructions have been given to the bank. At a particular date such a payment might have been made by the bank, but the payment might not have been shown in the firm's cash book on that date. Such standing orders can only be altered by the paying firm.

There are also payments which have to be made, and where the authority to get the money is given to the firm to whom the money is to be paid, instead of giving one's bank the instructions to pay certain amounts. Instead of one's bank remembering to make the payment, the creditor can automatically charge one's bank account with the requisite amount. These are called 'direct debits'. They are usually used for paying insurance premiums to insurance companies. If the person had to pay a premium to the Wonderful Insurance Company on a regular basis then he might give the Wonderful Insurance Company the right to take the required sum, as and when needed, from his bank account. There can also be cheques which have previously been banked by the firm, but have now been dishonoured and the firm has not been notified at this stage. All of these actions can result in payments being shown on the bank statement, without, at that time, any record being made in the bank column of the cash book.

4. Banking shown on the bank statement but not in the cash book. In the U.K. there is a system whereby one's customers can effect payment other than by sending cheques or cash. They are given the name and address of the bank at which the firm has its account, and also the reference number of the account. They can then pay their bills by instructing their own bank to transfer this amount to their creditor's account. Thus if G. Kelly, who had an account with Midland Bank at Birmingham, wanted to pay some money to H. Loftus, who had an account with Lloyds Bank in Stockport, he would instruct his bank to pay H. Loftus and give them details of the bank account of Loftus. The transfer would then be made through the banking system, and the amount would be shown in the account of Kelly at Birmingham as being paid out, whilst the account of Loftus in Stockport would show the payment into the account. Loftus would not know that the money had been paid into his account until he received a note from his bank (possibly also confirmed by one from Kelly) that payment had been received. The item would therefore be shown on the bank statement before it actually became recorded in the cash book of Loftus. These are usually called 'Trader's credits'. There are also cases where the bank receives dividends or interest on investments, and the firm has not yet been notified of their receipt.

Exhibit 13–1 shows a firm's cash book and its bank statement together with a bank reconciliation statement showing that the two balances are not incompatible.

Exhibit 13.1

Cash Book (bank columns only)

19–5	£	19–5	£
June 26 Total b/fwd	1,700	June 26 Total b/fwd	1,520
		„ 27 I. Glass	35
		„ 29 B. Turnock	40
		„ 30 Balance c/d	105
	1,700		1,700
July 1 Balance b/d	105		

Bank Statement

	Dr	*Cr*	*Balance*
	£		£
June 26 Balance b/fwd			180 CR
„ 30 I. Glass	35		145 CR

Bank Reconciliation Statement as on 30 June 19–5

	£
Balance in Hand as per Cash Book	105
Add unpresented cheque: Turnock	40
Balance in Hand as per Bank Statement	145

It would have been possible for the bank reconciliation statement to have started with the bank statement balance.

Bank Reconciliation Statement as on 30 June 19–5

	£
Balance in Hand as per Bank Statement	145
Less unpresented cheque: Turnock	40
Balance in Hand as per Cash Book	105

It will be noticed that the bank account is shown as a debit balance in the firm's cash book because to the firm it is an asset. In the bank's books the bank account is shown as a credit balance because this is a liability of the bank to the firm.

Exhibit 13–2 shows a firm with more differences between the bank statement and the cash book, together with a table showing the effect of the differences, followed by bank reconciliation statements prepared both ways.

Exhibit 13.2

Cash Book

19–5	£	19–5	£
Dec 27 Total b/fwd	2,000	Dec 27 Total b/fwd	1,600
„ 29 J. Peel	60	„ 28 J. Jacobs	105
„ 31 M. Johnson	220	„ 30 M. Coutts	15
		„ 31 Balance c/d	560
	2,280		2,280
19–6			
Jan 1 Balance b/d	560		

Bank Statement

19–5	*Dr* £	*Cr* £	*Balance* £
Dec 27 Balance b/fwd			400 CR
„ 29 Cheque		60	460 CR
„ 30 J. Jacobs	105		355 CR
„ „ Credit transfers		70	425 CR
„ 31 Bank commission	20		405 CR

Items not in both sets of books	Effect on Cash Book balance	Effect on Bank Statement	Adjustment required to one balance to reconcile it with the other: To Cash Book balance	To Bank Statement balance
1. Payment M. Coutts £15	reduced by £15	none—not yet entered	add £15	deduct £15
2. Banking M. Johnson £220	increased by £220	none—not yet entered	deduct £220	add £220
3. Bank Commission £20	none—not yet entered	reduced by £20	deduct £20	add £20
4. Credit Transfers £70	none—not yet entered	increased by £70	add £70	deduct £70

Bank Reconciliation Statement as on 31 December 19–5

	£	£
Balance in hand as per Cash Book		560
Add unpresented cheque	15	
Credit transfers	70	
		85
		645
Less Bank commission	20	
Bank lodgement not yet entered on bank statement	220	
		240
Balance in hand as per bank statement		405

Bank Reconciliation Statement as on 31 December 19–5

	£	£
Balance in hand as per bank statement		405
Add Bank commission	20	
Bank lodgement not yet entered on bank statement	220	
		240
		645
Less Unpresented Cheques	15	
Traders Credit Transfers	70	
		85
Balance in Hand as per Cash Book		560

Writing up the Cash Book Before Attempting a Reconciliation

It will soon become obvious that in fact the best procedure is to complete entering up the cash book before attempting the reconciliation, this being done by finding out the items that are on the bank statement but not in the cash book and remedying that fact. By this means the number of adjustments needed in the reconciliation statement are reduced. However, in examinations it is usual for the questions to ask for the reconciliation to take place before completing the cash book entries.

If, in Exhibit 13-2, the cash book had been written up before the bank reconciliation statement had been drawn up then they would have appeared as follows in Exhibit 13-3.

Exhibit 13.3

Cash Book

19–5	£	19–5	£
Dec 27 Total b/fwd	2,000	Dec 27 Total b/fwd	1,600
„ 29 J. Peel	60	„ 28 J. Jacobs	105
„ 31 M. Johnson	220	„ 30 M. Coutts	15
„ 31 Credit transfers (each one shown separately by name)	70	„ 31 Bank commission	20
		„ 31 Balance c/d	610
	2,350		2,350
19–6			
Jan 1 Balance b/d	610		

Bank Reconciliation Statement as on 31 December 19–5

	£
Balance in hand as per cash book	610
Add unpresented cheque	15
	625
Less Bank lodgement not yet entered on bank statement	220
Balance in hand as per bank statement	405

So that students can easily compare the entries on the bank statements with those in the cash book, the names of the persons to whom cheques have been paid have been shown in full on the bank statements. In fact, in most banks in the U.K. when cheques are paid out all that is shown on the bank statement is the cheque number which is printed on the cheque itself. In order to compare the bank statement with the cash book, therefore, the cheque counterfoils or returned cheques should be examined to establish the identity of the payees.

Bank Overdrafts

The adjustments needed to reconcile the bank overdraft according to the firm's books with that shown in the bank's books are the complete opposite of that needed when the account is not overdrawn. It should be noticed that most banks in the U.K. show that an account has been overdrawn by putting the letters O/D after the amount of the balance; this is obviously the abbreviation for overdraft.

Exhibit 13–4 shows a cash book fully written up to date, and the bank reconciliation statement needed to reconcile the cash book and bank statement balances.

Exhibit 13.4

Cash Book

19–4	£	19–4	£
Dec 5 I. Hunt	308	Dec 1 Balance b/f	709
„ 24 L. Mason	120	„ 9 P. Dennis	140
„ 29 K. Kilner	124	„ 27 J. Kearney	63
„ 31 G. Corrie	106	„ 29 United Trust	77
„ „ Balance c/f	380	„ 31 Bank Charges	49
	1,038		1,038

Bank Statement

	Dr	*Cr*	*Balance*
19–4	£	£	£
Dec 1 Balance b/f			709 O/D
„ 5 Cheque		308	401 O/D
„ 14 P. Dennis	140		541 O/D
„ 24 Cheque		120	421 O/D
„ 29 K. Kilner: Trader's credit		124	297 O/D
„ 29 United Trust: Standing order	77		374 O/D
„ 31 Bank Charges	49		423 O/D

Bank Reconciliation Statement as on 31 December 19–4

	£
Overdraft as per cash book	380
Add Bank Lodgements not on bank statement	106
	486
Less Unpresented cheque	63
Overdraft per bank statement	423

Exercises

13.1 Overleaf is an extract from the bank columns of the cash book of H. Beverley.

You are required to:

(*a*) Write the cash book up to date, and state the new balance as on 30 June 19–4, and then

(*b*) Draw up a bank reconciliation statement as on 30 June 19–4.

Dr		*Cr*	
19–4	£	19–4	£
June 1 Balance b/f	495	June 5 M. McIver	47
,, 8 P. King	76	,, 26 C. Clarence	106
,, 15 R. Sellars	54	,, 28 D. Simpson	42
,, 26 Cash	88	,, 30 Balance c/d	634
,, 30 F. Howard	116		
	829		829

He received the following bank statement from his manager:

	£	£	*Balance*
19–4	*Dr*	*Cr*	£
June 1 Balance b/f			495
,, 8 Cheque		76	571
,, 9 M. McIver	47		524
,, 15 Cheque		54	578
,, 26 Cash		88	666
,, 29 Credit transfer—C. Morgan		52	718
,, 30 Bank Charges	40		678

13.2. The bank columns in the cash book of G. Golden for the month of December 19–6 appeared as:

Dr		*Cr*	
19–6	£	19–6	£
Dec 1 Balance b/f	104	Dec 2 C. Masters	159
,, 6 T. Setters	208	,, 11 I. Hoe	115
,, 19 Cash	160	,, 24 D. Light	87
,, 31 P. Sidmouth	83	,, 29 T. Mossop	15
,, 31 T. Avon	109	,, 31 Balance c/d	288
	664		664

The following bank statement was obtained by him:

	Dr	*Cr*	*Balance*
19–6	£	£	£
Dec 1 Balance b/f			104
,, 5 C. Masters	159		55 O/D
,, 6 Cheque		208	153
,, 15 I. Hoe	115		38
,, 19 Cash		160	198
,, 29 Prudential: standing order	50		148
,, 30 C. Slater: trader's credit		89	237
,, 31 Bank Charges	48		189

You should:

(i) Write the cash book up to date to take the above into account, and then

(ii) Prepare a bank reconciliation statement as on 31 December 19–6.

13.3. The following were from the bank columns of the cash book of C. Smithson:

Dr		*Cr*	
19–5	£	19–5	£
Dec 4 C. Clarkson	108	Dec 1 Balance b/f	606
„ 21 Holt & Flynn	196	„ 8 J. Hatch	64
„ 31 A. Wood	119	„ 17 N. Ross	154
„ 31 Balance c/f	478	„ 29 M. Harry	77
	901		901

The details of the bank statement are as follows:

	Dr	*Cr*	*Balance*
19–5	£	£	£
Dec 1 Balance			606 O/D
„ 4 Cheque		108	498 O/D
„ 11 J. Hatch	64		562 O/D
„ 21 Cheque		196	366 O/D
„ 23 N. Ross	154		520 O/D
„ 28 M. Brindley: trader's credit		205	315 O/D
„ 30 UDT: standing order	57		372 O/D
„ 31 Bank Charges	30		402 O/D

You should:

(*a*) Write the cash book up to date to take the above items into account, and then

(*b*) Draw up a bank reconciliation statement as on 31 December 19–5.

13.4. On 31 March 19–5, the cash book of R. Brown, a trader, showed a balance at bank amounting to £471.

You are informed that:

1. A cheque for £28 received by Brown and entered in his cash book on 31 March 19–5, was not credited by the bank until 2 April.

2. No entry has been made in Brown's cash book for a remittance, by credit transfer, of £114, in settlement of a debt due by a customer. This amount was credited by the bank to Brown's account on 25 March 19–5.

3. Cheques drawn by Brown on 26 March 19–5, amounting to £268, were not paid by the bank until after 31 March.

4. In December 19–4, the bank debited Brown's account with £14 for interest and charges. No entry has been made in Brown's cash book.

5. In January 19–5, the bank paid, in accordance with a standing order from Brown, a trade subscription of £12. No entry has been made in Brown's cash book.

You are required to prepare statements showing:

(i) the balance which should appear in Brown's cash book on 3 March 19–5, after making all necessary corrections; and

(ii) a reconciliation of the balance shown by the bank statement on 31 March 19–5, with the corrected cash book balance.
(Institute of Bankers)

13.5. From the following details draw up a bank reconciliation statement:

	£
Cash at bank as per bank column of the Cash Book	678
Unpresented cheques	256
Cheques received and paid into the bank, but not yet entered on the bank statement	115
Credit transfers entered as banked on the bank statement but not entered in the Cash Book	56
Cash at bank as per bank statement	875

13.6. The cash book of H.S., a trader, showed the bank account with a debit balance of £273 on 31 May 19–5. This balance differed from that shown in the bank statement for the same date.

On investigation you find that the following discrepancies account for the difference:

1. Cheques from customers amounting to £550 were paid into bank on 31 May 19–5 but were not credited by the bank until the following day.
2. Cheques £247 drawn in favour of creditors on 30 May 19–5 were paid by the bank on 7 June 19–5.
3. A cheque paid for rates £67 on 10 May 19–5 had been entered in the cash book as £76.
4. A standing order for a trade subscription £12 was paid by the bank on 1 May 19–5 but no entry had been made in the cash book.
5. On 14 May 19–5 a cheque for £76 was received from a customer and paid into bank. The cheque was in payment of a debt of £80, £4 discount having been deducted. £80 had been entered in the bank column of the cash book.

Prepare:

(i) a statement showing the balance which should appear in the cash book on 31 May 19–5 after making all necessary corrections; and
(ii) a statement reconciling the corrected cash book balance with the balance as shown by the bank statement.
(Associated Examining Board 'A' Level)

13.7. The cash book of J.N., a trader, showed a balance of £970 at the bank on 30 September 19–4.

On investigation you find that:

1. Cheques from customers amounting to £386 which were entered in the cash book on 30 September 19–4, were not credited by the bank until the following day.
2. Cheques drawn by J.N. on 29 September 19–4, £618, in favour of trade creditors, entered in the cash book on that day, were paid by the bank in October.
3. On 17 August 19–4, a cheque for £196 was received from a customer and discount of £4 was allowed. £200 had been entered in the bank column of the cash book and credited to the customer. No entry for the discount was made in the books.
4. In accordance with a standing order from J.N., the bank had paid £18 for a trade subscription on 30 September 19–4, but no entry had been made in J.N.'s books. The subscription is in respect of the year to 30 September 19–5.
5. On 21 September 19–4, a credit transfer of £64, in settlement of the balance

in a customer's account, was received by the bank for the credit of J.N., but no entry had been made in J.N.'s books.

6. On 21 September 19–4, a cheque for £120 was received from a customer in settlement of his account and correctly entered in the books. This cheque was dishonoured and, on 26 September, the bank debited J.N.'s account, but no entry was made in J.N.'s books. It is considered that nothing will be recovered from this customer.

You are required to prepare:

(i) a statement showing the balance which should appear in the cash book on 30 September 19–4, after making all necessary corrections,

(ii) a statement showing your calculation of the balance shown by the bank statement on 30 September,

(iii) a statement reconciling the corrected cash book balance with the balance shown by the bank statement.

(Chartered Institute of Secretaries and Administrators)

13.8A. The following were from the bank columns of the cash book of V. White:

Dr			*Cr*		
19–0		£	19–0		£
Mar	1 Balance b/f	150	Mar	8 A. Roe	30
,,	6 Cash	75	,,	16 T. Salmon	15
,,	13 W. Wing	17	,,	28 A. Bird	29
,,	31 R. Nest	39	,,	31 Balance c/d	
		—			—
		═			═

On 31 March 19–0 he received the following bank statement from his bank:

		Dr	*Cr*	*Balance*
19–0		£	£	£
Mar	1 Balance (Cr.)			150
,,	6 Cash		75	225
,,	10 A. Roe	30		195
,,	13 W. Wing		17	212
,,	15 Credit transfer—B. Egg		16	228
,,	18 T. Salmon	15		213
,,	31 Charges	10		203

You are required to:

(*a*) Bring the cash book up to date, and state the new balance at 31 March 19–0.

(*b*) Prepare a statement, under its proper title, to reconcile the difference between the new up-to-date balance in the cash book and the balance in the bank statement on 31 March 19–0.

(University of Cambridge—Local Examinations—'O' Level)

13.9A. The bank columns of G. Shaw's cash book for the month of June 19–2 appeared as overleaf.

You are required to:

(i) Write the cash book up to date to take the necessary items into account, and then

(ii) Draw up a bank reconciliation statement as on 31 December 19–2.

Dr			Cr		
19–2		£	19–2		£
June	2 H. Wells	275	June	1 Balance b/f	807
,,	9 M. Kipps	140	,,	12 M. Polly	150
,,	20 L. Merton	45	,,	18 R. Jolly	49
,,	T. Cassius	72	,,	27 P. Strachan	63
,,	30 Balance c/d	537			
		1,069			1,069

The following is a copy of the bank statement for June:

		Dr	*Cr*	*Balance*
19–2		£	£	£
June	1 Balance b/f			807 O/D
,,	2 H. Wells		275	532 O/D
,,	15 M. Polly	150		682 O/D
,,	20 L. Merton		45	637 O/D
,,	24 R. Jolly	49		686 O/D
,,	28 Stockport Corporation: Standing Order	33		719 O/D
,,	30 H. Levinson: trader's credit		60	659 O/D
,,	30 Bank Charges	55		714 O/D

13.10A. J. Smith's cash book showed a balance at bank amounting to £849 on 30 June 19–7.

You are informed that:

1. A cheque for £71 drawn by Smith on 29 June 19–7 in favour of Peters had been entered in Smith's cash book but was not paid by his bank until early July 19–7.
2. Cheques received by Smith on 30 June 19–7 amounting to £244 were entered in his cash book on that date but were not credited by the bank until 1 July 19–7.
3. A credit transfer for £162 in settlement of a debt due by a customer was credited by the bank to Smith's account on 26 June 19–7 but had not been entered in his cash book.
4. On 25 June 19–7 the bank debited Smith's account with £22 for interest and charges. No entry had been made in Smith's cash book for this item.

Required:

A statement showing:

(*a*) the balance which would appear in Smith's cash book on 30 June 19–7 after making all the necessary corrections; and

(*b*) a reconciliation of the balance shown by the bank statement on 30 June 19–7 with the corrected cash book balance.

(Institute of Bankers)

13.11A. The following is a summary of a cash book as presented to you for the month of December 19–7:

	£		£
Receipts	1,469	Balance brought forward	761
Balance carried forward	554	Payments	1,262
	2,023		2,023

All receipts are banked and payments made by cheque.

On investigation you discover:

1. Bank charges of £136 entered on the bank statement had not been entered in the cash book.
2. Cheques drawn amounting to £267 had not been presented to the bank for payment.
3. Cheques received totalling £762 had been entered in the cash book and paid into the bank, but had not been credited by the bank until January 19–8.
4. A cheque for £22 had been entered as a receipt in the cash book instead of as a payment.
5. A cheque for £25 had been debited by the bank in error.
6. A cheque received for £80 had been returned by the bank and marked 'No funds available'. No adjustment had been made in the cash book.
7. All dividends receivable are credited directly to the bank account. During December amounts totalling £62 were credited by the bank and no entries made in the cash book.
8. A cheque drawn for £6 had been incorrectly entered in the cash book as £66.
9. The balance brought forward should have been £711.
10. The bank statement as on 31 December 19–7, showed an overdraft of £1,162.

You are required to:

(*a*) show the adjustments required in the cash book, and
(*b*) prepare a bank reconciliation statement as on 31 December 19–7.
(Institute of Chartered Accountants)

13.12A. The following is a summary from the cash book of the Hozy Company Limited for October 19–9:

Cash Book

	£		£
Opening balance b/d	1,407	Payments	15,520
Receipts	15,073	Closing balance c/f	960
	16,480		16,480

On investigation you discover that:

1. Bank charges of £35 shown on the bank statement have not been entered in the cash book.
2. A cheque drawn for £47 has been entered in error as a receipt.
3. A cheque for £18 has been returned by the bank marked 'refer to drawer', but it has not been written back in the cash book.
4. An error of transposition has occurred in that the opening balance in the cash book should have been carried down as £1,470.
5. Three cheques paid to suppliers for £214, £370 and £30 have not yet been presented to the bank.

6. The last page of the paying in book shows a deposit of £1,542 which has not yet been credited to the account by the bank.
7. The bank has debited a cheque for £72 in error to the company's account.
8. The bank statement shows an overdrawn balance of £124.

You are required to:

(*a*) show what adjustments you would make in the cash book, and
(*b*) prepare a bank reconciliation statement as at 30 October 19–9.

(Association of Certified Accountants)

14

The Journal

Previously it has been shown that the work of recording transactions is divided up into its different functions, there being a separate book (or some other sort of collection point for data) for each major function. The books in which entries are made prior to their posting to the ledgers are known as subsidiary books or as books of prime entry. Thus the sales, purchases, returns inwards and returns outwards books are all books of prime entry. The cash book is also regarded as a book of prime entry, although many would regard it as a ledger, as has been seen it originated from the cash and bank accounts being detached from the ledger. However, it is the book in which cash and bank entries are first made and from this point of view it may be taken as a book of prime entry.

It is to the firm's advantage if all transactions which do not pass through a book of prime entry are entered in a book called The Journal. The journal is a form of diary for such transactions. It shows:

1. The date.
2. The name of the account(s) to be debited and the amount(s).
3. The name of the account(s) to be credited and the amount(s).
4. A description of the transaction (this is called a 'narrative').

One would also expect to find a reference number for the documents supporting the transaction.

The advantages to be gained from using a journal may be summarized:

1. It eliminates the need for a reliance on the memory of the book-keeper. Some transactions are of a complicated nature, and without the journal the entries may be difficult, if not impossible, to understand. One must also bear in mind that if the book-keeper left the firm the absence of a journal could leave many unexplained items in the books.

2. Errors, irregularities and fraud are more easily effected when entries are made direct into the ledgers without any explanations being given. The journal acts as an explanation of the entries and details the necessary supporting evidence.

3. The risk of omitting the transaction altogether, or of making one entry only is reduced.

Despite these advantages there are many firms which do not have such a book.

Typical Uses of the Journal

Some of the main uses of the journal are listed below. It must not be thought that this list is exhaustive.

1. The purchase and sale of fixed assets on credit.
2. The correction of errors.
3. Opening entries. These are the entries needed to open a new set of books.
4. Other transfers.

The layout of the journal can now be shown:

The Journal

Date		*Folio*	*Dr*	*Cr*
	The name of the account to be debited. The name of the account to be credited. The Narrative.			

To standardize matters the name of the account to be debited should always be shown first. It also helps with the reading of the journal if the name of the account to be credited is written not directly under the name of the account to be debited, but is inset to the right-hand side.

It must be remembered that the journal is not an integral part of the double entry book-keeping system. It is purely a form of diary, and entering an item in the journal is not the same as recording an item in an account. Once the journal entry is made the necessary entry in the double entry accounts can then be effected.

Examples of the uses of the journal are now given.

1. Purchase and Sale on Credit of Fixed Assets

(*a*) A machine is bought on credit from Toolmakers Ltd for £550 on 1 July.

	Dr	Cr
	£	£
July 1 Machinery	550	
Toolmakers Ltd		550
Purchase of milling machine on credit, Capital Purchases invoice No. 7/159		

(*b*) Sale of a Motor Vehicle for £300 on credit to A. Barnes and Sons on 2 July.

	Dr	Cr
	£	£
July 2 A. Barnes and Sons	300	
Motor vehicles		300
Sales of Motor vehicles per Capital Sales Invoice No. 7/43		

2. *Correction of Errors*

These are dealt with in detail in Chapter 16.

3. *Opening Entries*

J. Brew, after being in business for some years without keeping proper records, now decides to keep a double entry set of books. On 1 July he establishes that his assets and liabilities are as follows:

Assets: Motor Van £840, Fixtures £700, Stock £390, Debtors—B. Neath £95, D. Blake £45, Bank £80, Cash £20.
Liabilities: Creditors—M. Line £129, C. Shaw £41.

The Assets therefore total £840+£700+£390+£95+£45+£80+£20 = £2,170; and, the Liabilities total £129+£41 = £170.

The Capital consists of: Assets—Liabilities, £2,170−£170 = £2,000

To start the books off on 1 July showing the existing state of the assets and liabilities and capital, these amounts therefore need entering in the relevant asset, liability and capital accounts. The asset accounts will be opened with debit balances and the liability and capital accounts will be opened with credit balances. The journal therefore shows the accounts which are to be debited and those which are to be credited and this is shown in Exhibit 14–1.

Now that the journal has been written up, the accounts can be opened.

Exhibit 14.1

The Journal Page 5

		Fol	Dr	Cr
			£	£
July 1	Motor Van	GL 8	840	
	Fixtures	GL 13	700	
	Stock	GL 19	390	
	Debtors—B. Neath	SL 45	95	
	D. Blake	SL 49	45	
	Bank	CB 12	80	
	Cash	CB 12	20	
	Creditors—M. Line	PL 81		129
	C. Shaw	PL 86		41
	Capital	GL 50		2,000
	Assets and liabilities at this date entered to open the books.			
			2,170	2,170

General Ledger

Motor Van Page 8

			£				
July 1	Balance	J 5	840				

Fixtures Page 13

			£				
July 1	Balance	J 5	700				

Stock Page 19

			£				
July 1	Balance	J 5	390				

Capital Page 50

							£
				July 1	Balance	J 5	2,000

Sales Ledger

B. Neath Page 45

			£				
July 1	Balance	J 5	95				

D. Blake Page 49

			£				
July 1	Balance	J 5	45				

Purchases Ledger

M. Line Page 81

			£
July 1	Balance	J 5	129

C. Shaw Page 86

			£
July 1	Balance	J 5	41

Cash Book Page 12

			Cash	Bank
			£	£
July 1	Balances	J 5	20	80

Once these opening balances have been recorded in the books the day-to-day transactions can be entered in the normal manner. The need for opening entries will not occur very often. They will not be needed each year as the balances from last year will have been brought forward. At the elementary level of examinations in book-keeping, questions are often asked which entail opening a set of books and recording the day-by-day entries for the ensuing period.

4. Other Transfers

These can be of many kinds and it is impossible to construct a complete list. However, two examples can be shown.
(*a*) S. Blake, a debtor, owed £200 on 1 July. He was unable to pay his account in cash, but offers a motor car in full settlement of the debt. The offer is accepted on 5 July.

The personal account is therefore discharged and needs crediting. On the other hand the firm now has an extra asset, a motor car, therefore the motor car account needs to be debited.

The Journal

		Dr	*Cr*
		£	£
July 5	Motor Car	200	
	S. Blake		200
	Accepted motor car in full settlement of debt per letter dated 5/7/–5		

(*b*) G. Grant is a creditor. On 10 July his business is taken over by A. Lee to whom the debt now is to be paid.

Here it is just the identity of one creditor being exchanged for another one. The action needed is to cancel the amount owing to G.

Grant by debiting his account, and to show it owing to Lee by opening an account for Lee and crediting it.

The Journal

		Dr	Cr
		£	£
July 10	G. Grant	150	
	A. Lee		150
	Transfer of indebtedness as per letter from Grant ref. G/1335		

Exercises

14.1. You are to open the books of K. Moggs, a trader, via the journal to record the assets and liabilities, and are then to record the daily transactions for the month of May. A trial balance is to be extracted as on 31 May.

May 1 *Assets*—Premises £2,000; Motor Van £450; Fixtures £600; Stock £1,289. Debtors—N. Hardy £40; M. Nelson £180. Cash at bank £1,254; Cash in hand £45.
Liabilities—Creditors: B. Blake £60; V. Raleigh £200.

May 1 Paid rent by cheque £15
,, 2 Goods bought on credit from: B. Blake £20; C. Hough £56; H. Gee £38; N. Lear £69
,, 3 Goods sold on credit to: K. Ollier £56; M. Bardsley £78; L. Skermer £98; N. Duffy £48; B. Green £118; M. Nelson £40
,, 4 Paid for motor expenses in cash £13
,, 5 Goods returned to: N. Lear £9; H. Gee £14
,, 7 Cash drawings by proprietor £20
,, 9 Goods sold on credit to: M. Bardsley £22; L. Pearson £67
,, 11 Goods returned to Moggs by: K. Ollier £16; L. Skermer £18
,, 14 Bought another motor van on credit from Better Motors Ltd £300
,, 16 The following paid Moggs their accounts by cheque less 5 per cent cash discount: N. Hardy; M. Nelson; K. Ollier; L. Skermer
,, 19 Goods returned by Moggs to N. Lear £20
,, 22 Goods bought on credit from: J. Johnson £89; T. Bamber £72
,, 24 The following accounts were settled by Moggs by cheque less 5 per cent cash discount: B. Blake; V. Raleigh; N. Lear
,, 27 Salaries paid by cheque £56
,, 30 Paid Rates by cheque £66
,, 31 Paid Better Motors Ltd a cheque for £300.

14.2. On 1 March 19–4 the financial position of L. Barker, a trader, was as follows:

	£
Freehold land and buildings	6,000
Cash at bank	1,500
Cash in hand	16
Trade debtors—A. Black	40
D. James	30
Plant and machinery	5,900

	£
Stock	2,200
Trade creditor—F. Robbins	60

Enter the above in the journal and post to the necessary accounts.

Post the following transactions for the month of March to the appropriate accounts, using where necessary the proper subsidiary books; extract a trial balance on 31 March 19–4.

Note:

Cheques received were banked on the day of receipt.

19–4

Mar 1 Sold goods to F. Morris, catalogue price £300, subject to 10 per cent trade discount

„ 3 A. Black was adjudicated bankrupt and a first and final dividend of 25 per cent was remitted to L. Barker by cheque

„ 5 Purchased goods from F. Robbins £60 (net)

„ 7 Paid F. Robbins by cheque the amount owing 1 March. Withdrew from bank £370 for office cash

„ 9 F. Morris returned goods sent on 1 March, catalogue price £50. Paid wages by cash £312

„ 11 D. James sent a cheque for £20 being a payment on account and was allowed £1 cash discount

„ 12 Cash sales £1,400

„ 19 Purchased from Goodall Ltd plant and machinery £3,000, Goodall Ltd taking in part exchange plant and machinery book value £900. The exchange value was the same as the book value

„ 21 Paid insurance premiums by cheque £30

„ 23 Paid for stationery by cash £26
Banked £1,350

„ 27 Purchased a vehicle for £1,700 paying by cheque

„ 31 L. Barker deposited £2,000 in the business bank account, this being the proceeds from the sale of two private cars. Purchased goods £400 paying by cheque.

(Northern Counties Technical Examinations Council)

14.3. On 1 March 19–5, the financial position of J. Taylor, a garage proprietor, was as follows:

	£
Freehold land and buildings	15,000
Cash at bank	10,500
Cash in hand	120
Trade debtor—A. Farmer	160
Trade creditor—Exe Garages Ltd	40
Fixtures and fittings	550
Stocks on hand—Vehicles	16,800
Petrol	115

Enter the above in the journal and post to the necessary accounts.

Post the following transactions for the month of March to the appropriate accounts, using where necessary the proper subsidiary books; extract a trial balance on 31 March 19–5.

Note.

Cheques received were banked on day of receipt.

19–5
Mar 4 Paid wages by cash £82
Withdrew from bank for office cash £150
Purchased National Insurance stamps £7 paying by cash
„ 6 A. Farmer paid one-half the amount owing on 1 March by cheque, deducting 2½ per cent cash discount from his remittance which J. Taylor disallowed
„ 10 Purchased stocks of petrol £250 from Wye Petroleum Co. Ltd, subject to 10 per cent trade discount
„ 12 Cash sales of petrol to date £136
„ 13 Banked £120
„ 15 Purchased four cars from 'Distributors' Ltd at £650 each subject to 20 per cent trade discount
„ 18 Paid wages in cash £94
„ 19 Cash sales of petrol to date £130
„ 20 Purchased a breakdown lorry and crane from Brights Garages Ltd for £1,600, one-half the amount being paid by cheque and liability admitted for the balance
„ 22 Sold a car to D. Davies for £720
„ 24 Dispatched invoices for repair work as follows:
C. Perrins £13; D. Adamson £42; J. Bell £80
„ 25 Cash sales of petrol to date £95
Cash received from emergency repair work £12
Paid wages in cash £74
„ 31 J. Bell paid his account in cash and was allowed 2½ per cent cash discount
Received petrol and oil £300 from Wye Petroleum Co Ltd subject to 10 per cent trade discount.

(Northern Counties Technical Examinations Council)

14.4A. I trade in typewriters and adding machines, and my assets and liabilities on 30 September 19–9 were:

		£
Cash held in the office		169
Bank overdraft		980
Stock of typewriters, worth		3,650
Stock of adding machines, worth		775
Equipment required by the business		688
Creditors:	L. Wright	79
	J. Gurney	143
	R. Pickard	320
Debtors:	J. Calne	435
	B. Swift	17
	K. Rogers	148
	R. Makston	76

(*a*) Enter these balances in the relevant books of account.
(*b*) Record the transactions for the month of October, (see below), in suitable books.
(*c*) Draw up a trial balance for 31 October 19–9, (all cheques are paid into the bank on the day of receipt).

Transactions for October:
Oct 1 Sold Elysium adding machine to J. Sanger for £145—paid for by cheque
„ 5 Paid off L. Wright's account by cheque for £79

„ „ Paid off £50 from J. Gurney's account as part payment—cheque sent
„ 9 K. Rogers sent a cheque for £148 to pay off his account
„ 9 Paid Elysium Machine Co £100 by cheque for 2 new machines
„ 10 Paid £10 in Cash for machine repair
„ 11 Paid monthly rental of premises, by cheque, £29
„ 14 Sold Eclipse typewriter to M. King for £85. Deposit of £40 received by cheque, with balance to be paid within 30 days
„ 16 Paid £5 cash for stationery
„ 20 Bought National Insurance stamps for cash, £8
„ 23 B. Swift sent his cheque for £17
„ 26 Paid cleaner's wages—cheque for £15
„ 28 J. Calne sent his cheque for £335
„ 30 Paid electricity bill £8 by cash.

(Southern Universities Joint Board—'O' Level)

14.5A. The following balances appear in the books of E. Eldon, grocer, on 1 May 19–9:

Shop furniture and equipment £880; Stock £1,269; P. Parker (a debtor) £40; Cash at bank £320; Cash in hand £15; H. Harman (a creditor) £16

Open the accounts in Eldon's books to show these balances—and his capital; then enter the following in the appropriate books, post to the ledger, extract a trial balance.

Note:

(i) Opening Journal entries are not required.
(ii) Cheques received are paid into the Bank immediately.
(iii) It is not necessary to rule off and balance the accounts other than those in the Cash Book.

19–9
May 1 Bought on credit from H. Harman: Canned goods invoiced at £90 less 33⅓ per cent trade discount; Packeted goods, invoiced at £80 less 25 per cent trade discount
„ „ Withdrew from bank for cash £30
„ 2 Received cheques:
(*a*) for sale of some of the Shop Equipment (valued in the books at £75), £60
(*b*) from P. Parker in settlement of his account less 5 per cent cash discount
„ „ Returned to H. Harman one-third of the canned goods received on 1 May, as damaged in transit
„ 5 Received from H. Harman, in place of goods returned on 2 May—canned goods invoiced at £32 less 25 per cent trade discount
„ „ E. Eldon's drawings: cash £20
„ 6 P. Parker's cheque banked on 2 May returned marked 'Refer to drawer'
„ „ Sold goods for cash £180
„ 7 Paid into bank from cash £200
„ „ Paid H. Harman by cheque the amount owing to him, less 5 per cent cash discount.

(Welsh Joint Education Committee—'O' Level)

14.6A.

Balance Sheet of C. Canon, Merchant
31 March 19–0

Liabilities	£	*Assets*	£
Capital	6,000	Equipment, etc.	2,400
Creditor: Y. Yard	480	Stock	3,800
Bank overdraft	320	Debtor: C. Crown	560
		Cash	40
	6,800		6,800

Open the accounts necessary to record the above particulars in the ledger and cash book of C. Canon; then record the transactions given below through the proper subsidiary books, post to the ledger, balance the cash book, and extract a trial balance as at 7 April 19–0.

Notes:
(i) Cheques received are paid into the bank immediately;
(ii) Opening journal entries are not required;
(iii) It is not necessary to rule off and balance the accounts other than those in the cash book.

19–0
Apr 1 Paid by cheques: Y. Yard in settlement of half the amount owing to him, less £12 cash discount
C. Canon's drawings £50
" 2 Cash sales £240; paid into bank £260
Received cheque from C. Crown in settlement of his account less 5 per cent cash discount
" 3 Paid by cash—wages £15
Bought on credit from Church Garage, motor van £660
" 4 Bought from Y. Yard goods invoiced at £120 less 25 per cent trade discount and other goods at £180 less $33\frac{1}{3}$ per cent trade discount
" 6 Returned to Yard one-third of the goods invoiced on 4 April at £180 less $33\frac{1}{3}$ per cent trade discount, as damaged in transit.
C. Canon withdrew for personal use, stock £30
" 7 C. Canon received bank statement showing he had been debited with £20 for bank charges and interest and with his annual subscription £10 to his trade association. He made the necessary entries in his books.
Wrote to C. Crown pointing out he was only entitled to $2\frac{1}{2}$ per cent cash discount and that he was accordingly being debited with half the amount he deducted on 2 April.

14.7A. After the preparation of a trial balance, an unexplained difference of DR £218 remains, and a Suspense Account is opened for that amount. Subsequent investigations reveal
(i) £35 received from A. Jones and credited to his account has not been entered in the Bank Account.
(ii) The owner of the business has taken goods which cost £69 for his own use. No entries have been made for this at all.
(iii) A payment of £47 to M. Smith has been credited to that account.

(iv) Discounts Allowed (£198) and Discounts Received (£213) have been posted to the discount accounts as credits and debits respectively.
(v) Bank Interest received of £111 has not been entered in the bank account.
(vi) £211 owing by A. Able has been debited incorrectly to B. Able.
(vii) The carriage outwards (£98) has been treated as a revenue.

Required:

(*a*) Prepare the Suspense Account making the entries necessary to eliminate the debit balance there is. Indicate clearly how you would deal with *all* of the errors discovered.
(*b*) To what extent is the balancing of a Trial Balance evidence of absence of error?

(Association of Certified Accountants)

APPENDIX 14.1

A Fully Worked Exercise

When learning to keep a set of books, and to draw up a Trading and Profit and Loss Account and Balance Sheet after the period is over, students learn the whole thing in parts. They learn to enter up a Cash Book, how to enter up the Sales Book and the Purchases Book, how to enter up the Sales Ledger, and so on. They are often very puzzled about various parts of the whole exercise when the complete task has to be undertaken, rather than simply one part of it. Some authors undertake this task by showing the complete records for a period. However, another problem then crops up for many students, and that is that they still do not understand how one period's accounts link up with those for the next period. In this Appendix, therefore, the full sets of records for two consecutive periods are examined, so that the full recording of a period, and its link with the next period, can both be seen properly.

Naturally enough, in a real business the number of transactions for a month may be exceedingly large. In this simulation of a business in this book, for reasons of space, the items will be kept to as low a number as possible. Details of the business are as follows:

G. Cheadle started in business on 1 January 19–5 by putting £20,000 into a bank account for the business.

19–5
Jan 2 He paid £160 cheque for rent for the two months January and February
" 2 Bought warehouse fixtures paying by cheque immediately for £2,400
" 3 Withdrew £300 cash from the bank for business use
" 4 Paid wages in cash for three weeks of January £240
" 5 Bought £1,400 goods paying for them immediately by cheque
" 6 Bought goods on credit from: T. Price £1,600; F. Ratcliffe Ltd £1,400; C. Norton & Co £1,100
" 8 Motor van bought by cheque £4,800
" 11 Paid for motor expenses by cash £30
" 12 Sold goods on credit to: K. Kitchen Ltd £640; E. Griffiths £1,400
" 13 Cash Sales £280
" 15 Paid for lighting and heating by cheque for the first two weeks of January £160
" 16 Paid Insurance by cheque £240 for the 12 months to 31 December 19–5
" 19 Bought goods on credit from: P. Goddard & Son £3,200
" 21 Sold goods on credit to: K. Kitchen Ltd £6,800; N. Fryer £240
" 24 Cheadle withdrew £400 by cheque for his personal use
" 26 Received cheques from: E. Griffiths £1,365 (after deducting £35 cash discount); K. Kitchen Ltd on account £1,000
" 27 Returned goods to: C. Norton & Co £240; F. Ratcliffe Ltd £200
" 29 Paid by cheque, after deducting 5 per cent cash discount, the accounts of T. Price and P. Goddard & Son
" 30 Goods returned to us by: K. Kitchen Ltd £80; N. Fryer £40
" 31 Cheadle withdrew £40 cash for his personal use.

Cash Book

Page 1

19–5			Discount £	Cash £	Bank £	19–5			Discount £	Cash £	Bank £
Jan 1	Capital	GL 1			20,000	Jan 2	Rent	GL 9			160
„ 3	Bank	C		300		„ 2	Warehouse fixtures	GL 7			2,400
„ 13	Sales	GL 5		280		3	Cash				300
„ 26	E. Griffiths	SL 2	35		1,365	„ 4	Wages	GL 10		240	
„ 26	K. Kitchen Ltd	SL 1			1,000	„ 5	Purchases	GL 3			1,400
						„ 8	Motor van	GL 8			4,800
						„ 11	Motor expenses	GL 11		30	
						„ 15	Light and heat	GL 12			160
						„ 16	Insurance	GL 13			240
						„ 24	Drawings	GL 2			500
						„ 29	T. Price	PL 1	30		570
						„ 29	P. Goddard & Son	PL 4	160		3,040
						„ 31	Drawings	GL 2		40	
						„ 31	Balance c/d			270	8,795
			35	580	22,365				190	580	22,365
Feb 1	Balances b/d			270	8,795						

Sales Book

Page 1

19–5		*Folio*	£
Jan 12	K. Kitchen Ltd	SL 1	640
„ 12	E. Griffiths	SL 2	1,400
„ 21	K. Kitchen Ltd	SL 1	6,800
„ 21	N. Fryer	SL 3	240
	Transferred to Sales Account	GL 5	9,080

Returns Inwards Book

Page 1

19–5		*Folio*	£
Jan 30	K. Kitchen Ltd	SL 1	80
„ 30	N. Fryer	SL 3	40
	Transferred to Returns Inwards Account	GL 6	120

Sales Ledger

K. Kitchen Ltd

Page 1

19–5			£	19–5			£
Jan 12	Sales	SB 1	640	Jan 26	Cash	CB 1	1,000
„ 21	Sales	SB 1	6,800	„ 30	Returns Inward	RI 1	80
				„ 31	Balance	c/d	6,360
			7,440				7,440
Feb 1	Balance	b/d	6,360				

Sales Ledger

E. Griffiths — Page 2

19–5			£				£
Jan 12	Sales	SB 1	1,400	Jan 26	Cash	CB 1	1,365
				„ 26	Discount	CB 1	35
			1,400				1,400

N. Fryer — Page 3

19–5			£	19–5			£
Jan 21	Sales	SB 1	240	Jan 30	Returns Inwards	RI 1	40
				„ 31	Balance	c/d	200
			240				240
Feb 1	Balance	b/d	200				

Purchases Book

Page 1

19–5		*Folio*	£
Jan 6	T. Price	PL 1	600
„ 6	F. Ratcliffe Ltd	PL 2	2,400
„ 6	C. Norton & Co	PL 3	1,100
„ 19	P. Goddard & Son	PL 4	3,200
	Transferred to Purchases Account	GL 3	7,300

Returns Outwards Book

Page 1

19–5		*Folio*	£
Jan 30	C. Norton & Co	PL 3	240
„ 30	F. Ratcliffe Ltd	PL 2	200
	Transferred to Returns Outwards Account	GL 4	440

Purchases Ledger

Page 1

T. Price

19–5			£	19–5			£
Jan 29	Bank	CB 1	570	Jan 6	Purchases	PB 1	600
„ 29	Discount	CB 1	30				
			600				600

Purchases Ledger

F. Ratcliffe Ltd Page 2

19–5			£	19–5			£
Jan 30	Returns Outwards	RO 1	200	Jan 6	Purchases	PB 1	2,400
,, 31	Balance	c/d	2,200				
			2,400				2,400
				Feb 1	Balance	b/d	2,200

C. Norton & Co Page 3

19–5			£	19–5			£
Jan 30	Returns Outwards	RO 1	240	Jan 6	Purchases	PB 1	1,100
,, 31	Balance	c/d	860				
			1,100				1,100
				Feb 1	Balance	b/d	860

P. Goddard & Son Page 4

19–5			£	19–5			£
Jan 29	Bank	CB 1	3,040	Jan 3	Purchases	PB 1	3,200
,, 29	Discount	CB 1	160				
			3,200				3,200

General Ledger

(before making adjustments and drawing up Trading and Profit and Loss Accounts and Balance Sheet)

Capital Page 1

				19–5			£
				Jan 1	Bank	CB 1	20,000

Drawings Page 2

19–5			£				
Jan 24	Bank	CB 1	500				
,, 31	Cash	CB 1	40				

Purchases Page 3

19–5			£				
Jan 5	Bank	CB 1	1,400				
,, 31	Credit Purchases for the month	PB 1	7,300				

General Ledger
(before making adjustments and drawing up Trading and Profit and Loss Accounts and Balance Sheet)

Returns outwards Page 4

				19–5			£
				Jan 31	Returns for the month	RO 1	440

Sales Page 5

				19–5			£
				Jan 13	Cash	CB 1	280
				,, 31	Credit Sales for the month	SB 1	9,080

Returns inwards Page 6

19–5			£				
Jan 31	Returns for the month	RI 1	120				

Warehouse fixtures Page 7

19–5			£				
Jan 2	Bank	CB 1	2,400				

Motor van Page 8

19–5			£				
Jan 8	Bank	CB 1	4,800				

Rent Page 9

19–5			£				
Jan 2	Bank	CB 1	160				

Wages Page 10

19–5			£				
Jan 4	Bank	CB 1	240				

Motor expenses Page 11

19–5			£				
Jan 11	Cash	CB 1	30				

Light & Heat Page 12

19–5			£				
Jan 15	Bank	CB 1	160				

Insurance Page 13

19–5			£				
Jan 16	Bank	CB 1	240				

General Ledger
(before making adjustments and drawing up Trading and Profit and Loss Accounts and Balance Sheet)

Discounts allowed Page 14

			£				
19–5							
Jan 31	Total for the month	CB 1	35				

Discounts received Page 15

							£
				19–5			
				Jan 31	Total for the month	CB 1	190

Now that all of the accounts have been entered up, the next step is to draw up a Trial Balance as on 31 January 19–5.

G. Cheadle
Trial Balance as on 31 January 19–5

			£	£
Capital		GL 1		20,000
Drawings		GL 2	540	
Purchases		GL 3	8,700	
Returns outwards		GL 4		440
Sales		GL 5		9,360
Returns inwards		GL 6	120	
Warehouse fixtures		GL 7	2,400	
Motor Van		GL 8	4,800	
Rent		GL 9	160	
Wages		GL 10	240	
Motor expenses		GL 11	30	
Light and heat		GL 12	160	
Insurance		GL 13	240	
Discounts allowed		GL 14	35	
Discounts received		GL 15		190
Bank		CB 1	8,795	
Cash		CB 1	270	
Debtors	per Sales Ledger		6,560	
Creditors	per Purchases Ledger			3,060
			33,050	33,050

Now that the Trial Balance has been seen to 'balance', the next step is to draw up a Trading and Profit and Loss Account for the month ended 31 January 19–5, followed by a Balance Sheet as at 31 January 19–5. Adjustments are needed for the following items (*a*) to (*e*) which were ascertained by G. Cheadle at the end of the working day of 31 January 19–5. He had:

(*a*) Valued his stock of goods at cost to be £2,360.
(*b*) Estimated that depreciation provisions should be at the rate of 10 per cent per annum for warehouse fixtures, and 20 per cent per annum for the motor van. In both cases the straight line method is to be used and salvage value is to be ignored. A full month's depreciation is to be given for January.
(*c*) He owed £180 for lighting and heating.
(*d*) He owed £60 for wages, and £80 for motor expenses.
(*e*) Noticed that the fire insurance was prepaid 11 months and rent is prepaid 1 month.

Of course, in real life, in a business as small as this it is unlikely that final accounts would be drawn up each month. However, it is much more simple to see the basic principles if a relatively few items are dealt with.

G. Cheadle
Trading and Profit and Loss Account for the month ended 31 January 19–5

		£			£
Purchases	8,700		Sales	9,360	
Less returns outwards	440	8,260	Less Returns inwards	120	9,240
Less closing stock		2,360			
Cost of goods sold		5,900			
Gross profits c/d		3,340			
		9,240			9,240
Wages		300	Gross profit b/d		3,340
Rent		80	Discounts received		190
Light and heat		340			
Insurance		20			
Motor expenses		110			
Discounts allowed		35			
Depreciation:					
Warehouse fixtures		20			
Motor van		80			
Net profit		2,545			
		3,530			3,530

In drawing up the Trading and Profit and Loss Account various transfers will have been made from the accounts in the General Ledger, such as the transfer from the Sales Account. It must be remembered that the Trading and Profit and Loss Accounts are part of the double entry system.

Balance Sheet as at 31 January 19–5

Capital		£	*Fixed Assets*		£
Cash introduced		20,000	Warehouse fixtures at		
Add net profit for the month		2,545	cost	2,400	
			Less depreciation to		
		22,545	date	20	2,380
Less drawings		540	Motor van at cost	4,800	
			Less Depreciation to		
			date	80	4,720
		22,005			7,100
Current liabilities			*Current Assets*		
Trade creditors	3,060		Stock	2,360	
Expenses accrued	320	3,380	Debtors	6,560	
			Prepaid expenses	300	
			Bank	8,795	
			Cash	270	18,285
		25,385			25,385

Theoretically, the Trading and Profit and Loss Account, as it is part of double entry, would be written up in the General Ledger as an account. In practice this would very rarely happen. It is usually allied to the Balance Sheet, and as this latter document is not part of a double entry system it would not, at least in theory, be found written up in a General Ledger. It would instead be written on separate sheets and kept in a file in the proprietor's filing cabinet etc.

All of the accounts in the General Ledger will now be shown after being completely written up for the month. These should be compared with the accounts as they appeared before being written up, so that the adjustments can be seen clearly. In a real firm each account would be shown once only, as it appears after being written up. For teaching purposes only the General Ledger is shown twice, once before the Trading and Profit and Loss Account has been drawn up, and once afterwards.

General Ledger

(after being fully written up)

Capital — Page 1

19–5			£	19–5			£
Jan 31	Drawings	GL 2	540	Jan 1	Bank	CB 1	20,000
,, 31	Balance	c/d	22,005	Jan 31	Net Profit for the month		2,545
			22,545				22,545
				Feb 1	Balance	b/d	22,005

General Ledger
(after being fully written up)

Drawings Page 2

			£				£
19–5				19–5			
Jan 24	Bank	CB 1	500	Jan 31	Capital	GL 1	540
,, 31	Cash	CB 1	40				
			540				540

Purchases Page 3

			£				£
19–5				19–5			
Jan 5	Bank	CB 1	1,400	Jan 31	Trading A/c		8,700
,, 31	Credit Purchases for the month	PB 1	7,300				
			8,700				8,700

Returns outwards Page 4

			£				£
19–5				19–5			
Jan 31	Trading A/c		440	Jan 31	Returns for the month	RO 1	440

Sales Page 5

			£				£
195				19–5			
Jan 31	Trading A/c		9,360	Jan 13	Cash	CB 1	280
				Jan 31	Credit Sales for the month	SB 1	9,080
			9,360				9,360

Returns inwards Page 6

			£				£
19–5				19–5			
Jan 31	Returns for the month	RI 1	120	Jan 31	Trading A/c		120

Warehouse fixtures Page 7

			£			£
19–5				19–5		
Jan 2	Bank	CB 1	2,400	(see note at end re balance)		

Motor van Page 8

			£
19–5			
Jan 8		CB 1	4,800

General Ledger
(after being fully written up)

Rent — Page 9

		£		£
19–5			19–5	
Jan 2 Bank	CB 1	160	Jan 31 Profit & Loss A/c	80
			Jan 31 Prepaid c/d	80
		160		160
Feb 1 Prepaid b/d		80		

Wages — Page 10

		£		£
19–5			19–5	
Jan 4 Bank	CB 1	240	Jan 31 Profit & Loss A/c	300
„ 31 Accrued c/d		60		
		300		300
			Feb 1 Accrued b/d	60

Motor expenses — Page 11

		£		£
19–5			19–5	
Jan 11 Cash	CB 1	30	Jan 31 Profit & Loss A/c	110
„ 31 Accrued c/d		80		
		110		110
			Feb 1 Accrued b/d	80

Light and heat — Page 12

		£		£
19–5			19–5	
Jan 15 Bank	CB 1	160	Jan 31 Profit & Loss A/c	340
„ 31 Accrued c/d		180		
		340		340
			Feb 1 Accrued b/d	180

Insurance — Page 13

		£		£
19–5			19–5	
Jan 16 Bank	CB 1	240	Jan 31 Profit & Loss A/c	20
			31 Prepaid c/d	220
		240		240
			Feb 1 Prepaid b/d	220

General Ledger
(after being fully written up)

Discounts allowed — Page 14

19–5			£	19–5			£
Jan 31	Total for the month	CB 1	35	Jan 31	Profit & Loss A/c		35
			=				=

Discounts received — Page 15

19–5			£	19–5			£
Jan 31	Profit & Loss A/c		190	Jan 31	Total for the month	CB 1	190
			=				=

Provision for depreciation: Motor van — Page 16

				19–5			£
				Jan 31	Profit & Loss A/c		80

Provision for depreciation: Warehouse fixtures — Page 17

				19–5			£
				Jan 31	Profit & Loss A/c		20

Stock — Page 18

19–5			£				
Jan 31	Trading A/c		2,360				

N.B. As the accounts on pages 7, 8, 16, 17 and 18 of the General Ledger contain one entry only, there is no point in carrying each item down as a balance. Each item is its own balance.

The following transactions for the month of February can now be listed and entered.

19–5
Feb 1 Bought warehouse fixtures paying in cash £480
" 3 Paid for lighting and heating by cheque £180
" 5 Bought goods on credit: C. Norton & Co £800; C. Stoddard Ltd £4,000; F. Ratcliffe Ltd £4,600
" 7 Paid cheque for a total of £210 motor expenses by cheque, including £80 owing from last month
" 10 Cash Sales £1,260
" 12 Sold goods on credit to: K. Kitchen Ltd £5,600; R. Antrobus & Co £660; N. Fryer £1,700
" 15 Paid wages owing for January, and those for the whole of February, a total by cash of £430
" 16 Cash Drawings £500
" 17 Returns received from: K. Kitchen Ltd £160; R. Antrobus & Co £60
" 18 Received cheque from K. Kitchen Ltd of £4,000 on account
" 20 We returned goods to: C. Stoddard Ltd £400; F. Ratcliffe Ltd £180
" 24 Received cheque from R. Antrobus & Co to settle account, after deducting $2\frac{1}{2}$ per cent discount

„ 25 Paid cheque of £3,420 to settle Stoddard's account. A cash discount of 5 per cent had been deducted
„ 25 Cash Sales paid direct into the bank £1,358
„ 26 Bought goods on credit from F. Ratcliffe Ltd £190
„ 28 Paid rent for the months of March and April by cheque £160
„ 28 Paid motor expenses by cash £45

Cash Book Page 2

		Discount	Cash	Bank			Discount	Cash	Bank
		£	£	£			£	£	£
Feb 1 Balances b/d			270	8,795	Feb 1 Warehouse fixtures	GL 7		480	
„ 10 Sales	GL 5		1,260		„ 3 Lighting and heating	GL 12			180
„ 18 K. Kitchen Ltd	SL 1			4,000	„ 7 Motor expenses	GL 11			210
„ 24 R. Antrobus & Co	SL 4	15		585	„ 15 Wages	GL 10		430	
„ 25 Sales	GL 5			1,358	„ 16 Drawings	GL 2		500	
					„ 25 C. Stoddard Ltd	PL 5	180		3,420
					„ 28 Rent	GL 9			160
					„ 28 Motor expenses	GL 11		45	
					„ 28 Balances c/d			75	10,768
		15	1,530	14,738			180	1,530	14,738
Mar 1 Balances b/d			75	10,768					

Sales Book Page 2

19–5		Folio	£
Feb 12	K. Kitchen Ltd	SL 1	5,600
„ 12	R. Antrobus & Co	SL 4	660
„ 12	N. Fryer	SL 3	1,700
	Transferred to Sales Account	GL 5	7,960

Returns Inwards Book Page 2

19–5		Folio	£
Feb 17	K. Kitchen Ltd	SL 1	160
„ 17	R. Antrobus & Co	SL 4	60
	Transferred to Returns Inwards Account	GL 6	220

Sales Ledger Page 1

K. Kitchen Ltd

19–5			£	19–5			£
Feb 1	Balance b/d		6,360	Feb 17	Returns Inwards	RI 2	160
„ 12	Sales	SB 2	5,600	„ 18	Bank	CB 2	4,000
				„ 28	Balance c/d		7,800
			11,960				11,960
Mar 1	Balance b/d		7,800				

Sales Ledger

N. Fryer — Page 3

19–5			£	19–5			£
Feb 1	Balance b/d		200	Feb 28	Balance c/d		1,900
„ 12	Sales	SB 2	1,700				
			1,900				1,900
Mar 1	Balance b/d		1,900				

R. Antrobus & Co — Page 4

19–5			£	19–5			£
Feb 12	Sales	SB 2	660	Feb 17	Returns inwards	RI 2	60
				„ 24	Bank	CB 2	585
				„ 24	Discount	CB 2	15
			660				660

Purchases Book

Page 2

19–5		Folio	£
Feb 5	C. Norton & Co	PL 3	800
„ 5	C. Stoddard Ltd	PL 5	4,000
„ 5	F. Ratcliffe Ltd	PL 2	4,600
„ 26	F. Ratcliffe Ltd	PL 2	190
	Transferred to Purchases Account	GL 3	9,590

Returns Outwards Book

Page 2

19–5		Folio	£
Feb 20	C. Stoddard Ltd	PL 5	400
„ 20	F. Ratcliffe Ltd	PL 2	180
	Transferred to Returns Outwards Account	GL 4	580

Purchases Ledger

Page 2

F. Ratcliffe Ltd

19–5			£	19–5			£
Feb 20	Returns outwards	RO 2	180	Feb 1	Balance b/d		2,200
„ 28	Balance c/d		6,810	„ 5	Purchases	PB 2	4,600
				„ 26	Purchases	PB 2	190
			6,990				6,990
				Mar 1	Balances b/d		6,810

Purchases Ledger

C. Norton & Co — Page 3

19–5			£	19–5			£
Feb 28	Balance c/d		1,660	Feb 1	Balance b/d		860
				,, 5	Purchases	PB 2	800
			1,660				1,660
				Mar 1	Balance b/d		1,660

C. Stoddard Ltd — Page 5

19–5			£	19–5			£
Feb 20	Returns outwards	RO 2	400	Feb 5	Purchases	PB 2	4,000
,, 25	Bank	CB 2	3,420				
,, 25	Discount	CB 2	180				
			4,000				4,000

General Ledger

(before making adjustments and drawings up Trading and Profit and Loss Accounts and Balance Sheet)

Capital — Page 1

				19–5			£
				Feb 1	Balance b/d		22,005

Drawings — Page 2

19–5			£				
Feb 16	Cash	CB 2	500				

Purchases — Page 3

19–5			£				
Feb 28	Credit purchases for the month	PB 2	9,590				

Returns outwards — Page 4

				19–5			£
				Feb 28	Returns for the month	RO 2	580

Sales — Page 5

				19–5			£
				Feb 10	Cash	CB 2	1,260
				,, 25	Bank	CB 2	1,358
				,, 28	Credit sales for the month	SB 2	7,960

General Ledger

(before making adjustments and drawings up Trading and Profit and Loss Accounts and Balance Sheet)

Returns inwards — Page 6

			£				£
19–5							
Feb 28	Returns for the month	RI 2	220				

Warehouse fixtures — Page 7

			£				£
19–5							
Jan 2	Bank	CB 1	2,400				
Feb 1	Cash	CB 2	480				

Motor van — Page 8

			£				£
19–5							
Jan 8	Bank	CB 1	4,800				

Rent — Page 9

			£				£
19–5							
Feb 1	Prepaid b/d		80				
,, 28	Bank	CB 2	160				

Wages — Page 10

			£				£
19–5				19–5			
Feb 15	Cash	CB 2	430	Feb 1	Accrued b/d		60

Motor expenses — Page 11

			£				£
19–5				19–5			
Feb 7	Bank	CB 2	210	Feb 1	Accrued b/d		80
,, 28	Cash	CB 2	45				

Light and heat — Page 12

			£				£
19–5				19–5			
Feb 3	Bank	CB 2	180	Feb 1	Accrued b/d		180

Insurance — Page 13

			£				£
19–5				19–5			
Feb 1	Prepaid b/d		220				

Discounts allowed — Page 14

			£				£
19–5							
Feb 28	Total for the month	CB 2	15				

Discounts received — Page 15

			£				£
				19–5			
				Feb 28	Total for the month	CB 2	180

General Ledger
(before making adjustments and drawings up Trading and Profit and Loss Accounts and Balance Sheet)

Provision for depreciation: Motor van Page 16

		£
19–5		
Jan 31	Profit & Loss A/c	80

Provision for depreciation: Warehouse fixtures Page 17

		£
19–5		
Jan 31	Profit & Loss A/c	20

The Trial Balance as on 28 February 19–5 can now be drawn up.

G. Cheadle
Trial Balance as on 28 February 19–5

		£	£
Capital	GL 1		22,005
Drawings	GL 2	500	
Purchases	GL 3	9,590	
Returns outwards	GL 4		580
Sales	GL 5		10,578
Returns inwards	GL 6	220	
Warehouse fixtures	GL 7	2,880	
Motor van	GL 8	4,800	
Rent	GL 9	240	
Wages	GL 10	370	
Motor expenses	GL 11	175	
Light and heat	GL 12	—	
Insurance	GL 13	220	
Discounts allowed	GL 14	15	
Discounts received	GL 15		180
Provision for depreciation, motor van	GL 16		80
Provision for depreciation, warehouse fittings	GL 17		20
Stock	GL 18	2,360	
Cash	CB 2	75	
Bank	CB 2	10,768	
Debtors—per Sales Ledger		9,700	
Creditors—per Purchases Ledger			8,470
		41,913	41,913

The Trading and Profit and Loss Account for the month ended 28 February 19–5 is now drawn up. Adjustments are needed for the following items (*a*) to (*d*) which were ascertained by G. Cheadle at the end of the working day of 28 February 19–5. He had:

(*a*) Valued his stock of goods at cost to be £4,830.
(*b*) He owed £270 for lighting and heating.

(*c*) He owed £40 for motor expenses.
(*d*) Noticed that insurance and rent had been prepaid.

G. Cheadle
Trading and Profit and Loss Account for the month ended 28 February 19–5

		£			£
Opening stock		2,360	Sales	10,578	
Add purchases	9,590		Less returns inwards	220	10,358
Less returns outwards	580	9,010			
		11,370			
Less closing stock		4,830			
Cost of goods sold		6,540			
Gross profit c/d		3,818			
		10,358			10,358
Wages		370	Gross profit b/d		3,818
Rent		80	Discounts received		180
Light & heat		270			
Insurance		20			
Motor expenses		215			
Discounts allowed		15			
Depreciation:					
Warehouse fixtures		24			
Motor van		80			
Net profit		2,924			
		3,998			3,998

General Ledger
(after all adjustments made to 28 February 19–5)

Capital — Page 1

19–5			£	19–5		£
Feb 28	Drawings	GL 2	500	Feb 1	Balance b/d	22,005
,, 28	Balance c/d		24,429	,, 28	Add Net Profit for the month	2,924
			24,929			24,929
				Mar 1	Balance b/d	24,429

Drawings — Page 2

19–5			£	19–5			£
Feb 16	Cash	CB 2	500	Feb 28	Capital	GL 1	500

Balance Sheet as at 28 February 19–5

Capital			*Fixed Assets*		
		£			£
Balance as at 1.2.19–5		22,005	Warehouse fixtures at cost	2,880	
Add Net Profit for the month		2,924	Less depreciation to date	44	2,836
		24,929	Motor van at cost	4,800	
Less drawings		500	Less depreciation to date	160	4,640
		24,429			7,476
Current Liabilities			*Current Assets*		
Trade creditors	8,470		Stock	4,830	
Expenses accrued	310	8,780	Debtors	9,700	
			Prepaid expenses	360	
			Bank	10,768	
			Cash	75	25,733
		33,209			33,209

General Ledger

Purchases — Page 3

19–5			£	19–5			£
Feb 28	Credit Purchases for the month	PB 2	9,590	Feb 28	Trading A/c		9,590

Returns outwards — Page 4

19–5			£	19–5			£
Feb 28	Trading A/c		580	Feb 28	Returns for the month	RO 2	580

Sales — Page 5

19–5			£	19–5			£
Feb 28	Trading A/c		10,578	Feb 10	Cash	CB 2	1,260
				Feb 25	Bank	CB 2	1,358
				Feb 28	Credit Sales for the month	SB 2	7,960
			10,578				10,578

General Ledger
(after all adjustments made to 28 February 19–5)

Returns inwards Page 6

19–5			£	19–5		£
Feb 28	Returns for the month	RI 2	220	Feb 28	Trading A/c	220

Warehouse fixtures Page 7

19–5			£	19–5		£
Jan 2	Bank	CB 1	2,400	Feb 28	Balance c/d	2,880
Feb 1	Cash	CB 2	480			
			2,880			2,880
Mar 1	Balance b/d		2,880			

Motor van Page 8

19–5			£
Jan 8	Bank	CB 1	4,800

Rent Page 9

19–5			£	19–5		£
Feb 1	Prepaid b/d		80	Feb 28	Profit & Loss A/c	80
„ 28	Bank	CB 2	160	„ 28	Prepaid c/d	160
			240			240
Mar 1	Prepaid b/d		160			

Wages Page 10

19–5			£	19–5		£
Feb 15	Cash	CB 2	430	Feb 1	Accrued b/d	60
				„ 28	Profit & Loss A/c	370
			430			430

Motor expenses Page 11

19–5			£	19–5		£
Feb 7	Bank	CB 2	210	Feb 1	Accrued b/d	80
„ 28	Cash	CB 2	45	„ 28	Profit & Loss A/c	215
„ 28	Accrued c/d		40			
			295			295
				Mar 1	Accrued b/d	40

General Ledger

(after all adjustments made to 28 February 19–5)

Light and heat — Page 12

19–5			£	19–5		£
Feb 3	Bank	CB 2	180	Feb 1	Accrued b/d	180
,, 28	Accrued c/d		270	,, 28	Profit & Loss A/c	270
			450			450
				Mar 1	Accrued b/d	270

Insurance — Page 13

19–5		£	19–5		£
Feb 1	Prepaid b/d	220	Feb 28	Profit & Loss A/c	20
			,, 28	Prepaid c/d	200
		220			220
Mar 1	Prepaid b/d	200			

Discounts allowed — Page 14

19–5			£	19–5		£
Feb 28	Total for the month	CB 2	15	Feb 28	Profit & Loss A/c	15

Discounts received — Page 15

19–5		£	19–5		£
Feb 28	Profit & Loss A/c	180	Feb 28	Total for the month	180

Provision for depreciation: Motor van — Page 16

19–5		£	19–5		£
Feb 28	Balance c/d	160	Jan 31	Profit & Loss A/c	80
			Feb 28	Profit & Loss A/c	80
		160			160
			Mar 1	Balance b/d	160

Provision for depreciation: Warehouse fixtures — Page 17

19–5		£	19–5		£
Feb 28	Balance c/d	44	Jan 31	Profit & Loss A/c	20
			Feb 28	Profit & Loss A/c	24
		44			44
			Mar 1	Balance b/d	44

General Ledger
(after all adjustments made to 28 February 19–5)

Stock

19–5		£	19–5		£
Jan 31	Trading A/c	2,360	Feb 28	Trading A/c	2,360
Feb 28	Trading A/c	4,830			

15

The Analytical Petty Cash Book and the Imprest System

With the growth of the firm it has been seen that it became necessary to have several books instead of just one ledger. As the firm further increased in size these books also were further sub-divided. An example of this is the splitting of the sales ledger into two or more ledgers on some convenient basis, such as alphabetical or geographical.

A further progression of these ideas can be extended to the cash book. It is obvious that in almost any firm there will be a great deal of small cash payments to be made. It would be an advantage if the records of these payments could be kept separate from the main cash book. Where a separate book is kept it is known as a Petty Cash Book.

The advantages of such an action can be summarized:

1. The task of handling and recording the small cash payments could be delegated by the cashier to a junior member of staff who would then be known as the petty cashier. Thus, the cashier, who is a relatively higher paid member of staff, would be saved from routine work easily performed by a junior and more lowly paid member of staff.

2. If small cash payments were entered into the main cash book these items would then need posting one by one to the ledgers. If travelling expenses were paid to staff on a daily basis this could involve over 250 postings to the Staff Travelling Expenses Account during the year. However, if a form of analytical petty cash book is kept it would only be the periodical totals that need posting to the general ledger. If this was done on a monthly basis, only 12 entries would be needed in the staff travelling expenses account instead of over 250. Thus the basic idea of taking unnecessary detail out of the general ledger is advanced one more step.

Each payment made by the petty cashier will have to be supported by vouchers showing the reason for the payment and signed by the person receiving the money.

The Imprest System

The basic idea of this system is that the cashier gives the petty cashier an adequate amount of cash to meet his needs for the ensuing period. At the end of the period the cashier ascertains the amount spent by the petty cashier, and gives him an amount equal to that spent. The Petty Cash in hand should then be equal to the original amount with which the period was started.
Exhibit 15–1 shows an example of this procedure:

Exhibit 15.1

		£
Period 1	The cashier gives the petty cashier	100
	The petty cashier pays out in the period	78
	Petty cash now in hand	22
	The cashier now reimburses the petty cashier the amount spent	78
	Petty cash in hand end of period 1	100
Period 2	The petty cashier pays out in the period	84
	Petty cash now in hand	16
	The cashier now reimburses the petty cashier the amount spent	84
	Petty cash in hand end of period 2	100

Of course, it may sometimes be necessary to increase the fixed sum, often called the cash 'float', to be held at the start of each period. In the above case if it had been desired to increase the 'float' at the end of the second period to £120, then the cashier would have given the petty cashier an extra £20, i.e. £84+£20 = £104.

One great advantage of the imprest system is the considerable control that one can exercise. It can be subject to check at any time, for the cash then in hand plus the amount spent in the period according to the vouchers should always equal the cash 'float'.

Illustration of an Analytical Cash Book

Sept	1	The cashier gives £50 as float to the petty cashier	
		Payments out of petty cash during September:	£
,,	2	Petrol	6
,,	3	J. Green—travelling expenses	3
,,	3	Postages	2
,,	4	D. Davies—travelling expenses	2
,,	7	Cleaning expenses	1
,,	9	Petrol	1
,,	12	K. Jones—travelling expenses	3
,,	14	Petrol	3

Exhibit 15.2

Petty Cash Book

Receipts	*Folio*	*Date*	*Details*	*Voucher No.*	*Total*	*Motor Expenses*	*Staff Travelling Expenses*	*Postages*	*Cleaning*	*Ledger Folio*	*Ledger Accounts*
£					£	£	£	£	£	£	£
50	CB 19	Sept 1	Cash								
		,, 2	Petrol	1	6	6					
		,, 3	J. Green	2	3		3				
		,, 3	Postages	3	2			2			
		,, 4	D. Davies	4	2		2				
		,, 7	Cleaning	5	1				1		
		,, 9	Petrol	6	1	1					
		,, 12	K. Jones	7	3		3				
		,, 14	Petrol	8	3	3					
		,, 15	L. Black	9	5		5				
		,, 16	Cleaning	10	1				1		
		,, 18	Petrol	11	2	2					
		,, 20	Postages	12	2			2			
		,, 22	Cleaning	13	1				1		
		,, 24	G. Wood	14	7		7				
		,, 27	C. Batsby	15	3					P: 18	3
		,, 29	Postages	16	2			2			
					44	12	20	6	3		3
						GL 17	GL 29	GL 44	GL 64		
44	CB 22	,, 30	Cash								
		,, 30	Balance	c/d	50						
94					94						
50		Oct 1	Balance	b/d							

		£
,,	15 L. Black—travelling expenses	5
,,	16 Cleaning expenses	1
,,	18 Petrol	2
,,	20 Postages	2
,,	22 Cleaning expenses	1
,,	24 G. Wood—travelling expenses	7
,,	27 Settlement of C. Batsby's account in the Purchases Ledger	3
,,	29 Postages	2
,,	30 The cashier reimburses the petty cashier the amount spent in the month.	

The Analytical Petty Cash Book containing the above items is shown in Exhibit 15–2.

The receipts column represents the debit side of the petty cash book. On giving £50 to the petty cashier on 1 September the credit entry is made in the cash book while the debit entry is made in the petty cash book. A similar entry is made on 30 September for £44.

The entries on the credit side of the petty cash book are first of all made in the totals column, and then are extended into the relevant expense column. At the end of the period, in this case a month, the payments are totalled, it being made sure that the total of the totals column equals the sum of the other payments totals, in this case £44. The expense columns have been headed with the type of expense.

To complete double entry, the total of each expense column is debited to the relevant expense account in the general ledger, the folio number of the page in the general ledger then being shown under each column.

The end column has been chosen as a ledger column. In this column items paid out of petty cash which need posting to a ledger other than the general ledger are shown. This would happen if a purchases ledger account was settled out of petty cash, or if a refund was made out of the petty cash to a customer who had overpaid his account.

Exercises

15.1. Enter the following transactions in a petty cash book, having analysis columns for motor expenses, postages and stationery, lighting and heating, sundry expenses, and a ledger column. This is to be kept on the imprest system, the amount spent to be reimbursed on the last day of the month. The opening petty cash float is £100.

19–6		£
May	1 Coal	3
,,	3 Speedy Garage—Petrol	2
,,	4 Postage stamps	5
,,	5 Envelopes	1
,,	6 Poison licence	1
,,	8 Unique Garage—Petrol	5

		£
,,	9 Corner Garage—Petrol	6
,,	11 Postage stamps	5
,,	12 F. Lessor—Ledger account	9
,,	13 H. Norris—Ledger account	4
,,	15 Fire lighters	2
,,	16 Bends Garage—petrol	7
,,	17 K. Kelly—Stationery	6
,,	19 Driving licences	1
,,	21 J. Green—Ledger account	7
,,	25 Coal	6
,,	27 Licence for guard dog	1
,,	28 Guard dog—Food	2
,,	31 Corner Garage—Petrol	5

15.2. Rule a petty cash book with four analysis columns for travelling expenses, office expenses, sundry expenses, and ledger accounts. The cash float is £50, and the amount spent is reimbursed on 31 March.

19–6
Mar 1 Received float of £50
,, 3 Paid—Petrol £3, hotel expenses £2
,, 5 Stationery £6
,, 7 G. George—Ledger account £4
,, 9 Petrol £2, postages £3, stationery £2
,, 11 Petrol £1, H. Hall—Ledger account £6
,, 20 Envelopes £2, Petrol £2, Sundries £2
,, 22 Petrol £4
,, 24 J. Jones—Ledger account £1
,, 20 Petrol £3
,, 30 Hotel expenses £5.

15.3A. Enter the following transactions in a petty cash book, having analysis columns for hotel charges, postages and stationery, motor expenses, sundry expenses and ledger accounts.

19–1
Apr 1 Received cash float of £200
,, 3 Paid sundry expenses £2, hotel charges £6
,, 4 Paid J. Jones' account £9
,, 5 F. Garner—Ledger account £4
,, 7 Petrol £2, Envelopes £3
,, 9 Sundry expenses £4, hotel expenses £7
,, 10 Postages £5
,, 11 Petrol £4, J. Jordan ledger account £2
,, 18 Stationery £3, Petrol £2, Hotel charges £7
,, 23 Sundry expenses £1, hotel charges £9
,, 25 Petrol £4, Postages £6, Ledger account Lucas £7
,, 26 Billheadings printed £3
,, 30 Received amount to bring petty cash balance up to £200.

15.4A. The following items are to be entered in a petty cash book. Analysis columns are to be headed up for travelling expenses, ledger accounts, postages, motor expenses, stationery, and sundry expenses. The book is to be kept on the imprest system, the amount spent to be reimbursed on the last day of each month. The opening petty cash float is £500 received on 1 March 19–3.

19–3			£
Mar	1	Manchester Garages: motor spares	22
„	3	Post Office: stamps	15
„	5	J. Hardy: ledger account	12
„	6	British Rail: train fare	19
„	8	Pear Tree Garage—petrol	10
„	9	E.P. & Co—stationery	8
„	10	Bus fares	2
„	11	Post Office: stamps	21
„	12	A. Hardacre: ledger account	16
„	13	Performing Rights licence	4
„	15	Food for office cat	2
„	16	Egan Reid—stationery	18
„	18	Banks Lane Garage—petrol	11
„	19	L. Mennies: ledger account	24
„	20	British Rail: train fare	13
„	21	Gordons: repairs to motor van	28
„	23	Post Office: stamps	17
„	24	A. & P. Baker: stationery	6
„	28	Donation to Charity	5
„	30	Offerton Lane Garage: petrol	12
„	31	Received reimbursement to bring cash float to desired level.	

16

Suspense Accounts, Types of Errors and their Correction

Errors Not Affecting the Agreement of the Trial Balance Totals

When discovered, the necessary correcting entries must be made in the accounts. To give fuller information as to the cause of errors and their remedy, a journal entry is made.

An example of each of these types of errors, already listed in Chapter 5, is now shown together with the journal entry recording the correction.

1. Error of Omission

The sale of goods, £59, to E. Gardner has been completely omitted from the books.

The Journal

	Dr	*Cr*
	£	£
E. Gardner	59	
Sales account		59
Correction of omission of sales Invoice No. ...... from sales journal.		

2. Error of Commission

A purchase of goods, £44, from C. Shaw was entered in error in C. Short's account.

The Journal

	Dr	*Cr*
C. Short	44	
C. Shaw		44
Purchase invoice No. ...... entered in wrong personal account, now corrected.		

3. *Error of Principle*

The sale of a machine, £200, is entered in a Sales Account instead of in a machinery disposals account.

The Journal

	Dr	Cr
	£	£
Sales account	200	
Machinery disposals account		200
Correction of error sale of fixed asset credited to revenue account.		

4. *Compensating Error*

The sales account is overcast by £200, as also is the wages account. This assumes that these are the only two errors found in the books.

The Journal

	Dr	Cr
	£	£
Sales Account	200	
Wages Account		200
Correction of overcasts of £200 each in the sales account and the wages account which compensated for each other.		

5. *Error of Original Entry*

A sale of £98 to A. Simpson was entered in the books as £89.

The Journal

	Dr	Cr
	£	£
A. Simpson	9	
Sales Account		9
Correction of error whereby sales were understated by £9.		

6. *Complete reversal of entries*

A payment of cash of £16 to M. Deakin was entered on the receipts side of the cash book in error and credited to M. Deakin's account. This is somewhat more difficult to adjust. First must come the amount needed to cancel the error, then comes the actual entry itself. Because of this, the entry is double the actual amount first recorded.

The Journal

	Dr	Cr
	£	£
M. Deakin	32	
Cash		32
Payment of cash £16 debited to cash and credited to Mr Deakin in error on ...... Error now corrected.		

Errors Affecting the Trial Balance

Besides the class of errors already described there is a class of errors which throw the totals of the trial balance out of agreement with one another. These are mainly concerned with incorrect additions and where an entry is made on only one side of the books.

Every effort should be made to find the errors immediately, but especially in examinations it is assumed that for one reason or other this is not possible. Making this assumption, the trial balance totals should be made to agree with each other by inserting the amount of the difference between the two sides in a Suspense Account.

Exhibit 16.1

Trial Balance as on 30 June 19–5

	Dr	Cr
	£	£
Totals after all the accounts have been listed	100,000	99,960
Suspense Account		40
	100,000	100,000

Suspense Account

			£
	19–5		
	June 30	Difference per trial balance	40

If the errors are not found before the final accounts are prepared, the balance of £40, being a credit balance, will be shown on the capital and liabilities side of the balance sheet. This, however, should never occur if the figure is a material one: the error must always be found. If the item is small, however, it may be added to current liabilities or current assets if a debit balance.

Whenever the error(s) are discovered they must be corrected, each one being supported by a journal entry. Assume that in the case in Exhibit 16–1 there were two errors, both found on 30 September 19–5, the undercasting of sales by £30 and the omission of the credit entry of cash received £10 in D. Scott's account. This would be corrected as in Exhibit 16–2.

Exhibit 16.2

Sales

				£
			Sept 30 Suspense	30

D. Scott

				£
			Sept 30 Suspense	10

Suspense

		£		£
Sept 30	Sales	30	Jul 1 Balance b/d	40
,, ,,	D. Scott	10		
		40		40

The Journal

	Dr	Cr
	£	£
Sept 30 Suspense	30	
Sales		30
Undercasting of sales by £30 in last year's accounts.		
Sept 30 Suspense	10	
D. Scott		10
Omission of credit entry of cash £10 in D. Scott's account during last year.		

Only those errors which do affect the agreement of the totals of the trial balance have to be corrected via the suspense account.

The Effect of Errors on Reported Profits

When errors are not discovered until a later period, it will often be found that the gross and/or net profits will have been incorrectly stated for the period when the errors were made but were undetected. If they are corrected in the period when they are found, then that period's profits will often be affected by the correcting of the errors. The statement of corrected net profits in Exhibit 16–3 shows how one period's profits were affected.

Exhibit 16.3

K. Black

Trading and Profit and Loss Account for the year ended 31 December 19–5

	£		£
Stock	500	Sales	8,000
Add Purchases	6,100		
	6,600		
Less Closing stock	700		
Cost of goods sold	5,900		
Gross profit c/d	2,100		
	8,000		8,000
Rent	200	Gross profit b/d	2,100
Rates	120	Discounts received	250
Lighting and heating	180		
Depreciation	250		
Net profit	1,600		
	2,350		2,350

Balance Sheet as at 31 December 19–5

Capital			*Fixed Assets*		
	£	£		£	£
Balance as at 1.1.19–5	1,800		Fixtures at cost	2,200	
Add Net profit	1,600		*Less* Depreciation to date	800	
	3,400				1,400
Less Drawings	900		*Current Assets*		
		2,500	Stock	700	
Current Liabilities			Debtors	600	
Creditors		600	Bank	340	
					1,640
			Suspense Account		60
		3,100			3,100

The following errors made in 19–5 were found in 19–6 and were then corrected:

	£
1. Sales overcast by	70
2. Rent undercast by	20
3. Rates overcast by	50
4. Cash payment to a creditor entered in the Cash Book only	30
5. Complete omission of drawings by cheque	15

	£
6. A purchase of £95 is entered in the books, debit and credit entries as £59	36
7. Discounts received undercast by	10

K. Black

Statement of Corrected Net Profit for the year ended 31 December 19–5

	£	£
Net Profit per the accounts		1,600
Add Rates overcast (3)	50	
Discounts received undercast (7)	10	
	—	60
		1,660
Less Sales overcast (1)	70	
Rent undercast (2)	20	
Purchases understated (6)	36	
	—	126
Corrected net profit for the year		1,534

Errors not affecting profit calculations:

4. All that happened was that creditors were overstated in the balance sheet by £30.

5. The profits are not affected. The bank item in the balance sheet is overstated by £15 and the drawings understated by £15.

The suspense account as corrected appears:

Suspense

19–5		£	19–6		£
June 30	Difference in trial balance	60	June 30	Sales	70
19–6			,, ,,	Rent	20
June 30	Rates	50	,, ,,	A creditor's account	30
,, ,,	Discounts received	10			
		120			120

Errors numbered 5 and 6, being errors which do not throw the totals of the trial balance out of agreement, are not corrected via this suspense account.

Exercises

16.1. A book-keeper extracts a trial balance which fails to agree. He places the difference in suspense account and then tries to find the errors which have caused his trial balance to disagree.

The following errors are found:

1. Sales day book overcast by £10.
2. Purchase of goods from Appleton Bros., £130 posted to their account in error as £100.
3. Balance on Blenkinsopp and Son's account of £35 in the sales ledger extracted in error as £55.
4. Discount allowed to Cantrell and Co £5 debited to their account.

Show the suspense account after the above errors have been adjusted therein, and the amount of the original error placed in suspense account.
(Union of Educational Institutions)

16.2. Ramsden and Camm are garage proprietors and prepare their own final accounts. The audit of the books for the year ending 31 December 19–2 revealed the following errors:

1. £27 paid for advertising charges had been debited to the personal account of the advertising contractor.
2. £800 paid for a car for resale had been treated as a fixed asset and depreciation written off at the rate of 25 per cent on cost.
3. £25 received from the sale of an old calculating machine (Book Value £40) had been credited to sales account.

You are required:

(*a*) to correct these errors by means of journal entries;
(*b*) to calculate the effect of these corrections on the net profit for the year which, before adjustment, was £4,036.

(Union of Educational Institutions)

16.3. On taking out a trial balance you discover that there is in fact a difference which you enter in a suspense account to await further investigation and also to use as a balancing figure for the trial balance.

Investigation locates the following errors:

1. A purchase of goods from A. Smith has been credited in error to A. Smith Ltd. The amount is £150.
2. A credit sale of goods, valued at £30, has been posted to the credit of L. Langford's account, instead of debit.
3. The purchase day book was undercast by £100.
4. The sales day book was undercast by £4.
5. Machinery purchased for £150 had been debited to the purchases account.

(*a*) Make the correcting journal entries.
(*b*) Show the entries in the suspense account, to eliminate the difference entered in the suspense account.

16.4. G.A. extracted the following trial balance from his ledgers at 30 May 19–4.

	£	£
Petty cash	20	
Capital		1,596
Drawings	1,400	
Sales		20,607
Purchases	15,486	
Purchases returns		210
Stock (1 January 19–4)	2,107	
Fixtures and fittings	710	
Sundry debtors	1,819	

	£	£
Sundry creditors		2,078
Carriage on purchases	109	
Carriage on sales	184	
Rent and rates	460	
Light and heat	75	
Postages and telephone	91	
Sundry expenses	190	
Cash at bank	1,804	
	24,455	24,491

The trial balance did not agree. On investigation G.A. discovered the following errors which had occurred during the month of May.

1. In extracting the schedule of debtors the credit side of a debtor's account had been overcast by £10.
2. An amount of £4 for carriage on sales had been posted in error to the carriage on purchases account.
3. A credit note for £17 received from a creditor had been entered in the correct subsidiary book but no entry had been made in the creditor's account.
4. £35 charged by Builders Ltd for repairs to G.A.'s private residence had been charged, in error, to sundry expenses account.
5. A payment of an electricity bill £21 had been entered correctly in the cash book but had been posted, in error, to the postages and telephone account as £12.

State what corrections you would make in G.A.'s ledger accounts and re-write the trial balance as it should appear *after* all the above corrections have been made.
(University of London 'O' Level)

16.5. J. Alton drew up the following balance sheet on 31 December 19–4.

Balance Sheet

	£	£		£	£
Capital (1.1.19–4)	4,569		*Fixed Assets*		
Add Net Profit	1,969		Furniture and fittings	560	
			Motor vans	1,240	
	6,538				1,800
Less Drawings	2,038		*Current Assets*		
		4,500	Stock	2,275	
Sundry Trade creditors		2,130	Sundry Debtors	1,345	
			Cash in hand and Balance at bank	1,210	
					4,830
		6,630			6,630

An audit of the books revealed the following:

1. Motor vans should have been depreciated by £280.
2. Goods £175 received on 30 December had been included in stock at 31 December 19–4. These were not invoiced and passed through the books until 3 January 19–5.

3. A debt of £65 owing by S. Bradford was considered to be bad and a provision of £40 was to be made for doubtful debts.
4. £45 outstanding for light and heat had not been entered in the accounts.
5. Rates charged in the rates account included £64 prepaid. No adjustment had been made.
6. Packing materials £132 had been charged in full to the profit and loss account. There was a stock of packing materials at 31 December 19–4 of £42.

You are required:
(*a*) to show your calculation of the correct net profit in account form, making adjustments for the above matters;
(*b*) to draw up a corrected balance sheet as at 31 December 19–4.
(Associated Examining Board 'O' Level)

16.6. F. W. Low's trial balance at 31 December 19–4 did not agree. He opened a suspense account for the difference, prepared his trading and profit and loss account and drew up the following balance sheet:

Balance Sheet

	£	£		£	£
Capital (1.1.19–4)	6,093		*Fixed Assets*		
Add Net Profit	2,970		Furniture and fittings	470	
			Motor vans	1,430	
	9,063				1,900
Less Drawings	2,500		*Current Assets*		
		6,563	Stock	3,146	
Sundry creditors		2,475	Sundry debtors	2,142	
Suspense Account		12	Cash in hand and		
			Balance at bank	1,862	
					7,150
		9,050			9,050

The following errors which accounted for the difference in the trial balance were subsequently discovered:
1. Bank charges £7 had been entered in the cash book but the double entry had not been completed.
2. Loss on the sale of an old motor van £12 had been correctly entered in the motor van account but had been charged to depreciation account as £21.
3. A cheque £86 for the purchase of a new typewriter had been correctly entered in the cash book but entered in the furniture and fittings account as £66.
4. A sale of goods to F. J. Bell £46 was correctly entered in the sales book but was posted to Bell's account as £64.
5. A credit note £17 received from R. Tate, a creditor, had been correctly entered in the subsidiary records but posted to Tate's account as £19.
6. The debit balance of £122 on R. S. Muir's account in the sales ledger, at 31 December 19–4 had been carried down as £132 and included in the trial balance at this figure.

You are required:
(*a*) to make the journal entries now required to correct the above errors;
(*b*) to show your calculation of the correct net profit in account form;
(*c*) to draw up a corrected balance sheet as at 31 December 19–4.
(Associated Examining Board 'O' Level)

16.7. The balance sheet of J. Holt as at 31 December 19–3 is given below:

	£	£		£
Capital, 1 January 19–3	5,000		Premises (at cost)	3,500
Add Net Profit for the year	1,840		Furniture (at cost)	1,800
			Delivery Van (at cost)	500
		6,840	Stock	1,250
Bank Loan		400	Debtors	460
Creditors		340	Cash and Bank	70
		7,580		7,580

(*a*) Explain by reference thereto the meanings of:
(i) Capital invested
(ii) Capital employed
(iii) Working capital.

(*b*) Redraft the balance sheet as it would appear after the following transactions had been completed.
(i) Part of the premises which cost £1,000 were sold for cash £1,400
(ii) Debtors to the extent of £300 paid £290 in cash, £10 being allowed to them as discount
(iii) Part of the stock included in the balance sheet at £80 was sold on credit for £100
(iv) New buildings were acquired at a cost of £850–£500 paid in cash and the balance was outstanding.

(Union of Lancashire and Cheshire Institutes)

16.8A. On checking a Profit and Loss Account for 19–8, it was found that the following errors had occurred in its preparation:

1. Power bills for £160 were outstanding and had not been paid. No entry had been made.
2. Premises were depreciated by £100; the amount should have been £200.
3. Expenses of £100 had been credited instead of being debited.
4. The Gross Profit had been entered as £35,000; it should have been £34,000.

If the net profit had been shown originally as £16,000, what should be the correct figure? Would any of the changes have affected the Balance Sheet?

(Southern Universities Joint Board—'O' Level)

16.9A. The trial balance of a trader, extracted as on 31 December 19–4, failed to agree. A trading and profit and loss account, prepared on the basis of this trial balance, but without writing off any difference on the books, showed a net profit of £7,080.

The following errors were afterwards discovered and the difference was eliminated:

1. A debit balance of £33 on sundry expenses account had been omitted from the trial balance.
2. The purchases journal had been over-cast by £200. The creditors are also overstated by £200 in the total balance.
3. The total of the returns outward journal for the month of December 19–4, amounting to £146, had been debited to returns inwards account.
4. On 31 December 19–4, a goods valued at £84 (selling price) were returned by

a customer. No entry for the return of these goods had been made in the books and they had not been included in the closing stock. The cost of these goods was £65.

5. A provision of £21 in respect of accrued charges for electricity at 31 December 19–3, debited in the lighting and heating account at that date, had not been brought forward to the credit of the account in 19–4, although it had been correctly shown as a liability in the balance sheet as on 31 December 19–3.

6. A balance at bank, £170, had been included in the trial balance as a credit balance, i.e. as if it had been a bank overdraft.

You are required:

(*a*) to show by how much the trial balance was out of balance and which side of the trial balance was in excess or deficiency by reason of each error; and

(*b*) to show your calculation of the correct net profit.

Note:

Tabulate your answer to (*a*) in the following form:

	excess of debit/deficiency of credit	*excess of credit/deficiency of debit*
(1)		

and so on for items 2. to 6.

(Institute of Bankers)

16.10A. Black and Co have produced a trial balance for the year ended 31 March 1970, which does not balance. A suspense account was opened for the difference. An examination of the company's books discloses the following errors:

1. An invoice from J. Jones amounting to £100, for goods purchased, has been omitted from the purchase day book and posted direct to purchases account in the nominal ledger but not to Jones' account in the purchase ledger.
2. The sales day book has been undercast by £240 and posted to the debtors control account accordingly.
3. Discount allowed for the month of March amounting to £489 has not been posted to the nominal ledger.
4. Goods received from CRT Ltd on 31 March 19–0, costing £2,410, have been included in stock but the invoice has not yet been received.
5. A cheque for £192 received from J. Crank, a debtor, has been posted direct to the sales account in the nominal ledger.
6. Sales account in the nominal ledger has been credited with a credit note for £250 being trade-in allowance given on a company van.

You are required:

(*a*) to give the journal entries, where necessary, to correct these errors, or if no journal entry is required, state how they will be corrected,

(*b*) to prepare a statement showing the effect the corrections would have on the company's profit for the year, and

(*c*) the net profit before the corrections are made is £20,000.

16.11A. Urr Ltd present you with the following Balance Sheet as at 31 December 19–7.

	£	£	Fixed Assets:	Cost £	Depreciation £	Net £
Ordinary Share Capital		35,000	Freehold property	65,000	-	65,000
Capital Reserve		12,500	Plant and Machinery	15,500	8,500	7,000
			Motor vehicles	3,250	1,850	1,400
		47,500	Goodwill	6,500	—	6,500
Profit and Loss Account		38,500				
5% Debentures		16,500		90,250	10,350	79,900
Trade creditors	22,300					
Accrued charges	1,500		Stock in trade		33,000	
Bank overdraft	12,250		Debtors		27,250	
		36,050	Cash in hand		550	
Suspense Account		2,150				60,800
		140,700				140,700

The item 'Suspense Account £2,150' represents the difference on the trial balance prior to the preparation of the accounts. On checking the books you discover the following errors:

1. A total in the purchase day book was carried forward as £5,975 instead of £5,795, the ultimate total being posted to purchases account.
2. The Stock Sheets were undercast by £1,000.
3. A Bank Deposit Account of £1,250 was omitted.
4. The cash in hand should be £55.
5. A page in the Sales Day Book totalling £2,275 was omitted from the amount posted to Sales Account.
6. No account has been taken of a liability for £125 Rent accrued to 31 December 19–7.
7. An invoice of £350 has been included in purchases and stock but not posted to the personal ledger.
8. An item in the Sales Day Book of £25 was posted in the Sales Ledger as £125.

You are required to show:

(*a*) Journal entries to correct the above errors.
(*b*) The Suspense Account.
(*c*) The corrected balance on the profit and loss account.

(Association of Certified Accountants)

17

Control Accounts

When all the accounts were kept in one ledger a trial balance could be extracted as a test of the arithmetical accuracy of the accounts. It must be remembered that certain errors were not revealed by such a trial balance. If the trial balance totals disagreed, the number of entries for such a small business being relatively few, the books could easily and quickly be checked so as to locate the errors. However, when the firm has grown and the accounting work has been so sub-divided that there are several or many ledgers, a trial balance the totals of which did not agree could result in a great deal of unnecessary checking before the errors were found. What is required in fact is a type of trial balance for each ledger, and this requirement is met by the Control Account. Thus it is only the ledgers whose control accounts do not balance that need detailed checking to find errors.

The principle on which the control account is based is simple, and is as follows. If the opening balance of an account is known, together with information of the additions and deductions entered in the account, the closing balance can be calculated. Applying this to a complete ledger, the total of opening balances together with the additions and deductions during the period should give the total of closing balances. This can be illustrated by reference to a sales ledger:

	£
Total of Opening Balances, 1 January 19–6	3,000
Add total of entries which have increased the balances	9,500
	12,500
Less total of entries which have reduced the balances	8,000
Total of closing balances should be	4,500

Because totals are used the accounts are often known as Total Accounts. Thus a control account for a sales ledger could be known either as a Sales Ledger Control Account or as a Total Debtors

Account. Similarly, a control account for a purchases ledger could be known either as a Purchases Ledger Control Account or as a Total Creditors Account.

It must be emphasized that control accounts are not necessarily a part of the double entry system. They are merely arithmetical proofs performing the same function as a trial balance to a particular ledger.

It is usual to find them in the same form as an account, with the totals of the debit entries in the ledger on the left-hand side of the control account, and the totals of the various credit entries in the ledger on the right-hand side of the control account.

Exhibit 17–1 shows an example of a sales ledger control account for a ledger in which all the entries are arithmetically correct.

Exhibit 17.1

	£
Sales Ledger No. 3.	
Debit balances on 1 January 19–6	1,894
Total credit sales for the month	10,290
Cheques received from customers in the month	7,284
Cash received from customers in the month	1,236
Returns Inwards from customers during the month	296
Debit balances on 31 January as extracted from the sales ledger	3,368

Sales Ledger Control

19–6		£	19–6		£
Jan 1	Balances b/f	1,894	Jan 31	Bank	7,284
,, 31	Sales	10,290	,, ,,	Cash	1,236
			,, ,,	Returns Inwards	296
			,, ,,	Balances c/d	3,368
		12,184			12,184

On the other hand Exhibit 17–2 shows an example where an error is found to exist in a purchases ledger. The ledger will have to be checked in detail, the error found, and the control account then corrected.

Exhibit 17.2

	£
Purchases Ledger No. 2.	
Credit balances on 1 January 19–6	3,890
Cheques paid to suppliers during the month	3,620
Returns outwards to suppliers in the month	95
Bought from suppliers in the month	4,936
Credit balances on 31 January as extracted from the purchases ledger	5,151

Purchases Ledger Control

19–6		£	19–6		£
Jan 31	Bank	3,620	Jan 1	Balances b/f	3,890
,, ,,	Returns Outwards	95	,, 31	Purchases	4,936
,, ,,	Balances c/d	5,151			
		8,866*			8,826*

* There is a £40 error in the purchases ledger.

Other Advantages of Control Accounts

Control accounts have merits other than that of locating errors. Normally the control accounts are under the charge of a responsible official, and fraud is made more difficult because transfers made (in an effort) to disguise frauds will have to pass the scrutiny of this person.

For management purposes the balances on the control account can always be taken to equal debtors and creditors without waiting for an extraction of individual balances. Management control is thereby aided, for the speed at which information is obtained is one of the prerequisites of efficient control.

Exhibit 17.3

Sales Book

Date	*Details*	*Total*	*Ledgers*		
			A–F	*G–O*	*P–Z*
19–6		£	£	£	£
Feb 1	J. Archer	58	58		
,, 3	G. Gaunt	103		103	
,, 4	T. Brown	116	116		
,, 8	C. Dunn	205	205		
,, 10	A. Smith	16			16
,, 12	P. Smith	114			114
,, 15	D. Owen	88		88	
,, 18	B. Blake	17	17		
,, 22	T. Green	1,396		1,396	
,, 27	C. Males	48		48	
		2,161	396	1,635	130

The Sources of Information for Control Accounts

To obtain the totals of entries made in the various ledgers, analytical journals and cash books are often used. Thus a firm with sales ledgers split on an alphabetical basis might have a sales book as per Exhibit

17–3. The totals of the A–F column will be the total sales figure for the sales ledger A–F control account, the total of the G–O column for the G–O control account and so on.

In machine accounting the control account is usually built in as an automatic by-product of the system.

Other Transfers

Transfers to bad debts accounts will have to be recorded in the sales ledger control account as they involve entries in the sales ledgers.

Similarly, a contra account whereby the same firm is both a supplier and a customer, and inter-indebtedness is set off, will also need entering in the control accounts. An example of this follows: G. Horn has supplied the firm with £880 goods, and the firm has sold him £600 goods. In the firm's books the £600 owing by him is set off against the amount owing to him, leaving a net amount owing to Horn of £280.

Sales Ledger

G. Horn

	£		£
Sales	600		

Purchases Ledger

G. Horn

	£		£
		Purchases	880

The set-off now takes place.

Sales Ledger

G. Horn

	£		£
Sales	600	Set-off: Purchases Ledger	600

Purchases Ledger

G. Horn

	£		£
Set-off: Sales Ledger	600	Purchases	880
Balance c/d	280		
	880		880
		Balance b/d	280

The transfer of the £600 will therefore appear on the credit side of the sales ledger control account and on the debit side of the purchases ledger control account.

Exhibit 17–4 shows a worked example of a more complicated control account.

Exhibit 17.4

19–6		£
Aug 1	Sales ledger—debit balances	3,816
„ 1	Sales ledger—credit balances	22
„ 31	Transactions for the month:	
	Cash received	104
	Cheques received	6,239
	Sales	7,090
	Bad debts written off	306
	Discounts allowed	298
	Returns inwards	164
	Cash refunded to a customer who had overpaid his account	37
	Dishonoured cheques	29
	At the end of the month:	
	Sales ledger—debit balances	3,879
	Sales ledger—credit balances	40

Sales Ledger Control Account

19–6		£	19–6		£
Aug 1	Balances b/d	3,816	Aug 1	Balances b/d	22
„ 31	Sales	7,090	„ 31	Cash	104
„ „	Cash refunded	37	„ „	Bank	6,239
„ „	Cash; dishonoured cheques	29	„ „	Bad debts	306
„ „	Balances c/d	40	„ „	Discounts allowed	298
			„ „	Returns inwards	164
			„ „	Balances c/d	3,879
		11,012			11,012

Control Accounts as Part of Double Entry

The control accounts may be treated as being an integral part of the double entry system, the balances of the control accounts being taken for the purpose of extracting a trial balance. In this case the personal accounts are being used as subsidiary records.

Self-Balancing Ledgers and Adjustment Accounts

Because ledgers which have a control account system are proved to be correct as far as the double entry is concerned they are sometimes called self-balancing ledgers. The control accounts where such terminology is in use are then often called 'Adjustment Accounts'.

Exercises

17.1. You are required to prepare a sales ledger control account from the following for the month of May:

19–6		£
May 1	Sales Ledger Balances	4,936
	Totals for May:	
	Sales Journal	49,916
	Returns Inwards Journal	1,139
	Cheques and Cash received from customers	46,490
	Discounts allowed	1,455
	Bad debts written off	99
	Balances in the Sales Ledger set off against credit balances in the Purchases Ledger	259
May 31	Sales Ledger Balances	5,410

17.2. You are required to prepare a purchases ledger control account from the following for the month of June. The balance of the account is to be taken as the amount of creditors as on 30 June.

19–6		£
June 1	Purchases Ledger Balances	3,676
	Totals for June:	
	Purchases Journal	42,257
	Returns Outwards Journal	1,098
	Cheques paid to suppliers	38,765
	Discounts received from suppliers	887
	Cash paid twice in error to a supplier, now refunded	188
	Balances in the Purchases Ledger set off against balances in the Sales Ledger	77
June 30	Purchases Ledger Balances	?

17.3. The trial balance of Queen and Square Ltd revealed a difference in the books. In order that the error(s) could be located it was decided to prepare purchases and sales ledger control accounts.

From the following prepare the control accounts and show where an error may have been made:

19–6		£
Jan 1	Purchases Ledger Balances	11,874
	Sales Ledger Balances	19,744
	Totals for the year 19–6:	
	Purchases Journal	154,562
	Sales Journal	199,662
	Returns Outwards Journal	2,648
	Returns Inwards Journal	4,556
	Cheques paid to suppliers	146,100
	Petty Cash paid to suppliers	78
	Cheques and Cash received from customers	185,960

	£
Discounts allowed	5,830
Discounts received	2,134
Bad Debts written off	396
Customers' cheques dishonoured	30
Balances on the Sales Ledger set off against balances in the Purchases Ledger	1,036

Dec 31 The list of balances from the purchases ledger shows a total of £14,530 and that from the sales ledger a total of £21,658.

17.4. The following figures relating to the year 19–3 were extracted from the books of a trader:

	£
Debit Balance on Sales Ledger Control Account, 1 January	5,082
Sales, per Sales Journal	61,318
Discounts allowed, per Cash Book	1,437
Receipts on account of Credit Sales	58,946

The book-keeper prepared a list of debit balances in the sales ledger as on 31 December 19–3, amounting to a total of £5,502. There were no credit balances.

After the extraction of the figures and the preparation of the list mentioned above, the following errors were discovered:

1. The sales journal had been overcast by £90.
2. The debit side of the personal account of a customer had been undercast by £209.
3. Discounts allowed, amounting to £48, had been credited to the personal accounts of customers, but were not entered elsewhere in the books.
4. Goods, invoiced to a customer at £16, had been returned by him. The return of these goods had not been recorded anywhere in the books.
5. A sales invoice of £132, entered in the sales journal, had not been posted to the customer's personal account.
6. A debit balance of £36 on the personal account of a customer had been omitted from the list of balances.

After the discovery of the above errors, the book-keeper prepared a sales ledger control account for the year 19–3 and a revised list of sales ledger balances as on 31 December 19–3.

You are required:

(*a*) to show the sales ledger control account for the year 19–3; and
(*b*) to show your calculation of the total of the revised list of sales ledger balances as on 31 December 19–3.

(Chartered Institute of Secretaries and Administrators)

17.5A.

(*a*) From the following particulars, which relate to the month of January 19–1, prepare a Sales Ledger Control Account.

	£
Sales	12,000
Returns Inwards	125
Cash received from customers	11,520
Discount Allowed	250
Bad Debts written off	500
Interest charged on overdue accounts	20
Balance 1 January 19–1	5,141

(*b*) The balance in this control account does not agree with the Schedule of Debtors extracted from the personal ledger which amounts to £4,074. An investigation revealed the following:

1. The Sales Day Book had been overcast by £100 on one occasion and £50 on another.
2. Discount £10, shown in the Sales Ledger has been omitted from the Cash Book.
3. Balances totalling £88 have been left off the list of debtors at 31 January.
4. The credit side of one sales ledger account is £50 too much.
5. Bad debts of £122 have been written off in the Sales Ledger but no entry has been made in the General Ledger.
6. An account of £224 in the Purchase Ledger has been set off against a contra account in the Sales Ledger but this is not recorded in either control account.
7. Discount allowed £6 entered in the Cash Book has not been carried to the customer's account.
8. An item of £93 in the Sales Day Book has been posted as £39 in the customer's account.

Show the adjustments necessary to:
(*a*) the balance in the Sales Ledger Control Account,
(*b*) the Schedule of Debtors.
(East Midland Educational Union)

17.6A. The following information relating to the year 19–8 has been extracted from the books of Steverton Ltd. All purchases and sales have been entered in personal accounts in the Purchases Ledger and Sales Ledger respectively.

	£
Sales Ledger debtor balances 1 January 19–8	4,491
Purchases ledger creditor balances 1 January 19–8	3,217
Receipts from customers (including £76 in respect of a debt written off as bad in 19–7)	54,642
Payments to suppliers	38,496
Sales	58,127
Purchases	41,742
Returns inwards	863
Returns outwards	425
Bad debts written off in 19–8	1,041
Increase in provision for doubtful debts at 31 December 19–8	124
Received from suppliers in respect of overpayment	48
Credit balance on sales ledger 31 December 19–8	82

Required:
The sales ledger control account and the purchases ledger control account for 19–8 showing the balance of debtors and creditors respectively at the year end.
(Institute of Bankers)

17.7A. During the course of the audit of Giles & Co it was found that the net total balances of £17,780, extracted from the Purchase Ledger on 30 June 19–9 did not agree with the balance on the Purchase Ledger Control Account.

Audit tests revealed the following errors and, when the necessary adjustments had been made, the books balanced:

1. Purchase ledger balances had been omitted from the list of balances as follows:

	£
Credits	270
Debits	20

2. Discounts received for the month of March, amounting to £15, had been recorded in the cash book and posted to the correct accounts in the purchase ledger, but no entry had been made in the Control Account.
3. The purchase returns day book had been overcast by £100.
4. Credit balances of £35 in the purchase ledger had been incorrectly listed as debit balances.
5. Payments for rates had been analysed as a purchase and posted to an account in the purchase ledger. The balance on this account, £180, had been transferred to the nominal ledger, but no entry had been made in the Control Account.
6. By arrangement, Burton's account in the sales ledger was set off by contra against the credit balance on his account in the purchase ledger. Transfers amounting to £450 had not been entered in the Control Account.
7. Johnson had been debited for goods returned to him, £40, and no entry had been made in the purchase returns day book.
8. An old debit balance on the purchase ledger of £2 had been written off as bad in June 19–9 but no entry had been made in the Control Account.
9. A June 19–9 payment of £120 had been correctly entered in the Control Account but had been posted to the purchase ledger as July 19–9.
10. The credit column of Taylor's account in the purchase ledger had been undercast by £10.

You are required to prepare:

(*a*) a statement reconciling the original net balances extracted from the purchase ledger with the adjusted final balance on the Purchase Ledger Control Account, and

(*b*) the Purchase Ledger Control Account showing the necessary adjustments and the balance on the account before these adjustments.

(Institute of Chartered Accountants)

17.8A. A business maintains a manual record of debtors' accounts, posting entries to the Sales Ledger from copies of invoices and credit notes. Cheques and discounts allowed are posted to the Sales Ledger from copies of daily cash sheets. Copy invoices and credit notes and daily cash sheets are totalled to provide for entries in the Control Account. All transfers into and out of the sales ledger are recorded through a Transfer Journal, which is totalled to provide for further entries in the Control Account.

At the end of March 19–5, the balances appearing in the Sales Ledger totalled to DR £9,275, and the balance in the Sales Ledger Control Account was DR £9,905.

An investigation of the difference revealed the following errors:

(i) A copy invoice for £80 has been posted to a customer's account as £8.
(ii) A copy credit note for £22 has been debited to a customer's account.
(iii) Discounts allowed of £14 shown on the daily cash sheets have not been posted to the customer's accounts.
(iv) An invoice for £135 for J. Brown has been posted to the debit of R. Brown's account.
(v) Two debit balances of £45 and £27 have been omitted from the list extracted from the Sales Ledger.
(vi) An account for £110 in the Sales Ledger has been settled by contra entry to

the Purchase Ledger, but no record has been made of this in the Transfer Journal.

(vii) A balance of £59 in a Sales Ledger account has been written off as irrecoverable, but has not been entered through the Transfer Journal.

(viii) The copy invoices were over-added by £325.

(ix) Cash of £25 paid in settlement of a customer's credit balance has been entered on the wrong side of the customer's account.

Required:

(*a*) Prepare a statement reconciling the Sales Ledger Total with the Sales Ledger Control Account.

(*b*) List the main benefits to be derived from the use of control accounts.

(Association of Certified Accountants)

18

Incomplete Records and Single Entry

This chapter is concerned with accounting systems which do not fully record the dual aspect of each accounting transaction. Some of them can hardly be graced with the word 'system'. They range from being almost full double entry down to a position where hardly any of the transactions have been entered in any form of account. Where a record of each transaction does exist, but not the dual aspect of it, then this is known as single entry. On the other hand, where records of only part of the transactions are available then this is known as incomplete records. In some of these latter cases calculations of profit depend very largely on the intuition, skill and perseverance of the person drafting the accounts, aided by the memory of the proprietor.

It is perhaps only fair to remember that accounting is after all supposed to be an aid to management, it is not something to be done as an end in itself. Therefore, many small firms, especially retail shops, can have all the information they want by merely keeping a cash book and having some form of record, not necessarily in double entry form, of their debtors and creditors. Many of these small businesses in fact would keep no books at all but for the requirements of the income tax authorities.

Probably the way to start is to recall that, barring an introduction of extra cash or resources into the firm, the only way that capital can be increased is by making profits. Therefore, the most elementary way of calculating profits is by comparing capital at the end of last period with that at the end of this period. If it is known that the capital at the end of 19–4 was £2,000 and that at the end of 19–5 it has grown to £3,000, and that there have been no drawings during the period nor has there been any fresh introduction of capital the net profit must therefore be £3,000–£2,000 = £1,000. If on the other hand the drawings had been £700, the profits must have been £1,700 calculated thus:

Last year's Capital +	Profits –	Drawings	= this year's Capital
£2,000 +	?	–£700	= £3,000

Filling in the missing figure by normal arithmetical deduction:

£2,000+£1,700−£700 = £3,000.

Exhibit 18–1 shows the calculation of profit where insufficient information is available to draft a trading and profit and loss account, only information of assets and liabilities being known.

Exhibit 18.1

H. Goddier provides information as to his assets and liabilities at certain dates.

At 31 December 19–5. *Assets*: Motor van £1,000; Fixtures £700; Stock £850; Debtors £950; Bank £1,100; Cash £100. *Liabilities*: Creditors £200; Loan from J. Blunt £600.

At 31 December 19–6. *Assets*: Motor van (after depreciation) £800; Fixtures (after depreciation) £630; Stock £990; Debtors £1,240; Bank £1,700; Cash £200. *Liabilities*: Creditors £300; Loan from J. Blunt £400; Drawings were £900.

First of all a Statement of Affairs is drawn up as at 31 December 19–5. This is the name given to what would have been called a balance sheet if it had been drawn up from a set of records. The capital is the difference between the assets and liabilities.

Statement of Affairs 31 December 19–5

	£		£	£
Capital (difference)	3,900	*Fixed Assets*		
		Motor Van		1,000
Long-Term Liability		Fixtures		700
Loan from J. Blunt	600			
				1,700
Current Liabilities		*Current Assets*		
Creditors	200	Stock	850	
		Debtors	950	
		Bank	1,100	
		Cash	100	
				3,000
	4,700			4,700

A statement of affairs is now drafted up at the end of 19–6. The formula of Opening Capital+Profit−Drawings = Closing Capital is then used to deduce the figure of profit.

Statement of Affairs 31 December 19–6

Capital		£	*Fixed Assets*		£
Balance at 1.1.19–6	3,900		Motor van		800
Add Net profit	?		Fixtures		630
					1,430
Less Drawings	900		*Current Assets*	£	
		?	Stock	990	
Long-term Liability			Debtors	1,240	
Loan from J. Blunt		400	Bank	1,700	
Current Liabilities			Cash	200	
Creditors		300			4,130
		5,560			5,560

Deduction of net profit
Closing Capital must be Assets – Liabilities = £5,560 – £400 – £300 = £4,860
Opening Capital + Net Profit – Drawings = Closing Capital
£3,900 + ? – £900 = £4,860
Therefore net profit = £1,860

Obviously, this method of calculating profit is very unsatisfactory as it is much more informative when a trading and profit and loss account can be drawn up. Therefore, whenever possible the comparisons of capital method of ascertaining profit should be avoided and a full set of final accounts drawn up from the available records. When doing this it must be remembered that the principles of calculating profit are still those as described in the compilation of a double entry trading and profit and loss account. Assume that there are two businesses identical in every way as to sales, purchases, expenses, assets and liabilities, the only difference being that one proprietor keeps a full double entry set of books while the other keeps his on a single entry basis. Yet when each of them draws up his final accounts they should be identical in every way. Exhibit 18–2 shows the method for drawing up final accounts from single entry records.

Exhibit 18.2

The accountant discerns the following details of transactions for J. Perkins' retail shop for the year ended 31 December 19–5:

1. The sales are mostly on a credit basis. No records of sales have been made, but £10,000 has been received, £9,500 by cheque and £500 by cash, from persons to whom goods have been sold.
2. Amount paid by cheque to suppliers during the year = £7,200.
3. Expenses paid during the year: By cheque, Rent £200, General Expenses £180; by cash, Rent £50.

4. J. Perkins took £10 cash per week (for 52 weeks) as drawings.

5. Other information is available:

	At 31.12.19–4	At 31.12.19–5
	£	£
Debtors	1,100	1,320
Creditors for goods	400	650
Rent Owing	—	50
Bank Balance	1,130	3,050
Cash Balance	80	10
Stock	1,590	1,700

6. The only fixed asset consists of fixtures which were valued at 31 December 19–4 at £800. These are to be depreciated at 10 per cent per annum.

The first step is to draw up a statement of affairs as at 31 December 19–4.

Statement of Affairs as at 31 December 19–4

	£		£	£
Capital	4,300	*Fixed Assets*		
		Fixtures		800
Current Liabilities		*Current Assets*		
Creditors	400	Stock	1,590	
		Debtors	1,100	
		Bank	1,130	
		Cash	80	
				3,900
	4,700			4,700

All of these opening figures are then taken into account when drawing up the final accounts for 19–5.

Next a cash and bank summary is drawn up:

	Cash	*Bank*		*Cash*	*Bank*
	£	£		£	£
Balances 31.12.19–4	80	1,130	Suppliers		7,200
Receipts from debtors	500	9,500	Rent	50	200
			General Expenses		180
			Drawings	520	
			Balances 31.12.19–5	10	3,050
	580	10,630		580	10,630

J. Perkins

Trading and Profit and Loss Account for the year ended 31 December 19–5

	£		£
Stock 1.1.19–5	1,590	Sales (*note 2*)	10,220
Add Purchases (*note 1*)	7,450		
	9,040		
Less Stock 31.12.19–5	1,700		
Cost of Goods Sold	7,340		
Gross Profit c/d	2,880		
	10,220		10,220
Rent (*note 3*)	300	Gross Profit b/d	2,880
General Expenses	180		
Depreciation: Fixtures	80		
Net Profit	2,320		
	2,880		2,880

Note 1. In double entry, purchases means the goods that have been bought in the period irrespective of whether they have been paid for or not during the period. The figure of payments to suppliers must therefore be adjusted to find the figures of purchases.

	£
Paid during the year	7,200
Less payments made, but which were for goods which were purchases in a previous year (creditors 31.12.19–4)	400
	6,800
Add purchases made in this year, but for which payment has not yet been made (creditors 31.12.19–5)	650
Goods bought in this year, i.e. purchases	7,450

The same answer could have been obtained if the information had been shown in the form of a total creditors account. the figure of purchases being the amount required to make the account totals agree.

Total Creditors

	£		£
Cash paid to suppliers	7,200	Balances b/f	400
Balances c/d	650	Purchases (missing figures)	7,450
	7,850		7,850

Note 2. The sales figure will only equal receipts where all the sales are for cash. Therefore, the receipts figures need adjusting to find sales. This can be done by constructing a total debtors account, the sales figures being the one needed to make the totals agree.

Total Debtors

	£		£
Balances b/f	1,100	Receipts: Cash	500
		Cheque	9,500
Sales (missing figures)	10,220	Balances c/d	1,320
	11,320		11,320

Note 3. Expenses are those consumed during the year irrespective of when payment is made. A rent account can be drawn up, the missing figure being that of rent for the year.

Rent Account

	£		£
Cheques	200	Rent (missing figure)	300
Cash	50		
Accrued c/d	50		
	300		300

The balance sheet can now be drawn up.

Incomplete Records and Missing Figures

In practice, part of the information relating to cash receipts or payments is often missing. If the missing information is in respect of one type of payment, then it is normal to assume that the missing figure is the amount required to make both totals agree in the cash column of the cash and bank summary. This does not happen with bank items owing to the fact that another copy of the bank statement can always be obtained from the bank. Exhibit 18–3 shows an example when the drawings figure is unknown, Exhibit 18–4 is an example where the receipts from debtors had not been recorded.

Balance Sheet as at 31 December 19–5

	£	£		£	£
Capital			*Fixed Assets*		
Balance at 1.1.19–5			Fixtures at 1.1.19–5	800	
(per opening Statement of Affairs)	4,300		*Less* Depreciation	80	720
Add Net Profit	2,320		*Current Assets*		
			Stock	1,700	
	6,620		Debtors	1,320	
Less Drawings	520		Bank	3,050	
		6,100	Cash	10	
Current Liabilities					6,080
Creditors	650				
Rent Owing	50				
		700			
		6,800			6,800

Exhibit 18.3

The following information of cash and bank receipts and payments is available:

	Cash	Bank
	£	£
Cash paid into the bank during the year	5,500	
Receipts from debtors	7,250	800
Paid to suppliers	320	4,930
Drawings during the year	?	—
Expenses paid	150	900
Balances at 1.1.19–5	35	1,200
Balances at 31.12.19–5	50	1,670

	Cash	Bank		Cash	Bank
	£	£		£	£
Balances 1.1.19–5	35	1,200	Banking C	5,500	
Received from debtors	7,250	800	Suppliers	320	4,930
Bankings C		5,500	Expenses	150	900
			Drawings	?	
			Balances 31.12.19–5	50	1,670
	7,285	7,500		7,285	7,500

The amount needed to make the two sides of the cash columns agree is £1,265. Therefore, this is taken as the figure of drawings.

Exhibit 18.4

Information of cash and bank transactions is available as follows:

	Cash	*Bank*
	£	£
Receipts from debtors	?	6,080
Cash withdrawn from the bank for business use (this is the amount which is used besides cash receipts from debtors to pay drawings and expenses)		920
Paid to suppliers		5,800
Expenses paid	640	230
Drawings	1,180	315
Balances 1.1.19–5	40	1,560
Balance 31.12.19–5	70	375

	Cash	*Bank*		*Cash*	*Bank*
	£	£		£	£
Balances 1.1.19–5	40	1,560	Suppliers		5,800
Received from debtors	?	6,080	Expenses	640	230
Withdrawn from Bank C	920		Withdrawn from Bank C		920
			Drawings	1,180	315
			Balances 31.12.19–5	70	375
	1,890	7,640		1,890	7,640

Receipts from debtors is, therefore, the amount needed to make each side of the cash column agree, £930.

It must be emphasized that balancing figures are acceptable only when all the other figures have been verified. Should for instance a cash expense be omitted when cash received from debtors is being calculated, then this would result in an understatement not only of expenses but also ultimately of sales.

Where there are Two Missing Pieces of Information

If both cash drawings and cash receipts from debtors were not known it would not be possible to deduce both of these figures. The only source lying open would be to estimate whichever figure was more capable of being accurately assessed, use this as a known figure, then deduce the other figure. However, this is a most unsatisfactory position as both of the figures are no more than pure estimates, the accuracy of each one relying entirely upon the accuracy of the other.

Margins and Mark-Ups and their Use in Deducing Missing Information

The purchase and sale of a good may be shown as

Cost Price+Profit = Selling Price.

The profit when expressed as a fraction, or percentage, of the cost price is known as the mark-up.

The profit when expressed as a fraction, or percentage, of the selling price is known as the margin.

Cost Price+Profit = Selling Price.
£4 + £1 = £5.

$$\text{Mark-up} = \frac{\text{Profit}}{\text{Cost Price}}$$ as a fraction, or if required as a percentage multiply by $\frac{100}{1}$

$$= \frac{£1}{£4} = \frac{1}{4}, \text{ or } \frac{1}{4} \times \frac{100}{1} = 25 \text{ per cent.}$$

$$\text{Margin} = \frac{\text{Profit}}{\text{Selling Price}}$$ as a fraction, or if required as a percentage multiply by $\frac{100}{1}$

$$= \frac{£1}{£5} = \frac{1}{5}, \text{ or } \frac{1}{5} \times \frac{100}{1} = 20 \text{ per cent.}$$

The following illustrations of the deduction of missing information assume that the rate of mark-ups and margins are constant, in other words the goods dealt in by the firm have uniform margins and mark-ups and they do not vary between one good and another. It also ignores wastages and pilferages of goods, also the fact that the market value of some goods may be below cost and therefore need to be taken into stock at the lower figure. These items will need to be the subject of separate adjustments.

1. The following figures are for the year 19–5:

	£
Stock 1.1.19–5	400
Stock 31.12.19–5	600
Purchases	5,200

A uniform rate of mark-up of 20 per cent is applied.
Find the gross profit and the sales figure.

Trading Account

	£		£
Stock 1.1.19–5	400	Sales	£
Add Purchases	5,200		
	5,600		
Less Stock 31.12.19–5	600		
Cost of goods sold	5,000		
Gross profit	?		

Answer: Cost of goods sold + Profit = Sales
Cost of goods sold + Percentage Mark-up = Sales
£5,000 + 20 per cent = Sales
£5,000 + £1,000 = £6,000
The gross profit is therefore £1,000 and the sales £6,000.

2. Another firm has the following figures for 19–6:

	£
Stock 1.1.19–6	500
Stock 31.12.19–6	800
Sales	6,400

A uniform rate of margin of 25 per cent is in use.
Find the gross profit and the figure of purchases.

Trading Account

	£		£
Stock 1.1.19–6	500	Sales	6,400
Add Purchases	?		
Less Stock 31.12.19–6	800		
Cost of goods sold	?		
Gross Profit	?		
	6,400		6,400

Answer: Cost of goods sold + Gross Profit = Sales

Therefore	Sales	−Gross Profit	= Cost of Goods Sold
	Sales	−25 per cent Margin	= Cost of Goods Sold
	£6,400	−£1,600	= £4,800

Now the following figures are known:

	£
Stock 1.1.19–6	500
Add Purchases (1)	?
(2)	?
Less Stock 31.12.19–6	800
Cost of goods sold	4,800

The two missing figures are found by normal arithmetical deduction:

No. (2) less £800 = £4,800
Therefore No. (2) = £5,600
So that: £500 opening stock + No. (1) = £5,600
Therefore No. (1) = £5,100

The completed trading account can now be shown:

Trading Account

	£		£
Stock 1.1.19–6	500	Sales	6,400
Add Purchases	5,100		
	5,600		
Less Stock 31.12.19–6	800		
Cost of goods sold	4,800		
Gross Profit	1,600		
	6,400		6,400

This technique is found very useful by retail stores when estimating the amount to be bought if a certain sales target is to be achieved. Alternatively, stock levels or sales figures can be estimated given information as to purchases and opening stock figures.

The Relationship Between Mark-Up and Margin

As both of these figures refer to the same profit, but expressed as a fraction or a percentage of different figures, there is bound to be a relationship. If one is known as a fraction, the other can soon be found.

If the mark-up is known, to find margin take the same numerator to be numerator of the margin, then for the denominator of the margin take the total of the mark-up's denominator plus the numerator. An example can now be shown:

Mark-up	*Margin*
$\frac{1}{4}$	$\frac{1}{4+1} = \frac{1}{5}$
$\frac{2}{11}$	$\frac{2}{11+2} = \frac{2}{13}$

If the margin is known, to find the mark-up take the same numerator to be the numerator of the mark-up, then for the denominator of the mark-up take the figure of the margin's denominator less the numerator:

Margin	*Mark-up*
$\frac{1}{6}$	$\frac{1}{6-1} = \frac{1}{5}$
$\frac{3}{13}$	$\frac{3}{13-3} = \frac{3}{10}$

Manager's Commission

Managers of businesses are very often remunerated by a basic salary plus a percentage of profits. It is quite common to find the percentage expressed not as a percentage of profits before such commission has been deducted, but as percentage of the amount remaining after deduction of the commission.

For example, assume that profits before the manager's commission was deducted amounted to £8,400, and that the manager was entitled to 5 per cent of the profits remaining after such commission was deducted. If 5 per cent of £8,400 was taken, this amounts to £420, and the profits remaining would amount to £7,980. However, 5 per cent of £7,980 amounts to £399 so that the answer of £420 is wrong.

The formula to be used to arrive at the correct answer is:

$$\frac{\text{Percentage commission}}{100+\text{Percentage commission}} \times \text{Profits before commission.}$$

In the above problem this would be used as follows:

$$\frac{5}{100+5} \times £8{,}400 = £400 \text{ manager's commission.}$$

The profits remaining are £8,000 and as £400 represents 5 per cent of it the answer is verified.

Commonly Used Accounting Ratios

There are some ratios that are in common use for the purpose of comparing one period's results against those of a previous period. Two of the ones most in use are the ratio of gross profit to sales, and the rate of turnover or stockturn.

(a) Gross Profit as Percentage of Sales

The basic formula is:

$$\frac{\text{Gross profit}}{\text{Sales}} \times \frac{100}{1} = \text{Gross profit as percentage of sales.}$$

Put another way, this represents the amount of gross profit for every £100 of sales. If the answer turned out to be 15 per cent, this would mean that for every £100 of sales £15 gross profit was made before any expenses were paid.

This ratio is used as a test of the profitability of the sales. Just because the sales are increased does not of itself mean that the gross profit will increase. The trading accounts in Exhibit 18–5 illustrates this.

Exhibit 18.5

Trading Accounts for the year ended 31 December

	19–6	*19–7*		*19–6*	*19–7*
	£	£		£	£
Stock	500	900	Sales	7,000	8,000
Purchases	6,000	7,200			
	6,500	8,100			
Less Stock	900	1,100			
Cost of goods sold	5,600	7,000			
Gross Profit	1,400	1,000			
	7,000	8,000		7,000	8,000

In the year 19–6 the gross profit as a percentage of sales was:

$$\frac{1{,}400}{7{,}000} \times \frac{100}{1} = 20 \text{ per cent.}$$

In the year 19–7 it became:

$$\frac{1,000}{8,000} \times \frac{100}{1} = 12\tfrac{1}{2} \text{ per cent.}$$

Thus sales had increased, but as the gross profit percentage had fallen by a relatively greater amount the actual gross profit has fallen.

There can be many reasons for such a fall in the gross profit percentage. Perhaps the goods being sold have cost more but the selling price of the goods has not risen to the same extent. Maybe in order to boost sales reductions have been made in the selling price of goods. There could be a difference in the composition of types of goods sold, called the sales-mix, between this year and last, with different product lines carrying different rates of gross profit per £100 of sales. Alternatively there may have been a greater wastage or pilferage of goods. These are only some of the possible reasons for the decrease. The idea of calculating the ratio is to highlight the fact that the profitability per £100 of sales has changed, and so promote an inquiry as to why and how such a change is taking place.

As the figure of sales less returns inwards is also known as turnover, the ratio is also known as the gross profit percentage of turnover.

(b) Stockturn or Rate of Turnover

This is another commonly used ratio, and is expressed in the formula:

$$\frac{\text{Cost of goods sold}}{\text{Average stock}} = \text{Number of times stock is turned over within the period}$$

Ideally, the average stock held should be calculated by taking a large number of readings of stock over the accounting year, then dividing the totals of the figures obtained by the number of readings. For instance, monthly stock figures added up then divided by twelve. It is a well-known statistical law that the greater the sample of figures taken the smaller will be the error contained in the answer.

However, it is quite common, especially in examinations or in cases where no other information is available, to calculate the average stock as the opening stock plus the closing stock and the answer divided by two. The statistical limitations of taking only two figures when calculating an average must be clearly borne in mind.

Using the figures in Exhibit 18–5:

$$\text{19–6} \quad \frac{5,600}{(500+900)\div 2} = \frac{5,600}{700} = 8 \text{ times per annum.}$$

$$\text{19–7} \quad \frac{7,000}{(900+1,100)\div 2} = \frac{7,000}{1,000} = 7 \text{ times per annum.}$$

In terms of periods of time, in the year 19–6 a rate of 8 times per annum means that goods on average are held 12 months÷8 = 1·5 months before they are sold.

For 19–7 goods are held on average for 12 months÷7 = 1·7 months approximately before they are sold.

When the rate of stockturn is falling it can be due to such causes as a slowing down of sales activity, or to keeping a higher figure of stock than is really necessary. The ratio does not prove anything by itself, it merely prompts inquiries as to why it should be changing.

Exercises

18.1. On 1 January 19–3, T. J. Wise began business by paying £800 into a bank account. He did not keep complete books of account, and used the bank account for both his private and business expenses.

On 31 March 19–3, Wise wished to ascertain his profit or loss for the quarter. On that date cash in hand was £10 and the balance at the bank £275. Stock-in-trade was valued at £840 and a motor van at £450. Trade creditors were £496 and trade debtors £189. Rent was prepaid £25 and an account for electricity £19 was outstanding.

An examination of bank withdrawals disclosed that £258 of these was for private expenses. Wise had also taken £217 for private expenses out of the business takings before paying them into the bank.

The motor van was brought into the business during the quarter at the same figure as the valuation on 31 March 19–3.

Prepare a statement to show the profit or loss of the business for the quarter ended 31 March 19–3.
(University of London 'O' Level)

18.2. Henry Connell is in business as a dealer in electrical equipment and has not kept proper books of account. His state of affairs on 31 March 19–2 was as follows:

	£
Cash in hand	45
Cash at bank	615
Stock-in-trade	1,323
Furniture and fittings	302
Sundry debtors	778
Sundry creditors	1,433

During the year ended 31 March 19–3 his drawings were £900 and he had also introduced fresh capital amounting to £600.

At the end of the year his assets and liabilities were: Cash in hand £32; Cash at bank £768; Stock-in-trade £1,470; Furniture and fittings £302; Motor van £600; Sundry debtors £863; Sundry creditors £1,278.

Prepare a statement setting out the profit or loss made by Connell for the year ending 31 March 19–3 after depreciating motor van by 25 per cent and creating a provision for bad debts of £43.
(Union of Educational Institutions)

18.3. On 1 April 19–4 J. B. Hill started business as a painter and decorator. He paid £100 into a bank account and drew a cheque £37 to pay for equipment.

On 30 June 19–4 Hill ascertained that for the quarter ended on that date:

1. he received £584 for decorating work and £26 was still owing to him
2. he drew cheques for:

	£	£
Decorating materials	210	
Rent, rates and insurance	126	
Sundry business expenses	27	
New decorating equipment	15	
Personal drawings	210	
	—	588

3. he still owed £14 for decorating materials and £3 for business expenses.

On 30 June 19–4 equipment was valued at £40.

(*a*) Prepare J. B. Hill's trading and profit and loss accounts for the quarter ended 30 June 19–4 and a balance sheet as at that date.

(*b*) What is the amount of Hill's turnover?

(University of London 'O' Level)

18.4. The following is a summary of the Bank Account of Dillon, a trader, for the year 19–3:

Bank Summary

	£		£
Balance 1 January 19–3	514	Payments to trade creditors for goods purchased	18,786
Cash sales and receipts on account of credit sales	24,372	Rent and rates	771
Balance, 31 December 19–3	118	General expenses	1,697
		Drawings	3,750
	25,004		25,004

All business takings had been paid into the bank except £2,118, out of which Dillon paid wages amounting to £1,280. He retained £838 for private purposes.

The following information is obtained from the books:

	31.12.19–2	*31.12.19–4*
	£	£
Stock-in-trade	2,430	3,150
Creditors for goods purchased	1,945	1,709
Debtors for goods sold	2,240	2,690
Amount owing to a customer (Smith) who had overpaid his account	60	—
Rates paid in advance	42	45
Creditors for general expenses	81	134
Furniture and fittings	1,000	1,000

Discounts received from trade creditors during 19–3 amounted to £150. No discounts were allowed to customers.

The amount due to Smith was set off against sales to him in 19–3.

You are required:

(*a*) to show your calculation of the balance on Dillon's capital account at 31 December 19–2, and

(*b*) to prepare a trading and profit and loss account for the year 19–3 and a balance sheet as on 31 December 19–3.

Note: Ignore depreciation of furniture and fittings.
(Institute of Bankers)

18.5. J. G., a trader, pays all his business takings into his bank account. All business payments are made by cheque. The following is a summary of his bank account for the year 19–3:

Bank Summary

	£		£
Balance, 31 December 19–2	240	Trade creditors	12,400
Received from debtors for goods	15,780	General expenses	1,262
		Rent	150
		Drawings	1,800
		Balance, 31 December 19–3	408
	16,020		16,020

The following information is obtained from the books:

	31.12.19–2	*31.12.19–3*
	£	£
Debtors for goods sold	950	1,172
Trade creditors	830	965
Creditors for general expenses	70	410
Stock-in-trade	1,020	924
Furniture and fittings	200	180

Discounts allowed to customers during 19–3 amounted to £300. No discounts were received from suppliers.

Throughout 19–3 J.G. occupied a building at a rent of £200 a year. The building is divided equally between business and private occupation.

You are required

(*a*) to show your calculation of the balance on J.G.'s capital account at 31 December 19–2, and

(*b*) to prepare the trading and profit and loss account for the year 19–3 and balance sheet as on 31 December 19–3.

(Chartered Institute of Secretaries and Administrators)

18.6. A. Naylor is a retail ironmonger and does not keep a complete set of accounting records. A summary of his banking account and cash book for the year to 31 March 19–2 was as follows:

Receipts	*Cash*	*Bank*
	£	£
Balance in hand 1 April 19–1	15	
Balance at bank 1 April 19–1		2,103
Cash sales		3,290
Credit sales		2,960
Rent of room sublet	52	
Proceeds of sale of old fixtures (written down value £30)	10	
Additional capital introduced		150
Income Tax Schedule 'D' refunded		25

Receipts

	£	£
Cash from bank	1,218	
	1,295	8,528

Payments

	£	£
Purchases for resale		4,220
General expenses	60	200
Rents and rates		295
Wages	560	
Personal drawings	650	
Income tax schedule 'D'		300
Cost of new showcases		160
Cash from bank		1,218
Balance at bank 31 March 19–2		2,135
Balance in hand 31 March 19–2	25	
	1,295	8,528

Inspection of the credit sales invoice books showed that customers owed £1,250 on 1 April 19–1 and £1,560 on 31 March 19–2 of which £58 and £68 respectively were expected to be bad debts.

Examination of the paid invoices for purchases disclosed creditors of £950 at 1 April 19–1 and £1,060 at 31 March 19–2.

Naylor estimates that he had taken goods from stock for his own domestic use costing £26 during the year, and had not paid for them.

At the beginning of the year the shop fixtures and fittings on which depreciation is charged at 5 per cent per annum, stood at £570.

Stock was valued at £950 on 1 April 19–1 and £900 on 31 March 19–2.

You are required to prepare a trading and profit and loss account for the year to 31 March 19–2 and a balance sheet as at that date. together with a statement of capital at 1 April 19–1.
(Association of Certified Accountants)

18.7 From the following trading account calculate:
(*a*) the rate of turnover of stock
(*b*) the ratio of gross profit to turnover:

Trading Account for the year ended 31 March 19–4

	£		£
Stock (1 April 19–3)	2,968	Sales	41,920
Purchases	30,744	Stock (31 March 19–4)	2,272
Gross Profit	10,480		
	44,192		44,192

If the ratio of gross profit to turnover was reduced by 5 per cent on turnover by how much would the rate of turnover of stock have to increase to maintain the same gross profit?

Assume that the opening and closing stocks remain at the same figures and that stock is valued at cost price.
(University of London 'O' Level)

18.8. The following details relate to J.B.'s business for the year ended 31 December 19–4:

	£
Sales	33,984
Sales returns and allowances	380
Stock (1 January 19–4) valued at cost price	1,378
Stock (31 December 19–4) valued at cost price	1,814
Gross Profit for the year	8,068

Calculate:
(*a*) the turnover for the year;
(*b*) the cost of goods sold during the year;
(*c*) the amount of purchases for the year;
(*d*) the rate of turnover of stock for the year;
(*e*) the percentage of gross profit to turnover (to nearest whole number).
(University of London 'O' Level)

18.9. T. Arrowsmith makes up his accounts annually on 31 December. Because of pressure of work, stock could not be taken until 5 January 19–5.
(*a*) From the following information ascertain the value of stock at cost price on 31 December 19–4:

		£
Stock at cost	5 January 19–5	3,300
Purchases	1–5 January 19–5	1,600
Sales	1–5 January 19–5	2,400
Sales returns	1–5 January 19–5	16

T. Arrowsmith makes a gross profit of $33\frac{1}{3}$ per cent on cost price of all goods sold.
(*b*) Show how the adjusted value for closing stock would appear in the books of Arrowsmith when his final accounts had been prepared.
(Northern Counties Technical Examinations Council)

18.10A. T. Fisher, a general dealer, had these assets and liabilities at 1 September 19–9: Freehold premises £4,600; Equipment £569; Vehicle £258; Stock £2,460; Sundry trade debtors £535; Cash in hand £26; Bank balance (overdrawn) £351; Sundry trade creditors £1,409.

The only book of account he uses is a Cash Book, and the following is a summary of the entries made in this book in the year ending 31 August 19–0:

Amounts paid:	£
for stock purchased for re-sale	8,817
for new equipment	224
for assistant's wages	765
for lighting and heating	114
for vehicle running expenses	133
for other general expenses	171

	£
Amounts paid:	
for household expenses (i.e. drawings)	860
for new vehicle	628
Amounts received:	
for goods sold	11,356
for vehicle disposed of (this vehicle was valued at £258 on 1 September 19–9)	190

You are asked to prepare Trading and Profit and Loss Accounts for the year ended 31 August 19–0 and the Balance Sheet at 31 August 19–0, taking these matters into account:

1. The fixed assets are to be shown in the balance sheet for 31 August 19–0 at these net amounts: freehold premises £4,600, Equipment £710, Vehicle £560.
2. At 31 August 19–0, the stock of goods for re-sale is valued at £2,654.
3. At 31 August 19–0, trade debtors total £480 and trade creditors £1,166.
4. Cash in hand at 31 August 19–0 amounts to £26.
5. A doubtful debts provision, £50, is required.
6. At 31 August 19–0, £25 is owing for lighting and heating.

(Oxford Local Examinations—'O' Level)

18.11A. T. White commenced business with £1,000 cash on 1 February 19–1. From his records, on 28 February 19–1, he extracted the following information:

Cash balance £20; Bank balance in hand £100; Creditors £400; Debtors £50; Drawings £80; Premises £800; Equipment £300; Stock in trade £60.

He considered that the equipment should be depreciated by 10%.

You are required to:

(*a*) Calculate the net profit or loss for February.
(*b*) Prepare a Balance Sheet as at 28 February 19–1.
(*c*) Calculate the estimated Profit and prepare an estimated Balance Sheet on 31 March 19–1, based on the following considerations:
  (i) Stock in trade at 31 March 19–1 would be 25% more.
  (ii) Trade creditors £360.
  (iii) The ratio of debtors to creditors was unchanged.
  (iv) Depreciation on equipment to be 10% on reduced balance.
  (v) Receipts and payments by cheque, £800 and £850 respectively, including £95 for drawings.
  (vi) All other assets remain unchanged.

N.B.—Show clearly all workings.
(Northern Counties Technical Examinations Council)

18.12A. The following information is extracted from the books of Denston at 31 December 19–9:

Total Bank Account for 19–9

	£		£
Opening balance	821	Cash paid to suppliers	18,624
Cash received from credit customers	24,264	Salaries	2,249
		Rent and rates	824

Total Bank Account for 19–9

	£		£
Closing balance	1,030	Lighting and heating	168
		General expenses	1,781
		Drawings	2,469
	26,115		26,115

	31 Dec. 19–8	*31 Dec. 19–9*
	£	£
Stock in trade	2,141	2,648
Debtors	3,219	3,388
Creditors for:		
purchases	1,842	1,891
lighting and heating	31	42
Rent and rates paid in advance	100	120
Fixed assets	2,200	see note

Required:
Denston's trading and profit and loss account for 19–9 and his balance sheet at 31 December 19–9.

Note: Depreciation at the rate of 10 per cent per annum on the opening balances is to be charged on fixed assets.
(Institute of Bankers)

18.13A. The balance sheet of Broadmoor's business as at 31 December 19–8 was as follows:

Balance Sheet as at 31 December 19–8

	£	£		£	£
Capital		8,628	Fixed Assets		6,250
Creditors:			Current assets:		
Goods	1,719		Stock	2,046	
Expenses	84		Debtors	1,492	
		1,803	Bank	643	
					4,181
		10,431			10,431

The following information about Broadmoor's financial position at 31 December 19–9 was extracted from his books:

	£
Stock	2,419
Debtors	1,328
Bank	1,021
Creditors:	
Goods	1,684
Expenses	91

Broadmoor drew £1,550 from the business during 19–9 for private purposes.

A depreciation charge of 10 per cent on the opening value of fixed assets should be made for 19–9.

Required:
A calculation of Broadmoor's profit for 19–9.
(Institute of Bankers)

18.14A. Ash is a small wholesaler of fancy goods. On 30 September 19–9 a fire occurred at his warehouse and the greater portion of his stock was destroyed. The value of the stock salvaged was agreed at £550.

His books were saved and the following is an extract from his last accounts for the year ended 31 March 19–9:

Trading Account

	£	£		£
Opening stock	34,240		Sales	98,000
Purchases	78,470			
	112,710			
Less Closing stock	29,410			
		83,300		
Gross profit		14,700		
		98,000		98,000

The stock was fully insured against fire risks.

Trade creditors on 31 March 19–9 amounted to £12,304. Sales for the period to 30 September 19–9 were £54,600 and amounts paid for purchases £44,008. On 30 September 19–9 trade creditors amounted to £11,056.

You are required to prepare a statement showing the amount Ash should claim from the insurance company for loss of stock.
(Institute of Chartered Accountants)

18.15A. Sparrow retired from his employment abroad and returned to this country, where he purchased a small retail business.

He took over the business on 1 July 19–9, acquiring the existing stock at a valuation of £1,142 and the rest of the purchase consideration was apportioned as to £1,500 for fixtures and fittings and the balance for goodwill.

He used his existing bank account and, other than bank statements and vouchers, the only record available was a till book recording cash payments from the till. Surplus cash was banked periodically during the year.

A summary of his bank account for the year ended 30 June 19–0, shows:

	£		£
Balance 1.7.–9	3,646	Purchase of business	3,192
Pension from former employment	975	Rent, 15 months to 30.9.–0	500
		Rates, 9 months to 31.3.–0	84
Bankings from shop	16,427	Electricity	92
		Hire of frozen food cabinet	80
		Purchases for resale	14,700
		Private cheques	1,122
		Balance, 30.6.–0	1,278

A summary of the till book for the year ended 30 June 19–0, shows:

	£
Cash purchases for resale	1,606
Staff wages	742
Sundry shop expenses	156
Cash drawings	520

On 30 June 19–0 stock, valued at cost, amounted to £1,542, amounts due from customers £74, and cash in hand amounted to £54. Depreciation is to be provided on fixtures and fittings at a rate of 10%.

Accounts outstanding on 30 June 19–0 were purchases £470 and rates for the year ending 31 March 19–1, £120.

You are required to prepare Sparrow's Trading and Profit and Loss Account for the year ended 30 June 19–0 and a Balance Sheet as on that date.
(Institute of Chartered Accountants)

18.16A. S. Bullock, a farmer, makes up his accounts to 31 March each year. The trial balance extracted from his books as at 31 March 19–6 was as follows:

	£	£
Purchases—Livestock, seeds, fertilizers, fodder, etc.	19,016	
Wages and National Insurance	2,883	
Rent, rates, telephone and insurance	1,018	
Farrier and veterinary charges	34	
Carriage	1,011	
Motor and tractor running expenses	490	
Repairs—Farm buildings	673	
Implements	427	
Contracting for ploughing, spraying and combine work	308	
General expenses	527	
Bank charges	191	
Professional charges	44	
Sales		29,162
Motor vehicles and tractors—as at 1 April 19–5	1,383	
Additions	605	
Implements—as at 1 April 19–5	2,518	
Additions	514	
Valuation as at 1 April 19–5:		
Livestock, seeds, fertilizers, fodder, etc.	14,232	
Tillages and growing crops	952	
Loan from wife		1,922
Minster Bank		4,072
S. Bullock—Capital at 1 April 19–5		6,440
Current Account at 1 April 19–5		6,510
Drawings during the year	1,280	
	48,106	48,106

On 31 March 19–6:

	£	£
Debtors and prepayments were: Livestock sales	1,365	
Motor licences	68	
Liabilities were: Seeds and fertilizers		180
Rent, rates and telephone		50
Motor and tractor running expenses		40
Professional charges		127
Contracting		179
General expenses		54

Included in the above-mentioned figure of £50 is £15 for rent and this is payable for the March 19–6 quarter. In arriving at this figure the landlord has allowed a deduction of £235 for materials purchased for repairs to the farm buildings, which were carried out by S. Bullock, and is included in the 'Repairs to Farm Buildings' shown in the trial balance. In executing these repairs it was estimated that £125 labour costs were incurred and these were included in 'Wages and National Insurance'. This cost was to be borne by S. Bullock.

The valuation as at 31 March 19–6 was:

	£
Livestock, seeds, fertilizers, fodder, etc.	12,336
Tillages and growing crops	898

Depreciation, calculated on the book value as at 31 March 19–6 is to be written off as follows:

Motor vehicles and tractors	25% per annum
Implements	12½% ,, ,,

You are requested to prepare:

(*a*) The Profit and Loss Account for the year ended 31 March 19–6, and
(*b*) The Balance Sheet as at that date.

18.17A. Z purchased a retail store and commenced business on 1 July 19–9. From the following information you are required to prepare, in as much detail as possible, a Trading and Profit and Loss Account for the year ended 30 June 19–0 and a balance sheet as that date.

	£
Capital introduced on 1 July 19–9	47,000
Drawings during the year	5,000
Working capital (current assets less current liabilities) at 30 June 19–0	23,000
Depreciation of fixed assets during the year, based on a rate of 10 per cent per annum on cost, was	3,000
The fixed assets were all purchased on 1 July 19–9	
Ratio of annual sales to year-end values of fixed assets plus working capital	2:1
Ratio of current assets to current liabilities at the year-end	2:1
Ratio of liquid assets (cash plus debtors) to current liabilities at 30 June 19–0	5:4

Debtors at the year-end are equal to 12 per cent of annual sales.

General expenses (excluding depreciation) are equal to 20 per cent of annual sales.

The current assets consist of stocks (which are unchanged throughout the year), debtors and cash.

Stocks are turned over four times during the year.

The current liabilities consist only of creditors.

(Institute of Cost and Management Accountants)

18.18A. Z, who is at present employed at a salary of £2,000 per annum, is considering investing his savings in a small shop with a flat above.

He has asked you to prepare a statement on which to base his decision, using the information given below for your calculations.

The price asked for the freehold property, shop fittings and goodwill is £6,200 and for the stock is £2,800, valued at cost. The stock consists of product P which cost £400, product Q costing £1,050 and product R which cost £1,350. Debtors and creditors would not be taken over and may be ignored.

The rates of gross profit on products P. Q and R, calculated as percentages of selling prices, are estimated at 40, 30 and 10 respectively, and the annual stock turnover rates (based on existing stock levels) are expected to be 3 for P, 4 for Q and 10 for R. Annual business expenses other than wages are estimated at £700.

If Z bought the shop he would work in it full time, and his wife would also give up her present part-time job at £350 per annum to help him. Z and his wife would give up their present accommodation which they rent at £300 per annum and would occupy the flat above the shop.

If Z does not buy the shop he can invest his savings at 10 per cent per annum, the degree of risk being about the same.

(Institute of Cost and Management Accountants)

18.19A. 12 Jan 19–7

Dear Mr Grey,

I am most relieved that you have agreed to assist me by sorting out the financial affairs of my second-hand business, which as you know commenced on 1 January 19–6. Such records as I have kept are, unfortunately, to be found on now rather scruffy scraps of paper stored in a large cardboard box. Doubtless you will want to examine these records for yourself, but I thought it might assist you if I were to summarize my business dealings up to 31 December 19–6 as I recall them.

In December 19–5 I was lucky enough to win £5,000 on the football pools, and this, together with £1000 loaned to me by a friend—I agreed, incidently, to pay him 10 per cent per year interest—formed the initial capital of £6,000. I put £5,500 into the bank immediately—in a separate business account. I needed a lorry to enable me to collect and deliver the second-hand goods, and I'm pleased to say I made a profit of £460 here; a dealer was asking £1,300 for a second-hand lorry, but I beat him down to £840. I've only paid by cheque £200 of this so far, but as I will finish paying the full £840 in three years, it will be mine before it falls to pieces in another five years from now.

I rent some business premises, and, as they are fairly dilapidated, I only pay £350 a year. I've paid this year's rent by cheque and also £50 in respect of next year.

My first bit of business was to buy a job lot of 2,000 pairs of jeans for £6,000. I've paid a cheque for £4,000 so far, and my supplier is pressing me for the balance. To date, I've sold 1,500 pairs, and received £5,800, but I reckon I'm still owed £500, most of which I should be able to collect. I promptly banked the £5,800 as it was all in cheques.

I bought 800 T-shirts for £1,200 out of my bank account. I've sold 700 of these for cash—£1,500 in all—but as the remainder have got damaged I'd be lucky if I get £50 for them.

I managed to get some pocket-calculators cheaply—50 of them only cost me £400, but I'm rather pleased I haven't paid for them yet, as I think there is something wrong with them. My supplier has indicated that he will in fact accept £200 for them, and I intend to take up his offer, as I reckon I can repair them for £1 each and then sell them at £8 a time—a good profit.

I haven't paid my cash into the bank at all, as the cash I got for the T-shirts and my initial float enabled me to pay for my petrol—£400—and odd expenses——£250. Also it enabled me to draw £20 per week for myself. As I've done so well I also took my wife on holiday—it made a bit of a hole in the bank account but it was worth all £600 of it.

Perhaps, from what I've told you, you can work out what profit I've made—only keep it as small as possible as I don't want to pay too much tax!

Yours sincerely,

Bert Huggins.

Required:

(*a*) From the data provided by Mr Huggins prepare a business Trading, and Profit and Loss Account for the period ended 31 December 1976, and a Balance Sheet as at that date. Show clearly all your workings and assumptions as notes to the accounts.

(*b*) Write a short report to Mr Huggins highlighting what you consider to be the most important features revealed by the accounts you have prepared.

(Association of Certified Accountants)

18.20A. D. M. opened a restaurant on 1 July 19–4. He is quite satisfied with his progress over the past three years and estimates that business increased by 25 per cent in the second year of operation and by a further 20 per cent over the second year in the year ending 30 June 19–7. However, D. M. feels that business has now stabilized, and he sees little or no scope for expansion in the foreseeable future. D. M. has been offered the position of restaurant manager of a nearby motel at a salary of £7,500, and this offer requires a prompt decision. He therefore asks for your professional advice as to whether he should accept this new post and dispose of his business primarily on financial considerations. His business accounting records are somewhat incomplete, but he supplies you with the following information:

	1 July 19–4	*30 June 19–7*	
	£	£	
Stock	960	1,890	
Equipment and fixtures at cost	1,440	2,190	(realizable value £1,500)
Bank	2,730	2,280	
Cash	15	30	
Freehold property at cost	9,600	9,600	(realizable value £12,300)
Amounts due from debtors	—	135	
	14,745	16,125	
Amounts due to creditors	750	540	
Net assets	£13,995	£15,585	

D. M. has made withdrawals from the business over the past three years as follows:

(i) Personal expenses of £750 in each of the first two years and £1,020 in the third year.

(ii) Transfer from business bank account to private bank account in each of the three years of £3,000, £7,200 and £8,700 respectively.

(iii) He has withdrawn from restaurant stock for private consumption purposes foodstuffs which carry an average gross profit of 25 per cent on selling price. These withdrawals over the three years, valued at selling price are as follows:

1st Year	£600
2nd Year	£720
3rd Year	£840

D. M. has stated he will have no problems in disposing of the business at the estimated value as at 30 June 19–7, together with £6,000 for goodwill. The proceeds of sale can be invested in a building society or similar institution to yield 8 per cent.

Required:

A report incorporating suitable financial data, advising D. M. on the action he should take on financial considerations alone.

Ignore taxation.

(Chartered Institute of Secretaries and Administrators)

18.21A. (*a*) Alec Mutton is considering going into business as a newsagent, having currently an opportunity to buy such a business for £10,000, comprising leasehold premises £7,250, shop fittings £1,250 and stock £1,500. Alec can provide £6,000 from his own funds—by realizing his deposit account with a Building Society which is currently paying interest of 8½ per cent per annum; the balance of the money will be borrowed from a loan company, paying interest at 12 per cent per year. He will use his own estate car exclusively in the business and he values this at £800. He will work full time in the business—giving up his own clerical job at a salary of £3,000. After examining the past records of the business Alec estimates his likely profit for the year as follows:

	£	£
Sales		25,600
Cost of goods sold		19,200
		6,400
Other expenses		
Assistant's wages	1,000	
Ground rent	100	
Electricity	150	
Rates	750	
Car—depreciation	170	
—running expenses	350	
Loan interest	480	
Miscellaneous	200	
		3,200
		3,200

Required:
Assuming that the estimates are realistic, advise Alec whether he should take the business.

(*b*) Alec decides to buy the business, and at the end of his first year of trading he presents you with the following summary:

1. Cash sales £23,950: debtors outstanding £1,050
2. Cash purchases £17,260: creditors for purchases outstanding £1,940 closing stock £700
3. Assistant's wages (part-time only) £470: wages owing £30
4. Rates paid £700: rates paid in advance £50
5. Car running expenses £250
6. Other expenses—as predicted.

Required:
Prepare a Trading, Profit and Loss Account for the period and comment upon the significant differences between this statement and the estimates prepared in (*a*) above.
(Ignore Taxation.)
(Association of Certified Accountants)

19

Receipts and Payments Accounts and Income and Expenditure Accounts

Clubs, associations and other non-profit making organizations do not have trading and profit and loss accounts drawn up for them, as their principal function is not trading or profit making. They are run to further the promotion of an activity or group of activities, such as playing cricket or chess, or engaging in drama productions. The kind of final accounts prepared by these organizations are either Receipts and Payments Accounts or Income and Expenditure Accounts.

Receipts and payments accounts are merely a summary of the cash book for the period. Exhibit 19–1 is an example.

Exhibit 19.1

The Homers Running Club
Receipts and Payments Account for the year ended 31 December 19–5

Receipts	£	*Payments*	£
Bank Balance 1.1.19–5	236	Groundsman's wages	728
Subscriptions received for 19–5	1,148	Upkeep of sports stadium	296
Rent from sub-letting ground	116	Committee expenses	58
		Printing and stationery	33
		Bank Balance 31.12.19–5	385
	1,500		1,500

However, when the organization owns assets and has liabilities, the receipts and payments account is an unsatisfactory way of drawing up accounts as it merely shows the cash position. What is required is a balance sheet, and an account showing whether or not the association's capital is being increased. In a commercial firm the latter information would be obtained from a profit and loss account. In a non-profit-making organization it is calculated in an account called the income and expenditure account. In fact the income and expenditure account follows all the basic rules of profit and loss accounts. Thus expenditure consists of those costs consumed during the period and income is the revenue earned in the period. Where income exceeds expenditure the difference is called 'Surplus of Income over Expenditure'. Where expenditure exceeds income the difference is called 'Excess of Expenditure over Income'.

There is, however, one qualification to the fact that normally such an organization would not have a trading or profit and loss account. This is where the organization has carried out an activity deliberately so as to make a profit to help finance the main activities. Running a bar so as to make a profit would be an example of this, or having dances or whist drives. For this profit-aimed activity a trading or profit and loss account may be drawn up, the profit or loss being transferred to the income and expenditure account.

If the books had been kept on a double entry basis, the income and expenditure account and balance sheet would be prepared in the same manner as the profit and loss account and the balance sheet of a commercial firm, only the titles of the accounts and terms like 'surplus' or 'excess' being different. It is perhaps more usual to find that the records have been kept in a single entry form. In this case the starting point is that as described in the last chapter, namely the drafting of an opening statement of affairs followed by a Cash Book Summary. If a receipts and payments account exists then this is in fact a cash book summary. The preparation of the income and expenditure account and the balance sheet then follows the normal single entry fashion. Exhibit 19–2 shows the preparation on such a basis.

Exhibit 19.2

Receipts and Payments Account for the year ended 31 December 19–6

Receipts		*Payments*	
	£		£
Bank Balance 1.1.19–6	524	Payment for bar supplies	3,962
Subscriptions received for:		Wages:	
19–5 (arrears)	55	Groundsman and assistant	939
19–6	1,236	Barman	624
19–7 (in advance)	40	Bar Expenses	234
Bar Sales	5,628	Repairs to pavilion	119
Donations Received	120	Ground upkeep	229
		Secretary's expenses	138
		Coach Hire	305
		Bank Balance 31.12.19–6	1,053
	7,603		7,603

The treasurer of the Lower Moultings Cricket Club has prepared a receipts and payments account, but members have complained about the inadequacy of such an account. He therefore asks an accountant to prepare a trading account for the bar, and an income and expenditure account and a balance sheet. The treasurer gives the accountant a copy of the receipts and payments account together with information of assets and liabilities at the beginning and end of the year:

Notes:

1.

	31.12.19–5	*31.12.19–6*
	£	£
Stocks in the bar—at cost	496	558
Owing for bar supplies	294	340
Bar expenses owing	25	36
Coach hire owing	—	65

2. The land and pavilion was valued at 31 December 19–5 at: land £4,000; pavilion £2,000: the pavilion is to be depreciated by 10 per cent per annum.
3. The equipment at 31 December 19–5 was valued at £550, and is to be depreciated at 20 per cent per annum.
4. Subscriptions owing by members amounted to £55 on 31 December 19–5, and £66 on 31 December 19–6.

From this information the accountant drew up the accounts and statements that follow.

Working of purchases and bar expenses figures:

Purchases Control

	£		£
Cash	3,962	Balances (creditors) b/f	294
Balances c/d	340	Trading Account (difference)	4,008
	4,302		4,302

Statement of Affairs as at 31 December 19–5

	£	£		£	£
Capital (difference)		7,306	*Fixed Assets*		
			Land		4,000
			Pavilion		2,000
Current Liabilities			Equipment		550
Creditors	294				
Bar expenses owing	25				6,550
		319			
			Current Assets		
			Stock in the bar	496	
			Debtors for subscriptions	55	
			Cash at bank	524	
					1,075
		7,625			7,625

The Lower Moultings Cricket Club

Bar Trading Account for the year ended 31 December 19–6

	£		£
Stock 1.1.19–6	496	Sales	5,628
Add Purchases	4,008		
	4,504		
Less Stock 31.12.19–6	558		
Cost of goods sold	3,946		
Gross Profit	1,682		
	5,628		5,628
Bar Expenses	245	Gross Profit b/d	1,682
Barman wages	624		
Net Profit to Income and Expenditure Account	813		
	1,682		1,682

Bar Expenses

	£		£
Cash	234	Balance b/f	25
Balance c/d	36	Trading Account (difference)	245
	270		270

The Lower Moultings Cricket Club

Income and Expenditure Account for the year ended 31 December 19–6

Expenditure	£	£	*Income*	£
Wages-Groundsman and assistant		939	Profit from the bar	813
			Subscriptions for 19–6	1,302
Repairs to pavilion		119	Donations received	120
Ground upkeep		229		
Secretary's expenses		138		
Coach hire		370		
Depreciation:				
Pavilion	200			
Equipment	110			
		310		
Surplus of income over expenditure		130		
		2,235		2,235

Workings on coach hire and subscriptions received figures:

Coach Hire

	£		£
Cash	305	Income and Expenditure	
Accrued c/d	65	Account	370
	370		370

Subscriptions Received

	£		£
Balance (debtors) b/f	55	Cash 19–5	55
Income and Expenditure		19–6	1,236
Account (difference)	1,302	19–7	40
Balance (in advance) c/d	40	Balance (owing) c/d	66
	1,397		1,397

It will be noted that subscriptions received in advance are carried down as a credit balance to the following period.

The Lower Moultings Cricket Club
Balance Sheet as at 31 December 19–6

Capital Account	£	£	*Fixed Assets*	£	£
Balance at 1.1.19–6	7,306		Land at valuation		4,000
Add Surplus of Income			Pavilion at valuation	2,000	
over Expenditure	130		*Less* Depreciation	200	
		7,436			1,800
			Equipment at		
			valuation	550	
			Less Depreciation	110	
					440
					6,240
Current Liabilities			*Current Assets*		
Creditors for bar			Stock of bar supplies	558	
Supplies	340		Debtors for		
Bar Expenses owing	36		Subscriptions	66	
Coach hire owing	65		Cash at bank	1,053	
Subscriptions received					1,677
in advance	40				
		481			
		7,917			7,917

Life Membership

In some clubs and societies members can make a payment for life membership. This means that by paying a fairly substantial amount now the member can enjoy the facilities of the club for the rest of his life.

Such a receipt should not be treated as Income in the Income and Expenditure Account solely in the year in which the member paid the money. It should be credited to a Life Membership Account, and transfers should be made from that account to the credit of the Income and Expenditure Account of an appropriate amount annually.

Exactly what is meant by an appropriate amount is decided by the committee of the club or society. The usual basis is to establish, on average, how long members will continue to use the benefits of the club. To take an extreme case, if a club was in existence which could not be joined until one achieved the age of 70, then the expected number of years' use of the club on average per member would be relatively few. Another club, such as a golf club, where a fair proportion of the members joined when reasonably young, and where the game is capable of being played by members until and during old age, would expect a much higher average of years of use per member. The simple matter is that the club should decide for itself.

In an examination the candidate has to follow the instructions set for him by the examiner. The credit balance remaining on the account, after the transfer of the agreed amount has been made to the credit of the Income and Expenditure Account, should be shown on the Balance Sheet as a liability. It is, after all, the liability of the club to provide amenities for the member without any further payment by him.

Outstanding Subscriptions and the Convention of Conservatism

The treatment of subscriptions owing has so far followed the normal procedures as applied to debtors in a commercial firm. However, as most treasurers of associations are fully aware, many members who owe subscriptions leave the association and never pay the amounts owing. This is far more prevalent than with debtors of a commercial firm. It can perhaps be partly explained by the fact that a commercial firm would normally sue for unpaid debts, whereas associations rarely sue for unpaid subscriptions. To bring in unpaid subscriptions as assets therefore contravenes the convention of conservatism which tends to understate assets rather than overstate them. With many clubs therefore, unpaid subscriptions are ignored in the income and expenditure account and balance sheet. If they are eventually paid they are then brought in as income in the year of receipt irrespective of the period covered by the subscriptions.

In examinations, the student should bring debtors for subscriptions into account unless he is given instructions to the contrary.

Exercises

19.1. A summary of the cash book of the Hydefield Social Club is shown below. From this construct an income and expenditure account for the year ended 31 December 19–4 and a balance sheet as at that date.

Cash Book Summary

	£		£
Balance 1.1.19–4	70	Prizes	22
Subscriptions	240	Games equipment	20
Profit on dances	148	Rent	105
Collections at football matches	25	Rates	30
Competition fees	18	Printing	16
Sales of refreshments	82	Stationery	22
		Postages	19
		Secretaries expenses	14
		Repairs to equipment	27
		Wages	120
		Refreshments	51
		Balance	137
	583		583

The rent was paid in advance £12. £4 is owing for printing.
(Union of Educational Institutions)

19.2. From the following details and the notes attached relating to the Westshire Tennis Club, prepare the final accounts of the club for the year ended 31 December 19–3.

On 1 January 19–3 the club's assets were:
Freehold club house £1,000
Equipment £70
Club subscriptions in arrear £8
Cash in Hand and balance at bank £76
The club owed £40 to Caterer's Ltd, for Christmas 19–2 dance catering.

Summary of Receipts and Payments for 19–4

Receipts	£	*Payments*	£
Subscriptions	164	Catering—19–2 dance (Caterer's Ltd)	40
Locker Rents	10		
Receipts from dances and social	139	19–3 dances and socials	95
Sale of used match tennis balls	15	Band Fees—19–3 dances	25
Sale of old lawn mower	8	New lawn mower	53
		Repairs to tennis nets	19
		Match tennis balls	31
		Match Expenses	17
		Repair and decoration of club house	65

Notes

(i) The book value on 1 January 19–3 of the old lawn mower sold during year was £3.
(ii) The club has 40 members and the subscription is £4 per annum. The subscriptions received in 19–3 included those in arrear for 19–2.
(iii) On 31 December 19–3 £11 was owed to Playfair Ltd for tennis balls supplied.
(iv) Equipment as at 31 December 19–3 is to be depreciated by 15 per cent per annum.
(v) Tennis balls are regarded as revenue expenditure.

(University of London 'O' Level)

19.3. The following were the assets and liabilities of the Newhaven Sports Club on 31 December 19–2:

	£
Assets	
Premises (at cost)	3,000
Furniture, etc., valued at	460
Investments—5 per cent Government Stock (at cost)	500
Sports equipment valued at	190
Stock of refreshments	38
Cash and bank balance	42
Liabilities	
Subscriptions for 19–3 received in advance	20
One quarter's rent of land	18
Creditor—Refreshments supplied	32

The Treasurer's cash book for the year to 31 December 19–3 shows:

Receipts	£	*Payments*	£
Balance in hand b/fwd	42	Rent of land	90
Subscriptions for 19–3	540	Wages	325
,, ,, 19–4	22	Purchase of sports equipment	140
Sale of refreshments	380	Dance Expenses	96
Sale of dance tickets	149	Refreshment supplies	194
Investment interest	25	Secretary's expenses	59
		Investment—5 per cent Goverment Stock	200
		Balance in hand c/fwd	54
	1,158		1,158

You are required to prepare the club's income and expenditure account for the year ended 31 December 19–3 and balance sheet on that date, after taking into account the following points:

1. There were no stocks of refreshments at 31 December 19–3.
2. Wages of £15 were due but unpaid at the year end.
3. Provide for depreciation of furniture, etc.—£60.
4. The sports equipment was valued at £300 on 31 December 19–3.
5. The purchase of investments this year was made on 31 December 19–3.

(Union of Lancashire and Cheshire Institutes)

19.4. The accounts of a social club are made up annually as at 31 December.

At 31 December 19–3 subscriptions in arrear amounted to £87 and subscriptions received in advance for the year 19–4 amounted to £71.

During 19–4 £1,214 was received in respect of subscriptions, including £87 arrears for 19–3, and £108 in advance for 19–5. At 31 December 19–4 subscriptions in arrear amounted to £53.

The annual income and expenditure account is credited with all subscriptions in respect of the year to which the account relates, on the assumption that all arrears will be subsequently collected.

You are required to set out the subscriptions account for the year 19–4, making therein the appropriate adjustments for subscriptions in arrear and for subscriptions in advance at the beginning and at the end of the year.
(Chartered Institute of Secretaries and Administrators)

19.5. The following is a summary of the Cash Book of the Near Country Club:

Receipts	£	*Payments*	£
Balance at bank 1 April 19–3	237	Staff wages	669
Members' subscriptions	1,786	Bar supplies	2,520
Entrance fees	160	Rent for 1½ years to 30.6.19–4	390
Bar takings	2,840	Rates	110
Competition receipts	382	Secretary's salary	156
Loan from treasurer	4	Lighting, heating and cleaning	385
		Competition prizes	185
		Printing, postages and sundries	300
		Deposited with Building Society	400
		Balance at bank 31 March 19–4	294
	5,409		5,409

The assets of the club on 1 April 19–3 were furniture and equipment £2,400, bar stocks £130, and prizes in hand £40: £260 was owing for bar supplies.

On 31 March 19–4 the bar stocks were £150, prizes £25 and £280 was owing for bar supplies.

It appeared from the register of members that subscriptions unpaid at 31 March 19–4 totalled £50. Subscriptions received during the year under review included £35 in respect of the previous year and £20 in respect of the year beginning 1 April 19–4.

The secretary is to be allowed £25 per annum for the use of his own motor car in connection with the club's affairs.

Interest on the building society deposit for the year to 31 March 19–4 was received on 1 April 19–4, amounting to £12.

It was agreed that the steward of the club should receive a bonus of 5 per cent of bar takings in excess of an average of £200 per month for the year to 31 March 19–4.

Write off depreciation on furniture and equipment at 10 per cent per annum.

Prepare an account showing the profit on the bar, an income and expenditure account for the year and a balance sheet as at 31 March 19–4.
(Association of Certified Accountants)

19.6A. The Alpha Social Club was formed on 20 October 19–8. The treasurer kept the accounts by double entry, and extracted the following trial balance on 19 October 19–9:

	£	£
Sundry creditors (for refreshments)		59
Members' subscriptions		336
Equipment	118	
Rent and rates	192	
Postage and stationery	59	
Dance expenses	73	
Sale of tickets for dances		119
Refreshments purchased	542	
Sale of refreshments		633
Sundry receipts (charges for games, etc.)		114
Lighting and heating	95	
Miscellaneous expenses	31	
Cash at bank	126	
Cash in hand	25	
	1,261	1,261

The treasurer asks you to check the entries in his books before the preparation of the annual accounts for the members. You obtain the following information:

1. Local firms gave the club £280 worth of equipment during the year, but no entry was made in the club's books.

2. In November 19–8, the treasurer had paid a club bill, for refreshments purchased, with a cheque for £11 drawn on his personal bank account. He made no entry in the club's books for the bill or for the payment and has forgotten to reimburse himself for this payment.

3. Entries in the Subscriptions Account include £16 paid by some members for their 19–9/19–0 subscriptions.

4. When the trial balance was extracted, no entry had been made in the books for certain amounts owing by the club: rent and rates £16, miscellaneous expenses £5, lighting and heating £24.

5. Allowance is to be made for depreciation of equipment, £30.

6. Stock of refreshments at 19 October 19–9 is valued at £15.

Prepare the club's Income and Expenditure Account for the year to 19 October 19–9 and Balance Sheet as at 19 October 19–9.
(Oxford Local Examinations—'O' Level)

19.7A. The Spear Throwers' Association was established in the United Kingdom by a group of Spear Throwers' Clubs to organize international matches. Its revenue is derived from:

1. international games and

2. subscriptions from member clubs.

International games are organized by the home country. The visiting country is entitled to reimbursement for approved expenses and to one third of the net gate.

The assets of the U.K. Association at 31 December 19–7 were:

	£
Debtors	
Clubs for subscriptions	25
Reimbursement of expenses for away matches	865
Furniture and equipment	2,000
Building	15,000
Investments in government securities	8,266
Bank balance	729

There was an unsettled claim from visiting countries for 19–7 travelling expenses amounting to £662.

The total bank account of the U.K. Association for 19–8 was as follows:

	£		£
Balance 1 January 19–8	729	Reimbursement of visiting counties for travel claims—	
Subscriptions from clubs—			
19–7	25	19–7	611
19–8	2,450	19–8	5,927
		General expenses of 19–8 home matches	3,461
Reimbursement of travelling expenses—		Cost of travel to 19–8 away matches	2,684
19–7	832		
19–8	2,179		
		Payments on account of 19–8 gates to away counties	1,400
Interest received	426		
Gates at home matches	14,268	Administration expenses	3,163
		Purchase of government securities	3,000
		Balance 31 December 19–8	663
	20,909		20,909

Debts due from clubs for subscriptions amounted to £50 on 31 December 19–8; at the same date claims by away teams for 19–8 travelling expenses reimbursement, amounting to £542, were received.

Furniture and equipment is to be charged with depreciation for the year at 15 per cent of the opening balance.

Claims by or against the Association outstanding at the end of each year in respect of that year are to be carried forward on the basis of the amount claimed. Adjustments that may be subsequently agreed to the amounts so carried forward are written off in the general income account of the following year.

Required:

(*a*) a balance sheet of the Spear Throwers' Association at 31 December 19–7;
(*b*) a games account for 19–8 calculating the net gate;
(*c*) a general income account for 19–8; and

(*d*) a balance sheet at 31 December 19–8.
Note: Ignore taxation.
(Institute of Bankers)

19.8A. The treasurer of the Walkover Cricket Club has prepared the following Receipts and Payments Account for the year ended 31 December 19–8:

Receipts		£	*Payments*		£
19–8			19–8		
Jan 1	Cash in hand	7	Dec 31	Groundsman's wages (including P.A.Y.E. National Insurance etc.)	641
	Balances at bank:			Rent of ground	100
	Current Account	159		Repairs to pavilion	69
	Deposit Account	617		Cricket equipment	34
19–8				New mower (*less* proceeds of sale of old mower £45)	155
Dec 31	Members' subscriptions	453		Bar purchases	1,524
	Bar takings	1,828		Secretarial expenses	47
	Surplus on dances	193		Insurance	48
	Bank Deposit Account interest	28		Cash in hand	15
	Donation	10		Balances at bank:	
				Current Account	111
				Deposit Account	551
		3,295			3,295

You are given the following additional information:

1. As on 31 December 19–7, the book values of the fixed assets were Pavilion £1,450 (cost £3,200) and Mower £15 (cost £135).

2. The other current assets and liabilities were as follows:

	On 31 December 19–7	*On 31 December 19–8*
	£	£
Value of bar stock at cost	131	110
Subscriptions due but not received	57	43
Creditors for bar purchases	40	33
Creditors for secretarial expenses	15	17
Insurance paid in advance	12	8
P.A.Y.E. payable to Inland Revenue	5	6

3. £150 is to be provided for depreciation of the pavilion for the year but no depreciation is to be provided on the new mower. Expenditure on cricket equipment is to be written off in the year in which it is incurred.

You are required to prepare:

(*a*) a statement showing the Accumulated Fund of the Club as on 31 December 19–7.

(*b*) the Income and Expenditure Account for the year ended 31 December 19 8 (showing separately the excess of bar sales over their cost), and
(*c*) the Balance Sheet as on 31 December 19–8.
(Institute of Chartered Accountants)

19.9A. The Happy Days Sports and Social Club consisted of two classes of members:

Social members—subscription £2 per annum.
Sporting members—subscription £3 per annum.
The Balance Sheet at 1 June 19–7, was as under:

		£	£			£	£
Accumulated Fund:				Sports equipment at cost		750	
Social section		2,400		*Less*: Depreciation to date		350	
Sports section		800					
			3,200				400
				Bar stocks		1,235	
Creditors:	£			Prepayment:	£		
Wines and spirits	310			Rent	100		
Artistes' fees	50			Rates	125		
		360				225	
Accruals—Light and heat		36		Bank balance		1,655	
Subscriptions in advance (including three Sports members)		19		Subscriptions in arrear (including twenty Sports members)		100	
			415				3,215
			3,615				3,615

The club was divided for accounts purposes into four sections: (*a*) Bar; (*b*) Entertainments; (*c*) Sports; (*d*) Social. Any profits or losses on the Bar and Entertainments were credited to or borne by the Social section. All members contribute towards the Social section, the additional portion of the Sports members' subscriptions being credited to the Sports section.

Each section is charged and credited with items relating to itself specifically, all general expenses being borne by the Social section.

A summary of the bank account shows the following:

	£		£
Bank balance 1.6.–7	1,655	Rent	350
Bar receipts	13,805	Rates	275
Entertainment Receipts	5,375	Heat and light	141
Subscriptions:		Telephone	56
Social members	1,196	Bar purchases	11,795
Sports members	1,311	Artistes' fees	4,805
Fees from Sports members for fixtures, table charges, etc.	275	Prizes at dances, shows, etc.	415
		Bar steward's wages	1,575
		Printing, entertainment	

	£		£
		programmes, tickets, etc.	390
		New sports equipment	400
		Repairs to sports equipment	75
		Repairs to property	34
		Club secretary's fee	1,200
		Sports section laundry	225
		Sports associations' subscriptions	115
		Printing and stationery	36
		Bank balance 31.5.–8	1,730
	23,617		23,617

You ascertain the following additional information:

1. Depreciation on sports equipment is charged at 25 per cent on reducing balance, a full year's charge being made in year of acquisition.

2. There are five Sports and five Social members' subscriptions in advance at 31 May 19–8.

3. There are ten Sports and fifteen Social members' subscriptions in arrears at 31 May 19–8.

4. Prepayments at 31 May 19–8: Rent £50; Rates £150.

5. Stocks in Bar 31 May 19–8, £1,315.

6. Creditors 31 May 19–8: Bar £75; Artistes' fees £20.

7. Light and Heat accrued charge 31 May 19–8, £30.

You are required to prepare in respect of the year ended 31 May 19–8:

(*a*) Bar Account.
(*b*) Entertainments Account.
(*c*) Sports Section Account.
(*d*) Social Section Account.
(*e*) Balance Sheet at 31 May 19–8.

20

Manufacturing Accounts

The final accounts prepared so far have all been for firms whose function is limited to that of merchandising, i.e. the buying and selling of goods. Obviously there are many firms whose main activity is in the manufacture of goods for sale. For these firms a Manufacturing Account is prepared in addition to the trading and profit and loss accounts.

Because the costs in the manufacturing account are involved with production there is an obvious link with the costing records, and the concepts of the manufacturing account are in fact really costing concepts. It will therefore be necessary to first of all examine the main elements and division of cost as used in costing. These may be summarized in chart form as follows:

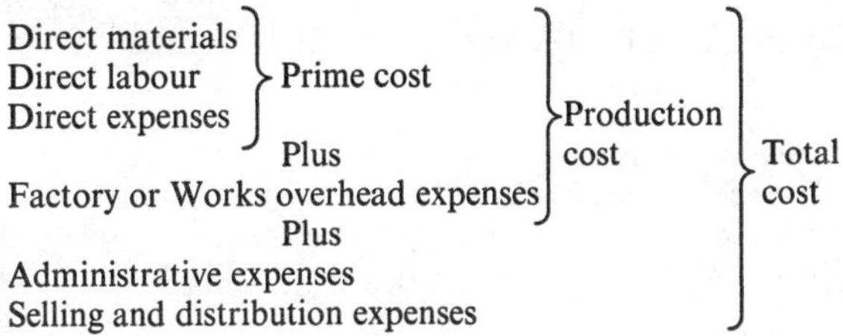

By 'direct' is meant that the materials, labour and expenses involved are traceable to the particular unit of goods being made, and that the trouble and labour involved in doing this are worthwhile. Labour such as that of a lathe operator will be direct labour, whereas that of a foreman who supervises many jobs cannot be easily traced down to each particular unit being produced and will accordingly be classified as indirect labour, forming part of the factory overhead expenses. The cost of direct materials will include the cost of carriage inwards on raw materials. Examples of direct expenses are the hire of special plant for a particular job, and royalties payable to inventors for use of a patent where a charge is levied on each unit produced.

Factory overhead expenses consist of all those expenses which occur in the factory where production is carried on, but which cannot easily be traced to the units being manufactured. Examples are wages of cleaners and crane drivers, rent and rates of the factory, depreciation of plant and machinery used in the factory, running of fork-lift trucks, factory power and lighting and heating.

Administration expenses consist of such items as managers' salaries, legal and accountancy charges, the depreciation of accounting machinery and secretarial salaries.

Selling and distribution expenses are items such as salesmen's salaries and commission, carriage outwards, depreciation of delivery vans, advertising and display expenses.

In the manufacturing account the production cost of goods completed during the accounting period is ascertained. This means that all the elements of Production cost, i.e. direct materials, direct labour, direct expenses and factory overhead expenses, are charged to the manufacturing account. All administration and selling and distribution expenses are charged to the profit and loss account. Note that the manufacturing account is concerned with the production cost of goods completed in the year irrespective of when work started on them. For this reason goods partly finished, known as work in progress, must be taken into account.

The necessary details required to draw up a manufacturing account can now be looked at. In the first example, Exhibit 20–1, it has been assumed that there was no work in progress, either at the beginning or end of the accounting period.

Exhibit 20.1

Details of production cost for the year ended 31 December 19–7:

	£
1 January 19–7, stock of raw materials	500
31 December 19–7, stock of raw materials	700
Raw materials purchased	8,000
Manufacturing (direct) wages	21,000
Royalties	150
Indirect wages	9,000
Rent of factory—excluding administration and selling and distribution blocks	320
Rates of factory	120
Depreciation of plant and machinery in factory	400
General indirect expenses	310

The production cost of goods completed, when ascertained, is carried down to the trading account, taking the place where normally purchases are shown. As this is a manufacturing concern selling its own products there will not usually be a figure for the purchase of finished goods. Sometimes, however, if a firm has produced less than the customers have demanded, then the firm may well have bought an outside supply of finished goods. In this case, the trading account will have both a figure for purchases and for production cost of goods completed

Manufacturing Account for the year ended 31 December 19–7

		£		£
Stock of			Production Cost of Goods	
Raw Materials 1.1.19–7		500	Completed c/d	39,100
Add Purchases		8,000		
		8,500		
Less Stock of				
Raw Materials 31.12.19–7		700		
Cost of Raw Materials				
Consumed		7,800		
Manufacturing Wages		21,000		
Royalties		150		
Prime Cost		28,950		
Factory Overhead Expenses	£			
Rent	320			
Rates	120			
Indirect Wages	9,000			
Depreciation	400			
General Expenses	310			
		10,150		
		39,100		39,100

When there is work in progress, i.e. goods only part completed at the beginning and end of an accounting period an adjustment is needed. To find the production cost of goods completed in the period the value of work in progress at the beginning must be brought into account as it will be work (provided it is not a job such as building a ship which will take more than a year) which is completed within the accounting period. On the other hand, work in progress at the end of the period must be carried forward to the next period, as it is completed within the next period. To do this, the value of work in progress at the beginning is added to the total production cost for the period, and the closing work in progress is deducted. An example is shown in Exhibit 20–2.

Exhibit 20.2

	£
1 January 19–7, Stock of raw materials	800
31 December 19–7, Stock of raw materials	1,050
1 January 19–7, Work in progress	350
31 December 19–7, Work in progress	420
Year to 31 December 19–7:	
Wages: Direct	3,960
Indirect	2,550

	£
Purchase of raw materials	8,700
Fuel and power	990
Direct expenses	140
Lubricants	300
Carriage inwards on raw materials	200
Rent and rates of factory	720
Depreciation of factory plant and machinery	420
Internal transport expenses	180
Insurance of factory buildings and plant	150
General factory expenses	330

Manufacturing Account for the year ended 31 December 19–7

		£		£
Stock of raw materials 1.1.19–7		800	Production cost of goods	
Add Purchases		8,700	Completed c/d	18,320
„ Carriage inwards		200		
		9,700		
Less Stock raw materials 31.12.19–7		1,050		
Cost of raw materials consumed		8,650		
Direct wages		3,960		
Direct expenses		140		
Prime cost		12,750		
Factory Overhead Expenses		£		
Fuel and power	990			
Indirect wages	2,550			
Lubricants	300			
Rent and rates	720			
Depreciation of plant	420			
Internal transport Expenses	180			
Insurance	150			
General factory expenses	330			
		5,640		
		18,390		
Add Work in progress 1.1.19–7		350		
		18,740		
Less Work in progress 31.12.19–7		420		
		18,320		18,320

The trading account is concerned with finished goods. If in the foregoing exhibit there had been £3,500 stock of finished goods at 1 January 19–7 and £4,400 at 31 December 19–7, and the sales of finished goods amounted to £25,000, then the trading account would appear:

Trading Account for the year 31 December 19–7

	£		£
Stock of Finished Goods 1.1.19–7	3,500	Sales	25,000
Add Production cost of goods completed b/d	18,320		
	21,820		
Less Stock of finished goods 31.12.19–7	4,400		
	17,420		
Gross profit c/d	7,580		
	25,000		25,000

The profit and loss account is then constructed in the normal way.

A complete worked example is now given. Note that in the profit and loss account the expenses have been separated so as to show whether they are administration expenses, selling and distribution expenses, or financial charges.

The trial balance overleaf has been extracted from the books of James Nelstrop, Toy Manufacturer, as on 31 December 19–7:

Notes at 31.12.19–7:

1. Stock of raw materials £2,400, stock of finished goods £4,000, work in progress £1,500.

2. Lighting and heating and rent, rates and insurance are to be apportioned: factory 5/6ths, administration 1/6th.

3. Depreciation on productive and accounting machinery at 10 per cent per annum on cost.

	Dr	Cr
	£	£
Stock of raw materials 1.1.19–7	2,100	
Stock of finished goods 1.1.19–7	3,890	
Work in progress 1.1.19–7	1,350	
Wages (direct £18,000; Factory indirect £14,500)	32,500	
Royalties	700	
Carriage inwards (on raw materials)	350	
Purchases of raw materials	37,000	
Productive machinery (cost £28,000)	23,000	
Accounting machinery (cost £2,000)	1,200	
General factory expenses	3,100	
Lighting and heating	750	
Factory power	1,370	
Administrative salaries	4,400	
Salesmen's salaries	3,000	
Commission on sales	1,150	
Rent and rates	1,200	
Insurance	420	
General administration expenses	1,340	
Bank charges	230	
Discounts allowed	480	
Carriage outwards	590	
Sales		100,000
Debtors and creditors	14,230	12,500
Bank	5,680	
Cash	150	
Drawings	2,000	
Capital as at 1.1.19–7		29,680
	142,180	142,180

James Nelstrop

Manufacturing, Trading and Profit and Loss Account for the year ended 31 December 19–7

	£	£		£
Stock of raw materials 1.1.19–7		2,100	Production cost of goods completed c/d	79,345
Add Purchases		37,000		
,, Carriage inwards		350		
		39,450		
Less Stock raw materials 31.12.19–7		2,400		

	£	£		£
Cost of raw materials consumed		37,050		
Direct labour		18,000		
Royalties		700		
Prime cost		55,750		
Factory Overhead Expenses				
General factory expenses	3,100			
Lighting and heating 5/6ths	625			
Power	1,370			
Rent and rates 5/6ths	1,000			
Insurance 5/6ths	350			
Depreciation of plant	2,800			
Indirect labour	14,500			
		23,745		
		79,495		
Add Work in progress 1.1.19–7		1,350		
		80,845		
Less Work in progress 31.12.19–7		1,500		
		79,345		79,345
		£		£
Stock of finished goods 1.1.19–7		3,890	Sales	100,000
Add Production cost of goods completed		79,345		
		83,235		
Less Stock of finished goods 31.12.19–7		4,000		
		79,235		
Gross profit c/d		20,765		
		100,000		100,000
Administration Expenses	£	£		£
Administrative salaries	4,400		Gross Profit b/d	20,765
Rent and rates 1/6th	200			
Insurance 1/6th	70			
General expenses	1,340			
Lighting and heating 1/6th	125			
Depreciation of accounting machinery	200			
		6,335		

	£	£		£
Selling and Distribution Expenses				
Salesmen's salaries	3,000			
Commission on sales	1,150			
Carriage outwards	590			
		4,740		
Financial Charges				
Bank charges	230			
Discounts allowed	480			
		710		
Net profit		8,980		
		20,765		20,765

J. Nelstrop

Balance Sheet as at 31 December 19–7

Capital	£	£	*Fixed Assets*	£	£
Balance as at 1.1.19–7	29,680		Productive machinery at cost	28,000	
Add Net profit	8,980		*Less* Depreciation to date	7,800	
	38,660				20,200
Less Drawings	2,000	36,660	Accounting machinery at cost	2,000	
Current Liabilities			*Less* Depreciation to date	1,000	1,000
Creditors		12,500			21,200
			Current Assets		
			Stocks:		
			Raw materials	2,400	
			Finished goods	4,000	
			Work in progress	1,500	
			Debtors	14,230	
			Bank	5,680	
			Cash	150	
					27,960
		49,160			49,160

Market Value of Goods Manufactured

The accounts of Nelstrop, just illustrated, are subject to the limitation that the respective amounts of the gross profit which are attributable to the manufacturing side or to the selling side of the firm are not known. A technique is sometimes used to bring out this additional information. By this method the cost which would have been involved if the goods had been bought in their finished state instead of being manufactured by the firm is brought into account. This is credited to the manufacturing account and debited to the trading account so as to throw up two figures of gross profit instead of one. It should be pointed out that the net profit will remain unaffected. All that will have happened will be that the figure of £20,765 gross profit will be shown as two figures instead of one.

The accounts, in summarized form will appear:

Manufacturing, Trading and Profit and Loss Account for the year ended 31 December 19–7

	£		£
Details as before		Market value of goods completed c/d	95,000
Production cost of goods completed	79,345		
Gross profit on manufacture c/d	15,655		
	95,000		95,000
Stock of finished goods 1.1.19–7	3,890	Sales	100,000
Add Market value of goods completed b/d	95,000		
	98,890		
Less Stock of finished goods 31.12.19–7	4,000		
	94,890		
Gross profit on trading c/d	5,110		
	100,000		100,000
		Gross Profit £	
		On manufacturing 15,655	
		On trading 5,110	20,765

Exercises

20.1. From the following ledger balances of AB Co prepare manufacturing, trading, and profit and loss accounts for the year ended 31 December 19–4.

Stocks at 1 January 19–4	£
Raw materials	6,300
Partly manufactured goods	8,000
Finished goods	6,000
Stocks at 31 December 19–4	
Raw materials	5,080
Partly manufactured goods	18,000
Finished goods	5,000
Other Balances	
Purchases of raw materials	22,000
Freight and carriage on raw materials	880
Productive wages	22,000
Rent, rates and taxes	1,000
Gas, fuel, water, light	1,800
Office salaries	2,300
Depreciation of productive machinery and plant	1,800
Sales	73,600

Rent and rates, and gas and fuel must be apportioned as to Factory $\frac{3}{4}$, Office $\frac{1}{4}$. If 100,000 articles are produced in one year, find the cost of producing one article.

Clearly indicate in answer prime cost.

(East Midland Educational Union)

20.2. The following figures, relating to the year 19–3, have been taken from the books of a manufacturing company:

	£
Stock of materials, 1 January, at cost	2,462
Materials purchased	31,318
Stock of materials, 31 December, at cost	3,015
Manufacturing wages	45,294
Sales	127,650
Factory expenses	12,347
Depreciation of plant and machinery	4,200
Depreciation of delivery vans	1,575
Factory power	2,825
Office and administration expenses	3,943
Advertising	500
Salesmen's salaries and expenses	5,035
Delivery van expenses	1,268

For purposes of the annual accounts, work in progress and stocks of finished goods are valued at factory cost. The work in progress (at factory cost) at 31 December 19–3, was £640 higher than at 31 December 19–2. The stock of finished goods (at factory cost) at 31 December 19–3, was £1,716 lower than at 31 December 19–2.

You are required to prepare a manufacturing and trading account and a profit and loss account for the year 19–3.

The accounts should show the factory cost of the goods completed during the year and the factory cost of the goods sold.

(Chartered Institute of Secretaries and Administrators)

20.3. C. Summers carries on business as a manufacturer and the trial balance extracted from his books on 31 March 19–4 is given below:

	£	£
Capital account		19,150
Drawings	1,600	
Light, heat, etc.: Office	138	
Factory	1,445	
Bank loan		5,600
Manufacturing wages	9,918	
Office salaries	2,116	
Advertising	856	
Stocks, 1 April 19–3: Raw materials	7,102	
Finished goods	7,278	
Trade Creditors		7,733
Sundry expenses: Office	399	
Factory	530	
Purchases—Raw materials	49,944	
Commission to salesmen	880	
Premises (at cost)	4,050	
Plant (cost £10,000)	7,500	
Sales of finished goods		71,580
Trade debtors	7,575	
Cash and bank	2,013	
Office machinery (cost £1,000)	500	
Rent, rates, etc.: Office	69	
Factory	150	
	104,063	104,063

You are required to prepare the manufacturing, trading and profit and loss accounts for the year ended 31 March 19–4, and balance sheet as on that date after giving effect to the following adjustments:

1. A provision for bad and doubtful debts equal to 4 per cent of trade debtors is to be made.

2. The stocks at 31 March 19–4, were valued at:
   Raw materials £7,064
   Finished goods £7,448.

3. Depreciation is to be provided on plant—5 per cent of cost and office machinery is valued at £400 on 31 March 19–4.

4. Wages due but unpaid at 31 March 19–4 amounted to £136 and advertising prepaid for the next year amounted to £48.

(Union of Lancashire and Cheshire Institutes)

20.4A. The following schedule of balances was extracted from the accounting records of STR Manufacturing Limited, as at 31 August 19–5:

	£
Stocks at 1 September 19–4:	
Raw materials	13,550
Work in progress	6,500
Finished goods	12,800
Purchases and Expenses for year to 31 August 19–5:	
Raw materials	237,650

	£
Indirect materials	1,850
Direct wages	53,230
Factory power	4,550
Factory heating and lighting	1,975
Office " " "	930
Printing and stationery	1,264
Postage and telephone	520
Factory salaries	11,500
Office salaries	9,900
Factory insurances	1,210
Other insurances	450
Depreciation: Factory equipment and machinery	5,000
Office " " "	650
Office expenses	1,680
Advertising	850
Sales of manufactured products to 31 August 19–5	378,150

The following additional information is relevant to the above accounting period:

(i) Finished goods manufactured during the accounting period are transferred from the factory at a manufacturing price of cost of production plus 10 per cent.

(ii) Stocks at 31 August 19–5:	£
Raw materials	24,000
Work in progress	7,987
Finished goods	18,050
(iii) Prepayments at 31 August 19–5:	
Factory insurances	116
Other insurances	45
(iv) Accruals at 31 August 19–5:	
Direct wages	1,342
Factory heating and lighting	197
Office " " "	43
Factory power	350

Required: for the year ending 31 August 19–5:
(*a*) Manufacturing account
(*b*) Trading account, and
(*c*) Profit and loss account.
(Chartered Institute of Secretaries and Administrators)

20.5A. The following accounts have been prepared by an inexperienced book-keeper. You are asked to redraft them in a more suitable form making any adjustments you think necessary.

Accounts for the year ended 31 December 19–0.
Manufacturing account:

	£		£
Stock at start:			
Raw materials	5,980	Stock at end	
Finished goods	6,250	Raw materials	7,532
Less loose tools at end	540	Finished goods	5,360

Accounts for the year ended 31 December 19–0.
Manufacturing account:

	£		£
	11,690		12,892
Purchases: Finished goods	13,540	*Less* loose tools at start	560
Raw materials	22,770		
Carriage outwards	940		12,332
Depreciation—Delivery vans	250	Discount received	424
	49,190	Trading Account	36,434

Trading account:

Manufacturing account	36,434	Sales	91,260
Productive wages	14,500	Work in progress	
General expenses (factory)	14,000	31 December 19–9	1,160
Carriage on raw materials	1,220		
Sales office salaries	3,740		
Travellers' commission	600		
Depreciation—Machinery	530		
Work in progress			
31 December 19–0	1,010		
Profit and Loss Account	20,386		
	92,420		92,420

Profit and Loss Account:

		£		£
Salaries: Manufacturing		2,500	Trading Account	20,386
Administration		4,000	Commission payable	
Legal charges		126	outstanding due to	
Audit fee		104	travellers	700
Advertising	1,500			
Add amount prepaid carried forward to next year	500			
		2,000		
Capital Account		12,356		
		21,086		21,086

Your accounts should show:

(*a*) Prime cost.
(*b*) Factory cost.
(*c*) Cost of sales.
(*d*) Gross profit.
(*e*) Net profit.

20.6A. Rock was the sole proprietor of a sweet manufacturing business and the following trial balance was extracted from his books as on 31 December 19–7: December 19–7:

	Dr. £	*Cr.* £
Capital Account: Rock		20,400
Freehold land and buildings at cost	15,000	
Plant and machinery at cost	14,500	
,, ,, provision for depreciation		7,000
Travellers' cars at cost	4,000	
,, ,, provision for depreciation		2,800
Loose tools and utensils at valuation on 1 January 19–7	1,200	
Stocks, 1 January 19–7: Raw materials	3,300	
Finished goods (25 tons)	6,000	
Purchases: Raw materials	18,500	
Tools and utensils	800	
Sales 210 tons		66,000
Wages: Factory	13,640	
Administration	5,400	
Sales department	3,000	
Rates and insurance	1,600	
Repairs to buildings	1,000	
Sales expenses including vehicle running costs	1,440	
Electricity and power	6,000	
Administration expenses	2,810	
Provision for doubtful debts		1,000
Sales Ledger balances	6,100	
Purchase Ledger balances		3,580
Bank		3,610
Cash in hand	100	
	104,390	104,390

You are given the following information:

1. Closing stocks on 31 December 19–7: Raw materials £2,800; Finished goods (15 tons) £3,900; Loose tools and utensils £1,600.

2. Provision is to be made for the following amounts owing on 31 December 19–7: Electricity and power £800; New machinery £500.

3. Payments in advance on 31 December 19–7, were as follows: Rates £300: Vehicle licences £40.

4. Annual depreciation on plant and machinery and travellers' cars is to be provided at the rate of 15 per cent and 20 per cent respectively on cost at the end of the year.

5. Bad debts amounting to £500 are to be written off and the provision for doubtful debts reduced to £600.

6. Expenses are to be allotted as follows:

	Works	*Administration*
Rates and insurance	$\frac{7}{10}$	$\frac{3}{10}$
Repairs	$\frac{4}{5}$	$\frac{1}{5}$
Electricity and power	$\frac{9}{10}$	$\frac{1}{10}$

Adjustments for bad debts and the provision for doubtful debts are attributable to selling and delivery expenses.

You are required to prepare:
(*a*) the Manufacturing, Trading and Profit and Loss Accounts for the year ended 31 December 19–7, showing the works cost and administration cost per ton produced, and
(*b*) the Balance Sheet as on that date.
(Institute of Chartered Accountants)

20.7A. Here are the balances at 31 December 19–9 extracted from ledger of V trading as V and Company, together with certain additional information.

You are required to prepare:
(*a*) manufacturing, trading and profit and loss accounts for the year ended 31 December 19–9; and
(*b*) a balance sheet as at that date.

	£
Capital account—V, at 1 January 19–9	85,000
Drawing—V	5,000
Freehold premises at cost	20,000
Plant and equipment at cost	70,000
Provision for depreciation at 31 December 19–9:	
freehold premises	2,000
plant and equipment	22,000
Stock of raw materials at 1 January 19–9	9,000
Work-in-progress at 1 January 19–9	7,000
Stock of finished products at 1 January 19–9	10,000
Trade debtors	12,000
Provision for doubtful debts at 1 January 19–9	500
Prepaid expenses at 1 January 19–9	900
Cash at bank and in hand	5,500
Trade creditors	11,000
Accrued expenses at 1 January 19–9	1,400
Sales	223,000
Purchases of raw materials	73,000
Manufacturing wages	36,000
Manufacturing expenses	53,000
Depreciation: freehold premises	500
plant and equipment	7,000
Administrative expenses	8,000
Selling and distribution expenses	23,000
General expenses	5,000

Additional information:

1. Stocks at 31 December 19–9 were as follows:

	£
Raw materials	10,000
Work-in-progress	5,500
Finished products	12,500

2. Details of prepaid expenses are:

	1 Jan 19–9	31 Dec 19–9
	£	£
Manufacturing expenses	100	—
Administrative expenses	500	400
Selling and distribution expenses	100	200
General expenses	200	100

3. Details of accrued expenses are:

	1 Jan 19–9	31 Dec 19–9
	£	£
Manufacturing expenses	200	300
Administrative expenses	200	300
Selling and distribution expenses	300	100
General expenses	700	400

4. The provision for doubtful debts is to be made equal to 5 per cent of the trade debtors. This item is traditionally regarded as a selling expense.

5. Depreciation and general expenses are to be apportioned as follows:

	Manufacturing expenses	*Administrative expenses*	*Selling and distribution expenses*
	%	%	%
Depreciation:			
freehold premises	70	20	10
plant and equipment	90	7	3
General expenses	$16\frac{2}{3}$	$16\frac{2}{3}$	$66\frac{2}{3}$

(Institute of Cost and Management Accountants)

APPENDIX 20.1

The Calculation of Wages and Salaries Payable to Employees

In the U.K. wages are generally taken to be the earnings paid on a weekly basis to employees, whilst salaries are those paid on a monthly basis.

The earnings of employees, whether paid monthly or weekly, are subject to various deductions. These can consist of the following items.

(1) Income Tax. In the U.K. the wages and salaries of all employees are liable to have income tax deducted from them. This does not mean that everyone will pay Income Tax, but that if Income Tax is found to be payable then the employer will deduct the tax from the employee's wages or salary.

Each person in the U.K. is allowed to set various personal reliefs against the amount earned to see if he/she is liable to pay Income Tax. The reliefs given for each person depend upon his or her personal circumstances. Extra relief is given to a man who is married, as compared to a single man; further extra relief will be given for factors such as having dependent relatives, and so on. The reliefs given are changed from time to time by Parliament. Most students will know of the 'Budget' which is presented to Parliament by the Chancellor of the Exchequer, in which such changes are announced. After discussion by Parliament, and subject to possible changes there, the changes will be incorporated into a Finance Act. This means that, for instance, a single man earning a given amount might pay Income Tax, whereas a married man who is eligible for extra reliefs might earn the same amount and pay no Income Tax at all.

Once the reliefs have been deducted from the earnings, any excess of the earnings above that figure will have to suffer Income Tax being levied on it. As the rates of Income Tax change regularly, all that can be given here are the basic principles; the rates given are for purposes of illustration only. A further complication arises because the rate of tax increases in steps when the excess of the earnings exceeds certain figures.

For instance, assume that the rates of Income Tax are (on the amount actually exceeding the reliefs for each person):

On the first £1,000	Income Tax at 20 per cent
On the next £5,000	Income Tax at 30 per cent
On the remainder	Income Tax at 50 per cent

The income Tax payable by each of four persons can now be looked at.

Miss Jones earns £1,500 per annum. Her personal reliefs amount to £1,700. Income Tax payable = Nil.

Mr Bland earns £4,000 per annum. His personal reliefs are £3,400. He therefore has £600 of his earnings on which he will have to pay Income Tax. As the rate on the first £1,000 taxable is 20 per cent, then he will pay £600 × 20 per cent = £120.

Mrs Hugo earns £6,500 per annum. She has personal reliefs amounting to £2,700. She will therefore pay Income Tax on the excess of £3,800. This will amount to:

On the first £1,000 tax at 20 per cent	=	200
On the remaining £2,800 tax at 30 per cent	=	840
Total Income Tax		£1,040

Mr Pleasance has a salary of £10,000 per annum. His personal reliefs amount to £3,560. He will therefore pay Income Tax on the excess of £6,440. This will amount to:

On the first £1,000 tax at 20 per cent	=	200
On the next £5,000 tax at 30 per cent	=	1,500
On the next £440 tax at 50 per cent	=	220
Total Income Tax		£1,920

The actual deduction of the Income Tax from the earnings of the employee is made by the employer. The tax is commonly called P.A.Y.E. tax, which represents the initial letters for Pay As You Earn. The amount of reliefs to which each employee is entitled is communicated to the employer in the form of a Notice of Coding, on which a code number is stated. The code number is then used in conjunction with special tax tables to show the amount of the tax deductible from the employee's earnings.

So far the amount of tax payable by anyone has been looked at on an annual basis. However, P.A.Y.E. means precisely that: it involves paying the tax as the earnings are calculated on each pay date, weekly or monthly, and not waiting until after the end of the year to pay the bill. The code numbers and the tax tables supplied to the employer by the Inland Revenue are so worked out that this is possible. It is outside the scope of this book to examine in detail how this is done. However, in the case of the three people already listed who will have to pay Income Tax, if we assume that Mrs Hugo is paid weekly, then from each week's wage she will have to pay one week's tax, in her case £1,040 ÷ 52 = £20. If Mr Bland and Mr Pleasance are paid on a monthly basis, then Mr Bland will have to pay £120 ÷ 12 = £10 per month, and Mr Pleasance £1,920 ÷ 12 = £160 per month.

It may well have crossed the reader's mind that, for many people, the year's earnings are not known in advance, and that the total amount payable, divided neatly into weekly or monthly figures, would not be known until the year was finished. The operation of the P.A.Y.E. system automatically allows for this problem. A book on Income Tax should be studied if the reader would like to investigate further how this is carried out.

(2) In the U.K. employees are also liable to pay National Insurance contributions. The deduction of these is carried out by the employer at the same time as the P.A.Y.E. Income Tax deductions are effected.

The payment of such National Insurance contributions is to ensure that the payer will be able to claim benefits from the State, if and when he is in a position to claim, such as unemployment benefit, sickness benefits, retirement pension and so on.

There is a lower limit for each employee below which no National Insurance is payable at all, and there is also a top limit, earnings above this amount being disregarded for National Insurance. These limits are changed by Parliament, usually annually. Any figures given in this book are by way of illustration only.

If it is assumed that the lower limit of earnings eligible for National Insurance contributions is £1,000, and that the top limit is £10,000, and that the rate of National Insurance payable by the employee is 5 per cent, then the following contributions would be made:

Mrs Jones: part-time cleaner, earns £900 per annum. National Insurance contribution nil.

Miss Hardcastle, earnings £3,000 per annum. National Insurance contribution £3,000 × 5 per cent = £150. The fact that there is a lower limit of £1,000 does not mean that the first £1,000 of the earnings are free of National Insurance contributions, but simply that anyone earning less than £1,000 will not pay any. Someone earning £1,100 would pay National Insurance of £1,100 × 5 per cent = £55.

Mr Evergreen earns £12,000 per annum. He would pay at the rate of 5 per cent on £10,000 only = £500.

As with the P.A.Y.E. Income Tax, the National Insurance contribution is payable per week or per month.

It should be noted that in the U.K. part of the National Insurance contributions are in respect of a supplement to the retirement pension. This supplement to the pension is based on the amount actually earned by the person during the years he was paying towards this supplement, and on the number of years he actually paid contributions. The more he earned, the more he would pay in contributions, and he would therefore get a bigger supplement than someone earning less and contributing less.

However, it was recognized when the scheme was started that some firms had special superannuation funds (dealt with later in this chapter), so that the employees in those firms would not necessarily wish to have an extra supplement from the State on top of their State retirement pension. At the same time they would therefore not want to pay as much in National Insurance as the man who wanted such a supplement. These firms were therefore given the right to 'opt out', and employees in these firms pay a lower percentage of their earnings in National Insurance contributions.

(3) Superannuation contributions. Many firms have superannuation schemes. These are schemes whereby the employee will receive a pension on retiring from the firm, plus, very often, a lump sum payment in cash. They also usually include benefits which will be paid to an employee's spouse if the employee dies before reaching retirement age.

Some of these schemes are non-contributory. This means that the firm pays for these benefits for its employees without deducting anything from the employee's earnings. The other schemes are contributory schemes whereby the employee will pay a part of the cost of the scheme by an agreed deduction from his earnings. The actual percentages paid by employees will vary from firm to firm. In addition the firm will pay part of the cost of the scheme without any cost to the employee. With the advent of the State scheme for a supplement to the retirement pension some firms opted out of the State supplement scheme, so that their employees rely on the firm's superannuation scheme instead. They still qualify for the basic State retirement pension, it will only be the supplement that they will not receive. Other firms carry on their own superannuation scheme and are also in the State scheme, so that their employees will get both the supplement from the State and the benefits from their firm's superannuation scheme on top as well.

Normally the contributions of employees to the superannuation schemes of their firms are tax deductible. This means that the part of their earnings taken as their contribution to the firm's scheme will escape Income Tax. This is not so with the contribution to any part of the State National Insurance scheme at the time that this book is being written.

Calculation of Net Wages/Salary Payable

Two illustrations of the calculation of the net pay to be made to various employees can now be looked at.

		£
(A) G. Jarvis:	Gross Earnings for the week ended 8 May 19–4	100
	Income Tax: found by consulting tax tables and employee's code number	12
	National Insurance 5%	

G. Jarvis: Payslip Week ended 8 May 19–4

	£	£
Gross pay for the week		100
Less Income Tax	12	
,, National Insurance	5	17
Net Pay		83

		£
(B) H. Reddish:	Gross earnings for the month of May 19–4	800
	Income Tax (from tax tables)	150
	Superannuation: 6% of gross pay	
	National Insurance 5% of gross pay	

H. Reddish: Payslip Month ended 31 May 19–4

		£
Gross pay for the month		800
Less Income Tax	150	
„ Superannuation	48	
„ National Insurance	40	238
Net Pay		562

National Insurance: Employer's Contribution

Besides the amount of the National Insurance which has to be suffered by the employee, the employer also has to pay a percentage based on the employee's pay as the firm's own contribution. This expense is suffered by the firm; it has no recourse against its employee. The percentage which the firm will have to pay varies as Parliament amends it to deal with the changing economic climate of the country. In this book it will be treated as though it is 10 per cent, but this figure is simply for illustration purposes. It does, however, at the time that this book is being written, equate to the approximate proportion which the employer pays as compared with that paid by the employee, the latter being about one-half of that suffered by the employer.

The entry of salaries and wages in the books of a firm can now be seen. A firm owned by H. Offerton has one employee, whose name is F. Edgeley. For the month of June 19–3 the payslip made out for Edgeley has appeared as:

F. Edgeley: Payslip month ended 30 June 19–3

		£
Gross Pay for the month		600
Less Income Tax	90	
„ National Insurance 5%	30	120
Net Pay		480

Additional to this, the firm will also have to pay its own share of the National Insurance contribution for Edgeley. This will be 10 per cent of £600 = £60. Therefore to employ Edgeley in the firm for this month has cost the firm the amount of his gross pay £600, plus £60 National Insurance, a total of £660. This means that when the firm draws up its Profit and Loss Account, the charge for the employment of this person for the month should be £660.

The firm has however acted as a collector of taxes and National Insurance on behalf of the government, and it will have to pay over to the government's agent, which is the Inland Revenue, the amount collected on its behalf. If it is assumed that the £90 deducted from pay for Income Tax, and the £30 deducted for National Insurance, are paid to the Inland Revenue on 30 June 19–3, then the cash book will appear as:

Cash Book (bank columns)

Dr		*Cr*		
		19–3		£
		Jun 30	Wages (cheque to Edgeley)	480
		,, ,,	Inland Revenue (see below)*	180

*Made up of:		
	Income Tax P.A.Y.E.	90
	National Insurance (employee's part)	30
	National Insurance (employer's part)	60
		180

In a firm as small as the one illustrated, both the figure of £480 and the £180 could be posted to a 'Wages and National Insurance Account', to give a total for the month of £660. In a larger firm such payments would be best posted to separate accounts for National Insurance and for P.A.Y.E. Income Tax, transfers then being made when the final accounts are drawn up.

Exercises to Appendix 20.1

20.8. H. Smith is employed by a firm of carpenters at a rate of £1.50 per hour. During the week to 18 May 19–5 he worked his basic week of 40 hours. The Income Tax due on his wages was £8, and he is also liable to pay National Insurance contributions of 5 per cent. Calculate his net wages.

20.9. B. Charles is employed as an undertaker's assistant. His basic working week consists of 40 hours, paid at the rate of £2 per hour. For hours worked in excess of this he is paid at the rate of 1½ times his basic earnings. In the week ended 12 March 19–6 he worked 60 hours. Up to £40 a week he pays no Income Tax, but he pays it at the rate of 30 per cent for all earnings above that figure. He is liable to pay National Insurance at the rate of 5 per cent. Calculate his net wages.

20.10. B. Croft has a job as a car salesman. He is paid a basic salary of £200 per month, with a commission extra of 2 per cent on the value of his car sales. During the month of April 19–6 he sells £30,000 worth of cars. He pays Income Tax at the rate of 30 per cent on all earnings above £100 per month. He also pays National Insurance at the rate of 5 per cent on the first £500 of his monthly earnings, paying nothing on earnings above that figure. Calculate his net pay for the month.

20.11. T. Penketh is an accountant with a firm of bookmakers. He has a salary of £500 per month, but he also has a bonus dependent on the firm's profits. The bonus for the month was £200. He pays National Insurance at the rate of 5 per cent on his gross earnings up to a maximum of £600 per month, there being no contribution for earnings above that figure. He pays Income Tax at the rate of thirty per cent on his earnings between £100 and £300 per month, and at the rate of 50 per cent on all earnings above that figure. However, before calculating earnings on which he has to pay Income Tax, he is allowed to deduct the amount of superannuation payable by him which is at the rate of 10 per cent on gross earnings. Calculate his net pay for the month.

20.12A. R. Kennedy is a security van driver. He has a wage of £100 per week, and danger money of £1 per hour in addition for every hour he spends in transporting gold bullion. During the week ended 16 June 19–3 he spends 20 hours taking gold bullion to London Airport. He pays Income Tax at the rate of 25 per cent on all his earnings above £80 per week. He pays National Insurance at the rate of 5 per cent on gross earnings. Calculate his net wage for the week.

20.13A. V. Mevagissey is a director of a company. She has a salary of £500 per month. She pays superannuation at the rate of 5 per cent. She also pays National Insurance at the rate of 5 per cent of gross earnings. Her Income Tax, due on gross salary less superannuation, is at the rate of 30 per cent after her personal reliefs for the month, other than superannuation, of £300 have been deducted. Calculate her net pay for the month.

20.14A. A firm employs John Jones at a standard rate of £1.10 per hour. Time and a half is paid for all hours worked in excess of 40. All employees pay a superannuation contribution of 5 per cent of all wages earned in a normal working week (40 hours). Time worked in excess of 40 hours is not subject to superannuation. National Insurance contributions are 5 per cent of gross wages. In the week ending 7 June John Jones has worked 45 hours. He pays income tax at 30 per cent on all he earns over £35 per week after superannuation has been deducted.

You are required to:

(i) calculate his gross wages.

(ii) show the value of each deduction and calculate his net wages.

(Royal Society of Arts)

21

Partnership Accounts: An Introduction

The final accounts so far described have, with the exception of income and expenditure accounts, been concerned with businesses each owned by one person. There must obviously come a time when it is desirable for more than one person to participate in the ownership of the business. It may be due to the fact that the amount of capital required cannot be provided by one person, or else that the experience and ability required to run the business cannot be found in any one person alone. Alternatively, many people just prefer to share the cares of ownership rather than bear all the burden themselves. Very often too there is a family relationship between the owners.

The form of business organization necessary to provide for more than one owner of a business formed with a view of profit is either that of a limited company or of a partnership. This chapter deals with partnerships, the governing act being the Partnership Act 1890. A partnership may be defined as an association of from two to twenty persons (except that there is no maximum limit for firms of accountants, solicitors, Stock Exchange members or other professional bodies which receive the approval of the Board of Trade for this purpose) carrying on business in common with a view of profit. A limited company would have to be formed if it was desired to have more than twenty owners.

With the exception of one special type of partner, known as a limited partner, each partner is liable to the full extent of his personal possessions for the whole of the debts of the partnership firm should the firm be unable to meet them. Barring limited partners, each partner would have to pay his share of any such deficiency. A limited partner is one who is registered under the provisions of the Limited Partnership Act 1907, and whose liability is limited to the amount of capital invested by him; he can lose that but his personal possessions cannot be taken to pay any debts of the firm. A limited partner may not however take part in the management of the partnership business. There must be at least one general partner in a limited partnership.

Limited partnerships were very rare indeed, but with the advent of Corporation Tax on limited companies in 1965 they became more common as partnerships then enjoyed several taxation advantages not available to limited companies.

Persons can enter into partnership with one another without any form of written agreement. It is, however, wiser to have an agreement drawn up by a solicitor, as this will tend to lead to fewer possibilities of misunderstandings and disagreements between the partners. Such a partnership deed or articles of partnership can contain as much, or as little, as the partners desire. It does not cover every eventuality. The usual accounting requirements covered can be listed:

1. The capital to be contributed by each partner.
2. The ratio in which profits (or losses) are to be shared.
3. The rate of interest, if any, to be given on capital before the profits are shared.
4. The rate of interest, if any, to be charged on partners' drawings.
5. Salaries to be paid to partners.

Some comments on the above are necessary.

(a) Ratio in Which Profits are to be Shared

It is often thought by students that profits should be shared in the same ratio as that in which capital is contributed. For example, suppose the capitals were Solway £2,000 and Firth £1,000, many people would share the profits in the ratio of ⅔rds to ⅓rd, even though the work to be done by each partner is similar. A look at the division of the first few years' profits on such a basis would be:

Years	*1*	*2*	*3*	*4*	*5*	*Total*
	£	£	£	£	£	£
Net profits	1,800	2,400	3,000	3,000	3,600	
Shared:						
Solway ⅔	1,200	1,600	2,000	2,000	2,400	9,200
Firth ⅓	600	800	1,000	1,000	1,200	4,600

It can now be seen that Solway would receive £9,200, or £4,600 more than Firth. Equitably the difference between the two shares of profit in this case, as the duties of the partners are the same, should be adequate to compensate Solway for putting extra capital into the firm. It is obvious that £4,600 extra profits is far more than adequate for this purpose.

Consider too the position of capital ratio sharing of profits if one partner put in £99 and the other put in £1 as capital.

To overcome the difficulty of compensating for the investment of extra capital, the concept of interest on capital was devised.

(b) Interest on Capital

If the work to be done by each partner is of equal value but the capital contributed is unequal, it is equitable to grant interest on the partners' capitals. This interest is treated as a deduction prior to the calculation of profits and their distribution according to the profit-sharing ratio.

The rate of interest is a matter for agreement between the partners, but it should theoretically equal the return which they would have received if they had invested the capital elsewhere.

Taking Solway and Firth's firm again, but sharing the profits equally after charging 5 per cent per annum interest on capital, the division of profits would become:

Years	*1*	*2*	*3*	*4*	*5*		*Total*
	£	£	£	£	£		£
Net Profit	1,800	2,400	3,000	3,000	3,600		
Interest on Capitals							
Solway	100	100	100	100	100	=	500
Firth	50	50	50	50	50	=	250
Remainder shared:							
Solway ½	825	1,125	1,425	1,425	1,725	=	6,525
Firth ½	825	1,125	1,425	1,425	1,725	=	6,525

Summary	*Solway*	*Firth*
	£	£
Interest on Capital	500	250
Balance of Profits	6,525	6,525
	7,025	6,775

Solway has thus received £250 more than Firth, this being adequate return (in the partners' estimation) for having invested an extra £1,000 in the firm for five years.

(c) Interest on Drawings

It is obviously in the best interests of the firm if cash is withdrawn from the firm by the partners in accordance with the two basic principles of: 1, as little as possible, and 2, as late as possible. The more cash that is left in the firm the more expension can be financed, the greater the economies of having ample cash to take advantage of bargains and of not missing cash discounts because cash is not available and so on.

To deter the partners from taking out cash unnecessarily the concept can be used of charging the partners interest on each withdrawal, calculated from the date of withdrawal to the end of the financial year. The amount charged to them helps to swell the profits divisible between the partners.

The rate of interest should be sufficient to achieve this end without being unduly penal.

Suppose that Solway and Firth have decided to charge interest on drawings at 5 per cent per annum, and that their year end was 31 December. The following drawings are made:

Solway

Drawings		*Interest*	
			£
1 January	£100	£100 × 5% × 12 months =	5
1 March	£240	£240 × 5% × 10 months =	10
1 May	£120	£120 × 5% × 8 months =	4
1 July	£240	£240 × 5% × 6 months =	6
1 October	£80	£80 × 5% × 3 months =	1
		Interest charged to Solway =	26

Firth

Drawings		*Interest*	
			£
1 January	£60	£60 × 5% × 12 months =	3
1 August	£480	£480 × 5% × 5 months =	10
1 December	£240	£240 × 5% × 1 month =	1
		Interest charged to Firth =	14

(d) Salaries

A partner may have some particular responsibility or extra task that the others have not got. It may in fact be of a temporary nature. To compensate him for this, it is best not to disturb the profit- and loss-sharing ratio. It is better to let him have a salary sufficient to compensate him for the extra tasks performed. This salary is deductible before arriving at the balance of profits to be shared in the profit-sharing ratio. A change in the profit- and loss-sharing ratio to compensate him would have meant bearing a larger share of any loss, hardly a fair means of compensation; or if there was only a small profit the extra amount received by him would be insufficient compensation, while if there was a large profit he may well be more than adequately compensated.

An Example of the Distribution of Profits

Barnes and Walls are in partnership sharing profits and losses in the ratio of Barnes 3/5ths, Walls 2/5ths. They are entitled to 5 per cent per annum interest on capitals, Barnes having £2,000 capital and Walls £6,000. Walls is to have a salary of £500. They charge interest on drawings, Barnes being charged £50 and Walls £100. The net profit, before any distributions to the partners, amounted to £5,000 for the year ended 31 December 19–7.

	£	£	£
Net Profit			5,000
Add Charged for interest on drawings:			
Barnes		50	
Walls		100	
			150
			5,150
Less Salary: Walls		500	
„ Interest on Capital:			
Barnes	100		
Walls	300		
		400	
			900
			4,250

	£	£
Balance of profits		
Shared:		
Barnes 3/5ths	2,550	
Walls 2/5ths	1,700	
		4,250

The £5,000 net profits have therefore been shared:

	Barnes	*Walls*
	£	£
Balance of profits	2,550	1,700
Interest on Capital	100	300
Salary	—	500
	2,650	2,500
Less Interest on drawings	50	100
	2,600	2,400

£5,000

The Final Accounts

If the sales, stock and expenses of a partnership were exactly the same as that of a sole trader then the trading and profit and loss account would be identical with that as prepared for the sole trader. However, a partnership would have an extra section shown under the profit and loss account. This section is called the profit and loss appropriation account, and it is in this account that the distribution of profits is shown. The heading to the trading and profit and loss account does not include the words 'appropriation account'. It is purely an accounting custom not to include it in the heading.

The trading and profit and loss account of Barnes and Walls from the details given would appear:

Barnes and Walls

Trading and Profit and Loss Account for the year ended 31 December 19–7

Trading Account—same as for sole trader					
		£			£
Profit and Loss Account—same as for sole trader					
	£	£		£	£
Net Profit c/d		5,000			
		£			£
Interest on Capitals:			Net Profit b/d		5,000
Barnes	100		Interest on drawings:		
Walls	300		Barnes	50	
		400	Walls	100	
					150
Salary: Walls		500			
Balance of profits:					
Barnes 3/5ths	2,550				
Walls 2/5ths	1,700				
		4,250			
		5,150			5,150

Fixed and Fluctuating Capital Accounts

There is a choice open in partnership accounts of:

(a) Fixed Capital Accounts Plus Current Accounts

The capital account for each partner remains year by year at the figure of capital put into the firm by the partners. The profits, interest on capital and the salaries to which the partner may be entitled are then credited to a separate current account for the partner, and the drawings and the interests on drawings are debited to it. The balance of the current account at the end of each financial year will then represent the amount of undrawn (or withdrawn) profits. A credit balance will be undrawn profits, while a debit balance will be drawings in excess of the profits to which the partner was entitled.

For Barnes and Walls, capital and current accounts, assuming drawings of £2,000 each, will appear:

Barnes—Capital

				£
			Jan 1 Balance b/d	2,000

Walls—Capital

				£
			Jan 1 Balance b/d	6,000

Barnes—Current Account

		£			£
Dec 31	Cash: Drawings	2,000	Dec 31	Profit and Loss Appropriation Account:	
,,	Profit and Loss Appropriation: Interest on Drawings	50		Interest on Capital	100
,, 31	Balance c/d	600		Share of Profits	2,550
		2,650			2,650
					£
			Jan 1	Balance b/d	600

Walls—Current Account

		£			£
Dec 31	Cash: Drawings	2,000	Dec 31	Profit and Loss Appropriation Account:	
,, 31	Profit and Loss Appropriation: Interest on Drawings	100		Interest on Capital	300
,, 31	Balance c/d	400		Share of Profits	1,700
				Salary	500
		2,500			2,500
					£
			Jan 1	Balance b/d	400

Notice that the salary of Walls was not paid to him, it was merely credited to his account. If in fact it was paid in addition to his drawings, the £500 cash paid would have been debited to the current account changing the £400 credit balance into a £100 debit balance.

(b) Fluctuating Capital Accounts

The distribution of profits would be credited to the capital account, and the drawings and interest on drawings debited. Therefore the balance on the capital account will change each year, i.e. it will fluctuate.

If Fluctuating Capital Accounts had been kept for Barnes and Walls they would have appeared:

Barnes—Capital

		£			£
Dec 31	Cash: Drawings	2,000	Jan 1	Balance b/d	2,000
,, 31	Profit and Loss Appropriation Account:		Dec 31	Profit and Loss Appropriation Account:	
	Interest on Drawings	50		Interest on Capital	100
,, 31	Balance c/d	2,600		Share of Profits	2,550
		4,650			4,650
			Jan 1	Balance b/d	2,600

Walls—Capital

		£			£
Dec 31	Cash: Drawings	2,000	Jan 1	Balance b/d	6,000
,, 31	Profit and Loss Appropriation Account:		Dec 31	Profit and Loss Appropriation Account:	
				Interest on Capital	300
	Interest on Drawings	100		Salary	500
,, 31	Balance c/d	6,400		Share of Profit	1,700
		8,500			8,500
			Jan 1	Balance b/d	6,400

Fixed Capital Accounts Preferred

The keeping of fixed capital accounts plus Current Accounts is considered preferable to fluctuating capital accounts. When partners are taking out greater amounts than the share of the profits that they are entitled to, this is shown up by a debit balance on the current account and so acts as a warning.

Also, the rule in *Garner* v. *Murray* (see page 369) will not apply inequitably if fixed capital accounts are used. This topic is dealt with in the chapter on partnership dissolution.

Where No Partnership Agreement Exists

Where no agreement exists, express or implied, Section 24 of the Partnership Act 1890 governs the situation. The accounting contents of this section states:

1. Profits and losses are to be shared equally.
2. There is to be no interest allowed on capital.
3. No interest is to be charged on drawings.
4. Salaries are not allowed.
5. If a partner puts a sum of money into a firm in excess of the capital he has agreed to subscribe, he is entitled to interest at the rate of 5 per cent per annum on such an advance.

This section applies where there is no agreement. There may be an agreement not by a partnership deed but in a letter, or it may be implied by conduct, for instance when a partner signs a balance sheet which shows profits shared in some other ratio than equally.

In some cases of disagreement as to whether agreement existed or not only the courts would be competent to decide.

The Balance Sheet

The capital and liabilities side of the balance sheet will appear:

Balance Sheet as at 31 December 19–7

		£	£
Capitals:	Barnes	2,000	
	Walls	6,000	
			8,000
Current Accounts	*Barnes*	*Walls*	
	£	£	
Interest on Capital	100	300	
Share of profits	2,550	1,700	
Salary	—	500	
	2,650	2,500	
Less Drawings	2,000	2,000	
Interest on drawings	50	100	
	600	400	
			1,000
Current Liabilities			
Creditors			2,000
			11,000

If one of the current accounts had finished in debit, for instance if the current account of Walls had finished up as £400 debit, the abbreviation Dr would appear and the balances would appear net in the totals column:

	Barnes	*Walls*	
	£	£	£
Closing balance	600	400 *Dr*	200

If the net figure turned out to be a debit figure then this would be deducted from the total of the capital accounts.

Exercises

21.1. Low, High and Broad are in partnership trading as Wide and Co, sharing profits and losses in the ratio 2:2:1 respectively. Interest is charged on partners' drawings at the rate of 5 per cent per annum and credited on partners' capital account balances at the rate of 5 per cent per annum.

High is the firm's sales manager and for his specialized services he is credited with a salary of £800 per annum.

During the year ended 30 April 19–5 the net profit of the firm was £6,200 and the partners' drawings were:

Low	£1,200
High	£800
Broad	£800

In each case, the above drawings were withdrawn in two equal instalments on 31 October 19–4, and 30 April 19–5.

On 31 October 19–4 the firm agreed that Low should withdraw £1,000 from his capital account and that Broad should subscribe a similar amount to his capital account.

The balances of the partners' accounts at 1 May 19–4 were as follows:

All Credit Balances

	Capital Accounts	*Current Accounts*
Low	£8,000	£640
High	£7,000	£560
Broad	£6,000	£480

Required:

(*a*) Prepare the firm's profit and loss appropriation account for the year ended 30 April 19–5.

(*b*) Prepare the partners' capital and current accounts for the year ended 30 April 19–5.

(Joint Royal Society of Arts and London Chamber of Commerce)

21.2. C. J. Ford is in a business and on 1 July 19–2 his assets and liabilities were:

	£
Sundry trade creditors	2,170
Sundry trade debtors	462

	£
Stock-in-trade	2,838
Motor vehicles	1,800
Furniture and fittings	300
Bank overdraft	630

On 1 July 19–2 W. S. Morris joined him as a partner on the following terms:

Morris paid £1,400 into the business bank account and brought in a motor van valued at £600. Each partner is to be allowed interest on capital at the rate of 6 per cent per annum, after which the balance of profit or loss is to be divided equally.

In 31 December 19–2 the following balances were extracted from the books of the firm:

	£
Cash in hand and balance at bank	1,076
Stock-in-trade	3,127
Sundry trade debtors	510
Sundry trade creditors	2,496
Sundry expense creditors	40
Motor vehicles	2,160
Furniture and fittings	285
Amounts prepaid	16
Current accounts:	
Ford—debit balance	750
Morris—debit balance	750
Net Trading Profit for the half year (before allowing for interest on capital)	1,538

Prepare the profit and loss appropriation account of the firm for the half year ended 31 December 19–2 and a balance sheet as on that date; ignore depreciation of Fixed Assets.

(University of London 'O' Level)

21.3. The following list of balances was extracted from the books of Messrs J. and L. Coat, as at 31 March 19–5:

	£
Capital at 1 April 19–4—J. Coat	5,000 credit
L. Coat	3,000 credit
Cash drawings—J. Coat	800
L. Coat	600
Freehold land and buildings at 1 April 19–4	5,100
Motor vehicles at 1 April 19–4	1,260
Stock of goods for resale at 1 April 19–4	3,600
Purchases	25,700
Sales	38,610
Debtors	3,960
Creditors	3,670
Wages and salaries	4,140
Motor vehicle running costs	1,480
Rates and insurances	964
General trade expenses	1,994
Cash at bank and in hand	782
Provision for bad and doubtful debts	100

Additional information:

1. Stock of goods for resale at 31 March 19–5—£4,100.
2. Provision is to be made for depreciation at the following rates:
   Motor vehicles—25 per cent per annum
   Freehold land and buildings—2 per cent per annum.
3. Reduce the provision for bad and doubtful debts to £75.
4. J. and L. Coat share profits and losses in the ratio 3:2 respectively.

Required:

(*a*) Prepare the Trading and Profit and Loss Account for the year ended 31 March 19–5 and a Balance Sheet as at that date.

(*b*) Calculate the firm's working capital as at 31 March 19–5.

(Joint Royal Society of Arts and London Chamber of Commerce)

21.4. James and Walls are in partnership and the trial balance extracted from their books on the 31 December 19–4 is shown below:

	£ *Debit*	£ *Credit*
Premises	6,000	
Carriage	100	
Bad Debts	50	
Purchases and sales	16,000	28,000
Returns	80	60
Salaries	1,400	
Rates and taxes	400	
Insurance	140	
Cash in hand and cash in bank	700	
Stock 1 January	3,500	
Fixtures and fittings	4,500	
Wages	2,600	
Capital:		
James		6,000
Walls		6,000
Current Account:		
James	100	
Walls		150
Drawings:		
James	800	
Walls	900	
Debtors and creditors	8,000	5,000
Provision for bad debts		250
Discount	100	20
Office expenses	110	
	45,480	45,480

Prepare trading, profit and loss, appropriation account and partners' current accounts for the year ended 31 December 19–4 and a balance sheet at that date, after making provision for the following:

1. Stock on 31 December 19–4 £2,800.
2. £60 of the carriage is for carriage in.

3. Depreciation of fixtures and fittings at 10 per cent per annum.
4. Interest at 5 per cent per annum on partners' capitals.
5. Partnership salary—£500 to James.
6. Wages accrued £400.
7. Residue of profits to be divided equally.
8. Provision for bad debts to equal 10 per cent of debtors.

(East Midland Educational Union)

21.5. You are required to prepare a trading and profit and loss account for the year ended 31 December 19–5, and a balance sheet as at that date from the following:

Trial Balance as at 31 December 19–5

	Dr	*Cr*
	£	£
Drawings:		
Perkins	1,750	
Hodson	1,429	
Capital:		
Perkins		9,000
Hodson		4,800
Current accounts as at 1 January 19–5:		
Perkins		880
Hodson	120	
Premises	10,000	
Motor vehicles	1,870	
Stock—1 January 19–5	2,395	
Returns inwards and outwards	110	286
Sales		28,797
Purchases	19,463	
Wages and salaries	4,689	
Carriage inwards	216	
Delivery expenses	309	
Rent and rates	485	
Insurances	116	
Debtors and creditors	3,462	1,899
Cash in hand	180	
General expenses	204	
Loan—T. Farthingale		2,000
Discounts allowed and received	392	404
Motor expenses	635	
Cash at bank	241	
	48,066	48,066

Notes at 31 December 19–5:

1. Stock £5,623
2. Depreciate motors 10 per cent
3. Insurance prepaid £12
4. Rates owing £57
5. Included in salaries is a salary to Hodson for the year £300

6. Allow 5 per cent interest on capitals
7. Charge interest on drawings: Perkins £58; Hodson £39
8. Goods value £75 have been taken by Perkins for his own use, no entry having yet been made in the books
9. Profit shared: Hodson 2/5ths; Perkins 3/5ths (calculations to nearest £)
10. Loan interest owing £140
11. Make a provision for bad debts £320.

21.6A. Black and White are in partnership, sharing profits and losses in proportion to their Capital Accounts. White is paid a salary of £500 per annum as Office Manager. On 31 December 19–6 the following balances were extracted from the partnership books:

		Dr	*Cr*
		£	£
Premises		3,500	
Fixtures and fittings		750	
Provision for bad debts			115
Carriage inwards		142	
Returns inwards and outwards		288	343
Purchases and sales		10,665	18,429
Discounts allowed and received		199	146
Stock on hand 1.1.–6		1,865	
Debtors and creditors		2,355	1,569
Salary—White		500	
Office salaries— General staff		2,550	
Insurance and rates		650	
Power bills		162	
Bank balance		522	
Current Account balances (1.1.–6):	Black	625	
	White	540	
Drawings:	Black	124	
	White	165	
Capital accounts:	Black		3,000
	White		2,000
		25,602	25,602

The following further information is available:

1. Value of stock on hand, 31 December 19–6, £2,560.
2. Depreciate premises, fixtures and fittings by 10%.
3. Bad debt provision is to be increased to £150.
4. An electricity bill of £52 is expected.
5. Rates are £125 in advance.

Prepare Trading Account, Profit and Loss Account and Appropriation Account for the year ended 31 December 19–6, and a Balance Sheet as at 31 December 19–6.

(Southern Universities Joint Board—'O' Level)

21.7A. R. Roe and D. Doe are in partnership sharing profits and losses equally. On 31 May 19–9 their trial balance is:

	Dr	*Cr*
	£	£
Bank Current Account		143
Bank Deposit Account	1,600	
Capital: R. Roe		8,000
D. Doe		6,000
Carriage inwards	128	
Carriage outwards	322	
Cash	28	
Commission		136
Debtors and creditors	1,478	1,865
Discounts	224	196
Drawings: R. Roe	1,200	
D. Doe	1,960	
Furniture and fittings	1,260	
General expenses	987	
Insurance	123	
Premises (at cost)	8,000	
Purchases and sales	14,090	23,538
Returns	458	234
Stock, 1 June 19–8	3,544	
Wages and salaries	4,710	
	40,112	40,112

Prepare Trading and Profit and Loss Accounts for the year ended 31 May 19–9, and a Balance Sheet as at that date, taking into consideration the following:

1. (i) For managing the business D. Doe is to be credited with a partnership salary of £2,000 a year.
(ii) Interest is to be allowed on the partners' Capitals at the rate of 6 per cent per annum, but no interest is to be charged on Drawings.
2. Value of stock 31 May 19–9, £5,240.
3. There are accrued (i) Carriage Inwards £12, (ii) Commission owing to an agent by the firm £58, and of the Insurance (£123) £28 is a payment in advance.
4. Furniture and fittings are revalued at £1,134.
5. Bad debts £38 are to be written off.
6. Two-thirds of the wages and salaries are to be charged to Trading Account, one-third to Profit and Loss Account.

(Welsh Joint Education Committee—'O' Level)

21.8A. Wave and Crest are in partnership sharing profits equally. Some of their books and records covering the year to 31 December 19–7 were accidentally destroyed and you are asked to prepare accounts for 19–7 from the records that are available. It has been possible to establish the amounts of the assets and liabilities, as follows:

	31 Dec 19–6	31 Dec 19–7
	£	£
Fixed assets	10,000	see below
Stock	3,829	4,137
Debtors for sales	2,961	3,128
Balance at bank	1,324	1,301
Creditors for purchases	2,273	2,184
Creditors for expenses	89	103

Note:
No fixed assets were acquired in 19–6 and none were sold or discarded; they are to be written down at an annual rate of 5 per cent calculated on the balance at the beginning of each year.

The total expenses of the business for the year 19–7, excluding depreciation, are £8,629.

The capital of Wave at 31 December 19–6 was £1,000 greater than that of Crest. During the year 19–7 Wave drew £2,149 and Crest drew £2,066 for personal expenses.

The rate of gross profit earned during 19–7 was at the uniform rate of 25 per cent on sales.

Required:
(*a*) A calculation of the net profit for 19–7;
and
(*b*) A trading and profit and loss account for 19–7 and a balance sheet at 31 December 19–7.
(Institute of Bankers)

21.9A. Rowe and Martin, partners in a manufacturing business, have prepared from the books of account the following draft Balance Sheet as on 31 December 19–9:

	Rowe	*Martin*			*Cost*	*Depre-ciation*	
	£	£	£		£	£	£
Capital 1 Jan 19–9	20,100	10,000		Freehold buildings	12,000	—	12,000
Profit for the year	4,770	4,770		Plant and machinery	15,000	7,000	8,000
				Motor vehicles	8,000	2,700	5,300
	24,870	14,770		Stocks			5,000
Less Drawings	2,000	3,800		Debtors			14,000
				Cash in hand			40
	22,870	10,970	33,840				
Creditors			7,800				
Bank overdraft			2,700				
			44,340				44,340

During the course of your examination of the books you ascertain that adjustments are required for the following items:

1. Freehold buildings are shown at cost less £3,000 being the proceeds of the sale during the year of premises costing £3,500.
2. Plant and machinery having a net book value of £215 had been scrapped during the year. The original cost was £615.

3. Motor vehicle licences for 12 month periods costing £100 had been written off, but did not expire until 30 June 19–0.
4. Debts to the value of £521 were considered to be bad, and a further £270 doubtful requiring 100 per cent provision. Provision had previously been made for £500 doubtful debts.
5. Stocks included at a value of £1,870 had a net realisable value of only £1,300, and scrap material having a value of £330 had been omitted from the stock valuation.
6. The cashier had misappropriated £35.
7. The cash book included payments amounting to £3,462, the cheques having been made out but not mailed to suppliers until 19–0.
8. Interest is to be allowed on partners' opening capital account balances less drawings during the year at 9 per cent.

You are required to prepare:

(*a*) a summary of adjustments to the Profit and Loss Account for the year and revised division of profit between the partners, and

(*b*) a revised Balance Sheet as on 31 December 19–9.

22

Bills of Exchange

When goods are supplied to someone on credit, or services performed for him, then that person becomes a debtor. The creditor firm would normally wait for payment by the debtor. Until payment is made the money owing is of no use to the creditor firm as it is not being used in any way. This can be remedied by factorizing the debtors. Another possibility is that of obtaining a bank overdraft, with the debtors accepted as part of the security on which the overdraft has been granted.

Yet another way that can give the creditor effective use of the money owing to him is for him to draw up a bill of exchange on the debtor. This means that a document is drawn up requiring the debtor to pay the amount owing to the creditor, or to anyone nominated by him at any time, on or by a particular date. He sends this document to the debtor who, if he agrees to it, is said to 'accept' it by writing on the document that he will comply with it and appends his signature. The debtor then returns the bill of exchange to the creditor. This document is then legal proof of the debt. The debtor is not then able to contest the validity of the debt but only for any irregularity in the bill of exchange itself. The creditor can now act in one of three ways:

(*a*) He can negotiate the bill to another person in payment of a debt. That person may also renegotiate it to someone else. The person who possesses the bill at maturity, i.e. the date for payment of the bill, will present it to the debtor for payment.

(*b*) He may 'discount' it with a bank. 'Discount' here means that the bank will take the bill of exchange and treat it in the same manner as money deposited in the bank account. The bank will then hold the bill until maturity when it will present it to the debtor for payment. The bank will make a charge to the creditor for this service known as a discounting charge.

(*c*) The third way open to the creditor is for him to hold the bill until maturity when he will present it to the debtor for payment. In this case, apart from having a document which is legal proof of the debt and could therefore save legal costs if a dispute arose, no benefit has been gained from having a bill of exchange. However, action (*a*) or (*b*) could have been taken if the need had arisen.

The creditor who draws up the bill of exchange is known as the *Drawer*. The debtor on whom it is drawn is the *Drawee*, when accepted he becomes the *Acceptor*, while the person to whom the bill is to be paid is the *Payee*. In fact it may be recognized that a cheque is a special type of bill of exchange where the drawee is always a bank and in addition is payable on demand. This chapter, however, refers to bills of exchange other than cheques.

To the person who is to receive money on maturity of the bill of exchange the document is known as a 'bill receivable', while to the person who is to pay the sum due on maturity it is known as a 'bill payable'.

Dishonoured Bills

When the debtor fails to make payment on maturity the bill is said to be dishonoured. If the holder is someone other than the drawer then he will have recourse against the person who has negotiated the bill to him, that person will then have recourse against the one who negotiated it to him, and so on until final recourse is had against the drawer of the bill for the amount of money due on the bill. The drawer's right of action is then against the acceptor.

On dishonour a bill is often 'noted'. This means that the bill is handed to a solicitor acting in his capacity as a notary public, who then represents the bill to the acceptor. The notary public then records the reasons for it not being discharged. With an inland bill, being one drawn and payable within the British Isles, this action is not legally necessary, but it does at least prevent any subsequent dispute as to the dishonour. The notary public's fee is known as a 'noting charge'. With a foreign bill, in addition to the bill being noted, it is necessary to 'protest' the bill in order to preserve the holder's rights against the drawer and previous endorsers. 'Protest' is the term which covers the legal formalities needed.

The action to be taken by the drawer depends entirely upon circumstances. Often the lack of funds on the acceptor's part is purely temporary. In this case the drawer will negotiate with the acceptor and agree to draw another bill, or substitute several bills of smaller amounts with different maturity dates, for the amount owing, frequently with an addition for interest to compensate for the extended period of credit. Negotiation is the keynote; it must not be thought that acceptors are always sued when they fail to make payment. They are customers, and where future dealings with them are expected to be profitable harsh measures are certainly to be avoided. Legal action should be the last action to be considered. Any interest charged to the acceptor would be debited to his account and credited to an Interest Receivable Account.

Discounting Charges and Noting Charges

From the acceptor's point of view the discounting of a bill is a matter wholly for the drawer or holder to decide. He, the acceptor, has been allowed a term of credit and will pay the agreed price on the maturity of the bill. Therefore the discounting charge is not one that he should suffer; this should be borne wholly by the person discounting the bill.

On the other hand, the noting charge has been brought about by the acceptor's default. It is equitable that his account should be charged with the amount of the expense of noting and protesting.

Retired Bills

Instead of waiting until maturity, bills may be retired, i.e. not allowed to run until maturity. They may be paid off before maturity, in which case a rebate is often allowed because the full term of credit has not been taken; or else renewed by fresh bills being drawn and the old ones cancelled, the new bills often including interest because the term of credit has been extended.

Exhibit 22.1

Drawer's Books

Goods had been sold by D. Jarvis to J. Burgon on 1 January 19–6 for £400. A bill of exchange is drawn by Jarvis and accepted by Burgon on 1 January 19–6, the date of maturity being 31 March 19–6. The following accounts show the entries necessary:

(*a*) If the bill is held by the drawer until maturity when the drawee makes payment.

J. Burgon

	£		£
19–6		19–6	
Jan 1 Sales	400	Jan 1 Bill Receivable	400

Bills Receivable

	£		£
19–6		19–6	
Jan 1 J. Burgon	400	Mar 31 Bank	400

Bank

	£		
19–6			
Mar 31	400		

(*b*) Where the bill is negotiated to another party by the drawer, in this case to I.D.T. Ltd on 3 January 19–6.

J. Burgon

19–6	£	19–6	£
Jan 1 Sales	400	Jan 1 Bill Receivable	400

Bills Receivable

19–6	£	19–6	£
Jan 1 J. Burgon	400	Jan 3 I.D.T. Ltd	400

(*c*) If the bill is discounted with the bank, in this case on 2 January 19–6, the discounting charges being £6.

J. Burgon

19–6	£	19–6	£
Jan 1 Sales	400	Jan 1 Bill Receivable	400

Bills Receivable

19–6	£	19–6	£
Jan 1 J. Burgon	400	Jan 2 Bank	400

Bank

19–6	£	19–6	£
Jan 2 Bills Receivable	400	Jan 2 Discounting Charges	6

Discounting Charges

19–6	£		
Jan 2 Bank	6		

Acceptor's Books

The instances (*a*), (*b*) and (*c*) in the drawer's books will result in identical entries in the acceptor's books. From the acceptor's point of view two things have happened, (1) The acceptance of the bill, and (2) its discharge by payment. The fact that (*a*), (*b*) and (*c*) would result in different payees is irrelevant as far as the acceptor is concerned.

D. Jarvis

19–6	£	19–6	£
Jan 1 Bill Payable	400	Jan 1 Purchases	400

Bills Payable

19–6	£	19–6	£
Mar 31 Bank	400	Jan 1 D. Jarvis	400

Bank

		19–6	£
		Mar 31 Bill Payable	400

Dishonoured Bills and Accounting Entries

These can be illustrated by reference to Exhibit 22–2.

Exhibit 22.2

On 1 April 19–7 A. Grant sells goods for £600 to K. Lee, a bill with a maturity date of 30 June 19–7 being drawn by Grant and accepted by Lee on 2 April 19–7. On 30 June 19–7 the bill is presented to Lee, but he fails to pay it and it is therefore dishonoured. The bill is noted, the cost of £2 being paid by Grant on 7 July 19–7.

The entries needed will depend on whether or not the bill had been discounted by Grant.

(a) Drawer's Books

(i) *Where the Bill had not been discounted or renegotiated*

K. Lee

19–7	£	19–7	£
Apl 1 Sales	600	Apl 2 Bill Receivable	600
Jun 30 Bill Receivable—dishonoured	600		
July 7 Bank: Noting Charge (A)	2		

Bills Receivable

19–7	£	19–7	£
Apl 2 K. Lee	600	June 30 K. Lee—bill dishonoured	600

Bank

		19–7	£
		July 7 Noting Charges—K. Lee (A)	2

Note:

(A) As the noting charges are directly incurred as the result of Lee's default, then Lee must suffer the cost by his account being debited with that amount.

(ii) *Where the Bill had been discounted with a bank*

The entries can now be seen as they would have appeared if the bill had been discounted on 5 April 19–7, discounting charges being £9.

K. Lee

		£			£
19–7			19–7		
Apl	1 Sales	600	Apl	2 Bill Receivable	600
June	30 Bank—bill dishonoured (C)	600			
July	7 Bank: Noting Charge	2			

Bills Receivable

		£			£
19–7			19–7		
Apl	2 K. Lee	600	Apl	5 Bank	600

Bank

		£			£
19–7			19–7		
Apl	5 Bills Receivable	600	Apl	5 Discounting Charges (B)	9
			June	30 K. Lee—bill dishonoured (C)	600
			July	7 Noting Charges—K. Lee	2

Discounting Charges

		£
19–7		
Apl	5 Bank (B)	9

Notes:

(B) The discounting charges are wholly an expense of A. Grant. They are therefore charged to an expense account. Contrast this with the treatment of the noting charges.
(C) On maturity the bank will present the bill to Lee. On its dishonour the bank will hand the bill back to Grant, and will cancel out the original amount shown as being deposited in the bank account. This amount is then charged to Lee's personal account to show that he is still in debt.

(b) Acceptor's Books

The entries in the acceptor's books will not be affected by whether or not the drawer had discounted the bill.

A. Grant

19–7		£	19–7		£
Apl 1	Bill Payable	600	Apl 1	Purchases	600
			June 30	Bill Payable—dishonoured	600
			July 7	Noting Charge (D)	2

Bills Payable

19–7		£	19–7		£
June 30	A. Grant—bill dishonoured	600	Apl 1	A. Grant	600

Noting Charges

19–7		£
July 7	A. Grant (D)	2

Note:
(D) The noting charges will have to be reimbursed to A. Grant. To show this fact A. Grant's account is credited while the Noting Charges Account is debited to record the expense.

Bills Receivable as Contingent Liabilities

The fact that bills had been discounted, but had not reached maturity by the Balance Sheet date, could give an entirely false impression of the financial position of the business unless a note to this effect is made on the Balance Sheet. That such a note is necessary can be illustrated by reference to the following Balance Sheets.

Balance Sheet as at 31 December 19–7

	(*a*)	(*b*)		(*a*)	(*b*)
	£	£		£	£
Capital	5,000	5,000	Fixed Assets	3,500	3,500
Current Liabilities	3,000	3,000	Current Assets:		
			Stock	1,000	1,000
			Debtors	1,200	1,200
			Bills Receivable	1,800	—
			Bank	500	2,300
	8,000	8,000		8,000	8,000

Balance Sheet (*a*) shows the position if £1,800 of bills receivable were still in hand. Balance Sheet (*b*) shows the position if the bills had been discounted, ignoring discounting charges. To an outsider,

Balance Sheet (*b*) seems to show a much stronger liquid position with £2,300 in the bank. However, should the bills be dishonoured on maturity the bank balance would slump to £500. The appearance of Balance Sheet (*b*) is therefore deceptive unless a note is added, e.g. *Note*: There is a contingent liability of £1,800 on bills discounted at the Balance Sheet date. This note enables the outsider to view the bank balance in its proper perspective of depending on the non-dishonour of the bills discounted.

Exercises

22.1. On 1 November 19–3 Acre sells goods for £800 to Wright and accepts a bill at four months in settlement. Defective goods, value £40, are returned by Wright on 30 November 19–3, credit being given for this amount. The bill is discounted with the bank at 5 per cent after one month, but on maturity is dishonoured. Acre induces Wright on 31 March 19–4 to accept another bill at one month for the outstanding account for a consideration of £5. This is duly met.

Noting charges amounted to £1.

Show the ledger accounts in:

(*a*) Acre's books (including cash book).

(*b*) Wright's books.

22.2. A. Todd commenced to trade on 1 May 19–6.

His diary recorded the following transactions:

May 1 Bought goods from T. Glue for £250.
„ 2 Sent Glue cheque for £120 and accepted bill drawn by him at one month for £100.
„ 8 Sold goods to P. Bacon for £120.
„ 9 Drew bill on Bacon for £120 at one month and discounted it at the bank for £118.
„ 14 Bought goods from C. Smith for £70 and paid him £40 on account.
„ 23 Sold goods to F. Webb for £50. Received cheque for £20 and a bill at one month for the balance.
„ 26 Endorsed Webb's bill and sent it to Glue in settlement of the open balance on his account.
June 4 Glue agreed to bill for £100 being withdrawn; sent him cheque for £60 and accepted another bill at one month for £40.
„ 13 Bacon's bill for £120 returned dishonoured.
„ 18 Webb returned goods invoiced to him for £15.
„ 20 Agreed with Bacon that he should return goods invoiced to him for £50 against a credit to him of £40. Agreed to accept 60 per cent of the balance of his account in full settlement if he paid by the end of July 19–6.
„ 26 Webb's bill duly honoured.

You are required to prepare the Personal Ledger Accounts recording the above transactions in Todd's books, and also the Bills Receivable Account and Bills Payable Account, bringing down any balances on 30 June 19–6.
(Institute of Chartered Accountants)

22.3. A.B. owed F.X. £320. A.B. accepted a Bill of Exchange at three months date for this amount which F.X. discounted for £316.

Before the due date of the bill F.X. was informed that A.B. was unable to meet the bill and was offering a composition of 37½ per cent of each £ to his creditors. This offer was accepted and cash equivalent to the composition was received.

Show the ledger entries to record the above in F.X.'s ledger.
(Associated Examining Board 'A' Level)

22.4. Prepare a creditors' Ledger control account and a debtors' ledger control account for April 19–7 from the following information:

	£
At 1 April 19–7	
Creditors' Ledger balances	3,282
Debtors' Ledger balances	8,884
Provision for bad debts	177
Totals for April 19–7	
Sales invoices sent	10,322
Purchases invoices received	9,389
Returns outward	528
Returns inward	280
Allowances by suppliers	89
Allowances to customers	23
Bills receivable accepted	392
Bad Debts written off	254
Receipts for cash sales	987
Bad debts previously written off, now recovered	18
Bills receivable dishonoured	33
Interest charged on customer's overdue account	3
Cash paid to suppliers	9,325
Cash received from customers	9,873
Cash discount allowed	89
Cash discount received	183
Dishonoured cheque included in total cash received from customers (above)	98
Cash discount which had been allowed on dishonoured cheque above)	2
Payments to suppliers for cash purchases	1,231

At 30 April 19–7

Contra item: B. Jones is both a customer and a supplier. In the purchases ledger he has a balance of £22 and in the sales ledger a balance of £56. A net balance is to be shewn.

	£
The account of A. Brown (a customer) has a credit balance of	27
Provision for bad debts	250

(Chartered Institute of Secretaries and Administrators)

22.5. The following information, relating to the year 19–4, has been extracted from the books of a trading company. All purchases and sales have been entered in personal accounts in the purchases ledger and sales ledger, respectively.

	£
Sales Ledger debit balances, 1 January	3,276
Purchases Ledger credit balances, 1 January	2,819

	£
Receipts from customers (including £56 recovered in respect of a debt written off as bad in 19–3, but exclusive of amounts received on maturity of bills of exchange)	43,664
Purchases	36,116
Sales	48,814
Returns inwards	627
Returns outwards	249
Discounts received	942
Discounts allowed	1,231
Bills receivable in hand, 1 January	350
Bills receivable in hand, 31 December	500
Cash received in respect of bills of exchange, on maturity	1,725
Sales Ledger Credit balances, 31 December	83
Payments to suppliers	34,480

All bills of exchange received during 19–4 were credited to personal accounts of customers in the sales ledger. No bills were dishonoured during the year and none was discounted.

During 19–4, debit balances in the sales ledger, amounting to £124, were transferred to the purchases ledger and set off against credit balances in that ledger.

You are required to prepare the sales ledger control account and the purchases ledger control account for the year 1964.
(Institute of Bankers)

22.6A. Indicate by Journal entries how the following would appear in the ledger accounts of (*a*) Prince, (*b*) Duke.

19–8
Jan 1 Duke sells goods £420 to Prince, and Prince sends to Duke a three months' acceptance for this amount.
,, 1 Duke discounts the acceptance with the Alpha Discount Co Ltd, receiving its cheque for £412.
Feb 29 One third of Prince's stock, valued at £3,600, is destroyed by fire. Prince claims on the underwriters at Lloyd's with whom he is insured.
Apr 1 The underwriters admit the claim for £3,000 only as the total stock was only insured for £9,000.
,, 4 In view of Prince's difficulties Duke meets the acceptance due today by giving his cheque for £420 to the Alpha Discount Co Ltd; he draws on Prince a further bill for one month for £430 (to include £10 interest) which Prince accepts.
,, 9 Prince receives cheque from the underwriters in settlement of the admitted claim.
May 7 Prince's bank honours the acceptance presented by Duke as due today.
(Welsh Joint Education Committee—'A' Level)

22.7A. Enter the following in the appropriate ledger accounts of Race:

19–0.
Jan 5 R. Race sold goods to P. Pound, £320, and Pound accepted Race's bill for three months for this amount.
,, 6 R. Race discounted Pound's bill at the Genuine Discount Co for £304, and pays this amount into his account at the bank.

Apr 8 The Genuine Discount Co notified Race that Pound's bill had been dishonoured. Race at once sent cheque to the Genuine Discount Co for the full amount of the bill plus £3 charges.

,, 14 Race agreed that Pound's bankers should accept a further bill for one month for the total amount owing plus £10 interest, and received the new acceptance.

May 18 Race's bank informed him the new bill had been paid.

(Welsh Joint Education Committee—'A' Level)

22.8A. On 1 June 19–2, X purchased goods from Y for £860 and sold goods to Z for £570.

On the same date, X drew a bill (No. 1) at three months on Z for £400 and Z accepted it.

On 12 June 19–2, Z drew a bill (No. 2) at three months on Q for £150 which Q accepted.

On 14 June, Z endorsed bill No. 2 over to X and, on 16 June, X endorsed this bill over to Y.

On 20 June, X accepted a bill (No. 3) at three months for £720 drawn by Y in full settlement of his account, including interest. On 23 June, Y discounted bill No. 3 at his bank.

On 17 September, Y informed X that Q's acceptance had been dishonoured and X sent a cheque for £150 to Y. The other bills were paid on the due dates.

On 20 September, X received a cheque from Z for half the amount due from him.

Show the entries to record these transactions in the ledger and cash book of X.

(Chartered Institute of Secretaries and Administrators)

23

Goodwill

When a firm has been in existence for some time, then if the owner(s) wanted to sell the business, they may well be able to obtain more for the business as a going concern than they would if the assets shown on the Balance Sheet were sold separately. To simplify matters, imagine that a man has a small engineering works, of which he was the originator, and that the business was started by him some twenty years ago. He now wishes to sell the business. If sold separately, the assets on the balance sheet would fetch a total of £40,000, being £12,000 for machinery, £25,000 for premises and the stock £3,000. As a complete going concern a purchaser may be willing to pay a total of £50,000 for it. The extra £10,000 that the purchaser will pay over and above the total saleable values of the identifiable assets is known in accounting as goodwill. This is a technical term used in accounting, it must not be confused with the meaning of goodwill in ordinary language usage.

The reasons why the purchaser would be willing to pay £10,000 for goodwill are not always capable of being identified with precision, nor is it often possible to place any particular value on any of the reasons which have induced him to make this offer. One fact only is obvious, and that is that no rational person would be willing to pay a higher figure for the entire going concern than he would pay for buying the identifiable assets separately, unless the expected rate of return on the purchase money spent was greater in the case of the entire going concern. While it is not possible to list all of the factors which induce purchasers to pay for goodwill, it may be useful to examine some possible motives.

(*a*) The business may have enjoyed some form of monopoly, either nationally or locally. There may not be sufficient trade for two such engineering firms to be carried on profitably. If the purchaser buys this firm then no one may set up in competition with him. On the other hand, if he buys the other assets separately and sets up his own firm, then the original business will still be for sale and the owner may well fix a price that will induce someone to buy it. Many prospective entrants would therefore be prepared to pay an extra amount in the hope of preserving the monopoly position. The monopoly may possibly be due to some form of governmental licence not otherwise easily available.

(*b*) The purchaser could continue to trade under the same name as that of the original firm. The fact that the firm was well known could mean that new customers would be attracted for this reason alone. The seller would probably introduce the purchaser to his customers. The establishment of a nucleus of customers is something that many new firms would be willing to pay for, as full profits could be earned from the very start of the business instead of waiting until a large enough body of customers is built up. There could be profitable contracts that were capable of being taken over only by the purchaser of the firm.

(*c*) The value of the labour force, including management skills other than that of the retiring proprietor. The possession of a skilled labour force, including that of management, is an asset that Balance Sheets do not disclose. To recruit and train a suitable labour force is often costly in money and effort, and the purchaser of a going concern would obviously normally be in a position to take over most of the labour force.

(*d*) The possession of trade marks and patents. These may have cost the original owner little or nothing, not be shown on the Balance Sheet, and could be unsaleable unless the business is sold as a going concern.

(*e*) The location of the business premises may be more valuable if a particular type of business is carried on rather than if the premises were sold to any other kind of business firm.

(*f*) The costs of research and development which have brought about cheaper manufacturing methods or a better product may not have been capitalized, but may have been charged as revenue expenditure in the periods when the expenditure was incurred. For any new firm starting up it could well cost a considerable amount of money to achieve the same results.

The amount which someone is prepared to pay for goodwill therefore depends on their view of the future profits which will accrue to the business due to the factors mentioned, or similar assets difficult to identify. The seller of the business will want to show these additional assets to their best advantage, while the buyer will discount those that he feels are inappropriate or over-stressed. The figure actually paid for goodwill will therefore often be a compromise.

The economic state of the country, and whether or not a boom or a recession is in the offing, together with the effects of a credit squeeze or of reflation, plus the relative position of the particular industry, trade or profession, will all affect people's judgements of future profits. In addition the shortage of funds or relatively easy access to finance for such a purchase will, together with the factors already mentioned, lead to marked differences of money paid for goodwill of similar firms at different points in time.

There are also instances where the amount that could be obtained for an entire going concern is less than if all the assets were sold separately. This, contrary to many a person's guess is not 'badwill', as this is just not an accounting term, but would in fact be negative goodwill. The owner would, if he was a rational man, sell all the assets separately, but it does not always hold true. The owner may well have a pride in his work, or a sense of duty to the community, and may elect to sell only to those who would carry on in the same tradition despite the fact that higher offers for the assets had been made. In accounting it is well to remember that figures themselves only tell part of the story.

Methods of Valuing Goodwill

Custom plays a large part in the valuation of goodwill in many sorts of businesses. Goodwill exists sometimes only because of custom, because if a somewhat more scientific approach was used in certain cases it would be seen that there was no justification for a figure being paid for goodwill. However, justification or not, goodwill exists where the purchaser is willing to pay for it.

The mere calculation of a figure for goodwill does not mean that someone will be willing to pay this amount for it. As with the striking of any bargain there is no certainty until the price is agreed.

A very important factor to take into account in the valuation of goodwill is based on the 'momentum' theory of goodwill. This can be stated to be that the profits accruing to a firm from the possession of the goodwill at a point in time will lose momentum, and will be gradually replaced by profits accruing from new goodwill created later on. Thus the old goodwill fades away or loses momentum, it does not last for ever, and new goodwill is gradually created. Therefore in a business goodwill may always exist, but it will very rarely be either of the same value or composed of the same factors.

Some of the methods used in goodwill valuation can now be looked at. The rule of thumb approach can be seen in particular in methods (i), (ii) and (iii) which follow. However, the accountant's role has often been not necessarily to find any 'true' figure which could be validated in some way, but has instead been to find an 'acceptable' figure, one which the parties to a transaction would accept as the basis for settlement. In particular trades, industries and professions, these methods while not necessarily 'true' have certainly been acceptable as the basis for negotiations.

(i) In more than one type of retail business it has been the custom to value goodwill at the average weekly sales for the past year multiplied by a given figure. The given figure will, of course, differ as between different types of businesses, and often changes gradually in the same types of businesses in the long term.

(ii) With many professional firms, such as accountants in public practice, it is the custom to value goodwill as being the gross annual fees times a given number. For instance, what is termed a two years' purchase of a firm with gross fees of £6,000 means goodwill = 2× £6,000 = £12,000.
(iii) The average net annual profit for a specified past number of years multiplied by an agreed number. This is often said to be *x* years purchase of the net profits.
(iv) The super-profits basis.

(a) The Traditional View

The net profits are taken as not representing a realistic view of the 'true' profits of the firm. For a sole trader, no charge has been made for his services when calculating net profit, yet obviously he is working in the business just as is any other employee. If the net profit is shown as £5,000, he can say that he is better off by £5,000 than he would otherwise have been? The answer must be negative, since if he had not owned a business he could have been earning money from some other employment. Also, if he had not invested his money in the business he could have invested it somewhere else. If these two factors are taken into account, the amount by which he would have been better off is given the name of 'super-profit'.

Exhibit 23.1

Hawks, a chemist, has a shop from which he makes annual net profits of £4,300. The amount of his capital invested in the business was £10,000. If he had invested it elsewhere in something where the element of risk was identical he would have expected a 5 per cent return per annum. If, instead of working for himself, he had in fact taken a post as a chemist he would have earned a salary of £1,800 per annum.

	£	£
Annual net profits		4,300
Less Remuneration for similar work	1,800	
,, Interest on capital invested £10,000 at 5 per cent	500	2,300
Annual Super-profits		2,000

If it is expected that super-profits can be earned for each of the next five years, then the value of the goodwill is the present value of receiving £2,000 extra for each of the next five years. A chapter in Volume 2 will illustrate the calculation of this more clearly. Assuming that the £2,000 extra is in fact received at the end of each year, then the figure that is needed is the amount that would now have to be invested at 5 per cent which would accumulate interest, but from which £2,000 would be taken each year so that at the end of five years the fund is completely exhausted by the last withdrawal of £2,000. This amount is in fact £8,659.

Sometimes the goodwill is calculated as x years purchase of the super-profits. If this were an eight-year purchase of super-profits of £5,000, then the goodwill would be stated to be worth £40,000.

(b) The Discounted Momentum Value Method

The momentum theory of goodwill has already been discussed briefly. The benefits to be gained from goodwill purchased fall as that goodwill gradually ceases to exist, while other benefits are gained from new goodwill created by the new firm. The principle may be further illustrated by reference to the fact that old customers die or may leave the firm, and new ones coming along to replace them are lightly to be due to the efforts of the new proprietors. Therefore when buying a business the goodwill should be assessed as follows:

(i) Estimate the profits that will accrue from the firm if the existing business is taken over.

(ii) Estimate the profits that would be made if, instead of buying the existing business, identical assets are bought (other than the goodwill) and the firm starts from scratch.

The difference in the profits to be earned will therefore be as a result of the incidence of the goodwill.

Exhibit 23.2

Years	*Estimated profits if existing business taken over*	*Estimated profits if new business set up*	*Excess profits caused by goodwill taken over*
	£	£	£
1	10,000	4,000	6,000
2	11,000	6,000	5,000
3	11,500	8,500	3,000
4	12,000	11,000	1,000
5	12,000	12,000	—
(and later years will show no difference in profits)			
			15,000

The value of obtaining £6,000 extra for year 1, £5,000 for year 2, £3,000 for year 3 and £1,000 in year 4 can now be calculated. Assume that the cost of capital (discussed in greater detail in Volume 2) is 7 per cent. Assuming that the extra profits are received at the end of each year the present value of these future amounts of profit are now calculated.

Present value of £1 is the given number of years hence		*Number of £s*	*Nearest £*
£0·93458	×	6,000	5,607
£0·87344	×	5,000	4,367
£0·81630	×	3,000	2,449
£0·76290	×	1,000	763
			13,186

Therefore it would be worth buying existing goodwill if it could be bought for less than £13,186, while an asking figure of more than £13,186 would mean that the prospective purchaser might as well set up his own business from scratch. This is assuming that the prospective purchaser does not value his leisure unduly, or that he does not place any value on the nervous stress and strain consequent on building up goodwill.

Sole Trader's Books

It would not be normal for goodwill to be entered in a sole trader's books unless he had actually bought it. Therefore the very existence of goodwill in the Balance Sheet would result in the assumption that the sole trader had bought the business from someone previously and was not himself the founder of the business.

Partnership Books

The partners may make any specific agreement between themselves concerning goodwill. There is no limit as to the ways that they may devise to value it or to enter it in the books, or to make adjusting entries in the books without opening a Goodwill Account. Whatever they agree will therefore take precedence over anything written in this chapter.

However, failing any agreement to the contrary, it is possible to state that a partner in a firm will own a share in the goodwill in the same ratio which he shares profits. Thus if A take one-quarter of the profits, then he will be the owner of one-quarter of the goodwill. This will hold true whether or not a Goodwill Account is in existence. Should a new partner be introduced who will take a share of one-third of the profits, he will, subject to there being any contrary agreement, be the owner of one-third of the goodwill. It is therefore essential that he should either pay something for goodwill when he enters the firm, or else an amount should be charged to his Capital Account.

This can probably be seen more clearly if a simple example is taken. A and B are in partnership sharing profits one-half each. A new partner, C, is admitted and A, B and C will now take one-third share of the profits, and therefore each will now own one-third of the goodwill. As A and B used to own one-half of the goodwill each they have therefore given part of the asset to C. A few months later the business is sold to a large company and £30,000 is obtained for goodwill. A, B and C will thus receive £10,000 each for their respective shares of the goodwill. If C had not been charged for goodwill, or have paid nothing for it, then A and B would have surrendered part of their ownership of the firm to C and received nothing in return.

Any change in profit sharing will, unless specifically agreed to the contrary, mean that the ownership of the goodwill will also change. As some partners give up their share, or part of their share, of an asset while other partners gain, it is therefore essential that some payment or adjustment be made whenever profit sharing is altered. This will take place whenever any of the following events occur:

1. There is a change in the profit-sharing ratios of existing partners.
2. A new partner is introduced.
3. A partner dies or retires.

In all these cases the whole of the goodwill is not sold. Only in (2) is part of the goodwill sold or charged to an outsider. In (3) the goodwill may be bought by the remaining partners, this is not necessarily the same figure that could be obtained by sale to an outsider. In the case of (2) it is usually assumed that if a new partner is to pay £1,000 to the old partners in satisfaction for a one-quarter share of the goodwill, then the entire goodwill is worth £4,000. The reasoning behind this is that if one-quarter could be sold for £1,000 then the total price would be in the same ratio, i.e. 25 per cent equals £1,000, therefore 100 per cent equals £4,000. This is very often just not true. A relatively higher price may be obtainable from someone who was to be a senior partner than from someone who was to be a junior partner. Thus a one-quarter share of the goodwill might fetch £1,000, but a three-quarters' share of the goodwill might fetch (say) £5,000 because of the factors of prestige and control that a senior partnership would give to the purchaser.

Similarly, with the retirement or death of a partner the amount payable to him or his representatives may not be directly proportional to the total value of goodwill. Circumstances vary widely, but personal relationships and other factors will affect the sum paid.

The question of the value to be placed on goodwill in all of these cases is therefore one of agreement between the partners, and is not necessarily equal to the total saleable value.

Goodwill Accounts and Partnerships

Unlike a sole trader, a partnership may therefore have a Goodwill

Account opened in its books even though the goodwill has never been purchased from an outside source. For instance, a Goodwill Account may be opened just because the partners have changed profit-sharing ratios even though they were the partners that were the founders of the firm, and had not therefore ever paid anything to an outsider for goodwill.

With some of the methods used a Goodwill Account is opened, whereas in others adjustments are made without the use of a Goodwill Account. It is not always advantageous to open a Goodwill Account. The mere existence of a Goodwill Account in the Balance Sheet may influence some prospective purchaser of the business, or of part of the business, in a way that was not intended when the Goodwill Account was opened. If a Goodwill Account showed a balance of £10,000 and the partners wanted to sell goodwill for £30,000, the purchaser's decision may be affected. He may have been quite content to pay £30,000 if a Goodwill Account had never existed, but he is now in the position of being asked to pay £30,000 for something which had been valued at £10,000 *x* years ago. On the other hand, suppose that the Goodwill Account was shown at £10,000 but that the price asked for it was only £4,000. Both of these cases may well put doubts into the mind of the purchaser that would never have existed if a Goodwill Account had never been shown. On the other hand, a lender of money may be happy to see the firm's belief in its goodwill valuation stated as an asset in the Balance Sheet. Business decisions can never be divorced from behavioural patterns. A feeling of 'he gave X £1,000 for it a year ago, why should I give £2,000 for it now?' is very often totally irrational, and would not exist if in fact the buyer never knew that the seller had bought it for that amount.

1. Where there is a change in the Profit-sharing Ratios of Existing Partners

This will normally occur when the effective contributions made by the partners in terms of skill or effort have changed in some way. A partner's contribution may be reduced because of ill-health or old age, or because he is now engaged in some other activity outside the partnership firm. A partner's contribution may have increased because of greater effort or skill compared with when he first joined the firm. The partners will then have to mutually agree to the new profit-sharing ratios. Lack of agreement could mean that the firm would have to be dissolved.

Taking the same basic data, the two methods used whereby (*a*) a Goodwill Account is opened, and (*b*) adjustments are made without the use of a Goodwill Account, can now be illustrated.

Exhibit 23.3

E, F and G have been in business for ten years. They have always shared profits equally. No Goodwill Account has ever existed in the books. On 31 December 19–6 they agree that G will take only a one-fifth share of the profits as from 1 January 19–7, this being due to the fact that he will be devoting less of his time to the business in future. E and F will then each take two-fifths of the profits. The summarized Balance Sheet of the business on 31 December 19–6 appears as follows:

Balance Sheet as at 31 December 19–6

	£		£
Capitals: E	3,000		
F	1,800	Net Assets	7,000
G	2,200		
	7,000		7,000

The partners agree that the goodwill should be valued at £3,000.

(a) Goodwill account opened. A Goodwill Account is opened and the total value of goodwill is debited to it. The credit entries are made in the partner's Capital Accounts, being the total value of goodwill divided between the partners in their old profit-sharing ratio.

The Balance Sheet items before and after the adjustments will appear as:

	Before	*After*		*Before*	*After*
	£	£		£	£
Capitals: E	3,000	4,000	Goodwill	—	3,000
F	1,800	2,800			
G	2,200	3,200	Other Assets	7,000	7,000
	7,000	10,000		7,000	10,000

(b) Goodwill account not opened. The effect of the change of ownership of goodwill may be shown in the following form:

Before			*After*		*Loss or Gain*	*Action Required*
		£		£		
E	One-third	1,000	Two-fifths	1,200	Gain £200	Debit E's Capital Account £200
F	One-third	1,000	Two-fifths	1,200	Gain £200	Debit F's Capital Account £200
G	One-third	1,000	One-fifth	600	Loss £400	Credit G's Capital Account £400
		3,000		3,000		

The column headed 'Action Required' shows that a partner who has gained goodwill because of the change must be charged for it by having his Capital Account debited with the value of the gain. A partner who has lost goodwill must be compensated for it by having his Capital Account credited.

The Balance Sheet items before and after the adjustments will therefore appear as:

	Before	*After*		*Before*	*After*
	£	£		£	£
Capitals: E	3,000	2,800	Net Assets	7,000	7,000
F	1,800	1,600			
G	2,200	2,600			
	7,000	7,000		7,000	7,000

It would appear at first sight that there is some disparity between the use of methods (*a*) and (*b*). Suppose however that very shortly after the above adjustments the business is sold, the time element being so short that there has been no change in the value of goodwill. If the other assets are sold for £7,000 and the goodwill for £3,000, then in method (*a*) the £10,000 would be exactly sufficient to pay the amounts due to the partners according to their Capital Accounts. In the method (*b*) the Capital Accounts total £7,000 and so the cash received from the sale of the other assets would be exactly enough to pay for those amounts due to the partners. In addition the goodwill has been sold for £3,000, and this sum can now be paid to the partners in the ratio which they owned goodwill, i.e. E two-fifths, £1,200, F two-fifths, £1,200 and G one-fifth, £600. This means that in total each would receive: E £2,800+£1,200 = £4,000; F £1,600+£1,200 = £2,800; and G £2,600+£600 = £3,200. These can be seen to be the same amounts as those paid under method (*a*). The two methods therefore bring about the same end result, the only difference being that one method utilizes a Goodwill Account whereas the other method avoids it.

2. *A New Partner is Introduced*

On the introduction of a new partner, unless he takes over the share of a retiring or deceased partner, then obviously the share of the profits taken by each of the partners must change. If A is taking two-thirds of the profits and B one-third, then with the introduction of C, the old partners must give up a share of the profits to him. They can do this by either (*a*) giving up the same proportion of their share of the profits so that the comparative ratios in which they share profits remain the same as before, or else (*b*) the sharing of profits becomes such that the relative profit-sharing ratios of the old partners change as between the new firm and the old firm.

If (*a*) applies, then with the advent of C the profits shared could become any of the following:

Some Possible Solutions

	A	B	C
1	$\frac{1}{2}$	$\frac{1}{4}$	$\frac{1}{4}$
2	$\frac{2}{5}$	$\frac{1}{5}$	$\frac{2}{5}$
3	$\frac{4}{7}$	$\frac{2}{7}$	$\frac{1}{7}$
4	$\frac{4}{9}$	$\frac{2}{9}$	$\frac{3}{9}$

A used to have two-thirds of the profit and B one-third of the profit. A therefore always had a share of the profits which was twice as great as that of B. In all of the above solutions A still takes twice as much as B, irrespective of whatever C takes.

On the other hand, if the ratios became A one-third, B one-third and C one-third, then A would have ceased taking twice as much profits as B. This has been referred to as (*b*).

Where (*a*) applies the only adjustments needed are those between C and the old partnership to compensate for C taking over part of the goodwill. If (*b*) applies, then there will still be adjustments necessary for the goodwill taken over by C, but there will also be adjustments necessary for the change in the relative shares of goodwill held by the old partners.

(a) No Change in the Old Partners' Relative Shares of Profits. The three basic methods in use have been designed to meet the particular wishes of the partners. Each one is used to meet a particular situation. Thus method (i) is suitable where the old partners want to be paid in cash privately, and (ii) applies where the cash is to be retained in the business, whereas (iii) will be used where an adjustment only is required, in all probability because the incoming partner has insufficient cash to pay separately for goodwill.

(i) The new partner pays a sum to the old partners privately which they share in their old profit-sharing ratios. Sometimes the money is paid into the business, only to be drawn out immediately, this is merely being a contra in the Cash Book.

(ii) The new partner pays cash into the business. This is debited to the Cash Book, then credited to the old partners' Capital Accounts in their old profit-sharing ratios.

(iii) A Goodwill Account is opened in which the total estimated value of goodwill is debited, and the credits are made in the old partner's Capital Accounts in their old profit-sharing ratios. No cash is paid in by the new partner specifically for goodwill. Any cash he does pay in, is in respect of capital and will therefore be credited to his Capital Account.

(b) Where the Old Partners' Relative Shares of Profits Change with the Introduction of a New Partner. The introduction of a new partner often takes place because of some fundamental change in the business, and it is often found that the relative shares of profits taken by the old partners need adjusting to preserve an equitable division of the profits to be made in the future. Either the partner will pay a premium for his share of the goodwill, or else an adjustment will be made to charge his Capital Account without any cash being paid by him.

(i) The New Partner Pays a Premium for a Share of Goodwill. Unless otherwise agreed, the assumption is that the total value of goodwill is directly proportionate to the amount paid by the new partner for the share taken by him. If a new partner pays £1,200 for a one-fifth share of the profits, then goodwill is taken to be £6,000. A sum of £800 for a one-quarter share of the profits would therefore be taken to imply a total value of £3,200 for goodwill.

It must be stressed that where a Goodwill Account had been in existence in the old partnership showing the full value of goodwill then the old partners will have been credited with their respective shares, and the following adjustments would not be applicable. These two methods are therefore dependent on adjustments for goodwill rather than the opening of a Goodwill Account.

Exhibit 23.4

Partners, J, K, L and M share profits in the ratio 2:3:4:1 respectively. (In other words, there are 2+3+4+1 parts = 10 parts in all, so that J takes two-tenths, K three-tenths, L four-tenths and M one-tenth of the profits.) A new partner N is to be introduced, to pay £1,000 as a premium for his share of the goodwill. The profits will now be shared between J, K, L, M and N in the ratios 2:1:2:2:1 respectively (8 parts in all). The effect of the changes in the ownership of goodwill is now shown in the form of a table. As £1,000 has been paid for one-eighth of the goodwill, the total goodwill is taken as £8,000.

Before			*After*		*Loss or gain*	*Action required*
		£		£		
J	Two-tenths	1,600	Two-eighths	2,000	Gain £400	Debit J's Capital Account £400
K	Three-tenths	2,400	One-eighth	1,000	Loss £1,400	Credit K's Capital Account £1,400
L	Four-tenths	3,200	Two-eighths	2,000	Loss £1,200	Credit L's Capital Account £1,200
M	One-tenth	800	Two-eighths	2,000	Gain £1,200	Debit M's Capital Account £1,200
N	—	—	One-eighth	1,000	Gain £1,000	Debit N's Capital Account £1,000
		8,000		8,000		

K and L are the partners who have given up part of their ownership of goodwill. They are therefore compensated by having their Capital Accounts increased, while the partners who have gained are charged, i.e. debited, with the goodwill taken over. The debit in N's Capital Account will be cancelled by the credit entry made when he actually pays in the premium of £1,000 as arranged. Thus the new partner will have paid for his share of the goodwill, while the others will have had their claims against the assets of the firm, i.e. their Capital Accounts, adjusted accordingly.

(ii) The New Partner Does Not Pay a Premium for Goodwill. Assuming that the facts were the same as in Exhibit 23–2, but that the new partner N was not to actually pay an amount specifically for goodwill yet the total value of goodwill was taken as £8,000, then the entries would be exactly the same as already shown. The only difference would be that the debit entry in N's Capital Account would not be cancelled out by an equal credit by an amount paid in specifically for the purpose. If N paid in £3,000 into the business, then the £1,000 debit for goodwill would reduce his capital to £2,000. Likewise if he only paid in £400 his Capital Account would show a debit balance of £600 until his share of the profits became sufficient to transform this into a normal credit balance.

3. A Partner Retires or Dies

When a partner leaves the firm, then he, or his personal representatives, will agree with the old partners as to how this shall be arranged. Perhaps the partnership deed will contain provisions for such an event, and if so this will normally be observed. Otherwise a new agreement will be arrived at. It would, of course, be normal for any agreement to take the course that the retiring partner was entitled to have his share of the goodwill credited to his Capital Account in his profit-sharing ratio. He could leave the amount due to him as a loan to the partnership, or else all or part of it be repaid to him either immediately or be repaid by instalments.

It could well be the case that a new partner takes over the retiring partner's share, all transactions being between him and the retiring partner, the other partners not interfering in any way. The only point that can be made with any certainty is that if the partners cannot agree as to the manner in which any settlement is to be made, then the partnership will have to be dissolved. In this case the procedures are outlined in the next chapter.

Many students are needlessly upset in examinations, because sometimes the examiner sets a question involving partnership goodwill in which the procedures to be carried out are quite unlike anything the student has ever seen before. It must be borne in mind that the partners can agree to payments or adjustments for goodwill in a manner decided by themselves. It does not have to bear any relationship to normal practice; it is purely a matter for agreement. Therefore the examiner is imagining such a situation, and the instructions the examination candidates are given are in accordance with such an imaginary agreement. If the student complies with the instructions he is therefore answering the question in the way required by the examiner.

A Company's Books

A limited company, as in the case of a sole trader, would normally open a Goodwill Account only when it had bought goodwill from some other firm.

Depreciation of Goodwill

There is certainly no consistency between firms regarding the depreciation of goodwill. On the one hand, some businessmen take a highly emotional view of the asset. They feel that there is something wrong about showing it as an asset because they do not feel that it is a 'real' asset. Their attitude is to depreciate it down to nothing as soon as possible and heave a sigh of relief when it ceases to appear on the Balance Sheet. Others say that goodwill is a permanent asset unless something occurs to affect it. Therefore they maintain that it should not be depreciated at all.

Both of these views are accepted; it is not that one view is right and that the other is wrong. Accounting practice is therefore quite flexible on this point, and it is a matter for the businessman to decide for himself. A comment that could be made on the attitude of the businessmen who prefer to write down goodwill in years when the profits shown are high, and therefore an extra provision for depreciation does not seem to matter so much as it would do in a year of low profits, is that provisions for depreciation of goodwill are being charged in the very years when it is shown to exist and even to grow because of the high profits. On the other hand, those who keep goodwill at its purchase price indefinitely on the grounds that goodwill still exists, are in fact stating that the goodwill that they bought is depreciating but is being replaced by new goodwill being created by the firm. They are therefore allowing the appreciation in the new goodwill to cancel out the depreciation of the old goodwill. It is therefore strictly contravening the 'cost' concept which shows assets at their cost less depreciation, because the asset that was bought was the old goodwill and that will certainly have depreciated.

Exercises

23.1. X and Y are in partnership, sharing profits and losses equally. They decide to admit Z. By agreement, goodwill valued at £6,000 is to be introduced into the business books. Z is required to provide capital equal to that of Y after he has been credited with his share of goodwill. The new profit sharing ratio is to be 4:3:3 respectively for X, Y and Z.

The Balance Sheet before admission of Z showed:

	£		£
Capital X	8,000	Fixed and Current Assets	15,000
Capital Y	4,000	Cash	2,000

	£		£
Current Liabilities	5,000		
	17,000		17,000

Show:
(*a*) Journal Entries for admission of Z.
(*b*) Opening Balance Sheet of new business.
(*c*) Journal entries for writing off the goodwill which the new partners decided to do soon after the start of the new business.
(East Midland Educational Union)

23.2. Wacks, Rouse and Patterson are in partnership sharing profits and losses in the ratios of 5:4:1 respectively. Their Capital Accounts show credit balances of Wacks £3,000, Rouse £5,000 and Patterson £4,000.

Two new partners are introduced, Pickering and Tinker. The profits are now to be shared: Wacks 3; Rouse 4; Patterson 2; Pickering 2; Tinker 1. Pickering is to pay in £3,000 for his share of the goodwill but Tinker has insufficient cash to pay immediately.

No Goodwill Account is to be opened. Show the Capital Accounts for all of the partners after Pickering has paid for his share of the goodwill.

23.3A. L, M and S are in partnership. They shared profits in the ratio 2:5:3. It is decided to admit R. It is agreed that goodwill was worth £10,000, but that this is not to be brought into the business records. R will bring £4,000 cash into the business for capital. The new profit sharing ratio is to be L 3:M 4:S 2:R 1.

The Balance Sheet before R was introduced was as follows:

	£		£
Capitals: L	3,000	Assets (other than cash)	11,000
M	5,000		
S	4,000		
		Cash	2,500
Creditors	1,500		
	13,500		13,500

Show:
(*a*) The entries in the Capital Accounts of L, M, S and R, the accounts to be in columnar form.
(*b*) The balance sheet after R has been introduced.

23.4A. Coy, Clark and Keers are partners. They share profits in the ratio of 5:3:2 respectively. Their capitals have credit balances of Coy £10,000, Clark £9,000 and Keers £7,000.

Two new partners are introduced, Wild and Duffy. The profits will now be shared Coy 3: Clark 4: Keers 2: Wild 2: Duffy 4. Duffy is to pay £2,000 for his share of the goodwill plus an extra £5,000 for capital. Wild has insufficient cash to pay immediately.

No Goodwill Account should be opened. Show the Capital Accounts for all the partners after Duffy has paid his amount into the firm.

24

Partnership Accounts Continued: Revaluation of Assets and Dissolution

Revaluation of Assets

It has been shown in Chapter 23 that adjustments or payments are required for goodwill in a partnership when a new partner is introduced, the partners change their relative profit-sharing ratios, or a partner retires or dies. Similarly, on each of those occasions the other assets may need to be revalued. Unless there is some agreement to the contrary, if the business is sold and the sale price of the assets exceeds their book values, then the resultant profit is shared between the partners in their profit- and loss-sharing ratios. Similarly, a loss would be borne by them in the same ratios. It is therefore essential that the assets on the Balance Sheet are not markedly out of touch with reality when any changes in partnerships occur. Exhibit 24–1 illustrates the necessity for the revaluation of assets.

Exhibit 24.1

The summarized Balance Sheet of a partnership business is as follows:

Balance Sheet as at 31 December 19–6

	£		£
Capitals: J	4,000	Property (at cost)	2,000
		Machinery (at cost *less*	
K	3,000	depreciation)	3,500
		Stock	1,500
L	5,000	Debtors	3,000
		Bank	2,000
	12,000		12,000

J, K and L started the business thirty years previously. They had always shared profits equally, but from 1 January 19–7 it was to change to J three-sevenths, K three-sevenths and L one-seventh. No revaluation of the assets took place. Six months later the business was sold because of friction between J and K. Because of the nature of the business the assets have to be realized separately and there is no goodwill. The firm had been extremely fortunate in the choice of its premises thirty years ago, they were now sold for £23,000, a profit of £21,000. With the machinery the firm had been negligent in not realizing that obsolescence had greatly reduced its value and the sale realized only £350—a loss of £3,150. The stock was sold for £1,500. The debtors included a debt of £2,100 from Long Ltd which had to be written off as a bad debt, all the other debts being realized in full. In fact it was L who had strongly recommended that Long Ltd was acceptable as a customer. None of the realized prices had been affected to any marked extent by events of the previous six months.

The profit on the premises £21,000 is divided as to J three-sevenths, £9,000, K three-sevenths, £9,000, and L one-seventh, £3,000. L's chagrin can be understood when it can be stated that if the partnership assets had been sold more than six months previously, then his share would have been one-third, £7,000 instead of £3,000.

The loss on the machinery is £3,150, shared J three-sevenths, £1,350, K three-sevenths, £1,350, and L one-seventh, £450. As the obsolescence factor is traceable back to more than six months ago, then L's advantage is not an equitable one.

The loss on debtors of £2,100 can be largely traceable to L's action in recommending an uncreditworthy customer. Yet the loss is shared: J three-sevenths, £900, K three-sevenths, £900 and L one-seventh, only £300.

The need for the assets to be revalued upon some change in the basis of the partnership is therefore obvious. The revised agreed values are amended quite simply. A Revaluation Account is opened, any increase in asset values being credited to it and the corresponding debits being in the asset accounts, while any reductions in asset values are debited to the Revaluation Account and credited to the asset accounts. If the increases exceed the reductions, then there is said to be a profit on revaluation, such a profit being shared by the old partners in their old profit-sharing ratio, the credit entries being made in the partners' Capital Accounts. The converse applies for a loss on revaluation. An illustration is now given in Exhibit 24–2.

Exhibit 24.2

The following is the summarized Balance Sheet of R, S and T who shared profits and losses in the ratios 3:2:1 respectively.

From 1 January 19–8 the profit-sharing ratios are to be altered to R 2:S 4:T 1. The following assets are to be revalued in the following amounts—Premises £7,000, Fixtures £1,800, Motor vehicles £1,300, and Stock to £1,500. The accounts needed to show the revaluation are as follows:

Balance Sheet as at 31 December 19–7

	£		£
Capitals: R	4,000	Premises (at cost)	4,500
S	5,000	Motor Vehicles (at cost *less* depreciation)	1,500
T	3,000	Fixtures (at cost *less* depreciation)	2,000
		Stock	1,800
		Debtors	1,600
		Bank	600
	12,000		12,000

Revaluation

	£	£		£
Assets reduced in value:			Assets increased in value:	
Fixtures		200	Premises	2,500
Motor Vehicles		200		
Stock		300		
Profit on Revaluation carried to Capital Accounts	£			
R three-sixths	900			
S Two-sixths	600			
T one-sixth	300	1,800		
		2,500		2,500

Premises

	£		£
Balance b/fwd	4,500		
Revaluation: Increase	2,500	Balance c/d	7,000
	7,000		7,000
Balance b/d	7,000		

Fixtures

	£		£
Balance b/fwd	2,000	Revaluation: Reduction	200
		Balance c/d	1,800
	2,000		2,000
Balance b/d	1,800		

Motor Vehicles

	£		£
Balance b/fwd	1,500	Revaluation: Reduction	200
		Balance c/d	1,300
	1,500		1,500
Balance b/d	1,300		

Stock

	£		£
Balance b/fwd	1,800	Revaluation: Reduction	300
		Balance c/d	1,500
	1,800		1,800
Balance b/d	1,500		

Capital: R

	£		£
		Balance b/fwd	4,000
Balance c/d	4,900	Revaluation: Share of profit	900
	4,900		4,900
		Balance b/d	4,900

Capital: S

	£		£
		Balance b/fwd	5,000
Balance c/d	5,600	Revaluation: Share of profit	600
	5,600		5,600
		Balance b/d	5,600

Capital: T

	£		£
Balance c/d	3,300	Balance b/fwd	3,000
		Revaluation: Share of profit	300
	3,300		3,300
		Balance b/d	3,300

The balances brought down are those used to start the recording of transactions for the following period.

Partnership Dissolution

Technically a partnership is dissolved whenever a new partner is admitted or a partner leaves the partnership firm; in addition there may be other reasons why the partnership can no longer be carried on, such as a court order insisting that the partnership be dissolved. Someone may cease to be a partner because of death, retirement, bankruptcy, insanity, etc. In their accepted sense, 'dissolution accounts' mean that the debts of the partnership are discharged and the assets distributed in accordance with the partnership deed or the provisions of the Partnership Act 1890. This is also the sense in which the term is used in examinations. However, the full dissolution of a partnership very rarely takes place just because of a change in partners. A full dissolution would in fact normally only take place when some disagreement between the partners that could not be settled amicably had occurred, or where the court had ordered it.

Upon a full dissolution of the partnership then, unless the partners otherwise agree, the amounts obtained from the realization of the assets plus any amounts paid in by partners to clear off debit balances on Capital or Current Accounts shall be disbursed in the following order:

1. In paying the debts and liabilities of the firm to persons who are not partners. It would in fact be an illegal act to pay any monies due to a partner before the creditors were paid, unless it was obvious that the creditors would be paid in full.

2. In paying to each partner the amount due to him in respect of advances as distinguished from capital. If the amount available is sufficient to pay (1) but not (2), then the amounts payable will be in proportion to the amount owing. For example, if there was only £3,000 left after (1) had been paid, and the advances to be repaid were £4,000 from A and £1,000 from B, then A would receive

$$\frac{£4,000}{£4,000+£1,000} \times £3,000 = £2,400, \text{ and B would receive}$$

$$\frac{£1,000}{£4,000+£1,000} \times £3,000 = £600.$$

3. To pay to each partner the amount finally due to him according to his Capital and Current Accounts. Any profit on realization will, subject to any agreement to the contrary, be credited to the partners' Capital Accounts in their profit- and loss-sharing ratio, while any loss will be debited in the same proportions. If a partner's final net balance on his Capital and Current Accounts is a debit balance, then he will be required to pay that amount into the partnership bank account. Should the partner not be able to meet all, or part, of such a deficiency, then the rule in *Garner* v. *Murray* will apply (see page 369) unless otherwise agreed.

When the business is being realized it is not necessary for all of the assets to be sold to outside parties. Very often one or more of the partners may take over some of the assets. The amount at which such assets will pass to him will be agreed to by all the partners. It is not necessary that he actually pays in an amount for them; it would be more normal for them to be charged to his Capital Account and so reduce the amount finally due to him.

The account opened to record the dissolution is the Realization Account. This is the account in which the profit or loss on realization is calculated, so that transfers can be made of the profits or losses to increase or reduce the amounts repayable to the partners, or by them, in respect of their Capital Accounts. To do this, the book values of the assets (with the exception of the cash and bank balances as these already represent 'realized' assets) are transferred to the debit of the Realization Account, while the amounts realized for them are credited to that account. As the Realization Account is nothing more than a Profit and Loss Account for a special purpose, an excess of credits over debits indicates a profit on realization, the converse represents a loss. Any costs of realizing the assets will also have been debited to the Realization Account. The profit or loss on realization will be divided between the partners in the profit- and loss-sharing ratio and will be transferred to their Capital Accounts.

It is a common failing of students to transfer the liabilities to the Realization Account. However, as realization for this purpose means 'sold' it will be obvious that liabilities are not realized, they are discharged, and it would therefore be an error of principle to show them in the Realization Account. As a matter of convenience it is often found that discounts on creditors, being a gain, are shown on the credit side of the Realization Account. They could instead be divided in the profit- and loss-sharing ratios and credited to the partners' Capital Accounts.

A fully worked example is shown in Exhibit 24–3. While every account is shown here, it would not be normal in examinations to show every account, the accounts normally shown in examinations have an (S) after the title of the account. This is because these accounts alone will demonstrate that the candidate understands the principles concerned. To show all the other accounts would only be time-consuming and would not really demonstrate the possession of any further knowledge. Of course, in real firms every account is shown.

Exhibit 24.3

On 31 December 19–8, P, Q and R decided to dissolve partnership. They had always shared profits in the ratio of P 3:Q 2:R 1.

Their goodwill was sold for £3,000, the machinery for £1,800 and the stock for £1,900. There were three motor-cars, all taken over by the partners at agreed values, P taking one for £800, Q one for £1,000 and R one for £500. The premises were taken over by R at an agreed value of £5,500. The amounts collected from debtors amounted to £2,700 after bad debts and discounts had been deducted. The creditors were discharged for £1,600, the difference being due to discounts received. The costs of dissolution amounted to £1,000.

Their last Balance Sheet is summarized as:

Balance Sheet as at 31 December 19–8

	£		£	£	£
		Fixed Assets			
Capital Account: P	6,000	Premises			5,000
Q	5,000	Machinery			3,000
R	3,000	Motor vehicles			2,500
	14,000				10,500
Current Accounts: P	200				
Q	100				
R	500				
	800				
Current Liabilities		*Current Assets*			
Creditors	1,700	Stock		1,800	
		Debtors	3,000		
		Less Provision for bad debts	200		
				2,800	
		Bank		1,400	
					6,000
	16,500				16,500

The accounts recording the dissolution are now shown. A description of each entry follows the accounts. The letters (A) to (K) against each entry indicates the relevant description.

Premises

	£			£
Balance b/fwd	5,000	Realization	(B)	5,000

Machinery

	£			£
Balance b/fwd	3,000	Realization	(B)	3,000

Motor Vehicles

	£			£
Balance b/fwd	2,500	Realization	(B)	2,500

Stock

	£			£
Balance b/fwd	1,800	Realization	(B)	1,800

Debtors

	£			£
Balance b/fwd	3,000	Provisions for bad debts	(A)	200
		Realization	(B)	2,800

Realization (S)

			£			£
Assets to be realized:				Bank: Assets sold		
Premises	(B)		5,000	Goodwill	(C)	3,000
Machinery	(B)		3,000	Machinery	(C)	1,800
Motor vehicles	(B)		2,500	Stock	(C)	1,900
Stock	(B)		1,800	Debtors	(C)	2,700
Debtors	(B)		2,800	Taken over by partners:		
Bank: Costs	(G)		1,000	P: Motor-car	(D)	800
Profit on realization:	(H)			Q: Motor-car	(D)	1,000
		£		R: Motor-car	(D)	500
P		600		R: Premises	(D)	5,500
Q		400		Creditors:		
R		200	1,200	Discounts	(F)	100
			17,300			17,300

Creditors

		£			£
Bank	(E)	1,600	Balance b/fwd		1,700
Realization (Discounts)	(F)	100			
		1,700			1,700

Bank (S)

		£			£
Balance b/fwd		1,400	Creditors	(E)	1,600
Realization: Assets sold			Realization: Costs	(G)	1,000
Goodwill	(C)	3,000	P: Capital	(K)	6,000
Machinery	(C)	1,800	Q: Capital	(K)	4,500
Stock	(C)	1,900			
Debtors	(C)	2,700			
R: Capital	(J)	2,300			
		13,100			13,100

P Capital (S)

		£			£
Realization: Motor-car	(D)	800	Balance b/fwd		6,000
Bank	(K)	6,000	Current Account transferred	(I)	200
			Realization: Share of profit	(H)	600
		6,800			6,800

Provision for Bad Debts

		£			£
Debtors	(A)	200	Balance b/fwd		200

P Current Account

		£			£
P: Capital	(I)	200	Balance b/fwd		200

Q Current Account

		£			£
Q: Capital	(I)	100	Balance b/fwd		100

Q Capital (S)

		£			£
Realization: Motor-car	(D)	1,000	Balance b/fwd		5,000
Bank	(K)	4,500	Current Account transferred	(I)	100
			Realization: Share of profit	(H)	400
		5,500			5,500

R Capital (S)

		£			£
Realization: Motor-car	(D)	500	Balance b/fwd		3,000
Realization: Premises	(D)	5,500	Current Account transferred	(I)	500
			Realization: Share of profit	(H)	200
			Bank	(J)	2,300
		6,000			6,000

R Current Account

		£		£
R: Capital	(I)	500	Balance b/fwd	500

Description of transactions:

(A) The provision accounts are transferred to the relevant asset accounts, so that the net balance on the asset accounts may be transferred to the Realization Account. Dr Provision Accounts, Cr Asset Accounts.

(B) The net book values of the assets are transferred to the Realization Account. Dr Realization Account, Cr Asset Accounts.

(C) Assets sold. Dr Bank Account, Cr Realization Account.

(D) Assets taken over by partners. Dr Partners' Capital Accounts, Cr Realization Account.

(E) Liabilities discharged. Cr Bank Account, Dr Liability Accounts.

(F) Discounts on creditors. Dr Creditors' Account, Cr Realization Account.

(G) Costs of dissolution. Cr Bank Account, Dr Realization Account.

(H) Profit or Loss split in profit/loss-sharing ratio (subject to contrary agreement). Profit—Dr Realization Account, Cr Partners' Capital Accounts. The converse if a loss.

(J) Transfer the balances on the partners' Current Accounts to their Capital Accounts.

(J) Any partner with a Capital Account in deficit, i.e. debits exceed credits, must now pay in the amount needed to cancel his indebtedness to the partnership firm. Dr Bank Account, Cr Capital Account.

(K) The credit balances on the partners' Capital Accounts can now be paid to them. Cr Bank Account, Dr Partners' Capital Accounts.

The payments made under (K) should complete the elimination of all the balances in the partnership books. It should be checked that the balance in hand at the bank, after all other payments and receipts have been made, should exactly equal the amounts to be repaid to the partners. If it does not, then an error has been made. This fact often bewilders students meeting it for the first time. The fact that it should be true is a further reiteration of the accounting equation. The steps in a partnership dissolution may be shown thus for a firm where A takes three-quarters of the profit and B takes one-quarter.

(*a*) Capital + Liabilities = Assets
A £3,000 + B £2,000 + Creditors £1,000 = £6,000

(*b*) Liabilities discharged
Capital = Assets
A £3,000 + B £2,000 = (£6,000–£1,000) £5,000

(*c*) Assets sold at a loss of £1,200
Capital = Assets
A (£3,000 − $\frac{3}{4}$ loss £900) £2,100 + B (£2,000 − $\frac{1}{4}$ loss £300) £1,700
= (£5,000 − £1,200) £3,800 Bank

The final bank balance of £3,800 therefore exactly equals the totals of the balances on the partners' Capital Accounts. The equality of Capital + Liabilities = Assets must always hold true, and after the liabilities have been discharged, then it becomes Capital = Assets. The assets are all converted into a final bank balance, any loss on sale having been deducted not only on the assets side but also from the Capital Accounts. The final asset, i.e. the bank balance, will therefore always equal the final balances on the Capital Accounts.

The Rule in Garner *v.* Murray

It sometimes happens that a partner's Capital Account finishes up with a debit balance. Normally the partner will pay in an amount to clear his indebtedness to the firm. However, sometimes he will be unable to pay all, or part, of such a balance. In the case of *Garner* v. *Murray* in 1904 the court ruled that, subject to any agreement to the contrary, such a deficiency was to be shared by the other partners *not* in their profit- and loss-sharing ratios but in the ratio of their 'last agreed capitals'. By 'their last agreed capitals' is meant the credit balances on their Capital Accounts in the normal Balance Sheet drawn up at the end of their last accounting period. It must be borne in mind that the balances on their Capital Accounts after the assets have been realized may be far different from those on the last Balance Sheet. Where a partnership deed is drawn up it is commonly found that agreement is made to use normal profit- and loss-sharing ratios instead, thus rendering the *Garner* v. *Murray* rule inoperative.

Exhibit 24.4

After completing the realization of all the assets, in respect of which a loss of £4,200 was incurred, but before making the final payments to the partners, the Balance Sheet appears:

Balance Sheet

	£		£
Capitals: R	5,800	Cash at bank	6,400
S	1,400	Capital: Q debit balance	1,200
T	400		
	7,600		7,600

According to the last Balance Sheet drawn up before the dissolution, the partners' Capital Account credit balances were: Q £600; R £7,000; S £2,000; T £1,000; while the profits and losses were shared Q 3:R 2:S 1:T 1.

Q is unable to meet any part of his deficiency. Each of the other partners therefore suffer the deficiency as follows:

$$\frac{\text{Own capital per Balance Sheet before dissolution}}{\text{Total of all solvent partners' capitals per same Balance Sheet}} \times \text{Deficiency}$$

This can now be calculated.

$$\text{R} \quad \frac{£7{,}000}{£7{,}000+£2{,}000+£1{,}000} \times £1{,}200 = £840$$

$$\text{S} \quad \frac{£2{,}000}{£7{,}000+£2{,}000+£1{,}000} \times £1{,}200 = £240$$

$$\text{T} \quad \frac{£1{,}000}{£7{,}000+£2{,}000+£1{,}000} \times £1{,}200 = £120$$

$$£1{,}200$$

When these amounts have been charged to the Capital Accounts, then the balances remaining on them will equal the amount of the bank balance. Payments may therefore be made to clear their Capital Accounts.

	Credit balance B/fwd		*Share of deficiency now debited*		*Final credit balances*
	£		£		£
R	5,800	−	840	=	4,960
S	1,400	−	240	=	1,160
T	400	−	120	=	280
Equals the bank balance					6,400

The rule has often been criticized, many parties maintaining that it would be more equitable if the normal profit- and loss-sharing ratios were used. The basic idea behind the rule is that an agreement to share profits and losses refers to those accruing from trading operations, the fact that a partner may not honour his obligations concerning capital is a risk which attaches to capital only. However, in a case such as that shown in Exhibit 24–4 it is possible, if fluctuating Capital Accounts had been used, that both R, S and T could each have started with £1,000 capital each some years ago. R allows a much greater part of his profits to remain in the business than the other partners. It would seem a strange way of rewarding him for the financing benefits which have flowed from R's behaviour to make him suffer a more than proportionate share of Q's deficiency. The rule would act as a deterrent to a partner wishing to leave undrawn profits in the firm. The use of separate agreements to ignore the rule and of Current Accounts which are ignored for this purpose, have been the ways used by the accounting profession to circumvent the *Garner* v. *Murray* decision.

Piecemeal Realization of Assets

Frequently the assets may take a long time to realize. The partners will naturally want payments made to them on account as cash is received. They will not want to wait for payments until the dissolution is completed just for the convenience of the accountant. There is, however, a danger that if too much is paid to a partner, and he is unable to repay it, then the person handling the dissolution could be placed in a very invidious position.

Therefore the convention of conservatism is brought into play. The view taken is to treat each receipt of sale money as being the last money receivable. Any loss then calculated is shared between the partners in their profit- and loss-sharing ratio. Should any partner's Capital Account then show a debit balance it is assumed that he will be unable to meet such a deficit, and this will be shared (subject to any contrary agreement) between the other partners using the *Garner* v.

Murray rule. After payment of the liabilities and the costs of dissolution the remaindeı of the cash is then paid to the partners.

In this manner, even if no further money was received, or should a partner become insolvent, the division of the available cash would be strictly in accordance with the legal requirements. Exhibit 24–5 shows such a series of calculations.

Exhibit 24.5

The following is the summarized Balance Sheet of H, I, J and K as at 31 December 19–5. The partners had shared profits in the ratios H 6:I 4:J 1:K 1.

Balance Sheet as at 31 December 19–5

	£		£
Capitals:		Assets	8,400
H	600		
I	3,000		
J	2,000		
K	1,000		
Creditors	1,800		
	8,400		8,400

On 1 March 19–6 some of the assets were sold for cash £5,000. Out of this the creditors £1,800 and the cost of dissolution £200 are paid, leaving £3,000 distributable to the partners.

On 1 July 19–6 some more assets are sold for £2,100. As all of the liabilities and the costs of dissolution have already been paid, then the whole of the £2,100 is available for distribution between the partners.

On 1 October 19–6 the final sale of the assets realized £1,200.

First Distribution: 1 March 19–6	*H*	*I*	*J*	*K*
	£	£	£	£
Capital balances before dissolution	600	3,000	2,000	1,000
Loss if no further assets realized— Assets £8,400 – Sale £5,000 = £3,400+ Costs £200 = £3,600 loss				
Loss shared in profit/loss ratios	1,800	1,200	300	300
	1,200 Dr	1,800 Cr	1,700 Cr	700 Cr
H's deficiency shared in *Garner* v. *Murray* ratios		$\frac{3}{6}$ 600	$\frac{2}{6}$ 400	$\frac{1}{6}$ 200
Cash paid to partners (£3,000)		1,200	1,300	500

Second Distribution: 1 July 19–6	*H*	*I*	*J*	*K*
	£	£	£	£
Capital balances before dissolution	600	3,000	2,000	1,000
Loss if no further assets realized— Assets £8,400 – Sales (£5,000 + £2,100) = £1,300 + costs £200 = £1,500 loss.				
Loss shared in profit/loss ratios	750	500	125	125
	150 Dr	2,500 Cr	1,875 Cr	875 Cr
H's deficiency shared in *Garner* v. *Murray* ratios		75	50	25
		2,425	1,825	850
Less first distribution already paid		1,200	1,300	500
Cash now paid to partners (£2,100)		1,225	525	350
Third and Final Distribution: 1 October 19–6				
Capital balances before dissolution	600	3,000	2,000	1,000
Loss finally ascertained— Assets £8,400 – Sales (£5,000 + £2,100 + £1,200) = £100 + costs £200 = £300 loss.				
Loss shared in profit/loss ratios	150	100	25	25
	450 Cr	2,900 Cr	1,975 Cr	975 Cr
(No deficiency now exists on any Capital Account)				
Less first and second distributions	—	2,425	1,825	850
Cash now paid to partners (£1,200)	450	475	150	125

In any subsequent distribution following that in which all the partners have shared, i.e. no partner could then have had a deficiency left on his Capital Account, all receipts of cash are divided between the partners in their profit- and loss-sharing ratios. Following the above method would give the same answer for these subsequent distributions but obviously an immediate division in the profit- and loss-sharing ratios would be quicker. The reader is invited to try it to satisfy himself that it would work out at the same answer.

Exercises

24.1. Hill, Vale and Dale were partners in a firm sharing profits and losses in the proportions of one-half, one-third and one-sixth respectively.

On 31 May 19–6 Hill retired from the firm and it was agreed that in order to ascertain the balance due to him certain of the assets should be revalued.

The original balance sheet at 31 May 19–6 was:

	£		£
Hill Capital	40,000	Freehold premises	21,000
Vale Capital	34,000	Plant	32,000
Dale Capital	14,000	Equipment	4,200
Sundry creditors	6,400	Investment	20,000
		Debtors	5,400
		Bank	11,800
	94,400		94,400

It was agreed to revalue the premises at £42,000, plant at £28,000 and equipment at £3,600, and to value goodwill at £11,200. The investment was transferred to Hill at book value, together with £6,000 cash, in part payment of the amount due to him, the balance being left on loan account.

Draw up the initial balance sheet of the new firm immediately after Hill's retirement, after giving effect to the above.
(Union of Educational Institutions)

24.2. Birch, Rose and Larch were in partnership sharing profits and losses: Birch one-half, Rose one-third, Larch one-sixth.

The draft Balance Sheet as on 31 March 19–7 was as follows:

	£	£		£	£
Capital Accounts:			Freehold premises		6,000
Birch	12,000		Plant and equipment		9,400
Rose	6,000		Stock		4,600
Larch	3,000		Debtors	6,200	
		21,000	*Less* Provision for		
Current Accounts:			doubtful debts	600	
Birch	960				5,600
Rose	840		Balance at bank		8,060
Larch	560				
		2,360			
Loan—Birch		2,500			
Provision for staff pensions		3,000			
Creditors		4,800			
		33,660			33,660

Birch retired on 31 March 19–7, and Rose and Larch continued in Partnership, sharing profits and losses: Rose two-thirds, Larch one-third. Birch's loan was repaid on 1 April 19–7, and it was agreed that the remaining balance due to him, other than that on his current account, should remain on loan to the partnership.

It was agreed that the following adjustments were to be made to the Balance Sheet as on 31 March 19–7:

(i) The freehold premises were to be revalued at £12,000 and the plant and equipment at £7,900.
(ii) The provision for bad debts was to be increased by £200.
(iii) A provision of £250 included in creditors was no longer required.
(iv) The provision for staff pension was to be increased by £2,000.

(v) £600 was to be written off the stock in respect of damaged and obsolete items included therein.

(vi) Provision of £120 was to be made for professional charges in connection with the revaluations.

The partnership agreement provided that on the retirement of a partner, goodwill was to be valued at an amount equal to the average annual profits of the three years expiring on the date of the retirement. The relevant profits were:

	£
Year ended 31 March 19–5	6,520
Year ended 31 March 19–6	8,420
Year ended 31 March 19–7	7,210 (as shown by the draft accounts)

It was agreed that, for the purpose of valuing goodwill, the revaluation of the fixed assets, the adjustment to the provision for staff pensions and the professional charges should not be regarded as affecting the profits.

No account for goodwill was to be maintained in the books, adjusting entries for transactions between the parties being made in their capital accounts.

You are required to prepare:

(*a*) the Revaluation Account,

(*b*) Birch's account, showing the balance due to him, and

(*c*) the Balance Sheet of Rose and Larch as on 1 April 19–7.

(Institute of Chartered Accountants)

24.3. Black, White and Green carried on a manufacturing business in partnership sharing profits and losses: Black two-fifths, White two-fifths, Green one-fifth. They agreed to amalgamate as on 31 December 19–6 with Frost who carried on a similar business.

The summarized Balance Sheets of the two firms as on 31 December 19–6 were as follows:

	Black, White and Green		*Frost*		*Black, White and Green*		*Frost*
	£	£	£		£	£	£
Capital Accounts				Freehold premises		6,000	—
Black	8,000			Plant and motor			
White	6,000			vehicles		3,600	2,400
Green	4,000						
		18,000	—			9,600	2,400
Frost		—	3,000	Stocks		6,000	2,500
Trade creditors		9,000	2,000	Debtors	7,400		3,600
Bank overdraft		—	3,500	*Less:* Provision for			
				doubtful debt	400		
						7,000	
				Balance at bank		4,400	—
		27,000	8,500			27,000	8,500

The terms on which the businesses were amalgamated were as follows:

(i) Black was to retire on 31 December 19–6, any balance due to him being left on loan with the new firm.

(ii) Profits were to be shared: White one-half, Green one-quarter, Frost one-quarter.

(iii) The values of goodwill were agreed at £10,000 for the firm of Black, White and Green and £4,000 for Frost.

(iv) The new firm was to take over all the assets and discharge all the liabilities of the two businesses, but certain of the assets were to be revalued as follows:

	Black, White and Green	Frost
	£	£
Freehold premises	8,000	—
Plant and motor vehicles	3,200	2,900
Debtors	6,800	3,160

(v) The capital of the new firm was to be £10,000 and was to be contributed by the partners in their profit-sharing ratios, any surplus or deficiency being transferred to Current Accounts.

No account for goodwill was to be maintained in the books, adjusting entries for transactions between the partners being made in the partners' Capital Accounts.

You are required to give:
(*a*) the partners' Capital Accounts in the books of the old and the new firms, recording these transactions, and
(*b*) the opening Balance Sheet of the new firm.
(Institute of Chartered Accountants)

24.4. C and D were in partnership sharing profits and losses three-fifths and two-fifths respectively after allowing D a salary of £1,200 per annum. No interest was allowed on capital.

On 1 April 19–6 E was admitted as a partner on the following terms:

(i) E to pay £2,000 as capital;
(ii) E to pay £400 for his share of unrecorded goodwill, this sum to remain in the business;
(iii) D to continue to be entitled to a salary of £1,200 per annum and E to be entitled to a salary of £800 per annum;
(iv) interest to be allowed on fixed capitals at 5 per cent per annum;
(v) profits and losses to be shared C two-fifths, D two-fifths, E one-fifth;
(vi) final accounts to continue to be prepared annually to 31 December.

The following was the firm's trial balance at 31 December 19–6:

	£	£
Capitals: C		6,000
D		4,000
E		2,000
Current Accounts: C		50
D		80
Drawings: C	1,800	
D	1,900	
E	900	
Payment by E—for goodwill		400
Fixed Assets	10,000	
Stock 1 January 19–6	4,100	
Debtors and creditors	330	3,200
Purchases and sales	15,800	22,000
General expenses	1,120	
Bank balance	1,780	
	37,730	37,730

At 31 December 19–6:

1. No entries had been made for (i) goods withdrawn by D for private use, valued at £100, (ii) partners' interest and salaries;

2. Stock was valued at £4,200;

3. Depreciation of fixed assets is to be provided for at 8 per cent per annum;

4. It was discovered that no entries had been made in the accounts for the year 19–5 in respect of D's salary of £1,200 for that year, and it was decided to make the appropriate adjustments by entries in the partners' current account.

Gross profit is to be apportioned on the basis of sales, which for the first three months of the year amounted to £4,400. General expenses accrued evenly throughout the year.

You are required to prepare:

(*a*) The firm's trading account for the year;
(*b*) in columnar form, the profit and loss and appropriation accounts for the periods before and after the admission of E;
(*c*) D's current account.

Note:
A balance sheet is *not* required.
(Associated Examining Board 'A' Level)

24.5. Feet and Yard were in partnership sharing profits and losses: Feet three-fifths, Yard two-fifths. The following was the summarized Balance Sheet of the partnership as on 31 December 19–4:

	£	£		£	£
Capital Accounts:			Buildings, plant, machinery and equipment		8,400
Feet	7,516		Investments		3,200
Yard	4,408		Current assets:		
		11,924	Stock	4,000	
Loan: Feet	3,000		Debtors	3,500	
Interest accrued	80				7,500
		3,080			
Creditors		2,500			
Bank overdraft		1,596			
		19,100			19,100

1. Feet and Yard, wishing to dissolve partnership, accepted the offer of Measures Ltd to purchase the business. The company agreed:

(i) to take over the stock and the buildings, plant, machinery, and equipment, with the exception of two motor-cars whose book values were £800 and £400 respectively, and
(ii) that the consideration, £20,000, was to be satisfied by a cash payment of £11,000 and the balance by the transfer to the partners of 21,000 ordinary shares of £0.5 each.

2. Feet took over the first-mentioned motor-car at a valuation of £850 and Yard the other at a valuation of £350.

3. Feet's loan, together with the interest accrued thereon, was transferred to his Capital Account.

4. Cash realized on the sale of investments amounted to £2,800. The debtors realized £3,300 and the creditors were settled for £2,400.

5. Costs incurred were £150.

6. The partners agreed to divide the ordinary shares in proportion to the balances on their capital accounts after realization, settling their final balances by cash.

You are required to prepare:
(*a*) the Realization Account,
(*b*) the Bank Account, and
(*c*) Partners' Capital Accounts showing the final settlement between them.
(Institute of Chartered Accountants)

24.6. Saunders, Thomas and Baker are in partnership sharing profits and losses in the ratio of 3:2:1. The following is their balance sheet as at 1 April 19–6.

	£		£
Creditors	3,500	Cash	1,790
Current Accounts:		Debtors	2,440
Saunders	860	Stock	3,000
Thomas	520	Investments	3,164
Capital Accounts:		Plant and machinery	5,704
Saunders	9,200	Freehold buildings	2,932
Thomas	4,600	Current Account:	
Baker	2,300	Baker	1,950
	20,980		20,980

It has been decided that the partnership should be dissolved, Saunders agreeing to take over the stock, plant and machinery and freehold buildings for £10,200. The investments are sold for £1,720, creditors are settled for £3,400 and debtors realize £2,112.

Baker is declared insolvent, a payment of 25 per cent of each £ being received from his estate.

Show how the above transactions would be dealt with in the Realization, Bank and Capital Accounts of the partners. The final settlement made by or to the partners should be shown.
(Northern Counties Technical Examinations Council)

24.7 A, B and Z who were in partnership sharing profits and losses A three-eighths, B three-eighths and Z one-quarter decided to close down their business on 1 January 19–5. The Balance Sheet on that date was as follows.

Balance Sheet

Capital Account	£	£	£		£	£
A		6,000		Goodwill (at cost)		3,000
B		4,000		*Fixed Assets*		
Z	1,000			Freehold premises (at cost)		10,000
Less Debit balance				Fixtures, Fittings (at cost		
on Current A/c	170	830		*less* depreciation)		1,500
			10,830	*Current Assets*		
Current Accounts				Stock		3,240
A	200			Sundry debtors	2,400	

B	300		*Less* Provision for bad debts	200	
		500			2,200
Sundry creditor		4,820	Cash in hand		10
Bank overdraft		3,800			
		19,950			19,950

Goodwill was written off, freehold premises were sold at book value and fixtures and fittings realized £250. Stock was sold by auction for £2,400. All book debts, with the exception of a balance of £160, were collected subject to discounts amounting to £110. Expenses of realization of the assets amounted to £360 which was paid by cheque.

Out of the proceeds of the realization the bank overdraft and the creditors were paid in full.

Accounts were then drawn up to show the amount due to or from each partner. Nothing could be recovered from Z in respect of his deficiency.

You are required to show the Realization Account and the closing entries in each partner's Capital Account and in the Cash Book.
(Associated Examining Board 'A' Level)

24.8A. Hand and Glove, who share profits and losses equally, decide to dissolve their partnership as at 31 March 19–1.

Their balance sheet on that date was as follows:

	£		£
Capital Account: Hand	2,000	Buildings	800
Glove	1,500	Tools and fixtures	850
		Debtors	2,800
	3,500	Cash	1,800
Sundry creditors	2,750		
	6,250		6,250

The debtors realized £2,700, the buildings £400 and the tools and fixtures £950. The expenses of dissolution were £100 and discounts totalling £200 were received from creditors.

Prepare the accounts necessary to show the results of the realization and of the disposal of the cash.
(Royal Society of Arts and London Chamber of Commerce—Joint Scheme)

24.9A. Black and Green were in partnership sharing profits in the ratio of 3:2. The balance sheet of the firm on 31 December 19–7 was as follows:

	£		£
Capital: Black	9,620	Fixed assets	13,100
Green	7,219	Current assets	8,453
	16,839		
Creditors	4,714		
	21,553		21,553

On 31 December 19–8 current assets amounted to £9,426 and creditors were £4,187. Each partner drew £1,000 in 1968. There had been no capital expenditure during the year.

On 1 January 19–9 Black and Green agreed to wind up their business and ceased trading on that day. During January 19–9 they sold the plant for £12,100 and current assets (other than cash) at their book value and the creditors were paid off in full. On 31 January 19–9 the partners withdrew the amounts due to them.

Required:

(*a*) a calculation of profit for 19–8 (ignore depreciation); and

(*b*) realization account, cash account and partners' capital accounts to record the realization.

Note: Ignore taxation.
(Institute of Bankers)

24.10A. *Balance Sheet of X, Y and Z as at 31 March 19–0*

	£		£
Capitals: *X*	8,000	Premises	12,000
Y	4,000	Furniture, etc.	1,312
Z	4,000	Stock	3,200
		Debtors	848
	16,000		
Creditors	1,100		
Bank overdraft	260		
	17,360		17,360

X, *Y* and *Z* share profits and losses in proportion to their Capitals.

The partnership is being dissolved as on 31 March 19–0.

Y is continuing in business on his own account and it is agreed he shall take over the stock at a valuation of £3,600, the furniture for £1,100, and the Debtors at £820.

Y also takes over the premises. These are re-valued at £21,000. *Y* secures a mortgage of £16,000 and a cheque for this amount is paid into the partnership banking account. By agreement the balance which *Y* owes to the partnership is to be treated as a loan from *X* for the time being, settlement (with agreed interest) to be made within a year.

The creditors of the partnership are paid in full.

Show the entries in the ledger of the partnership to give effect to the foregoing.
(Welsh Joint Education Committee—'A' Level)

24.11A. Long, Tall and Short were in partnership sharing profits and losses: Long 40 per cent, Tall 35 per cent and Short 25 per cent.

The draft Balance Sheet of the partnership as on 30 September 19–9, was as follows:

	£	£		£	£
Capital accounts:			Leasehold premises at cost		7,500
Long	9,000		Plant and equipment at cost	8,000	
Tall	5,000		*Less* Provision for depreciation	2,800	

	£	£		£	£
Short	3,000				5,200
		17,000			
Current accounts:			Stock		4,200
Long	1,200		Debtors	3,400	
Tall	800		*Less* Provision for doubtful		
Short	600		debts	600	
		2,600			2,800
Loan—Tall		3,000	Balance at bank		6,700
Creditors		3,800			
		26,400			26,400

Tall retired on 30 September 19–9, and Long and Short continued in partnership, sharing profits and losses: Long 60 per cent, Short 40 per cent. Half of Tall's loan was repaid on 1 October 19–9, and it was agreed that £8,000 of the balance remaining due to him should remain on loan to the partnership.

It was agreed that adjustments were to be made to the Balance Sheet as on 30 September 19–9, in respect of the following:

1. The leasehold premises which had been acquired two years previously on 1 October 19–7, and were leased for a period of 15 years were to be written off over the period of the lease.
2. The plant and equipment was to be revalued at £5,800.
3. The provision for doubtful debts was to be increased by £120.
4. Creditors for expenses amounting to £500 had been omitted from the books.
5. £400 was to be written off the stock in respect of obsolete items included therein.
6. Provision of £120 was to be made for professional charges in connection with the revaluation.

The partnership agreement provided that on the retirement of a partner, goodwill was to be valued at an amount equal to the average annual profit of the three years expiring on the date of retirement and that, in arriving at the profits, a notional amount of £8,000 should be charged for partners' salaries. The relevant profits before charging such salaries were:

		£
Year ended 30 September:	19–7	14,400
	19–8	16,800
	19–9	18,820 (as shown by the draft accounts)

It was agreed that, for the purpose of valuing goodwill, the revaluation of the plant and equipment and the professional charges should not be regarded as affecting the profits.

No account for goodwill was to be maintained in the books, adjusting entries of transactions between the partners being made in their capital accounts.

You are required to prepare:

(*a*) The Revaluation Account,
(*b*) Partners' Capital Accounts (in columnar form),
(*c*) Tall's account showing the balance due to him, and
(*d*) the Balance Sheet of Long and Short as on 1 October 19–9.

(Institute of Chartered Accountants)

25

Departmental Accounts

Accounting information varies in its usefulness. For a retail store with five departments, it is obviously better to know that the store has made £10,000 gross profit than to be completely ignorant of this fact. The figure of £10,000 gross profit unfortunately does not give the owners the insight into the business necessary to control it much more effectively. What would be far more meaningful would be the knowledge of the amount of gross profit or loss for each department. Assume that the gross profits and losses for the departments were as follows:

Department	*Gross profit*	*Gross loss*
	£	£
A	4,000	
B	3,000	
C	5,000	
D		8,000
E	6,000	
	18,000	8,000

Gross profit of the firm, £10,000.

Ignoring the overhead expenses for the sake of simplicity, although in practice they should never be ignored, can any conclusions be drawn from the above? It may well appear that if department D was closed down then the store would make £18,000 gross profit instead of £10,000. This could equally well be true or false depending on circumstances. Department D may be deliberately run at a loss so that its cheap selling prices may attract customers who, when they come to the store, also buy goods in addition from departments A, B, C and E. If department D were closed down perhaps most of the customers would not come to the store at all. In this case all the other departments would only have small gross profits because of the falls in sales and if this happened the gross profits might well be—departments: A £1,000, B £500, C £2,500 and E £2,000, a total of £6,000. Therefore department

D operating at a loss because of cheap prices would have increased the gross profit of the firm.

The converse could, however, hold true. If department D were closed down the sales in the other departments might rise. Department D could be a wine and spirits department at the entrance to the store through which all customers have to walk to the other departments. Teetotallers may therefore avoid the store because they would not like to be seen going into a department where alcohol was being sold. To close down the department, leaving it merely as an access route to the other departments, may result in higher sales in these other departments because the teetotallers who had previously shunned the store might now become customers. The effect on the existing non-teetotal customers could also be considered as well as the possibility of the re-location of the wine and spirits department.

Accounting information therefore seldom tells all the story. It serves as one measure, but there are other non-accounting factors to be considered before a relevant decision for action can be made.

The various pros and cons of the actions to be taken to increase the overall profitability of the business cannot therefore be efficiently considered until the departmental gross profits or losses are known. It must not be thought that departmental accounts refer only to departmental stores. They refer to the various facets of a business. Consider the simple case of a barber who does shaving, shampoos and haircutting. He may find that the profit from shaving is very small, and that if he discontinues shaving he will earn more from extra haircutting because he does not have to turn customers away because of lack of time. The principle of departmental accounts is concerned just as much with the small barber's shop as with a large department store. The reputation of many a successful businessman has been built up on his ability to utilize the departmental account principle to guide his actions to increase the profitability of a firm. The lesson still has to be learned by many medium-sized and small firms. It is one of accounting's greatest, and simplest, aids to business efficiency.

Expenses

The expenses of the firm are often split between the various departments, and the net profit for each department then calculated. Each expense is divided between the departments on what is considered to be the most logical basis. This will differ considerably between businesses. An example of a Trading and Profit and Loss Account drawn up in such a manner is shown in Exhibit 25–1.

Exhibit 25.1

The Lazarus Company have three departments in their store:

	(*a*) Cosmetics	(*b*) Ladies hairdressing	(*c*) Millinery
	£	£	£
Stock of goods or materials, 1 January 19–8	2,000	1,500	3,000
Purchases	11,000	3,000	15,000
Stock of goods or materials, 31 December 19–8	3,000	2,500	4,000
Sales and work done	18,000	9,000	27,000
Wages of assistants in each department	2,800	5,000	6,000

The following expenses cannot be traced to any particular department:

	£
Rent and rates	3,500
Administration expenses	4,800
Heating and lighting	2,000
General expenses	1,200

It is decided to apportion rent and rates together with heating and lighting in accordance with the floor space occupied by each department. These were taken up in the ratios of (*a*) one-fifth, (*b*) half, (*c*) three-tenths. Administration expenses and general expenses are to be split in the ratio of sales and work done.

Lazarus Company
Trading and Profit and Loss Account for the year ended 31 December 19–8

	(*a*) Cos-metics	(*b*) Hair-dressing	(*c*) Mil-linery		(*a*) Cos-metics	(*b*) Hair-dressing	(*c*) Mil-linery
	£	£	£		£	£	£
Stock 1 January 19–8	2,000	1,500	3,000	Sales and work done	18,000	9,000	27,000
Add Purchases	11,000	3,000	15,000				
	13,000	4,500	18,000				
Less Stock 31 December 19–8	3,000	2,500	4,000				
Cost of goods or materials	10,000	2,000	14,000				
Gross profit c/d	8,000	7,000	13,000				
	18,000	9,000	27,000		18,000	9,000	27,000
Wages	2,800	5,000	6,000	Gross profit b/d	8,000	7,000	13,000
Rent and rates	700	1,750	1,050				
Administration expenses	1,600	800	2,400				
Heating and lighting	400	1,000	600				
General expenses	400	200	600				
Net profit	2,100		2,350	Net loss		1,750	
	8,000	8,750	13,000		8,000	8,750	13,000

This way of calculating net profits and losses seems to imply a precision that is lacking in fact, and would often lead to an interpretation that the hairdressing department has lost £1,750 this year, and that this amount would be saved if the department was closed down. It has already been stated that different departments are very often dependent on one another, therefore it will be realized that this would not necessarily be the case. The calculation of net profits and losses are also dependent on arbitrary division of overhead expenses. It is by no means obvious that the overheads of department (*b*) would be avoided if it were closed down. Assuming that the sales staff of the department could be discharged without redundancy payments or other forms of compensation, then £5,000 would be saved in wages. The other overhead expenses shown under department (*b*) would not, however, necessarily disappear. The rent and rates may still be payable in full even though the department were closed down. The administration expenses may turn out to be only slightly down, say from £4,800 to £4,600, a saving of £200; heating and lighting down to £1,500, a saving of £500; general expenses down to £1,100, a saving of £100. Therefore the department, when open, costs an additional £5,800 compared with when the department is closed. This is made up as follows:

	£
Administration expenses	200
Heating and lighting	500
General expenses	100
Wages	5,000
	5,800

But when open, assuming this year is typical, the department makes £7,000 gross profit. The firm is therefore £1,200 a year better off when the department is open than when it is closed, subject to certain assumptions. These are:

(*a*) That the remaining departments could not be profitably expanded into the space vacated to give greater proportionate benefits than the hairdressing department.

(*b*) That a new type of department which would be more profitable than hairdressing could not be set up.

(*c*) That the department could not be leased to another firm at a more profitable figure than that shown by hairdressing.

There are also other factors which, though not easily seen in an accounting context, are still extremely pertinent. They are concerned with the possible loss of confidence in the firm by customers generally; what appears to be an ailing business does not usually attract good customers. Also the effect on the remaining staff should not be ignored. The fear that the dismissal of the hairdressing staff may mirror what is also going to happen to themselves may result in the loss of staff, especially the most competent members who could easily find work elsewhere, and so the general quality of the staff may decline with serious consequences for the firm.

A far less misleading method of drafting departmental accounts is by showing costs which are in the nature of direct costs allocated entirely to the department, and which would not be payable if the department was closed down, in the first section of the Trading and Profit and Loss Account. The second section is left to cover those expenses which need arbitrary apportionment or which would still be payable on the closing of the department. The surpluses brought down from the first section represent the 'contribution' that each department makes to cover the other expenses and profit. The contributions can thus be seen to be the results of activities which are under a person's control, in this case the departmental managers concerned. The sales revenue has been generated by the workforce, etc., all under their control, and the costs charged have been under their control, so that the surpluses earned (or deficits incurred) are affected by the degree of their control. The other costs in the second section are not, however, under their control. The departmental managers cannot directly affect to any extent the costs of rent and rates or of heating and lighting, so that the contributions from the sections of the business must more than cover all these expenses if the business is to earn a profit. From the figures given in Exhibit 25–1 the accounts would appear as follows:

Lazarus Company

Trading and Profit and Loss Account for the year ended 31 December 19–8

	(a) *Cos-metics*	*(b)* *Hair-dressing*	*(c)* *Mil-linery*		*(a)* *Cos-metics*	*(b)* *Hair-dressing*	*(c)* *Mil-linery*
	£	£	£		£	£	£
Stock 1 January 19–8	2,000	1,500	3,000	Sales and work done	18,000	9,000	27,000
Add Purchases	11,000	3,000	15,000				
	13,000	4,500	18,000				
Less Stock 31 December 19–8	3,000	2,500	4,000				
Cost of goods or materials	10,000	2,000	14,000				
Wages	2,800	5,000	6,000				
Surpluses c/d	5,200	2,000	7,000				
	18,000	9,000	27,000		18,000	9,000	27,000

	All Departments		*All Departments*
	£		£
Rent and rates	3,500	Surplus b/d:	
Administration expenses	4,800	Cosmetics	5,200
Heating and lighting	2,000	Hairdressing	2,000
General expenses	1,200	Millinery	7,000
Net profit	2,700		
	14,200		14,200

None the less, frustrating though it may be, in examinations students must answer the questions as set, and not give their own interpretations of what the question should be. Therefore if an examiner gives details of the methods of apportionment of expenses, then he is really looking for an answer in the same style as Exhibit 25–1.

The Balance Sheet

The Balance Sheet does not usually show assets and liabilities split between different departments.

Exercises

25.1. J. Spratt is the proprietor of a shop selling books, periodicals, newspapers and children's games and toys. For the purposes of his accounts he wishes the business to be divided into two departments:

Department A Books, periodicals and newspapers.
Department B Games, toys and fancy goods.

The following balances have been extracted from his nominal ledger at 31 March 19–6:

	Dr	*Cr*
	£	£
Sales Department A		15,000
Sales Department B		10,000
Stocks Department A, 1 April 19–5	250	
Stocks Department B, 1 April 19–5	200	
Purchases Department A	11,800	
Purchases Department B	8,200	
Wages of sales assistants Department A	1,000	
Wages of sales assistants Department B	750	
Newspapers delivery wages	150	
General office salaries	750	
Rates	130	
Fire insurance—buildings	50	
Lighting and heating	120	
Repairs to premises	25	
Internal telephone	25	
Cleaning	30	
Accountancy and audit charges	120	
General office expenses	60	

Stocks at 31 March 19–6 were valued at:
Department A £300
Department B £150

The proportion of the total floor area occupied by each department was:

Department A One-fifth
Department B Four-fifths

Prepare J. Spratt's Trading and Profit and Loss Account for the year ended 31 March 19–6, apportioning the overhead expenses, where necessary, to show the Department profit or loss.

25.2. The Supply-All Stores has various departments. The Directors desired to know the separate approximate net profits of departments 5, 8 and 9 for the four months ended 31 December 19–1. It was found impracticable to take stock on that date. However, there is a good system of departmental accounting in operation and it is known that the normal rates of gross profit on turnover for the departments in question are 35 per cent, 33⅓ per cent and 25 per cent respectively.

The following is the information available:

	Departments		
	5	*8*	*9*
Stock on hand 1 September 19–1	5,000	4,400	6,000
Sales during the period	10,000	5,400	10,800
Purchases during the period	5,700	5,000	6,000
Direct expenses during the period	1,710	850	1,280

The indirect expenses during the period, including those attributable to other departments, amounted in total to £4,698, and the sales of all the departments in total amounted to £78,300.

Indirect expenses are charged to each department in proportion to turnover.

Prepare a statement for submission to the directors providing for each department a stock reserve of 12 per cent on the estimated value as at 31 December 19–1.

25.3A. From the following list of balances you are required to:

1. Prepare a departmental trading and profit and loss account in columnar form for the year ended 31 March 19–0, in respect of the business carried on under the name of S.V.A. Trading Company.

		£	£
Rent and rates			2,100
Delivery expenses			1,200
Commission			1,920
Insurance			450
Purchases:	Dept. A	26,400	
	B	21,800	
	C	17,400	
			65,600
Discounts received			984
Salaries and wages			15,750
Advertising			972
Sales:	Dept. A	40,000	
	B	32,000	
	C	24,000	
			96,000
Depreciation			1,470
Opening Stock:	Dept. A	7,300	
	B	5,620	
	C	4,560	
			17,480

		£	£
Administration and general expenses			3,945
Closing stock:	Dept. A	6,200	
	B	4,327	
	C	4,873	
			15,400

Except as follows, expenses are to be apportioned equally between the departments.

Delivery expenses—proportionate to sales.
Commission—two per cent of sales.
Salaries and wages; Insurance—in the proportion of 6:5:4.
Discounts received—1·5 per cent of purchases.

2. What advantages do you see in preparing final accounts in this form?
(Union of Educational Institutions)

25.4A. A, B, C and D were partners in a garage business comprising (i) petrol sales, (ii) repairs and servicing and (iii) second-hand car dealing.

A was responsible for petrol sales, B for repairs and servicing, C for second-hand car deals whilst D acted purely in an advisory capacity.

The partnership agreement provided the following:

(i) Interest on fixed capital at 10 per cent per annum.
(ii) Each working partner to receive commission of 10 per cent of the gross profit of his own department.
(iii) Profits were shared as follows:

A: $\frac{2}{10}$
B: $\frac{3}{10}$
C: $\frac{3}{10}$
D: $\frac{2}{10}$

(iv) Accounts to be made up annually to 30 September.

A Trial Balance extracted from the books at 30 September 19–7 showed the following balances:

		Dr	*Cr*
		£	£
A	Capital Account		3,500
	Current Account		1,350
	Drawings Account	6,000	
B	Capital Account		7,500
	Current Account		7,500
	Drawings Account	13,250	
C	Capital Account		6,500
	Current Account		5,500
	Drawings Account	10,500	
D	Capital Account		12,500
	Current Account		2,150
	Drawings Account	3,500	
Freehold premises at cost		25,000	
Goodwill at cost		10,000	
Servicing tools and equipment at cost		9,000	

	Dr	Cr
	£	£
Servicing tools and equipment—accumulated depreciation to 1 October 19–6		1,350
Bank Balance		10,105
Stocks at 1 October 19–6—Petrol	950	
Spares	525	
Second-hand cars	6,350	
Debtors	4,350	
Cash in hand	125	
Creditors		2,350
Sales—Petrol		68,650
Servicing and repairs		86,750
Cars		156,000
Purchases—Petrol	58,500	
Spares	51,650	
Second-hand cars	118,530	
Wages—Forecourt attendants	5,750	
Mechanics	31,350	
Car salesmen	8,550	
Office personnel	1,850	
Rates	2,500	
Office expenses	1,800	
Heating and lighting	550	
Advertising	775	
Bank interest	350	
	371,705	371,705

The following additional information is obtained:

1. Stocks at 30 September 19–7

	£
Petrol	1,050
Spares	475
Second-hand cars	9,680

2. Depreciation on tools and equipment is to be provided at 5 per cent per annum by the straight-line method.

3. Your fees for preparation of the accounts will be £175.

4. The service department did work valued at £11,300 on the second-hand cars.

5. The service department used old cars valued at £550 for spare parts in services and repairs.

You are required to prepare:

(*a*) Trading and Profit and Loss Account for the year ended 30 September 19–7.
(*b*) Balance Sheet at 30 September 19–7.
(*c*) Partners' Current Accounts in columnar form for the year.

APPENDIX 25.1

Columnar Day Books: Sales and Purchases

In Appendix 9–2 the reader will have been shown how to draw up Purchases Analysis Books. The basic idea of having a total column, and analysing the items under various headings, can be carried one stage further. This could be the case where it was desired to ascertain the profits of a firm on a departmental basis.

In such a case the Purchases Analysis Books already described could have additional columns so that the purchase of goods for each department could be easily ascertained. Taking the Purchases Analysis Book per Exhibit 9–4, assume that the firm had three departments, Sports Department, Household Department and Electrical Department. Instead of one column for Purchases there could be three columns, each one headed with the title of a Department. When the invoices for purchases were being entered in the enlarged Purchases Analysis Book, the amount of each invoice could be split as between each department, and the relevant figures entered in each column. The total figure of all the three columns would represent the total for Purchases, but it would also be known how much of the Purchases were for each department. This would help when the final accounts were being drafted in a departmental fashion. The Purchases Analysis Book per Exhibit 9–4 might appear instead as follows in Exhibit 25–3.

Exhibit 25.2

Purchases Analysis Book Page 105

Date 19–5	*Name of Firm*	*PL Folio*	*Total*	*Sports Dept.*	*Household Dept.*	*Electrical Dept.*	*Stationery*	*Motor*	*Carriage Inwards*
			£	£	£	£	£	£	£
May 1	D. Watson Ltd	129	296	80	216				
,, 3	W. Donachie & Son	27	76	76					
,, 5	Barnes Motors Ltd	55	112					112	
,, 6	J. Corrigan & Co	88	65				65		
,, 8	C. Bell Ltd	99	212	92		120			
,, 10	Barnes Motors Ltd	55	39					39	
,, 13	A. Hartford & Co	298	35				35		
,, 16	M. Doyle Ltd	187	243			243			
,, 20	G. Owen	222	58						58
,, 21	B. Kidd & Son	188	135	135					
,, 24	K. Clements	211	122	70		52			
,, 24	Channon Haulage	305	37						37
,, 26	C. Bell Ltd	99	111		111				
,, 28	A. Hartford & Co	298	49				49		
,, 29	B. Kidd & Son	188	249	60	103	86			
,, 31	Barnes Motors Ltd	55	280					280	
			2,119	513	430	501	149	431	95
				GL 77	GL 77	GL 77	GL 97	GL 156	GL 198

The Purchases Account in the General Ledger could also have three columns, so that the purchases for each department could be entered in separate columns. Then, when the Trading Account is drawn up the respective totals of each department could be transferred to it. The items shown in Exhibit 25–2 will be used in Exhibit 25–3 later.

Of course, a Purchases Day Book could be kept, strictly for Purchases only, without the other expenses, such as Stationery, Motor Expenses and Carriage Inwards. In this case there would simply be the total column with an analysis column for each separate department's purchase.

With Purchases, the use of an analysis book with columns for other expenses is very useful. When looking at Sales, however, the need to split Sales between departments is not usually accompanied by the need to show analysis columns for other items of income. Involved in the expenditure of a firm are many items of expense besides Purchases. With income, the main part of income is represented by the Sales. The amount of transactions in such items as the selling of a fixed asset are relatively few. The Sales Analysis Book, or Columnar Sales Book as it might be called, therefore usually consists of the sales of goods only.

A columnar Sales Book for the firm in Exhibit 25–2 might appear as in Exhibit 25–3.

Exhibit 25.3

Columnar Sales Day Book

Date		*Name of Firm*	*SL Folio*	*Total*	*Sports Dept.*	*Household Dept.*	*Electrical Dept.*
19–5			£	£	£	£	£
May	1	N. Coward Ltd	87	190		190	
,,	5	L. Olivier	76	200	200		
,,	8	R. Colman & Co	157	307	102		205
,,	16	Aubrey Smith Ltd	209	480			480
,,	27	H. Marshall	123	222	110	45	67
,,	31	W. Pratt	66	1,800		800	1,000
				3,199	412	1,035	1,752
					GL 88	GL 88	GL 88

The Sales Account, and the Purchases Account, in the General Ledger could be in columnar form. From Exhibits 25–2 and 25–3 the Purchases and Sales Accounts would appear as:

General Ledger

Sales — page 88

					19–5		*Sports Dept.*	*Household Dept.*	*Electrical Dept.*
							£	£	£
					May 31	Credit Sales for the month	412	1,035	1,752

page 77 — Purchases

19–5		*Sports Dept.*	*Household Dept.*	*Electrical Dept.*		
May 31	Credit Purchases for the month	513	430	501		

The Purchases and Sales Accounts would then accumulate the figures for these items, so that when the final accounts were being drawn up the total figures for each department could be transferred to the

Trading Account. There is, of course, nothing to stop a firm having one account for Purchases (Sports Dept.), another for Purchases (Household Dept.) and so on. The Stock Account could be kept in a columnar fashion as well, to aid the transfer of stock values to the respective departmental columns in the Trading Account.

The personal accounts in the Sales and Purchases Ledgers would not be in columnar form. As an instance of this, the personal account of W. Pratt in the Sales ledger would simply be debited with £1,800 in respect of the goods sold to him, there being no need to show the analysis between Household and Electrical Departments in his account. If the firm wanted to have columnar personal accounts then there is nothing to stop them keeping them, but this would not normally be the case.

Sales Analysis Books and VAT

All that would be needed would be an extra column for VAT. In the example that follows the debtors would be charged up with the gross amounts, whilst the VAT £184 would be credited to the VAT Account, and the Sales figures of £1,040, £410 and £390 credited to the Sales Account.

Columnar Sales Day Book

Date	*Name of Firm*	*SL Folio*	*Total*	*VAT*	*Furniture Dept.*	*Hardware Dept.*	*General Dept.*
19–4			£	£	£	£	£
May 1	H. Smedley	133	220	20	200		
„ 6	T. Sarson	297	528	48	210	100	170
„ 16	H. Hartley Ltd	444	286	26		110	150
„ 31	H. Walls	399	990	90	630	200	70
			2,024	184	1,040	410	390
				GL 65	GL 177	GL 177	GL 177

Exercise to Appendix 25.1

25.5A. D. Jones, a wholesale dealer in electrical goods, has three departments: (*a*) Hi Fi, (*b*) TV, and (*c*) Sundries. The following is a summary of D. Jones' Sales Invoices during the period 1 to 7 February 19–7:

	Customer	*Invoice No.*	*Department*	*List price less trade discount*	*VAT*	*Total invoice price*
				£	£	£
Feb. 1	P. Small	261	TV	2,600	208	2,808
2	L. Goode	262	Hi Fi	1,800	144	1,944
3	R. Daye	263	TV	1,600	128	1,728
5	B. May	264	Sundries	320	Nil	320
7	L. Goode	265	TV	900	72	972
	P. Small	266	Hi Fi	3,400	272	3,672

(*a*) Record the above transactions in a columnar book of original entry and post to the General Ledger in columnar form.

(*b*) Write up the Personal Accounts in the appropriate ledger.

N.B.—Do NOT balance off any of your ledger accounts.

(Royal Society of Arts)

26

Joint Venture Accounts and Consignment Accounts

Joint Venture Accounts

Sometimes it is to the mutual advantage of two or more persons or firms to tackle a particular business venture together instead of engaging in it separately. These are known as joint ventures. Early versions of Joint Venture Accounts being kept were by the Venetian merchants trading in the Mediterranean in the fifteenth century. One merchant might provide the ship, another the goods and another the capital. Any profits or losses would then be split in an agreed ratio. Present-day versions are to be found in certain parts of the United Kingdom where early vegetables are grown. A produce merchant provides the capital, the transport to market and the selling skills, while the farmer actually grows the produce. The profits are then shared between them. Joint ventures may seem to be exactly the same as partnerships. In fact a joint venture is a form of partnership, but it is limited to a particular transaction. There may be several joint ventures as between the same parties, but each one is a separate venture, and the agreements may be different for each one, e.g. in respect of the sharing of profits and losses.

Some joint ventures may be of such magnitude that a bank account is opened especially for the venture and separate books kept. The calculation of the profits and the eventual withdrawal of their money by the parties involved is quite a straightforward matter. However, it is usually found that each party will record in his own books only those transactions with which he has been concerned. No one party to the venture will therefore have a full record of all the transactions. An example of this is now given:

Exhibit 26.1

Black, of London, Johnson, of Manchester, and Graham, of Glasgow, enter into a joint venture. Black and Johnson are both to supply some of the materials, while only Johnson and Graham will sell the finished goods. Profits are to be shared, Black 3: Johnson 2: Graham 1.

Details of the transactions are:

	£
Black supplied materials costing	450
Johnson supplied materials costing	300
Black paid wages	180
Black paid storage expenses	40
Johnson paid for carriage	90
Graham paid selling expenses	120
Johnson received cash from sales	800
Graham received cash from sales	1,100

Each party has entered in his own books the transactions which have been his concern. He will have opened a 'Joint Venture (with the names of the other two parties) Account'. Payments will have been credited to his Cash Book and debited to the Joint Venture Account. Goods supplied will be credited to his Purchases Account and debited to the Joint Venture Account. This Joint Venture Account will appear as follows:

Black's Books (in London)

Joint Venture with Johnson and Graham

	£		
Purchases: Materials	450		
Cash: Wages	180		
Cash: Storage expenses	40		

Johnson's Books (in Manchester)

Joint Venture with Black and Graham

	£		£
Purchases: Materials	300	Cash: Sales	800
Cash: Carriage	90		

Graham's Books (in Glasgow)

Joint Venture with Black and Johnson

	£		£
Cash: Selling Expenses	120	Cash: Sales	1,100

Now, as things stand, each party knows only the details concerning the transactions he has recorded in his own books. Each one is unaware of (i) the amount of his share of the profit, and (ii) how much he will have to pay to, or receive from, the other parties in final settlement of the joint venture. The only way that this can be settled is for each person to take a copy of his own Joint Venture Account and to send it to the other parties. Each one will then have the account in his own books and one copy of each of the accounts in the other person's books. As this consists of all records of transactions from the start to the completion of the venture, then the profit or loss is now capable of being calculated by each party to the venture. Each person will therefore draw up a Profit and Loss Account for the venture. This will be called a Joint Venture Memorandum Account. It is a memorandum account because the account itself is not going to be incorporated into each person's double entry recording. All that will be required is an entry in each set of books to record their shares of the profits or losses.

Black, Johnson and Graham

Memorandum Joint Venture Account

		£		£
Materials		750	Sales	1,900
Wages		180		
Storage expenses		40		
Carriage		90		
Selling expenses		120		
Net Profit:				
Black (one-half)	360			
Johnson (one-third)	240			
Graham (one-sixth)	120			
	—	720		
		1,900		1,900

Now that each person's share of the profit is known an entry can be made. The share of the net profit on the venture will need to be credited to that person's Profit and Loss Account. The debit is to the source of the profit, the Joint Venture Account. After the entries have been made the balance on the Joint Venture Account can be carried down. If the balance carried down is a credit one then the person has received more from the joint venture than he is entitled to keep, and he will have to pay this amount to the person(s) who has received less than his entitlement, this being shown by a debit balance.

The Joint Venture Accounts now completed can be shown.

Black's Books (in London)

Joint Venture with Johnson and Graham

	£		£
Purchases: Materials	450	Balance c/d	1,030
Cash: Wages	180		
Cash: Storage expenses	40		
Share of profit transferred to Profit and Loss Account	360		
	1,030		1,030
Balance b/d	1,030	Cash received in settlement:	
		From Johnson	170
		From Graham	860
	1,030		1,030

Johnson's Books (in Manchester)

Joint Venture with Black and Graham

	£		£
Purchases: Materials	300	Cash: Sales	800
Cash: Carriage	90		
Share of Profit transferred to Profit and Loss Account	240		
Balance c/d	170		
	800		800
Cash in settlement to Black	170	Balance b/d	170

Graham's Books (in Glasgow)

Joint Venture with Black and Johnson

	£		£
Cash: Selling expenses	120	Cash: Sales	1,100
Share of profit transferred to Profit and Loss Account	120		
Balance c/d	860		
	1,100		1,100
Cash in settlement to Black	860	Balance b/d	860

Consignment Accounts

A consignment of goods is the sending of them by the owner (the consignor) to his agent (the consignee) who agrees to collect, store and sell them on behalf of the owner. When the two parties are both trading in this country it is not difficult for sales of goods consigned to an agent to be recorded in the owner's books, in the same manner as sales of goods stored in his own premises. When the owner is in this country and the agent is overseas, modern methods of communication enable the consignor to similarly record sales made on his behalf by the agent, which is, perhaps, the reason why consignment accounts are not met as frequently today. However, in the days before telecommunications and air travel it was usually too difficult for sales by the agent to be entered in the consignor's books, using separate accounts for the overseas customers, so the practice grew of allowing the agent to collect the money from the overseas customers supplied by him, deduct his expenses and commission, and remit the balance to the consignor.

Consignor's Records

The difficulty of recording individual overseas sales led to an interesting development in profit measurement long before today's advanced techniques. By drawing up consignment accounts it was possible to measure the profit or loss on each consignment thus allowing the consignor to compare the performance of different agents and to separate such profits or losses from those of his main business.

A consignment account is, in effect, a combined Trading and Profit and Loss Account related solely to the consignment. On the debit side is entered the cost of the goods, transport costs, agent's disbursements such as import duties, dock charges, warehouse rent and distribution expenses, and agent's commission, while on the credit side is entered the proceeds of sales. The difference between the two sides represents the profit or loss. If the agent completes the sales before the end of the consignor's financial year, the accounting work is simple. An example to illustrate the entries in the consignor's books can now be seen.

Exhibit 26.2

Robson, whose financial year ends on 31 December, consigned goods to Iturbi, his Agent in Spain, on 16 January 19–8. Robson had purchased the goods for £500 and paid £50 on 28 February for carriage and freight to Spain. Iturbi paid £25 import duty and £30 distribution expenses. He sold the goods for £750, deducted his disbursements and his commission which was at the rate of 6 per cent of the sales, and, on 20 April 19–8, remitted the balance to Robson. Of course, Iturbi's transactions were in pesetas but all items were converted into sterling for inclusion in Robson's books.

While the student at this stage will readily follow the Consignment Account, he must not consider it in isolation. If he does not understand the other parts of the double entry he will share the unnecessary difficulty regularly experienced by students.

The first occurrence to be recorded is the separation of the £500 cost of the goods from Robson's other purchases. Even if they were bought specially for the consignment it is desirable that they should first be entered in the Purchases Account. If the goods were those normally traded in and were simply diverted to the consignment they would already be included in the purchases total or, if they were in stock when the last Trading Account was drawn up, they would be included in the balance on Stock Account. In either event the £500 would be included eventually somewhere on the debit of the Trading Account which must therefore be credited to show the transfer of the goods from the principal trading activity. The entry on the credit side of the Trading Account would read 'Goods sent on Consignment' and the corresponding debit would be on the Consignment Account—if it were not for a practical difficulty. At the time when the Consignment Account is being entered, the Trading Account will not be set up; also there might be several consignments in the financial period for which the Trading Account will be prepared. Therefore there is need for an intermediate account to 'hold' the credit destined for the Trading Account and to permit the accumulation of a total for all consignments so that the Trading Account can be relieved of unnecessary detail. This intermediate account is called simply, 'Goods Sent on Consignments Account'. At the end of the financial year it is closed by a transfer to the Trading Account. The first entry, letter A, in Robson's books for his consignment to Spain is therefore

Debit—Consignment to Iturbi, Madrid, Spain
Credit—Goods sent on Consignments

Note that Iturbi, the agent, has not been debited—the goods are still the property of Robson and Iturbi has so far incurred no financial obligation to him.

Expenses incurred by the consignor for carriage and freight, letter B, are debited to the Consignment Account and credited to the Cash Book bank columns, unless they are not paid separately, in which case the credit will be on the account of the carrier.

Robson makes no further entries until he receives a report from his agent. This is usually called an 'Account Sales' and it is shown in traditional form in Exhibit 26–3. Robson received it on 23 April and made the recording entries necessary to incorporate its contents into his books.

The sales are entered, letter C, by crediting the Consignment Account (instead of the main Trading Account) and by debiting the agent (who stands in place of the separate overseas customers).

Expenses incurred on Robson's behalf and paid by Iturbi, letter D, are entered by a debit on the Consignment Account (instead of the main Profit and Loss Account) and a credit on the agent's account.

The commission due to the agent, normally by way of a percentage on sales, letter E, is debited to the Consignment Account and credited to Iturbi's.

The account of the agent is closed by recording, letter F, his payment of the balance due which is usually by bank transfer or bill of exchange. The bank column of the Cash Book is debited and the agent's account is credited.

Referring to the Consignment Account, it is noted that the credit side exceeds the debit by £100 which is the measure of the profit. A transfer to Profit and Loss Account would close it but, because the firm does not wish to wait until the Profit and Loss Account is prepared at the end of the accounting period, another intermediate account is needed to 'hold' the amount in the meantime. This account will also serve the purpose of combining the profits and losses of all consignments in the accounting period. To close the Consignment Account, letter G, it is debited with the £100 and 'Profit and Loss on Consignments' is credited.

Exhibit 26.2

Consignment to Iturbi, Madrid, Spain

		£			£
Jan 16	(A) Goods sent on consignments	500	Apl 23	(C) Iturbi: Sales	750
Feb 28	(B) Bank: carriage and freight	50			
Apl 23	(D) Iturbi:				
	Import duty	25			
	Distribution	30			
	(E) Commission	45			
	(G) Profit and loss on consignment	100			
		750			750

Goods sent on Consignments

		£			£
Dec 31	Trading Account	...	Apl 23	(A) Consignment to Iturbi	500
					...
					...
					...

Iturbi, Madrid, Spain

		£			£
Apl 23	(G) Consignment: sales	750	Apl 23	Consignment:	
				(D) Import duty	25
				distribution	30
				(E) Commission	45
				(F) Bank	650
		750			750

Profit and Loss on Consignments

		£		£
Dec 31	Profit and loss	...	Apl 23 (G) Consignment to Iturbi	100
				...
				...
				...
		—		—
		═		═

Exhibit 26.3

Account Sales
(Converted into sterling)

Iturbi,
Madrid,
Spain.

Consignment of electrical goods ex M.V. Don Juan sold on behalf of Robson, Manchester, England.

	£	£
Sales per attached schedule (not reproduced)		750
Payments:		
Import duty	25	
Distribution expenses	30	
Commission: 6 per cent of £750	45	
	—	100
		—
Balance due for which sight draft enclosed		650
		═

Madrid, 20 April 19–8. (signed) Iturbi.

Consignor's Accounting Year and Incomplete Consignments

When the consignor's accounting year comes to a close and there is an incomplete consignment, the agent will be required to submit an interim report or 'Account Sales'. Two related problems arise:

1. How is the unsold stock to be valued?
2. What is the profit earned up to date?

It should be appreciated that these two are so connected that the calculation of one of them will produce the answer to the other.

Unsold stock is valued at cost unless net realizable value or replacement price, as appropriate, is lower. Cost includes all expenditure incurred in bringing the goods to a saleable condition and location and so an appropriate part of carriage, freight, insurance and import duty can properly be included in the valuation. On the Consignment

Account the stock so valued is credited above, and debited below, the line. The difference between the two sides above the line is the measure of profit earned up to date and the balance below the line is the asset, or part of it, shown in the Balance Sheet as stock on consignments. Instead of including part of the carriage, etc., in the stock figure, some might prefer to carry it forward as a prepayment but this method is not recommended. For it to be followed to its logical conclusion, any carriage inwards paid on ordinary trading stock would also need to be shown as a prepayment and this would be absurd. Care must be taken to distinguish between expenditure which can be regarded as part of the cost of unsold stock and that which refers only to goods which have been sold, e.g. selling expenses and commission.

Before working through another example which will demonstrate the points discussed, there are two terms to be explained which often feature in consignments.

The first is *del credere commission.* This is an Italian term, based on creed or faith, which refers to additional commission paid to an agent who guarantees the debts incurred by customers supplied by him. To the consignor it is a form of credit insurance.

Second is *pro forma.* In the home trade this refers to an invoice sent to a customer who is required to pay for goods before they are delivered to him. It is used when the supplier does not know the credit-worthiness of the customer. When used in the context of consignments, the term means either a value to be used for overseas customs purposes or a minimum selling price. In either case the figure is not brought into the accounts although a student might have to calculate the cost of the goods from the *pro forma* figure. For instance, a problem might use the phrase, 'invoiced *pro forma* at £1,000 being cost plus 25 per cent'. The student is properly expected to be able to calculate the cost figure of £800.

Exhibit 26.4

On 19 August 19–8 Shaw, a merchant in Preston, sent a consignment of 50 cases of goods to O'Grady, his agent in Cork, Eire. On 26 August Shaw received O'Grady's acceptance of a six months' bill of exchange for £2,000 drawn by Shaw and immediately discounted it for £1,950. The goods had cost Shaw £40 per case and carriage, freight and insurance paid by him on 30 September amounted to £50. During the voyage two cases of the consignment were completely destroyed by fire and on 31 October Shaw received the appropriate compensation from the insurance company.

Shaw's accounting year ended on 31 December 19–8 and O'Grady sent him an interim Account Sales made up to that date. It disclosed that 28 cases had been sold for £60 each and landing charges and import duty, £192, and distribution expenses, £20, had been paid. Commission at 5 per cent on sales plus $2\frac{1}{2}$ per cent *del credere* was charged.

On 15 March 19-9, Shaw received the final Account Sales showing that the remainder of the consignment had been sold for £62 per case, distribution charges, £32, had been paid, and commission was deducted. A bill of exchange was enclosed for the balance due to Shaw.

The accounts are shown in Exhibit 26–4 and the accounts sales in 26–5. Explanations are limited to those entries which are additional to those in the previous example.

The bill of exchange was drawn by the consignor by way of security and he had the choice of holding it until maturity or discounting it. That he chose the latter in order to have use of the money is not directly concerned with the consignment, and so the discount charges are best debited in the general Profit and Loss Account because the main business activities benefited.

An insurance claim will normally cover the full cost of the goods up to the time of loss, but not the expected profit. In our example, the cost per case is £41 made up of original cost £40 and carriage, etc., £1.

In valuing the stock unsold at 31 December, the original cost and carriage, etc., have been apportioned over 50 cases, whereas the landing charges, etc., have been related to the 48 cases landed. The distribution expenses are regarded as selling expenses.

While noting that the £274 profit up to 31 December is the balance of the Consignment Account after carrying down the value of unsold stock, it should be realized that the profit can be checked as follows:

	£		£
Sales	28 at 60		1,680
Cost per case:			
Original	40		
Carriage, etc.	1		
Landing charges, etc.	4		
	—	£	
	28 at 45	1,260	
Distribution expenses		20	
Commission		126	
			1,406
Profit			274

This, of course, demonstrates the relationship between stock valuation and profit mentioned at the beginning of this section.

Exhibit 26.4

Bills Receivable

	£		£
Aug 26	2,000	Aug 26 Bank	1,950
		Discount charges	50
	2,000		2,000

Consignment to O'Grady, Cork, Eire

		Cases	£			Cases	£
Aug 19	Goods sent on consignments	50	2,000	Oct 31	Bank: insurance claim	2	82
Sep 30	Bank: Carriage freight and Insurance		50	Dec 31	O'Grady: Sales	28	1,680
Dec 31	O'Grady:				Stock c/d	20	
	Landing charges and duty		192		20/50 × 2,050	820	
	Distribution		20		20/48 × 192	80	
	Commission		126			—	900
	P. & L. on consignments		274				
		50	2,662			50	2,622
Jan 1	Stock b/d	20	900	Mar 15	O'Grady: Sales	20	1,240
Mar 15	O'Grady:						
	Distribution		32				
	Commission		93				
	P. & L. on consignments		215				
		20	1,240			20	1,240

O'Grady, Cork, Eire

		£			£
Dec 31	Consignment: Sales	1,680	Aug 26	Bill Receivable	2,000
	Balance c/d	658	Dec 31	Consignment:	
				Landing charges and duty	192
				Distribution	20
				Commission	126
		2,338			2,338
Mar 15	Consignment: Sales	1,240	Jan 1	Balance b/d	658
			Mar 15	Consignment:	
				Distribution	32
				Commission	93
				Bank	457
		1,240			1,240

Exhibit 26.5

Interim Account Sales

O'Grady, Cork, Eire.

Consignment of goods ex M.V. Preston Maid sold on behalf of Shaw, Preston, England.

		£	£	£
Sales	28 cases at £60 each			1,680
Payments: Landing charges and import duty at £4 per case			192	
Distribution expenses			20	
Commission at 5 per cent		84		
at 2½ per cent *del credere*		42		
		—	126	
			—	338
				1,342
Acceptance				2,000
Balance in my favour, carried forward				658

Cork, Eire, 31 December 19–8 (signed) O'Grady

Extract from the Final Account Sales

		£	£	£
Sales	20 cases at £62			1,240
Payments: Distribution expenses			32	
Commission at 5 per cent		62		
at 2½ per cent *del credere*		31		
		—	93	
			—	125
				1,115
Balance in my favour, brought forward				658
Sight draft herewith				457

Cork, Eire, 15 March 19–9

Consignee's Records

In considering the consignee's records of a consignment the reader should again refer to Chapter 7 of this Volume where basic concepts are described. The first two, money measurements and business entity, are especially relevant in helping to decide which aspects of the consignment should be entered.

When the agent receives the goods he is under an obligation to sell them on behalf of the owner but that obligation cannot really be measured in monetary terms. Although the original cost might be known to the agent, it does not concern him and it should not be entered in his accounts. He will, of course, need to keep a stock record of quantities held but this will be quite separate from the double entry accounts, as it is for any trader. The reader will have seen earlier that because purchases and sales of goods are entered at different price levels the Purchase and Sales Accounts do not provide a record of stock held.

The consignee's transactions usually commence when he takes possession (but not ownership) of the goods. He will probably pay landing charges and customs duties on behalf of the owner, and he will expect to be reimbursed eventually by subtracting such amounts from those received from the sales of goods. The entries are simply: debit the personal account of the consignor; credit the Bank Account. A Balance Sheet of the agent drawn up just after such a payment would include as a current asset the amount due from the consignor but would not include the stock of goods held on his behalf.

As the sales are made the debits will be either on the Cash or Bank Account, if they are cash sales; or on the personal accounts of the customers, if they are credit sales. The credits will be on the personal account of the consignor and not on the Sales Account (if any). The reader might object here and suggest that it is being inconsistent in refusing to enter the receipt of the goods, on the grounds that they are not the property of the consignee, while advocating entering the sales of them. It is submitted that each sale directly affects the agent in so far as he is obliged to account to the owner for that particular amount of money. The possibility of a bad debt not covered by *del credere commission* does not alter this for the agent is still required to take all reasonable steps to obtain payment. If the agent also sells his own goods it is clearly necessary for him to carefully distinguish between sales of them and sales of goods sent to him on consignment.

Commission earned by the consignee is debited to the consignor's Personal Account and credited to a commission account for subsequent transfer to the agent's own Profit and Loss Account.

By way of illustration, the accounts of O'Grady, the consignee in the second example in the previous section, are shown in Exhibit 26–6. Additional information is introduced in order to show a more complete picture. Assume that O'Grady sold 15 cases on credit and 2 for cash during October, 7 cases on credit in November, and 4 cases on credit in December. The landing charges and import duty were paid on 31 August and the distribution expenses on 29 December. During 19–9, 20 cases were sold on credit in February and the distribution expenses were paid on 10 March.

Exhibit 26.6

(Books of O'Grady)
Shaw, Preston, England

		£			£
Aug 26	Bill Payable	2,000	Oct 31	Debtors	900
,, 31	Bank: Landing charges and import duty	192		Bank	120
			Nov 30	Debtors	420
			Dec 31	Debtors	240
Dec 29	Bank: Distribution charges	20		Balance c/d	658
,, 31	Commission	126			
		2,338			2,338
Jan 1	Balance b/d	658	Feb 28	Debtors	1,240
Feb 28	Commission	93			
Mar 10	Bank: Distribution charges	32			
,, 15	Bill payable	457			
		1,240			1,240

Commission

					£
Dec 31	P. & L. a/c	...	Dec 31	Shaw	126
					...
					...

For simplicity, the financial year of O'Grady has been taken as the same as Shaw's. The coincidence will not often occur in practice and the student should realize that the entries for commission can be made on a monthly basis so that the amount earned in the consignee's year can be properly included.

Before concluding this section, it should be mentioned that there might be special circumstances in which it was desirable to vary the above procedures and include as a purchase the goods received from the consignor. A skilled accountant could produce a system which would accommodate this requirement but it would need to have built into it a number of cancelling entries, so that whenever the final accounts were prepared, the correct amount of indebtedness to the consignor could be shown and any balance of stock eliminated for Balance Sheet purposes.

Exercises

26.1. Charles and Jones enter a joint venture, to share profits or losses equally, resulting from dealings in second-hand cars. Both parties take an active part in the business, each recording his own transactions. They have no joint banking account or separate set of books.

19–3
Jan 1 Charles buys three cars for £900.
„ 31 Charles pays for repairs and respraying of vehicles £60.
Mar 1 Jones pays garage rental £20 and advertising expenses £10.
Apr 12 Jones pays for licence and insurance renewal of vehicles, £36.
Aug 10 Jones buys a vehicle in excellent condition for £100.
„ 31 Charles sells the four vehicles, to various clients, the sales being completed on this date, totalling £1,600.

Show the relative accounts in the books of both partners.
(East Midland Educational Union)

26.2. Brown and Turner agreed to enter into a joint venture to buy and sell second-hand ice-cream vehicles and to share profits and losses in the ratio 5:3 respectively. It was agreed that Brown would record all details of the venture in his books of account.

On 21 December 19–5 Turner purchased two vehicles and paid cash of £2,000. On 2 January 19–6 he spent sums of £248 on repairs, £24 on drivers' wages and £36 on temporary insurance cover. He sold the vehicles a week later for £2,800 subject to a 2 per cent cash discount if paid within seven days. He paid the proceeds of sale into his bank account on 10 January 19–6.

On 31 January 19–6 Brown purchased five vehicles for £5,000, of which he managed to sell three for £3,600 for cash on the same day, without incurring any expenses. The fourth vehicle was sold for £1,350 and on 7 February 19–6 he received a bill receivable to be presented for payment in three months' time.

On 31 March 19–6 the fifth vehicle was still unsold and it was agreed that Turner should take over this vehicle at a valuation of £750.

On 31 March 19–6 the parties made a settlement between each other, Brown agreeing to take the bill receivable at a value of £1,318.

You are required to prepare:

(*a*) the Joint Venture Account, and
(*b*) Turner's Account,

as they would appear in the books of Brown.
(Institute of Chartered Accountants)

26.3. Plant, Hoe & Reap entered into a joint venture for dealing in carrots. The transactions connected with this venture were:

19–1
Jan 8 Plant rented land cost £156
„ 10 Hoe supplied seeds cost £48
„ 17 Plant employed labour for planting £105
„ 19 Hoe charged motor expenses £17
„ 30 Plant employed labour for fertilizing £36
Feb 28 Plant paid the following expenses: Sundries £10, Labour £18, fertilizer a/c £29
Mar 17 Reap employed labour for lifting carrots £73

„ 30 Sale expenses London paid by Reap £39
„ 31 Reap received cash from sale proceeds gross £987—

You are required to show the joint venture accounts in the books of Plant, Hoe & Reap. Also show in full the method of arriving at the profit on the venture which is to be apportioned: Plant seven-twelfths; Hoe three-twelfths; Reap two-twelfths.

Any outstanding balances between the parties are settled by cheque on 30 April.

26.4. On 8 February 19–5 P.J., a London trader, consigned 120 cases of goods to M.B., an agent in New Zealand

The cost of the goods was £25 a case. P.J. paid carriage to the port £147 and insurance £93.

On 31 March 19–5 P.J. received an Account Sales from M.B., showing that 100 cases had been sold for £3,500 and M.B. had paid freight, at the rate of £2 a case, and port charges amounting to £186. N.B. was entitled to a commission of 5 per cent on sales. A sight draft for the net amount due was enclosed with the Account Sales.

You are required to show the accounts for the above transactions in the ledger of P.J. and to show the transfer to Profit and Loss Account at 31 March 19–5.

(Chartered Institute of Secretaries and Administrators)

26.5. On 1 August 19–5 Hope & Sons of London consigned 100 cases of goods to Lintang & Co of Singapore. The cost of the goods was £30 per case. Hope & Sons drew on Lintang & Co for £2,000 at three months date and discounted the bill for £1,980. Hope & Sons paid carriage, freight and insurance £75.

On arrival at Singapore Lintang & Co paid landing and customs charges £30.

Lintang & Co were entitled to a commission of 5 per cent on sales and an additional *del credere* commission of 1 per cent on sales.

Lintang & Co sold 50 cases at £45 per case and 10 cases at £40 per case and on 31 December 19–5 Hope & Sons received an Account Sales for these transactions. A banker's draft was enclosed for the balance due on these sales.

Hope & Sons balanced their accounts on 31 December 19–5 and prepared final accounts.

Show (*a*) the entries relating to the above consignment in the books of Hope & Sons, and balance the accounts as at 31 December 19–5; (*b*) the account of Hope & Sons in the books of Lintang & Co.

(Associated Examining Board 'A' Level)

26.6A. Port and Starboard agreed to enter into a joint venture to buy and sell speedboats. Profits and losses were to be divided: Port two-thirds, Starboard one-third.

On 3 May 19–9 Port purchased three speedboats for £730, £820 and £950 respectively. He bought a reconditioned engine costing £120 which he installed in one of the boats, the old engine being scrapped. On 31 May 19–9 he sold two of the boats for £900 each, paying the proceeds into his private bank account.

On 15 June 19–9 he sold the other boat for £1,000, which amount he paid over to Starboard, who paid it into his bank account.

On 4 May 19–9 Starboard purchased a speedboat for £675 and, having incurred expenditure of £40 on repainting, sold it on 12 May 19–9 for £750, paying the proceeds into his own bank account. This boat developed mechanical trouble and on 25 May 19–9 Starboard agreed to take the boat back at a price of £720, which he paid out of his bank account. The boat was still unsold at 30 June 19–9 and it was agreed that Starboard should take it over for his personal use at a valuation of £700.

Other expenditure incurred was as follows.

	Port	*Starboard*
	£	£
Harbour dues	10	3
Marine insurance	20	6

Port paid into his bank net receipts of £24 in respect of speedboat trips.

On 1 July 19–9 the sum required in full settlement as between Port and Starboard was paid by the party accountable.

You are required to prepare:

(*a*) the Account of the Joint Venture with Port as it would appear in the books of Starboard, and

(*b*) the Memorandum Joint Venture Account, showing the net profit.

(Institute of Chartered Accountants)

26.7A. On 15 November 19–5, Hugo of Holland consigned 300 bicycles to Pedlar of London. On 31 December 19–5, Pedlar forwarded an account sales, with a draft for the balance, showing the following transactions:

1. 250 bicycles sold at £20 each and 50 at £18 each.
2. Port and duty charges £720.
3. Storage and carriage charges £410.
4. Commission on sales 5%+1% *del credere*.

You are required to:

(*a*) prepare the Account Sales, and

(*b*) show the Consignment Inward Account in the books of Pedlar.

Ignore interest.

(Institute of Chartered Accountants)

26.8A. Stone consigned goods to Rock on 1 January 19–6, their value being £12,000, and it was agreed that Rock should receive a commission of 5 per cent on gross sales. Expenses incurred by Stone for freight and insurance amount to £720. Stone's financial year ended on 31 March 19–6, and an Account Sales made up to that date was received from Rock. This showed that 70 per cent of the goods had been sold for £10,600 but that up to 31 March 19–6, only £8,600 had been received by Rock in respect of these sales. Expenses in connection with the goods consigned were shown as being £350, and it was also shown that £245 had been incurred in connection with the goods sold. With the Account Sales, Rock sent a sight draft for the balance shown to be due, and Stone incurred bank charges of £12 on 10 April 19–6, in cashing same.

Stone received a further Account Sales from Rock made up to 30 June 19–6, and this showed that the remainder of the goods had been sold for £4,800 and that £200 had been incurred by way of selling expenses. It also showed that all cash due had been received with the exception of a debt for £120 which had proved to be bad. A sight draft for the balance due was sent with the Account

Sales and the bank charged Stone £9 on 1 July 19–6, for cashing same. You are required to write up the necessary accounts in Stone's books to record these transactions.
(Association of Certified Accountants)

26.9A. Wild, Wood and Bine enter into a joint venture for dealing in antiques. The following transactions took place:

19–4
Mar 1 Wild rented a shop, paying 3 months' rent £150
,, 2 Wood bought a motor van for £2,700
,, 4 Wood bought antiques for £650
,, 15 Bine received cash from sale proceeds of antiques £3,790
,, 28 Wild bought antiques for £1,200
Apr 11 Motor Van broke down. Bine agreed to use his own van for the job, until cessation of the joint venture, at an agreed charge of £400
,, 13 Motor van bought on May 2 was sold for £2,100. Proceeds were kept by Wild
,, 15 Sales of antiques, cash being kept by Wood £780
,, 18 Lighting and heating bills paid for shop by Bine £120
,, 30 Bine bought antiques for £440
May 4 General expenses of shop paid for £800, Bine and Wild paying half each
,, 19 Antiques sold by Bine £990, proceeds being kept by him
,, 31 Joint venture ended. The antiques still in stock were taken over at an agreed valuation of £2,100 by Wood.

You are required to show the joint venture accounts in the books of each of the three parties. Show in full the workings needed to arrive at the profit on the venture. The profit or loss was to be split: Wood one-half; Wild one-third; Bine one-sixth. Any outstanding balances between the parties were settled on 31 May 19–4.

27

An Introduction to the Final Accounts of Limited Liability Companies

The two main disadvantages of a partnership are that the number of owners cannot normally exceed twenty, and that their liability, barring limited partners, is not limited to the amount invested in the partnership but extends to the individual partners' private possessions. This means that the failure of the business could result in a partner losing both his share of the business assets and also part or all of his private assets as well.

The form of organization to which these two limitations do not apply are known as Limited Liability Companies. There are companies which have unlimited liability, but these are not dealt with in this volume. From this point any reference to a company means a limited liability company.

The capital of a limited company is divided into Shares. These can be of any denomination, such as £5 shares or £1 shares. To become a Member of a limited company, alternatively called a Shareholder, a person must buy one or more shares. He may either pay in full for the shares that he takes up, or else the shares may be partly paid for, the balance to be paid as and when the company may arrange. The liability of a member is limited to the shares that he holds, or where a share is only partly paid he is also liable to have to pay the amount owing by him on the shares. Thus, even if a company loses all its assets a member's private possessions cannot be touched to pay the company's debts, other than in respect of the amount owing on partly paid shares.

Companies thus fulfil the need for the capitalization of a firm where the capital required is greater than that which twenty people can contribute, or where limited liability for all members is desired.

Private and Public Companies

There are two classes of company, the Private Company and the Public Company. In fact there are more than 500,000 active companies, and private companies outnumber public companies by a ratio of more than twenty to one. A private company is one which has a minimum membership of two and fulfils the following conditions:

1. Restricts the right to transfer its shares.

2. Limits the number of its members to fifty, excluding employees and ex-employees of the company.

3. Prohibits any invitation to the public to subscribe for any shares or debentures of the company.

Any company which does not fulfil the above conditions is a public company. These have a minimum membership of seven and no maximum limit.

The day-to-day business of a company is not carried on by the shareholders. The possession of a share normally confers voting rights on the holder, who is then able to attend general meetings of the company. At one of these the shareholders will meet and will vote for Directors, these being the people who will be entrusted with the running of the business. At each Annual General Meeting the directors will have to report on their stewardship, and this report is accompanied by a set of Final Accounts for the year.

Share Capital

A shareholder of a limited company obtains his reward in the form of a share of the profits, known as a Dividend. The directors consider the amount of profits and decide on the amount of profits which are placed to reserves. Out of the profits remaining the directors then propose the payment of a certain amount of dividend to be paid. It is important to note that the shareholders cannot propose a higher dividend for themselves than that already proposed by the directors. They can however propose that a lesser dividend should be paid, although this action is very rare indeed. If the directors propose that no dividend be paid then the shareholders are powerless to alter the decision.

The decision by the directors as to the amount proposed as dividends is a very complex one and cannot be fully discussed here. Such points as Government directives to reduce dividends, the effect of taxation, the availability of bank balances to pay the dividends, the possibility of take-over bids and so on will all be taken into account.

The dividend is usually expressed as a percentage. Ignoring income tax, a dividend of 10 per cent in Firm A on 500,000 Ordinary Shares of £1 each will amount to £50,000, or a dividend of 6 per cent in Firm B on 200,000 Ordinary Shares of £2 each will amount to £24,000. A shareholder having 100 shares in each firm would receive £10 from Firm A and £12 from Firm B.

There are two main types of share, Preference Shares and Ordinary Shares. A preference share is one whose main characteristic is that it is entitled to a specified percentage rate of dividend before the ordinary shareholders receive anything. On the other hand the ordinary shares would be entitled to the remainder of the profits which have been appropriated for dividends.

For example, if a company had 10,000 5 per cent preference shares of £1 each and 20,000 ordinary shares of £1 each, then the following dividends would be payable:

Years	*1*	*2*	*2*	*4*	*5*
	£	£	£	£	£
Profits appropriated for Dividends	900	1,300	1,600	3,100	2,000
Preference Dividends (5%)	500	500	500	500	500
Ordinary Dividends	(2%) 400	(4%) 800	(5½%) 1,100	(13%) 2,600	(7½%) 1,500

There are two main types of preference share, these being Non-cumulative Preference Shares and Cumulative Preference Shares. A non-cumulative preference share is one which is entitled to a yearly percentage rate of dividend, and should the available profits be insufficient to cover the percentage dividend then the deficiency cannot be made good out of future years' profits. On the other hand, any deficiency on the part of cumulative preference shares can be carried forward as arrears, and such arrears are payable before the ordinary shares receive anything.

Illustrations of the two types of share should make this clearer:

Illustration 1: A company has 5,000 £1 ordinary shares and 2,000 5 per cent non-cumulative preference shares of £1 each. The profits available for dividends are: year 1 £150, year 2 £80, year 3 £250, year 4 £60, year 5 £500.

Year	*1*	*2*	*3*	*4*	*5*
	£	£	£	£	£
Profits	150	80	250	60	500
Preference Dividend (limited in years 2 and 4)	100	80	100	60	100
Dividends on Ordinary Shares	50	—	150	—	400

Illustration 2: Assume that the above preference shares had been cumulative, the dividends would have been:

Year	*1*	*2*	*3*	*4*	*5*
	£	£	£	£	£
Profits	150	80	250	60	500
Preference Dividend	100	80	120*	60	140*
Dividends on Ordinary Shares	50	—	130	—	360

* including arrears.

The total of the Share Capital which the company would be allowed to issue is known as the Authorized Share Capital, or alternatively as the Nominal Capital. The share capital actually issued to shareholders is known as the Issued Capital. Obviously, if the whole of the share capital which the company is allowed to issue has in fact been issued then the authorized and the issued share capital will be the same figure.

Where only part of the amount payable on each share has been asked for, then the total amount asked for on all shares is known as the Called-up Capital. The Uncalled Capital is therefore that part of the amount payable on all the shares for which payment has not been requested. Calls in arrear relate to amounts requested (called for) but not yet received, while calls in advance relate to moneys received prior to payment being requested.

Trading and Profit and Loss Accounts

From the viewpoint of the preparation of trading and profit and loss accounts, there are no differences as between public and private limited companies. The accounts now described are those purely for internal use by the company. Obviously, if a full copy of the trading and profit and loss accounts were given to each shareholder, the company's rivals could easily obtain a copy and would then be in a position to learn about details of the company's trading which the company would prefer to keep secret. The Companies Act therefore states that only certain details of the trading and profit and loss account must be shown. Companies can, if they so wish, disclose more than the minimum information required by law, but it is simply a matter for the directors to decide whether or not it would be in the company's interest. A discussion of the minimum information required is contained in Volume 2.

The trading account of a limited company is no different from that of a sole trader or of a partnership. The profit and loss account also follows the same pattern as those of partnerships or sole traders except for some types of expense which are peculiar to limited companies. The two main expenses under this heading are:

1. Directors' remuneration. This is obvious, since only in companies are directors found.

2. Debenture interest. The term debenture is used when money is received on loan to the company and written acknowledgement is given, usually under seal. Thus a loan to a partnership is known as a loan, while usually a loan to a company is known as a debenture. The interest payable for the use of the money is an expense of the company, and is payable whether profits are made or not. This means that debenture interest is charged as an expense in the Profit and Loss Account itself. Contrast this with dividends which are dependent on profits having been made.

The Appropriation Account

Next under the profit and loss account is a section called, as it would also be in a partnership, the profit and loss appropriation account. The net profit is brought down from the profit and loss account, and in the appropriation account is shown the manner in which the profits are to be appropriated, i.e. how the profits are to be used.

First of all, if any of the profits are to be put to reserve then the transfer is shown. To transfer to a reserve means that the directors wish to indicate that that amount of profits is not to be considered as available for dividends in that year. The reserve may be specific, such as a Fixed Asset Replacement Reserve or may be a General Reserve.

Out of the remainder of profits the dividends are proposed and the unused balance of profits is carried forward to the following year, where it goes to swell the profits then available for appropriation. It is very rare, assuming the firm has not been incurring losses, for there not to be any unappropriated balance of profits carried forward even if it is the policy of the firm to declare the greatest possible dividends, because dividends are normally proposed either as a whole percentage or to a one-half or one-quarter per cent. Arithmetically it is uncommon for the profits remaining after transfers to reserves to equal such a figure exactly.

Exhibit 27–1 shows the profit and loss appropriation account of a new business for its first three years of business.

Exhibit 27.1

I.D.O. Ltd has an Ordinary Share Capital of 40,000 ordinary shares of £1 each and 20,000 5 per cent preference shares of £1 each.

The net profits for the first three years of business ended 31 December are: 19–4, £5,967; 19–5, £7,864, and 19–6, £8,822.

Transfers to reserves are made as follows: 19–4 nil; 19–5, general reserve, £1,000, and 19–6, fixed assets replacement reserve, £1,500.

Dividends were proposed for each year on the preference shares and on the ordinary shares at: 19–4, 10 per cent; 19–5, 12½ per cent; 19–6, 15 per cent.

Profit and Loss Appropriation Accounts

(1) *For the year ended 31 December 19–4*

	£		£
Proposed dividends:		Net profit brought down	5,967
Preference Dividend of 5%	1,000		
Ordinary Dividend of 10%	4,000		
Balance carried forward to next year	967		
	5,967		5,967

(2) *For the year ended 31 December 19–5*

	£		£
General reserve	1,000	Net profit brought down	7,864
Proposed dividends:			
Preference Dividend of 5%	1,000	Balance brought forward from last year	967
Ordinary Dividend of 12½%	5,000		
Balance carried forward to next year	1,831		
	8,831		8,831

(3) *For the year ended 31 December 19–6*

	£		£
Fixed assets replacement Reserve	1,500	Net profit brought down	8,822
Proposed Dividends:			
Preference Dividend of 5%	1,000	Balance brought forward from last year	1,831
Ordinary Dividend of 15%	6,000		
Balance carried forward to next year	2,153		
	10,653		10,653

The Balance Sheet

The balance sheet must conform to the regulations specified in the Companies Act. A specimen balance sheet appears on page 419, and the following notes are applicable to it:

Notes:

1. Fixed assets should normally be shown either at cost or alternatively at some other valuation. In either case, the method chosen should be clearly stated.

2. The total depreciation from date of purchase to the date of the balance sheet should be shown.

3. The authorized share capital, where it is different from the issued share capital, is shown as a note.

4. Reserves consist either of those unused profits remaining in the appropriation account, or transferred to a reserve account appropriately titled, e.g. General Reserve, Fixed Assets Replacement Reserve,

etc. Volume 2 of this book will examine these in rather more detail. At this juncture all that needs to be said is that any account labelled as a reserve has originated by being charged as a debit in the appropriation account and credited to a reserve account with an appropriation title. These reserves are shown in the balance sheet after share capital under the heading of 'Reserves'.

One reserve that is in fact not labelled with the word 'reserve' in its title is the Share Premium Account. For reasons which will be explained in Volume 2, shares can be issued for more than their face or nominal value. The excess of the price at which they are issued over the nominal value of the shares is credited to a Share Premium Account. This is then shown with the other reserves in the Balance Sheet.

5. Where shares are only partly called up, then it is the amount actually called up that appears in the balance sheet and not the full amount.

6. The share capital and reserves should be totalled so as to show the book value of all the shares in the company.

Balance Sheet as at 31 December 19–7

Share Capital	£	£	*Fixed Assets*			
Authorized				*Cost*	*Depreciation to date*	*Net*
20,000 shares of £1 each		20,000				
Issued 12,000 Ordinary shares of £1 each, fully paid		12,000		£	£	£
			Buildings	15,000	6,000	9,000
Reserves			Machinery	8,000	2,400	5,600
Share premium	1,200		Motor Vehicles	4,000	1,600	2,400
General reserve	3,800					
Profit and Loss Account	1,000					
		6,000				
				27,000	10,000	17,000
		18,000				
Debentures			*Current Assets*			
Six per cent Debentures		6,000	Stock		6,000	
Current Liabilities			Debtors		3,000	
Proposed Dividend	1,000		Bank		2,000	
Creditors	3,000					11,000
		4,000				
		28,000				28,000

Taxation

At the time of writing the form of tax levied on companies is Corporation Tax. Here also a fuller discussion is a feature of Volume 2. All that needs to be stated here is that Corporation Tax should be shown as a charge in the Appropriation Account, and until it is paid it will be shown as a current liability in the balance sheet.

Director's Current Accounts

With a great many private limited companies the directors are the only shareholders of the company, or alternatively the directors hold the great majority of the shares. In such circumstances it is natural that the relationships between the company and the directors are rather more informal than in public companies. In these cases therefore it is natural for directors to take drawings from the firm either in cash or in goods. It is also quite normal for the remuneration of the directors to be agreed after the accounts year has ended, by this way the amount of taxation liability of the company and of the directors can be kept to a minimum. There is nothing illegal in this, it is just a matter of saying that the rewards of the directors cannot be properly assessed until the profits are known.

It is thus usual for the directors to each have a current account with the company, rather in the way that partners have current accounts in partnerships. The director is debited with his drawings of goods and cash, and credited with the amount of remuneration voted to him. The balance on the account is then shown as a current liability in the Balance Sheet.

Exhibit 27–2 is an example, albeit rather an exaggerated one, of a limited company for its first two years of operation.

Exhibit 27.2

B.T.Y. Ltd Trial Balance as on 31 December 19–4

	£	£
Sales		100,000
Purchases	90,000	
General expenses	20,000	
Debenture interest	840	
Debentures		12,000
Ordinary share capital		30,000
Eight per cent Preference Shares		10,000
Plant and machinery at cost	10,000	
Motor vehicles at cost	5,000	
Creditors		21,600
Debtors	40,000	
Drawings of Directors: A. Blake	1,200	
B. Charles	900	
Bank	5,660	
	173,600	173,600

A company has issued 30,000 ordinary shares of £1 each and 10,000 8 per cent preference shares of £1 each. The authorised share capital is 40,000 ordinary shares of £1 each and 20,000 8 per cent preference shares of £1 each. There are two directors who own the greater part of the shares.

At the end of the first year the trial balance was as shown.

Notes:

1. The stock on hand at 31.12.19–4 was £30,000.
2. The preference dividend will be paid on 8 January 19–5.
3. Corporation tax based on the year's profits will be £5,000 and will be paid on 1 October 19–5.
4. The two directors are to have remuneration of £2,000 each.
5. A dividend is to be proposed of 15 per cent on the ordinary shares.
6. Depreciate plant and machinery £2,000 and motor vehicles £1,000.
7. Transfer £1,000 to a General Reserve.

B.T.Y. Ltd Trading and Profit and Loss Account
for the year ended 31 December 19–4

	£		£
Purchases	90,000	Sales	100,000
Less stock in hand	30,000		
Cost of goods sold	60,000		
Gross profit carried down	40,000		
	100,000		100,000
General expenses	20,000	Gross profit brought down	40,000
Directors' remuneration	4,000		
Debenture interest	840		
Depreciation: Plant and machinery	2,000		
Motor vehicle	1,000		
Net profit carried down	12,160		
	40,000		40,000
Corporation tax	5,000	Net Profit brought down	12,160
Preference Dividend	800		
Proposed Ordinary Dividend of 15 per cent	4,500		
Transfer to General Reserve	1,000		
Balance carried forward to next year	860		
	12,160		12,160

Balance Sheet as at 31 December 19–4

				Cost	*Depreciation to date*	*Net*
Share Capital		£	*Fixed Assets*	£	£	£
Authorized						
40,000 Ordinary Shares of £1 each		40,000	Plant and machinery	10,000	2,000	8,000
20,000 8 per cent Preference Shares of £1 each		20,000	Motor vehicles	5,000	1,000	4,000
		60,000		15,000	3,000	12,000
Issued			*Current Assets*			
30,000 Ordinary Shares of £1 each		30,000	Stock		30,000	
10,000 8 per cent Preference Shares of £1 each		10,000	Debtors		40,000	
			Bank		5,660	
						75,660
		40,000				
Reserves	£					
General Reserve	1,000					
Profit and Loss Account	860					
		1,860				
		41,860				
Seven per cent Debentures		12,000				
Current Liabilities						
Preference Dividend	800					
Proposed Ordinary Dividend	4,500					
Corporation tax	5,000					
Creditors	21,600					
Directors' Current Accounts	1,900					
		33,800				
		87,660				87,660

Note: The Directors' Current Account figure listed under Current Liabilities is made up of remuneration 2 × £2,000 = £4,000 *less* drawings £2,000 = £1,900.

At the end of the second year the trial balance was as follows:

Trial Balance as on 31 December 19–5

	£	£
Sales		150,000
Purchases	100,000	
General expenses	28,000	
Debenture interest	840	
Debentures		12,000
Ordinary Share Capital		40,000
Share Premium		1,000
Eight per cent Preference Shares		10,000
Plant and machinery at cost	16,000	
Motor vehicles	7,000	
Profit and Loss Account as at 31.12.19–4		860
Creditors		17,240
Debtors	50,000	
General Reserve		1,000
Drawings of Directors: A. Blake	2,300	
B. Charles	1,800	
Provisions for depreciation: Plant and machinery		2,000
Motor vehicles		1,000
Bank	1,060	
Stock at 31.12.19–4	30,000	
Directors' Current Account Balances		1,900
	237,000	237,000

Notes:

1. The stock on hand at 31 December 19–5 was £40,000.
2. The preference dividend for 19–5 will be paid on 10 January 19–6.
3. Corporation tax based on the year's profit will be £8,000 and will be paid on 1 October 19–6.
4. The two directors are to have remuneration of £3,500 each.
5. A dividend is to be proposed of 25 per cent on the ordinary shares.
6. Depreciate plant and machinery £3,200 and motor vehicles £1,400.
7. Transfer £1,200 to General Reserve.

B.T.Y. Ltd Trading and Profit and Loss Account
for the year ended 31 December 19–5

	£		£		£
Stock at 31.12.19–4		30,000	Sales		150,000
Add Purchases		100,000			
		130,000			
Less Stock at 31.12.19–5		40,000			
Cost of goods sold		90,000			
Gross profit carried down		60,000			
		150,000			150,000
General expenses		28,000	Gross profit brought down		60,000
Debenture interest		840			
Directors' remuneration		7,000			
Depreciation:	£				
Plant and machinery	3,200				
Motor vehicles	1,400				
		4,600			
Net profit carried down		19,560			
		60,000			60,000
Corporation tax		8,000	Net profit brought down		19,560
Preference Dividend		800	Balance brought forward from last year		860
Proposed Ordinary Dividend of 25 per cent		10,000			
Transfer to General Reserve		1,200			
Balance carried forward to next year		420			
		20,420			20,420

Exercises

27.1. A limited liability company has an authorized capital of £200,000 divided into £20,000 6 per cent preference shares of £1 each and 180,000 ordinary shares of £1 each. All the preference shares are issued and fully paid: 100,000 ordinary shares are issued with 75*p* per share paid on each share.

On 31 December 19–2, the company's revenue reserves were £30,000, current liabilities £7,500, current assets £62,750, fixed assets (at cost) £90,000 and provisions for depreciation on fixed assets £20,250.

Make a summarized balance sheet as at 31 December 19–2 to display this information. Set out the balance sheet in such a way as to show clearly the net value of current assets.

(University of London 'O' Level)

Balance Sheet as at 31 December 19–5

				Cost	*Depreciation to date*	*Net*
Share Capital		£	*Fixed Assets*	£	£	£
Authorised						
40,000 Ordinary Shares of £1 each		40,000	Plant and machinery	16,000	5,200	10,800
20,000 8 per cent Preference Shares of £1 each		20,000	Motor vehicles	7,000	2,400	4,600
		60,000		23,000	7,600	15,400
Issued			*Current Assets*			
40,000 Ordinary Shares of £1 each		40,000	Stock		40,000	
			Debtors		50,000	
10,000 8 per cent Preference Shares of £1 each		10,000	Bank		1,060	
						91,060
		50,000				
Reserves						
Share Premium Account	1,000					
General Reserve	2,200					
Profit and Loss	420					
		3,620				
		53,620				
Seven per cent Debentures		12,000				
		65,620				
Current Liabilities						
Preference Dividend	800					
Proposed Ordinary Dividend	10,000					
Corporation tax	8,000					
Creditors	17,240					
Directors' Current Account	4,800					
		40,840				
		106,460				106,460

Note: The Directors' Current Account figure listed under Current Liabilities is made up of Balances brought forward £1,900+remuneration £7,000 = £8,900 *less* drawings £4,100 = £4,800.

27.2. The Quick Trading Co Ltd has an authorized capital of £300,000 divided into 300,000 shares of £1 each, of which 200,000 shares are issued and fully paid.

The following information relates to the position of the company at 31 December 19–4.

	£
Revenue Reserves	15,000
Balance of Profit and Loss Account	1,500
Current Liabilities	3,500
Current Assets	114,000
Fixed Assets (at cost)	185,000
Provision for depreciation of Fixed Assets	79,000

Draft a summarized balance sheet of the company as at 31 December 19–4.

27.3. The following Trial Balance was extracted from the books of H.D.L. Ltd as on 31 December 19–3:

Trial Balance

	£	£
Share Capital, authorized and issued:		
40,000 Ordinary Shares of £1 each		40,000
Trade creditors		13,970
Provision for depreciation of motor vans to 31 December 19–2		2,845
Motor vans, at cost (£5,750) *less* sale on 1 January 19–3	5,510	
Freehold Land and Buildings, at cost	37,000	
Stock-in-trade, 31 December 19–2	9,500	
Purchases	92,000	
Sales		132,025
Trade debtors	12,618	
Wages and salaries	15,312	
Motor and delivery expenses	1,481	
Rates and insurances	639	
General expenses	6,984	
Cash in hand	46	
Balance at bank	11,750	
Directors' fees	4,500	
Profit and Loss Account, Balance at 31 December 19–2		8,500
	197,340	197,340

You are given the following information:

1. Stock-in-trade, 31 December 19–3, £8,800.
2. Provision for depreciation of motor vans is to be made at the rate of 20 per cent per annum, on cost.
3. A motor van which had cost £800 was sold on 1 January 19–3 for £240. Depreciation provided for this van up to 31 December 19–2 was £520.
4. Rates and insurances paid in advance at 31 December 19–3 £112.
5. The cash in hand shown in the trial balance (£46) includes a post-dated cheque for £28 which had been cashed for a customer on 31 December 19–3.
6. The amounts shown in the trial balance for sales and trade debtors include goods sent out on sale or return, invoiced at £300, which represented cost plus 50 per cent. These goods were returned on 3 January 19–4.
7. In December 19–3 goods, the cost of which was £725, were destroyed by fire. The insurance company has agreed to pay in full a claim for this amount, but no entry has been made in the company's books.

8. The directors have decided to recommend a dividend of 10 per cent for the year 19–3.

You are required to prepare the trading and profit and loss account for the year 19–3 and the balance sheet as on 31 December 19–3.

Ignore taxation.

(Chartered Institute of Secretaries and Administrators)

27.4. The trial balance extracted from the books of Hillgate Ltd at 31 December 19–4 was as follows:

	£	£
Share capital		100,000
Profit and Loss Account 31 December 19–3		34,280
Freehold premises at cost	65,000	
Machinery at cost	55,000	
Provision for depreciation on machinery account as at 31 December 19–3		15,800
Purchases	201,698	
Sales		316,810
General expenses	32,168	
Wages and salaries	54,207	
Rents and rates	4,300	
Lighting and heating	1,549	
Bad debts	748	
Provision for doubtful debts at 31 December 19–3		861
Debtors	21,784	
Creditors		17,493
Stock in trade 31 December 19–3	25,689	
Bank balance	23,101	
	485,244	485,244

You are given the following additional information:

(i) The authorised and issued share capital is divided into 100,000 shares of £1 each.
(ii) Stock in trade at 31 December 19–4, £29,142.
(iii) Wages and salaries due at 31 December 19–4 amounted to £581.
(iv) Rates paid in advance at 31 December 19–4 amounted to £300.
(v) A dividend of £10,000 is proposed for 19–4.
(vi) The provision for doubtful debts is to be increased to £938.
(vii) A depreciation charge is to be made on machinery at the rate of 10 per cent per annum on cost.

Required:

A trading and profit and loss account for 19–4 and a balance sheet at 31 December 19–4.

(Royal Society of Arts)

27.5A. The following balances have been extracted from the books of the XY Co Ltd at 31 December 19–0:

	£	£
Capital—authorised and issued:		
60,000 Ordinary Shares of £1, each fully paid		60,000

	£	£
30,000 6 per cent Preference Shares of £1, each fully paid		30,000
Share Premium Account		10,000
General Reserve		20,000
Profit and Loss Account Balance, 1 January 19–0		28,000
5 per cent Debentures (Secured)		60,000
Debtors, Creditors	40,000	45,000
Balance at bank		15,000
Land and buildings at cost	160,000	
Plant and machinery at cost	190,000	
Stock	30,000	
Cash	1,000	
Provision for bad debts, 1 January 19–0		2,000
Provisions for depreciation to 1 January 19–0:		
Land and buildings		40,000
Plant and machinery		70,000
Gross profit		120,000
Discounts	1,000	4,000
Administrative expenses	45,000	
Selling and distribution expenses	35,000	
Debenture interest paid	2,000	
	504,000	504,000

Prepare in good form Profit and Loss Account for the year to 31 December 19–0 and a Balance Sheet at that date, taking into account the following additional information:

1. Provide depreciation on land and buildings at 2½ per cent p.a. on cost.
2. Provide depreciation on plant and machinery at 10 per cent p.a. on cost.
3. The Provision for bad debts is to be 2½ per cent of Debtors.
4. Rates accrued, £1,000.
5. The Directors decide to:
   (i) transfer £10,000 to General Reserve,
   (ii) pay Preference Dividend for the year,
   (iii) recommend a Dividend of 10 per cent on the Ordinary Shares.

(Welsh Joint Education Committee)

27.6A. The Basford Trading Co Ltd was formed on 1 April 19–0 with an authorised capital of £100,000 divided into £1 shares. The whole of the capital was issued on the same day at a premium of 10p per share and fully paid up.

In addition to any balances arising on the issue of shares, the following amounts appeared in the company's ledger on 31 March 19–1, after the Trading Account had been prepared.

	£
Eight per cent Debentures (issued 1.4.19–0)	40,000
Land and buildings at cost	90,000
Plant and machinery at cost	30,000
Provision for depreciation on plant and machinery	3,000
Fixtures and fittings at cost	5,450
Stock 31 March 19–1	31,926

	£
Debtors	21,500
Bad debts	170
Creditors	10,900
Discount received	1,800
General expenses	250
Directors' Fees	750
Salaries	14,483
Insurance	90
Rates	450
Discount allowed	198
Debenture interest ($\frac{1}{2}$ year to 30.9.19–0)	1,600
Bank balance	7,455
Interim Dividend paid	2,000
Gross profit	40,622

Note:
(i) Provide for debenture interest outstanding.
(ii) Insurance prepaid at 31 March 19–1, £12.
(iii) Create a provision of £500 against future bad debts.
(iv) Write 10 per cent off Fixtures and Fittings.
(v) Transfer £5,000 to General Reserve.
(vi) Provide for a final dividend of 8 per cent, making 10 per cent for the year.

Prepare the Profit and Loss Account and Appropriation Account for the year to 31 March 19–1 and a Balance Sheet at that date.
(East Midland Educational Union)

27.7A. A. Keen and Sharp Ltd is a manufacturing company with an authorised Share Capital of:

100,000 £1 Ordinary Shares
60,000 £1 Preference Shares (6 per cent)

A trial balance as at 31 March 19–0, was as follows:

	£	£
Issued Share Capital:		
80,000 £1 Ordinary Shares		80,000
40,000 £1 Preference Shares (6 per cent)		40,000
Profit and Loss Account balance b/f		1,020
Stocks: Raw materials	5,226	
Work in progress	10,117	
Finished goods	6,121	
Factory rent	1,417	
Factory lighting and power	3,820	
Factory salaries	6,808	
Administrative expenses	4,752	
Raw material purchases	24,592	
Wages	26,261	
Sales		90,814
Plant and machinery (at cost)	60,000	
Plant and machinery depreciation provision		17,540
Fixtures (at cost)	7,500	
Fixtures depreciation provision		2,500
Premises (at cost)	76,800	

	£	£
Debtors	42,000	
Cash at bank	10,000	
Creditors		51,620
Bad debts provision		1,920
	285,414	285,414

The following adjustments are required:

1. Amount due for factory power £285.
2. Factory rent prepaid £142.
3. Depreciation provision for the year to be 10 per cent on the reducing balance method for plant and machinery and fixtures.
4. Provision for doubtful debts to be 5 per cent of total debtors.
5. Stocks as at 31 March 19–0:

Raw materials	£8,134
Work in progress	£7,115
Finished goods	£6,002

You are required to prepare Manufacturing, Trading and Profit and Loss Accounts for the year and a Balance Sheet as at 31 March 19–0. (Ignore taxation and dividends on all shares.)
(Royal Society of Arts and London Chamber of Commerce—Joint Scheme)

27.8A. The following balances remained in the books of Home Counties Ltd at 31 October 19–9, after the preparation of the Trading Account. Prepare the Profit and Loss Account, and Appropriation Account, for the year to 31 October 19–9 and a Balance Sheet at that date.

	£
Ordinary Share Capital Account (£1 shares)	40,000
Eight per cent Preference Share Capital Account (£1 shares)	12,000
Debtors	8,300
Creditors	5,200
Gross profit	34,000
Stock (at 31 October 19–9)	12,000
Wages accrued (at 31 October 19–9)	480
Fixed Assets	60,000
Provision for depreciation—Fixed assets	9,400
Bank	19,400
Administration expenses	6,600
Debenture interest	900
Selling expenses	9,200
Interim Dividend—Preference Shares	480
P and L Balance, 1 November 19–8 (credit)	800
six per cent Debentures	15,000

Take into account the following:

1. Administration expenses prepaid £200.
2. Dividends—Provide for 12½ per cent on Ordinary Shares and the remainder of the Preference Dividend.
3. Transfer to General Reserve £3,500.

4. Provide £7,500 for Corporation tax.
5. Authorised Capital of Home Counties Ltd:
   50,000 £1 Ordinary Shares £50,000
   20,000 £1 8 per cent Preference Shares £20,000.

(Northern Counties Technical Examination Council)

27.9A. The following list of balances was extracted from the books of the W.T. Co Ltd at 31 March 19–9:

	£
Share capital, authorised and issued:	
160,000 Ordinary Shares of £1 each	160,000
80,000 8 per cent Cumulative Preference shares of £1 each	80,000
Retained earnings	20,000
Seven per cent loan stock	40,000
Freehold property at cost	280,000
Motor vehicles (cost £32,000)	27,200
Stock in trade, 1 April 19–8	49,600
Bank overdraft	11,752
Cash in hand	1,558
Sales	696,000
Purchases	535,000
Wages and salaries	65,460
Motor expenses	7,910
Rates and insurance	3,600
General expenses	22,536
Preference dividend, paid for half year to 30 September 19–8	3,200
Debtors	63,374
Creditors	53,944
Director's current accounts:	
A.T. (debit balance)	7,680
W.T. (credit balance	2,400
Provision for bad debts	3,120

The following errors have since been discovered and now require to be corrected:

1. an invoice for motor expenses of £30 had been completely omitted from the books;

2. a sale of £166 had been entered in the sales day book but not debited to the customer's account;

3. a purchase of £194 had been credited to the account of the wrong supplier;

4. the debit side of the cash column of the cash book had been overadded by £68.

The following information is also available:

(i) Bad debts amounting to £340 are to be written off, and the provision for bad debts is to be adjusted to 5 per cent of total debtors.
(ii) Stock in trade at 31 March 19–9, was valued at £39,400.
(iii) Rates and insurance paid in advance at 31 March 19–9, amounted to £1,000 and wages outstanding amounted to £3,360.
(iv) The directors are entitled to salaries of £8,000 each. Their cash drawings have been recorded in their current accounts, but no entries have been made

in respect of these salaries or for stock withdrawn by W.T. At cost price, his drawings of stock during the year amounted to £1,300.

(v) Depreciation on motor vehicles is to be provided at 20 per cent per annum of cost.

(vi) The directors have proposed a dividend of 10 per cent on the ordinary share capital.

(vii) No interest has been paid or provided for on the loan stock for the year.

Required:

(*a*) Trading, Profit and Loss and Appropriation Accounts for the year ended 31 March 19–9.

(*b*) A balance sheet at that date.

Notes:

Ignore taxation.

Journal entries or a trial balance are not required.

Show corrections inset as adjustments to amounts entered in the final accounts.

State any assumptions you consider it necessary to make.

(Chartered Institute of Secretaries and Administrators)

APPENDIX 27.1

Examinations at Stage One Level

As an author I can now change my writing style here into that of the first person singular, as I want to put across to you a message about examinations, and I want you to feel that I am writing this for you as an individual rather than simply as one of the considerable number of people who have read the technical part of the book.

When you think about it, you have spent a lot of hours trying to master such things as double entry, balance sheets, suspense accounts and goodness knows what else. Learning accounting/bookkeeping does demand a lot of discipline and practice. Compared with the many hours learning the stuff, most students spend very little time actually considering in detail how to tackle the examination. You are probably one of them, and I would like you to take some time away from your revision of the various topics in the syllabus, and instead I want you to think about the examination.

Let me start by saying that if you want to understand anything about examinations then you have got to understand examiners, so let us look together at what these peculiar creatures get up to in an examination. The first thing is that when they set an examination they are looking at it on the basis that they want good students to get a pass mark. Obviously anyone who doesn't achieve the pass mark will fail, but the object of the exercise is to find those who will pass rather than to find the failures. This means that if you have done your work properly, and if you are not sitting for an examination well above your intellectual capabilities, then you should manage to get a pass mark. By now you are probably falling asleep, but it was important to stress that before I could get down to the details of setting about the task.

There are, however, quite a large number of students who will fail, not because they haven't put in enough hours on their studies, not because they are unintelligent, but simply because they throw away marks unnecessarily by poor examination technique. If you can read the rest of this piece, and then say honestly that you wouldn't have committed at least one of the mistakes that I am going to mention, then you are certainly well outside the ordinary range of students.

Before thinking about the examination paper itself, let us think about how you are going to get to the examination room. If it is at your own college then you have no problems as to how you will get there. On the other hand it may be at an external centre. Do you know exactly where the place is? If not, you had better have a trip there if possible. How are you going to get there? If you are going by bus or train do you know which bus of train to catch? Will it be the rush hour when it may well take you much longer than mid-day? Quite a large proportion of students lose their way on their way to the examination room, or else arrive, breathless and flustered, at the very last minute. They then start off the attempt at the examination in a somewhat nervous state, a recipe for disaster for a lot of students. So plan how you are going to get there, and give yourself enough time.

Last minute learning of stuff for your examination will be of little use to you. The last few days before the examination should not be spent in cramming. You can look at past examination papers and rework some of them. This is totally different from trying to cram new facts into your head. On the way to the exam don't read textbooks, try reading the newspaper or something similar.

This is probably the first examination you will have taken in book-keeping/accounting. At this level the examiner is very much concerned with your practical ability in the subject. Accounting is a practical subject, and your practical competence is about to be tested. The examiner will therefore expect the answers to be neat and well set out. Untidy work with figures spread over the sheet in a haphazard way, badly written figures, and columns of figures in which the vertical columns are not set down in straight lines, will incur the examiner's displeasure.

Really, what you should say to yourself is: 'Suppose I was in charge of an office, doing this type of book-keeping work, what would I say if one of my assistants put on my desk a sheet of paper with book-keeping entries on it written in the same manner as my own efforts in attempting this examination question?'. Just look at some of the work you have done in the past in book-keeping. Would you have told your assistant to go back and do the work again because it is untidy? If you would say that about your own work then why should the examiner think any different?

Anyone who works in Accounting knows full well that untidy work leads to completely unnecessary errors. Therefore the examiner insisting on clear, tidy, well laid-out work is not being Victorian in approach, he/she wants to ensure that you are not going to mess up the work of an Accounting department. Imagine going to the Savings Bank and the manager says to you 'We don't know whether you've got £5 in the account or £5,000. You see the work of our clerks is so untidy that we can never sort out exactly how much is in anybody's account.' I would guess that you wouldn't want to put a lot of money into an account at that bank. How would you feel if someone took you to court for not paying a debt of £100 when in fact you owed them nothing? All of this sort of thing would happen all the time if we simply allowed people to keep untidy accounts. The examiner is there to ensure that the person to whom he gives a certificate will be worthy of it, and will not continually mess up the work of any firm at which he/she may work in the future.

I can imagine quite a few of you groaning at all of this, and if you don't want to pass the examination then please give up reading here. If you do want to pass, and your work is untidy, then what can you do about it! Well, the answer is simple enough: start right now to be neat and orderly in your work Quite a lot of students have said to me over the years 'I may be giving you untidy work now, but when I actually get in the exam room I will then do my work neatly enough.' This is as near impossible as anything can be. You cannot suddenly be able to do accounting work neatly, and certainly not when you are under the stress and strain of an examination. Even the neatest worker may well find that in an examination that his/her work may not be of its usual standard because of the fact that nervousness will see them make mistakes. If this is true, then if you are an untidy worker now your work in an examination is likely to be even more untidy. Have I convinced you yet?

The next thing is that work should not only be neat and well laid out. Headings should always be given, and any dates needed should be inserted. The test you should apply is to imagine that you are a partner in a firm of professional accountants and you are away on holiday for a few weeks. During that time your assistants have completed all sorts of work including reports, drafting final accounts, various forms of other computations and so on. All of this work is deposited on your desk while you are away. When you return you look at each item in the pile of stuff awaiting your attention. Suppose the first item is a Trading and Profit and Loss Account for the year ended 31 December 19–5 in respect of J. King, one of your clients. When you looked at it you could see that it was a Trading and Profit and Loss Account, but that you didn't know for which client, nor did you know which year it was for. Would you be annoyed with your staff?—of course you would. So therefore in an examination why should the examiner accept as a piece of your work a Trading and Profit and Loss Account answer without the name of the business on top, the fact that it was Trading and Profit and Loss Account also written across the top, and in addition the period covered by it? Similarly a bank reconciliation statement should also state that fact and show the date and the name of the client. If proper headings are not given you will lose a lot of marks, even though the actual calculations of the gross and net profits are correct. Always therefore put in the headings properly; don't wait until your examination to start this correct practice.

If you have now got the right attitude about setting out your work, we must now look at the way in which you should tackle the examination paper when the time comes. One of the troubles about book-keeping/accounting examinations is that the student is expected to do a lot of work in a relatively short time. I have personally campaigned against this attitude, but the tradition is of long-standing and I am therefore afraid that you are stuck with it. It will be the same for every other student taking your examination, so it is not unfair as far as any one student is concerned. Working at speed does bring about various disadvantages, and makes the way you tackle the examination of even greater importance than for examinations where the pace is more leisurely.

Very approximately, the marks allotted to each question will give you some idea as to how long you should take over the question. At this level quite a few of the papers are of 2 hours' duration. This means 100 possible marks for 120 minutes work. If your arithmetic is any good you will be able to see that to work out how long a question should take, the thing to do is to take the number of marks for the question and add one-fifth of that figure to equal minutes available. For example, a question with 30 marks should take 30+one-fifth of 30 = 30+6 = 36 minutes, or a question worth 10 marks should take 10+one-fifth of 10 = 10+2 = 12 minutes. In a 3-hour examination the easiest way to calculate it is to double the number given for marks and then subtract one-tenth of that total, so that a 25-mark question should take 25 × 2 = 50 less one-tenth, i.e. 5 = 45 minutes, or a 10-mark question should take 10 × 2 = 20 less one-tenth 2 = 18 minutes. Get used to working out, for your particular examination, how long questions should take.

However, the calculation of minutes to be spent on each question is an approximate one. If you are working in an examination room and you are beating the clock—for instance in a 2-hour examination—if, after half an hour you have attempted questions with a possible total of 30 marks, then you will feel more confident, as in that amount of time on a strict apportionment of marks as already described, you will have been expected to have attempted questions with a total of possible marks of 25. If, on the other hand, you have spent half an hour and are still struggling only part way through a long question worth 20 marks altogether, then it would not be surprising if you were becoming rather anxious. In fact examiners usually set what might be called 'warm-up' questions. These are usually fairly short, and not very difficult, questions and the examiner will expect you to tackle these questions first of all. You will probably be able to do these questions in less time than the time normally allocated. The examiner is trying to be kind to you. He knows that there is a certain amount of nervousness on the part of a student taking an examination, and he will want to give you the chance to calm down by letting you tackle these short, relatively easy questions, first of all, and generally settle down to your work.

	£
Opening Stock	4,000
Add Purchases	11,500
	15,500
Less Closing Stock	3,800
	12,700

One golden rule which should always be observed is 'show all of your workings'. Suppose for instance you have been asked to work out the Cost of Goods Sold, not simply as part of a Trading Account but for some other reason. On a scrap of paper you work out the answers above.

You put down the answer as £12,700. The scrap of paper with your workings on it is then crumpled up by you and thrown in the waste-paper basket as you leave the room. You may have noticed in reading this that in fact the answer should have been 11,700 and not 12,700, as the arithmetic was incorrect. The examiner may well have allocated, say, 4 marks for this bit of the question. What will he do when he simply sees your answer as £12,700? Will he say: 'I should imagine that the candidate mis-added to the extent of £1,000, and, as I am not unduly penalising for arithmetic, I will give the candidate 3½ marks.' I'm afraid the examiner cannot do this; the candidate has got the answer wrong, there is no supporting evidence, and so the examiner gives marks as nil. If you had only attached the workings to your answer, and the workings could be easily related to your answer, then I have no doubt that you would have got 3½ marks at least.

On the other hand, do not expect that these 'warm-up' questions will be numbered 1 and 2 on your examination paper. Most accounting examinations start off with a rather long-winded question, worth quite a lot of marks, as question number 1 on the paper. Over the years I have advised students not to tackle these questions first. A lot of students are fascinated by the fact that such a question is number 1, that it is worth a lot of marks, and their thinking runs: 'If I do this question first, and make a good job of it, then I am well on the way to passing the examination.' I do not deny that a speedy and successful attempt at such a question would probably lead to a pass. The trouble is that this doesn't usually happen, and many students have told me afterwards that their failure could be put down to simply ignoring this advice. What happens, very often, is that the student starts off on such a question, things don't go very well, a few mistakes are made, the student then looks at the clock and sees that he/she is not 'beating the clock' in terms of possible marks, and then panic descends on him/her. Leaving that question very hastily the student then proceeds to the next question, which normally might have been well attempted, but because of the state of mind a hash is made of that one as well, and so you may fail an examination which you had every right to think you could pass.

At this stage there are not usually many essay-type questions. Before I discuss these I want you to look at two questions set recently at this stage. Having done that visualise carefully what you would write in answer to them. Here they are:

(a) You are employed as a book-keeper by G. Jones, a trader. State briefly what use you would make of the following documents in relation to your book-keeping records.

(i) A bank statement.

(ii) A credit note received to correct an overcharge on an invoice.

(iii) A paying-in slip.
(iv) Petty cash voucher.

(b) Explain the term 'depreciation'. Name and describe briefly two methods of providing for depreciation of fixed assets.

Now we can test whether or not you would have made a reasonably good attempt at the questions. With question (*a*) a lot of students would have written down what a bank statement is, what a paying-in slip is, what a petty cash voucher is and so on. Marks gained by you for an answer like that would be . . . nil. Why is this? Well you simply have not read the question properly. The question asked what USE you would make of the documents, and not instead to describe what the documents were. The bank statement would be used to check against the bank column in the cash book or cash records to see that the bank's entries and your own were in accordance with one another, with a bank reconciliation statement being drawn up to reconcile the two sets of records. The petty cash voucher would be used as a basis for entering up the payments columns in the petty cash book. Therefore the USE of the items was asked for, not the DESCRIPTIONS of the items.

Let us see if you have done better on question (*b*). Would you have written down how to calculate two methods of depreciation, probably the reducing balance method and the straight line method? But have you remembered that the question also asked you to EXPLAIN THE TERM DEPRECIATION? In other words, what is depreciation generally. A fair number of students will have omitted that part of the question. My own guess is that far more students would have made a rather poor attempt at question (*a*) rather than question (*b*). In both cases the questions should have been read very carefully, and it is good practice to underline the key words in a question. If you had set out to underline the key words, to get at the core of the question, then you would have underlined the word USE as one of the keywords in question (*a*), and consequently have not been guilty of writing about descriptions of things instead of describing to what USE these things are put.

The next point is concerned with familiarizing yourself with the type of examination for which you are studying. You should get hold of as many of the past examination papers as you can manage. Work through as many of them as you can. By doing this you will get some idea as to how long it will take you to finish the paper, or how much you can manage before time runs out. It will also give you the feel of the examination, as the style of examinations vary.

Later on in *Business Accounting 2* I will deal with further problems which arise at the more advanced stages of the examinations. What I would like you to do now is to attempt the following two papers which are fairly typical of papers at this stage. Full and complete answers are shown at the back of the book. What I do not want you to do is simply to look at the questions and then turn to the answers and compare them. Practice at tackling accounting examinations is something you actually have to do; it is simply no use at all getting hold of the answers and then ticking off on them the appropriate figures. You have to do these papers without looking at the answers. I also want you to devote a full two hours to them, so that you can see just how much you can get through in the time.

Answers at the back of the book

THE ROYAL SOCIETY OF ARTS
EXAMINATIONS BOARD
Single-Subject Examinations

Book-Keeping

Stage I (Elementary)

(TWO HOURS ALLOWED)

All questions in Section A and TWO *questions in Section B are to be attempted.*

SECTION A

1. Re-draft the following Balance Sheet of Kandy Stores in its correct form:

Balance Sheet for the Year Ended 31 December 19–5

	£		£
Capital	20,000	Cash	248
Trade Debtors	6,420	Bank Overdraft	1,500
Prepaid Expenses	460	Trade Creditors	5,140
Net Profit for the Year	7,364	Stock-in-Trade	4,656
		Drawings	3,000
		Freehold Premises	12,000
		Furniture and Fittings	2,500
		Motor Vehicles	4,960
		Accrued Expenses	240
	34,244		34,244

(23 *marks*)

2. The following extract is from the bank columns of the Cash Book of J. Coral:

19–6		£	19–6		£
April 26	Balance b/f	260	April 27	M. Turner	53
,, 27	L. Brown	84	,, 30	K. Jones	21
,, 29	Cash	100	,, 30	S. Cooper	42
,, 30	H. Cane	62		Balance c/f	390
		506			506

On 30 April, he received the following bank statement from the bank:

		Payments	Receipts	Balance
19–6		£	£	£
April 26	Balance (credit)			260
„ 28	Brown		84	
„ 28	Credit Transfer—S. King		48	392
„ 29	Cash		100	492
„ 30	Turner	53		
„ 30	Charges	25		414

You are required to:

(*a*) Bring the Cash Book up to date, and carry down the new balance at 30 April 19–6; and

(*b*) Prepare a statement under its proper title to reconcile the difference between the revised balance in the cash book and the balance in the bank statement on 30 April 19–6.

(14 *marks*)

3. On 1 January 19–5, S. Drive started business as a wholesaler. The following were among the balances extracted from his books on 31 December 19–5. From this information prepare S. Drive's Trading and Profit and Loss Accounts for the year ended 31 December 19–5.

	£
Purchases	15,750
Sales	20,500
Returns Inwards	456
Returns Outwards	278
Motor-van Expenses	320
Carriage on Purchases	84
Advertising	240
Wages	2,500
Office Expenses	470
Insurance	125
Heat and Light	75
Interest on Loan (debit)	30
Discount Allowed	210
Discount Received	140
Rent and Rates	725

You are given the following additional information:

(*a*) Stock-in-hand at 31 December 19–5 £4,750.

(*b*) Provide £100 for Doubtful Debts.

(*c*) A van which cost £1,500 is to be depreciated by 20 per cent on cost.

(*d*) A half-year's interest, £30, is due on the loan.

(*e*) Rates prepaid amount to £70.

(*f*) Insurance accrued, £20.

(26 *marks*)

4. Rule a Petty Cash Book with four analysis columns for Travelling Expenses; Office Expenses; Postages and Stationery; and Ledger Accounts. The cash float is £100 and the amount spent is reimbursed on 27 February 19–6.

Enter the following transactions and balance at the end of February:

19–6			£
Feb.	2	Received float of	100
		Paid:	
,,	5	Document Folders	6
,,	6	S. Haines—Ledger a/c	15
		Office Cleaner	5
,,	9	Petrol for Office Car	5
		Postages	3
,,	10	Sundry Fares	1
		Desk Calendar	2
,,	13	Office Cleaner	5
,,	20	Postages	2
		Sundry Fares	3
,,	24	Biros and Pencils	3
,,	27	H. Carter—Ledger a/c	12
		Office Cleaner	5

(13 *marks*)

SECTION B

5. In your answer book write the words which are missing from the following sentences:

(*a*) The total of the Purchases Returns Book is posted to the .... side of the .... account.

(*b*) Discount Payable is to be found on the .... side of the .... account.

(*c*) Items in the Purchases Day Book are posted to the .... side of personal accounts and items in the Sales Returns Book are posted to the .... side of personal accounts.

(*d*) Asset accounts have .... balances and accounts for liabilities have .... balances.

(*e*) The excess of the total of current assets over the total of current liabilities is known as the .... of the business.

(10 *marks*)

6. In your answer book rule a table as indicated below. Show how the following transactions would affect the amount of the net capital and the working capital of a business.

Indicate in your table an increase by the sign + and a decrease by the sign −. If there is no effect write the words 'No effect'.

(*a*) £500 was paid to trade creditors.

(*b*) Stock valued at £300 was sold on credit for £375.

(*c*) Furniture and Fittings was depreciated by £250.

(*d*) Trade debtors totalling £120 were written off as bad debts.

(*e*) Office furniture valued in the books at £90 was sold for £75.

Item	Effect on Capital	Effect on Working Capital
(*a*)		
(*b*)		
etc.		

(10 *marks*)

7. Prepare the Journal entries and brief narrations in the books of C. Shell, a boat builder, to correct the following errors:

(*a*) £560 had been included in the Wages Account and £240 in the Materials Account, which amounts represented expenditure on C. Shell's private sailing yacht.

(*b*) A cheque payment of £84 to A. H. Clark had been debited to H. Clarkson's account.

(*c*) The purchase of a calculating machine for the office, value £300, had been posted to the Purchases account.

(10 *marks*)

Answers at the back of the book

The London Chamber of Commerce and Industry

Book-Keeping

Elementary Stage

(TWO HOURS ALLOWED)

Instructions to Candidates

(*a*) All questions should be attempted.
(*b*) Marks may be lost by lack of neatness.
(*c*) Journal entries are not required unless requested.

1. A sole trader, whose knowledge of book-keeping is very poor, prepared the following document from his records:

Dr *Balance Sheet for the year ending 31 October 19–6* *Cr*

	£		£
Capital 1 November 19–5	1,980	Cash in Hand	40
		Debtors	1,670
Bank Balance	480	Office Furniture	300
Net Profit for Year	1,380	Drawings	1,160
Creditors	930	Bad Debts	90
Discount Received	80	Discount allowed	120
		Stock	1,470
	4,850		4,850

The items shown in the above document have been correctly extracted from the Ledger, i.e. those on the left hand side are credit balances whereas those on the right hand side are debit balances.

Required:

(*a*) Commencing with the <u>incorrect</u> Net Profit figure of £1,380 calculate the correct Net Profit.

(*b*) Redraft the above document so that it conforms with modern practice.

(20 *marks*)

2. Robert is in business as a sole trader and his Trading Account for the year 19–5 is given below:

	£		£
Stock 1 January 19–5	1,360	Sales	11,000
Purchases	8,930		
	10,290		
Less Stock 31 Dec 19–5	1,490		
Cost of goods sold	8,800		
Gross Profit for year	2,200		
	11,000		11,000

On 15 April 19–6 Robert's warehouse was destroyed by fire—including all his Stock-in-Trade. Fortunately his book-keeping records were saved and these disclosed the following figures:

Purchases	1 January 19–6 to 15 April 19–6	£2,180
Sales	1 January 19–6 to 15 April 19–6	£3,000

All goods purchased during the period 1 January 19–6 to 15 April 19–6 were received in the warehouse *before* the fire and all goods sold in that period were despatched before the fire.

Required:

(*a*) Calculate the percentage of Gross Profit to Sales for 19–5.

(*b*) To enable Robert to submit a fire insurance claim calculate what the stock would have been at the date of the fire. For this purpose you must assume that the percentage of *Gross Profit* to *Sales* for 19–6 would be the same as the percentage for the year 19–5.

Note:
Calculations must be shown.

(25 *marks*)

3. The following figures have been extracted from the records of a sole trader who does not keep a full record of his transactions on the double entry system:

		£
1 November 19–5	Debtors	920
	Creditors	360
	Stock	670
31 October 19–6	Debtors	1,030
	Creditors	440
	Stock	720

All goods were sold on credit and all purchases were made on credit. During the year ending 31 October 1976 Cash received from Debtors amounted to £4,870 whilst Cash paid to Creditors amounted to £3,130.

Required:

(*a*) Calculate the amount of Sales and Purchases for the year ending 31 October 19–6.

(*b*) Draw up the Trading Account for the year ending 31 October 19–6.

Note:
Calculations must be shown.

(25 *marks*)

4. George Holt, a sole trader extracted from his books the following Trial Balance as at the close of business on 31 October 19–6:

	Dr	Cr
	£	£
Stock 1 November 19–5	1,970	
Debtors and Creditors	2,350	1,680
Wages and Salaries	1,520	
Rent, Rates and Insurance	280	
Bad Debts	110	
Discounts	130	90
Fixtures and Fittings	400	
Purchases and Sales	5,930	9,620
Bank Overdraft		260
Cash in Hand	30	
Capital Account 1 November 19–5		2,700
Drawings	1,440	
General Office Expenses	190	
	14,350	14,350

Notes:
(*a*) Rent prepaid at 31 October 19–6 £40.
(*b*) Stock 31 October 19–6 £1,780.
(*c*) Depreciation £100 for fixtures and fittings.

Required:
Prepare the Trading and Profit and Loss Accounts for the year ending 31 October 19–6 together with a Balance Sheet as at that date.

(30 *marks*)

Full paper without answers

THE ROYAL SOCIETY OF ARTS EXAMINATIONS BOARD
Single-Subject Examinations

Book-Keeping

Stage I (Elementary)

(TWO HOURS ALLOWED)

All questions in Section A and TWO *questions in Section B are to be attempted.*

SECTION A

1. P. Brown is in practice as a professional adviser. The figures below relate to his affairs for the year ended 31 May 19–6. Prepare a Profit and Loss Account for the year ended 31 May 19–6 and a Balance Sheet on that date.

	£	£
Capital 1 June 19–5		6,200
Drawings	4,000	
Office furniture and equipment (at cost)	1,400	
Subscriptions to professional bodies	120	
Money held in trust for clients		2,000
Postage and stationery	450	
Rent and rates	700	
Interest on bank deposit account		150
Money on deposit account	3,000	
Professional charges for services		12,000
Unpaid accounts for services	400	
Petty cash	30	
Cash in bank	5,500	
Salaries office staff	4,000	
Travelling expenses	750	
	20,350	20,350

The following should be taken into consideration:

(*a*) Salaries unpaid, £80.

(*b*) Rent and rates unpaid for April and May may be calculated from the figure of £700 which covers ten months.

(*c*) Travelling expenses for private journeys by P. Brown (included in the £750 travelling expenses), £50.

(*d*) Of the interest received the following amount is interest on client's money, £100.

(*e*) Depreciate furniture and equipment by 10 per cent on cost.

(25 *marks*)

2. A fire in the accounts section of G. Illington had destroyed all the sales records for the year ended 31 May 19–6. However, you are asked to prepare a trading account from the information which is available.

Stock in trade: 1 June 19–5, £8,500; 31 May 19–6, £7,900.
Purchases during year, £29,000.
Gross profit is always 25 per cent of the cost of goods sold.

G. Illington's Balance Sheet on 31 May 19–5 showed debtors £3,400. Cash received for credit sales during the year amounted to £36,000.

What should be the figure for debtors in the Balance Sheet on 31 May 19–6?

(10 *marks*)

3. Enter the following transactions in the appropriate accounts in the Sales and Purchases ledgers. Balance the accounts at the end of May 19–6.

19–6			*List price*	*VAT*
			£	%
May	1	Bought goods from P. Ellison (20 per cent trade discount is allowed)	150	10
,,	3	Sold goods to G. Brandon	300	10
		Sold goods to R. Strong	200	10
,,	7	Returned goods to P. Ellison	50	10
,,	8	G. Brandon returned goods	40	10
,,	10	Settled P. Ellison's account less 2½ per cent cash discount		
,,	13	Sold goods to R. Strong	200	10
,,	18	Sold goods to G. Brandon	300	10
,,	24	G. Brandon settled his account		
,,	28	Received information that R. Strong's premises had been completely destroyed by fire. The premises were not insured and R. Strong had disappeared.		
,,	29	Bought goods from P. Ellison. (This transaction subject to 25 per cent trade discount)	200	10

(*b*) Write up the VAT account in the general ledger. (Note 10 per cent may not be the rate ruling at the time of the examination, but it is selected for its convenience in calculations.)

(25 *marks*)

4. Rule up a petty cash book with columns for the following. Purchases of stock, Proprietor's drawings, Postage and stationery, Miscellaneous items and Value added tax.

Enter the following transactions:

19–6			£
May	1	Cash balance	50.00
		Bought sundry items for stock	10.00 (plus 10% VAT)
„	3	Journey by works foreman	5.10
„	7	Private journey by proprietor	3.50
„	8	Flowers for proprietor to take home to his wife	0.70
„	11	Postage stamps	3.00
„	17	Bought stationery	1.00 (plus 10% VAT)
„	21	Bought soap, etc., for washroom	1.50
„	24	Proprietor took for his own use	5.00

Replenish the imprest on 24 May 19–6.

(16 *marks*)

SECTION B

5. S. Trader has never kept any books and has decided to set up a double entry system. Draft an opening journal entry using the following valuations on 1 June 19–6:

	£
Premises	10,000
Stock	1,500
Motor van	700
Creditors	250
Cash in hand	70
Cash at bank	150

S. Trader informs you that in addition to the above he has a mortgage of £2,000 on the premises, and that the rates are paid for the six months April to September 19–6 (inclusive), £120.

(10 *marks*)

6. (*a*) Smith receives his bank statement showing a balance in bank of £1,340 on 31 May 19–6. Cheques totalling £130 paid to creditors have not yet been presented for payment, and a sum of £75 credit transfer received by the bank has not been entered in his cash book. Calculate the balance which Smith's cash book should show before any corrections are made.

(*b*) Smith receives a statement of account from one of his suppliers. It shows a balance due of £180. The account in Smith's ledger indicates that the amount due is only £50. Explain how this difference could arise without any mistakes being made.

(10 *marks*)

7. Distinguish between:

(*a*) Cash discount and trade discount.

(*b*) Turnover and rate of stock turnover.

(*c*) Bad and doubtful debts and provision for bad and doubtful debts.

(*d*) A trial balance and a balance sheet.

(10 *marks*)

Full paper without answers

The London Chamber of Commerce and Industry

Book-Keeping

Elementary Stage

(TWO HOURS ALLOWED)

Instructions to Candidates

(*a*) All questions should be attempted.
(*b*) Marks may be lost by lack of neatness.
(*c*) Journal entries are not required unless requested.

1. Thomas Dawson, a sole trader, has the following purchases and sales on credit for the month of February 19–7.

19–7 February 1 Purchased from Smith Bros.—linen £37, silk £25
„ 4 Purchased from W. Mills—woollen goods £46, cotton goods £33
„ 8 Sold to A. Thompson—linen £21, cotton goods £26
„ 12 Purchased from F. Jackson—cotton goods £39, silk £28
„ 17 Sold to T. Robinson—linen £17, silk £18, cotton goods £24
„ 23 Sold to J. Williams—woollen goods £30, linen £14

Required:

(*a*) Enter the above transactions at the Purchases Day Book and the Sales Day Book of Thomas Dawson and post to the personal accounts concerned.

(*b*) Total the two Day Books—posting the totals to Purchases Account and Account and Sales Account.

(25 *marks*)

2. The following Trial Balance was extracted from the books of Adam Jenkins at the close of business on 28 February 19–7.

	Dr.	Cr.
	£	£
Purchases and Sales	3,760	6,580
Cash at Bank	380	
Cash in Hand	70	
Capital Account 1 March 19–6		3,300
Drawings	950	
Office Furniture	480	
Rent and Rates	340	
Wages and Salaries	860	
Discounts	230	120
Debtors and Creditors	1,640	830
Stock 1 March 19–6	990	
Provision for Bad and Doubtful Debts 1 March 19–6		90
Delivery van	800	
Van running costs	150	
Bad Debts written off	270	
	10,920	10,920

Notes:
(*a*) Stock 28 February 19–7—£1,170.
(*b*) Wages and Salaries accrued at 28 February 19–7—£30.
(*c*) Increase the provision for Bad and Doubtful Debts by £20.
(*d*) Provide for depreciation as follows:
Office Furniture £60 Delivery Van £160

Required:
Draw up the Trading and Profit and Loss Accounts for the year ending 28 February 19–7 together with a Balance Sheet as on 28 February 19–7.

(30 *marks*)

3. Robert Church and Frederick Gill—two sole traders—decided to enter into partnership as from 1 March 19–7. On that date, their separate Balance Sheets were as follows:

Robert Church
Balance Sheet as at 1 March 19–7

	£			£
Capital Account	3,250	*Fixed Assets*		
Creditors	610	Office Furniture		360
		Current Assets		
		Stock	1,630	
		Debtors	1,480	
		Cash at bank	390	
				3,500
	3,860			3,860

Frederick Gill
Balance Sheet as at 1 March 19–7

	£			£
Capital Account	3,800	*Fixed Assets*		
Creditors	920	Office Furniture		440
		Current Assets		
		Stock	1,810	
		Debtors	1,940	
		Cash at bank	530	
				4,280
	4,720			4,720

The partnership takes over all the assets (including Cash at Bank) and liabilities of the two sole traders. For this purpose, however, Office Furniture is to be revalued as follows:

Church £300. Gill £400.

In addition, it is agreed that Bad Debts—as below—be written off *before* the new partnership opens its books:

Church £40. Gill £60.

Required:

(*a*) Calculate the opening capital of each partner. (*N.B.*—Calculations must be shown.)

(*b*) Draw up the opening Balance Sheet of the partnership after giving effect to the above.

(25 *marks*)

4. At the close of business on 26 February 19–7, Alfred Bishop, a sole trader, extracted a Trial Balance from his books. The Trial balance did not agree, but Bishop entered the difference in a Suspense Account. He then prepared his Trading and Profit and Loss Accounts for the year ending 28 February 19–7 in the normal way. The Profit and Loss Account so prepared showed a Net Profit amounting to £2,370.

During March 19–7, Bishop discovered the following errors in his books and these accounted for the entire difference in the Trial Balance:

(*a*) Bad Debts Account had been debited with items of £31 and £27 in respect of bad debts but the *personal accounts* of the individual debtors had not been credited.
(*b*) The Sales Day Book was overcast by £70.
(*c*) Cash £36 received from Simon Jones had been correctly entered in the Cash Book but the double entry had been made on the *wrong side* of Jones' Personal Account in Alfred Bishop's ledger.
(*d*) The Discount allowed total in the Cash Book—£42—has not been entered in the Discount Account.

Required:

(i) State how, and to what extent, each of the above errors would have affected the Trial Balance, e.g. Debit overstated £......

(ii) Calculate the correct figure for Net Profit.

N.B.—Calculations must be shown.

(20 *marks*)

APPENDIX 27.2

Answers to Exercises

1.1 (*a*) 10,700
(*b*) 23,100
(*c*) 4,300
(*d*) 3,150
(*e*) 25,500
(*f*) 51,400.

1.2 (*a*) −Cash, −Creditors
(*b*) −Bank, +Fixtures
(*c*) +Stock, +Creditors
(*d*) +Cash, +Capital
(*e*) +Cash, +Loan
(*f*) +Bank, −Debtors
(*g*) −Stock, −Creditors
(*h*) +Premises, −Bank.

1.3 (i) Asset
(ii) Liability
(iii) Asset
(iv) Asset
(v) Liability
(vi) Asset

1.4 Wrong: Assets: Loan from C. Smith; Creditors; Liabilities: Stock of Goods; Debtors.

1.5 Assets: Motor 2,000; Premises 5,000; Stock 1,000; Bank 700; Cash 100 = total 8,800: Liabilities: Loan from Bevan 3,000; Creditors 400 = total 3,400. Capital 8,800−3,400 = 5,400.

1.6 Assets: Buildings 3,000; Motor 1,800; Stock 350; Bank 1,010. Capital 5,000; Loan 1,000; Creditor 160. Totals 6,160.

2.1 (*a*) Dr Motor Van, Cr Cash
(*b*) Dr Office machinery, Cr J. Sumner & Son
(*c*) Dr Cash, Cr Capital
(*d*) Dr Bank, Cr J. Crawshaw
(*e*) Dr U. Cope, Cr Cash

2.2 (*a*) Dr Machinery, Cr A. Loft & Son
(*b*) Dr A. Loft & Son, Cr Machinery
(*c*) Dr Cash, Cr Debtor
(*d*) Dr Bank, Cr J. Smith (Loan)
(*e*) Dr Cash, Cr Office machinery

2.3 Capital Cr 1,000, Cash Dr 1,000 Cr 60 and 698, Speed & Sons Dr 698 Cr 698, Motor lorry Dr 698, Office machinery Dr 60.

2.4 Bank Dr 2,500, Cr 150 & 600 & 750 & 280, Capital Cr 2,500, Office furniture Dr 150, Cr 60, Machinery Dr 750 & 280, Planers Dr 750, Cr 750, Motor van Dr 600, J. Walker Dr 60, Cr 60, Cash Dr 60.

2.5 Cash Dr 2,000 & 75 & 100, Cr 1,800, Bank Dr 1,800 & 500, Cr 950 & 58 & 100, Capital Cr 2,000, Office furniture Dr 120, Cr 62, Betta Built Dr 62 & 58, Cr 120, Motor van Dr 950, Evans & Sons Cr 560, Works machinery Dr 560, Cr 75, J. Smith (Loan) Cr 500.

2.6 Cash Dr 500 & 400 & 200; Cr 350 & 50: Bank Dr 10,000 & 1,000 & 350 & 1,000 & 1,800; Cr 3,000 & 2,000: Manchester Garages Dr 2,000; Cr 3,600: R. Jones Dr 3,000; Cr 1,000 & 1,800 & 200: J. Davidson Ltd, Dr 200; Cr 700: Loan J. Hawkins Cr 400: Loan H. Townsley Cr 1,000: Motor Van Dr 3,000 & 3,600: Cr 3,000: Office Equipment Dr 7,000 & 50; Cr 200: Capital Cr 10,000 & 500.

3.1 (*a*) Dr Purchases, Cr Cash
(*b*) Dr Purchases, Cr E. Flynn
(*c*) Dr C. Grant, Cr Sales
(*d*) Dr Cash, Cr Motor van
(*e*) Dr Cash, Cr Sales.

3.2 (*a*) Dr H. Poirot, Cr Returns outwards
(*b*) Dr Purchases, Cr P. Wimsey
(*c*) Dr S. Templar, Cr Sales
(*d*) Dr Returns inwards, Cr M. Spillane
(*e*) Dr Purchases, Cr Bank.

3.3 Totals—Purchases Dr 307, Sales Cr 89, Returns outwards Cr 15, C. Breeze Dr 15, Cr 72, C. Farr Cr 90, Cash Dr 25, E Rase Dr 64, A. Price Cr 145.

3.4 Totals—Cash Dr 597 Cr 173, Capital Cr 500, Purchases Dr 299, Sales Cr 97, Returns outwards Cr 47, E. Mitting Dr 116, Cr 116, A. Lot Dr 19 Cr 98, A. Knight Dr 55 Cr 55.

3.5 Totals—Cash Dr 1,028 Cr 955, Bank Dr 1,000 Cr 710, Purchases Dr 133, S. Holmes Dr 78 Cr 78, Capital Cr 1,000, Motor van Dr 500, Sales Cr 126, P. Moriarty Dr 98, Returns outwards Cr 18, Fixtures Dr 150, M/c Equipt Co Dr 150 Cr 150, Watson (Loan) Cr 100.

3.6 Capital Cr 10,000 & 500: Bank Dr 10,000 & 250; Cr 1,070 & 2,600: Cash Dr 400 & 200 & 70 & 500; Cr 250 & 220 & 100: Purchases Dr 840 & 3,600 & 370 & 220: Sales Cr 200 & 180 & 220 & 190 & 320 & 70: Returns Inwards Dr 40 & 30: Returns Outwards Cr 140 & 110: Motor Van Dr 2,600: Office Furniture Dr 600 & 100: Cr 160: Loan from T. Cooper Cr 400: F. Jones Dr 140 & 1,070; Cr 840 & 370: S. Chipchase Dr 110; Cr 3,600: C. Percy Dr 180; Cr 40: J. Noel Dr 220: H. Morgan Dr 190; Cr 30: J. Peat Dr 320: Stockport Motors Dr 2,600; Cr 2,600: Faster Supplies Dr 160; Cr 600.

4.1 (*a*) Dr Rates, Cr Bank
(*b*) Dr Wages, Cr Cash
(*c*) Dr Bank, Cr Rent received
(*d*) Dr Bank, Cr Insurance
(*e*) Dr General expenses, Cr Cash.

4.2 Totals—Bank Dr 1,200 Cr 289, Cash Dr 120 Cr 33, Purchases Dr 381, X. Press Cr 296, C. Moore Cr 85, Capital Cr 200, U. Surer (Loan) Cr 1,000, Motor van Dr 250, Sales Cr 105, Motor expenses Dr 15, Wages Dr 18, Insurance Dr 22, Commission Cr 15, Electricity Dr 17.

4.3 Totals—Bank Dr 2,005, Cr 450, Capital Cr 2,000, Purchases Dr 289, Micawber Dr 23 Cr 175, Fixtures Dr 150, Cash Dr 275 Cr 203, S. Weller Cr 114, Rent Dr 15, Stationery Dr 27, Returns outwards Cr 23, Rent received Cr 5, U. Heap Dr 77, Sales Cr 352, Motor van Dr 300, Wages Dr 117, Drawings Dr 44.

4.4 Totals—Cash 1,549 Cr 1,186, Capital Cr 1,500, Purchases Dr 421, Rent Dr 28, Bank Dr 1,000 Cr 689, Sales Cr 132, Linklater Dr 54 Cr 14, Stationery Dr 15, Returns outwards Cr 17, A. Christie Dr 296 Cr 296, S. Maugham Dr 29, Repairs Dr 18, Returns inwards Dr 14, Motor van Dr 395, Motor expenses Dr 15, Fixtures Dr 120, A. Waugh Cr 120.

5.1 *Trial Balance*—Drs: Cash 215, Purchases 459, Rent 30, Bank 96, Hughes

129, Spencer 26, Carriage 23; Crs: Capital 250, Sales 348, Males 130, Booth 186, Lowe 64. Totals: 978.

5.2 *Trial Balance*—Drs: Purchases 360, Bank 361, Cash 73, Wages 28, Lane 74, Shop fixtures 50, Motor van 400, Elliot 35; Crs: King Loan 60, Buckley 134, Heyworth 52, Capital 800, Sales 291, Returns outwards 44. Totals: 1,381.

5.3 *Trial Balance*—Drs: Bank 267, Cash 84, Purchases 871, Norris 57, Motor van 256, Motor expenses 17, Barnes 24, K. Liston 71, Moores 65, Returns inwards 11, Drawings 34, Postages 4, Edgar 67; Crs: Capital 650, Jones 673, Sales 438, Returns outwards 67. Totals: 1,828.

5.4 Trial Balance—Drs: Cash 55; Bank 7,081; Office Fixtures 363; Purchases 2,220; Returns Inwards 60; Rent 100; Wages 160; Office Stationery 310; Drawings 250; Sundry Expenses 5; J. Garner & Son 430; P. Gould 340; T. Sutherland 110; T. Bourne Ltd, 120; Crs: Capital 8,000; Sales 1,534; Returns Outwards 104; Leah & Co, 900; P. McDonald 320; K. Beverley Ltd 366; C. Rose 160; E.P. & Co, 220. Totals 11,604.

6.1 *Trading:* Dr Stock 3,249, Purchases 11,380 *less* Closing Stock 2,548 Cr Sales 18,462, Dr Gross Profit 6,381. *Profit and Loss:* Dr Salaries 2,150, Motor expenses 520, Rent and rates 670, Insurance 111, General 105, Net profit 2,825. *Balance Sheet*—Capital 5,424, *add* Net profit 2,825, *less* Drawings 895, 7,354. *Liabilities:* Creditors 1,538. *Assets:* Premises 1,500, Motors 1,200, Stock 2,548, Debtors 1,950, Bank 1,654, Cash 40. Totals: 8,892.

6.2 *Trading:* Dr Stock 2,375, Purchases 21,428, *less* Stock 4,166, Gross profit 9,157, Cr Sales 28,794. *Profit and Loss:* Dr Salaries 3,164, Rent 854, Lighting 422, Insurance 105, Motor expenses 1,133, Trade expenses 506, Net profit 2,973. *Balance Sheet*—Capital: 65,900, *add* Net profit 2,973, Drawings 2,400, Creditors 1,206. Assets: Buildings 50,000, Fixtures 1,000, Motors 5,500, Stock 4,166, Debtors 3,166, Bank 3,847. Totals: 67,679.

6.3 Rent receivable: Dr Balance b/d 90, In advance c/d 90, Profit and Loss 1,980, Cr Balance b/d 75, Cash T 750, Cash B 1,260, Balance c/d 75.

6.4 Rent payable: Dr Cash 750, Accrued c/d 250, Cr Profit and Loss 1,000. Rent receivable: Dr Arrears b/d 75, In advance c/d 75, Profit and Loss 500, Cr In advance b/d 50, Hill 150, 75, 75, 150, Pine 100, In arrears c/d 50.

6.5 Fuel Account: Dr Stock b/f 35; Cash 260; Accrued c/f 145; Cr Accrued b/f 60; Profit and Loss 330; Stock c/f 50.

6.6 *Trading:* Dr Stock 2,368, Purchases 12,389, *less* Stock 2,946, Gross profit 7,111, Cr Sales 18,922. *Profit and Loss:* Dr Salaries 3,862, Rent 564, Insurance 66, Motor expenses 664, Office 216, Lighting 198, General 314, Net Profit 1,227. *Balance Sheet*—Assets: Premises 5,000, Motors 1,800, Fixtures 350, Stock 2,946, Debtors 3,896, Prepaid 12, Bank 482, Capital: 12,636, *add* Net profit 1,227, *less* Drawings 1,200, 12,663, Creditors 1,731, Expenses owing 92. Totals: 14,486.

6.7 *Trading:* Dr Stock 3,776, *add* Purchases 12,556, *less* Stock 4,998, Gross profit 7,621. Cr Sales 18,955. *Profit and Loss:* Dr Salaries 2,447, Motor 720,

Rent 480, Rates 100, Insurance 111, Packing 276, Lighting 665, Sundry 141, Net profit 2,681. *Balance Sheet*—Assets: Fixtures 600, Motors 2,400, Stock 4,998, Debtors 4,577, Prepaid 55, Bank 3,876, Cash 120. Liabilities: Capital 12,844, *add* Net Profit 2,681, *less* Drawings 2,050, 13,475, Creditors 3,045, Expenses owing 106. Totals: 16,626.

6.8 Credits: Sales 25,500; Creditors 5,680; Loan 1,000 = 32,180+Capital = ? All other items are debit balances—total 38,856. Therefore Capital is 6,676.

8.1 Totals: Cash 363, Bank 731, Balances—Cash 184, Bank 454.

8.2 Totals: Cash 380, Bank 2,700, Balances—Cash 98, Bank 2,229.

8.3 Totals: Discounts allowed 25, Cash 135, Bank 1,564, Discounts received 36, Balances—Cash 47, Bank 421.

8.4 Totals: Discounts allowed 119, Cash 254, Bank 4,601, Discounts received 26, Balances—Cash 112, Bank 3,940.

9.1 Sales Journal total 881.

9.2 Totals: Purchases 1,096, Returns outwards 46.

9.3 Totals: Sales 1,062, Purchases 644, Returns inwards 54, Returns outwards 48.

9.7 (i) Invoice after Trade Discount 700+VAT 70 = 770
(ii) Books of D. Wilson Ltd Sales Cr 700; VAT Cr 70; G. Christie & Son Dr 770
Books of G. Christie & Son Purchases Dr 700: VAT Dr 70: D. Wilson Ltd, Cr 770.

9.8 Sales Book totals Net 520: VAT 52.
General Ledger: Sales Cr 520; VAT Cr 52.
Sales Ledger: M. Sinclair & Co Dr 165; M. Brown & Associates Dr 286; A. Axton Ltd Dr 88; T. Christie Dr 33.

9.9 Sales Book totals Net 590; VAT 59.
Purchases Book totals Net 700; VAT 70.
Sales Ledger: Dr B. Davies & Co 165; C. Grant Ltd 242 and 154; B. Karloff 88.
Purchases Ledger: Cr G. Cooper & Son 440; J. Wayne Ltd 209; B. Lugosi 55; S. Hayward 66.
General Ledger: Sales Cr 590: Purchases Dr 700: VAT Dr 70; Cr 59; Balance c/d 11.

9.13 Purchases Analysis Book: Totals of columns:
Total 2,252; Purchases 1,346; Light and Heat 246; Motor Expenses 376; Stationery 137; Carriage Inwards 147.

9.14 General Ledger: Purchases Dr 1,346; Light and Heat Dr 246; Motor Expenses Dr 376; Stationery Dr 137; Carriage Inwards 147.

Purchases Ledger: Credits in all accounts: L. Gladstone Ltd 220; E. Heath & Co 390; Northern Electricity 88; H. Wilson & Son 110 and 116; Disraeli Motors 136 and 55 and 185; W. Pitt Ltd 77; North Gas Board 134; A. Palmerston 200; O. Cromwell Ltd 24; H. MacMillan 310; R. MacDonald 85; J. Callaghan Ltd 60; D. Melbourne Ltd 62.

10.1 Motor vans Dr 3,800, Provision for depreciation Cr 620.

10.2 Machinery Dr 800, 1,000, 600, 200, Provision for depreciation −3, 80, −4, 145, −5, 240, −6, 255. *Balance Sheet:* −3, 800 *less* 80, −4, 2,400 *less* 225, −5, 2,400 *less* 465, −6, 2,600 *less* 720.

10.3 Machinery Dr 640, 720, Fixtures Dr 100, 200, 50; Provision for: Depreciation machinery −5, 80, −6, 160, Depreciation fixtures −5, 30, −6, 32. *Balance Sheets:* −5, F 300 *less* 30, M 640 *less* 80, −6, F 350 *less* 62, M 1360 *less* 240.

10.4 Plant Dr −4, 900, 600, −6, 550, Cr −7, 900, Depreciation Dr −7, 675, Cr −4, 210, −5, 300, −6, 355, −7, 365. Disposals Dr Plant 900, Profit to Profit and Loss 50, Cr Depreciation 675, Cash 275. *Balance Sheet:* −4, 1,500 *less* 210, −5, 1,500 *less* 510, −6, 2,050 *less* 865, −7, 1,150 *less* 555.

10.5 Machinery Dr Bal b/f 52,590, Cash 2,480, Cr Disposals 2,800, Balance c/d 52,270, Office furniture Dr Balance b/f 2,860, Cash 320, Cr Balance c/d 3,180, Depreciation M. Dr Disposals 1,120, Balance c/d 29,777, Cr Balance b/f 25,670, Profit and Loss 5,227, Depreciation O.F. Dr Balance c/d 1,649, Cr Balance b/d 1,490, Profit and Loss 159. *Balance Sheet:* M. 52,270 *less* 29,777, O.F. 3,180 *less* 1,649.

10.6 Red. Balance: ABC 800 *less* 160, 102, 82, 66 = 262, DEF 860 *less* 172, 138, 110, 88 = 352, GHJ 840 *less* 168, 134, 108 = 430, KLM 950 *less* 190, 152 = 608, NOP 980 *less* 196 = 784.
Straight Line: ABC 800 *less* 156×5 = 20, DEF 860 *less* 168×4 = 188, GHJ 840 *less* 164×3 = 348, KLM 950 *less* 186×2 = 578, NOP 980 *less* 192 = 788.
Adjustments: Cr Prov for Dep A/c ABC 242, DEF 164, GHJ 82, KLM 30,
Dr Prov for Dep A/c NOP 4.
19–4 Depreciation: ABC nil, GHJ 164, KLM 186, NOP 192, QRS 188, *loss* on DEF 128.

11.1 (i) Bad Debts Dr H. Gordon 110; D. Bellamy Ltd 64; J. Alderton 12; Provision c/d 220; Cr Profit and Loss 406.
(ii) 406.
(iii) Debtors 6,850 *less* Provision for Bad Debts 220.

11.2 (i) Bad Debts 19–6 Dr W. Sykes & Son 85; S. D. Kidd Ltd 140; Provision c/d 550: Cr Profit and Loss 775.
Bad Debts 19–7 Dr L. J. Silver & Co 180; N. Kelly 60; A. Capone & Associates 250; Provision c/d 600. Cr Profit and Loss 540.
(ii) 19–6 Bad Debts 775: 19–7 Bad Debts 540.
(iii) 19–6 Debtors 40,500 *less* Provision for Bad Debts 550: 19–7 Debtors 47,300 *less* Provision for Bad Debts 600.

11.3 (i) Bad Debts Dr Various 540; Provision c/d 310: Cr Provision b/f 260; Profit and Loss 590.
(ii) Dr Bad Debts 590.
(iii) Debtors 6,200 *less* Provision for Bad Debts 310.

11.4 (i) Bad Debts 19–5 Dr Various 656; Provision c/d 1,100 Cr Profit and Loss 1,756. 19–6 Dr Various 1,805; Provision c/d 2,800; Cr Provision b/d 1,100; Profit and Loss 3,505, 19–7 Dr Various 3,847: Provision c/d 3,600: Cr Provision b/d 2,800; Profit and Loss 4,647.
(ii) Debtors 19–5: 22,000; 19–6: 40,000; 19–7: 60,000; Less Provisions for Bad Debts 19–5: 1,100; 19–6: 2,800; 19–7: 3,600.

11.5 (i) Bad Debts 19–5 Dr Various 656; Cr Profit and Loss 656: 19–6 Dr Various 1,805; Cr Profit and Loss 1,805; 19–7 Dr Various 3,847; Cr Profit and Loss 3,847. Provision for Bad Debts 19–5 Dr Provision c/d 1,100; Cr Profit and Loss 1,100: 19–6 Dr Provision c/d 2,800; Cr Provision b/d 1,100; Profit and Loss 1,700: 19–7 Dr Provision c/d 3,600; Cr Provision b/d 2,800; Profit and Loss 800.
(ii) Same as for (ii) in question 11.4.

11.6 Provision for doubtful debts: Dr Profit and Loss—reduction 32, Balance c/d 640, Cr balance b/f 672.
Provision for discounts on debtors: Dr Profit and Loss—reduction 15, Balance c/d 304, Cr Balance b/f 319.

11.7 Provision for bad debts: Cr Balance b/f 3,900, Profit and Loss 100. Provision for discounts allowed: Cr Profit and Loss 1,800.

11.8 *Trading:* Dr Stock 6,300, Purchases (*less* own goods) 46,300 *less* stock 8,800; Gross profit: 17,100, Cr Sales 60,900.
Profit and Loss: Dr Wages 8,924, Rates 203, Bad debts 359, Repairs 198, Car expense 212, Discounts allowed 1,061, General 1,586, Net profit 5,411. Cr. Gross profit 17,100, Reduction in bad debts provision 40, Discounts received 814. *Balance Sheet:* Assets—Land 10,650, Furniture 1,460, Car 950, Stock 8,800, Debtors 5,213 *less* Bad debts Provision 100, Prepaid 45, Bank 540. Capital: 20,500 *add* Net profit 5,411 *less* Drawings 2,706, 23,205, Creditors 4,035, Wages owing 318. Totals: 27,558.

11.9 *Trading:* Dr Stock 6,100, Purchases 58,700, *less* Stock 8,500, Gross profit 13,000, Cr Sales 69,300. *Profit and Loss:* Cr Rents Receivable 300. Discounts 925, Dr Wages 7,460, Bad debts 325, *Bad Debts Provision* 60, General 865, Rates 250, Loan interest 60, Discounts allowed 1,320, Net profit, 3,885. *Balance Sheet*—Assets: Land 7,000, Furniture 1,400, Stock 8,500, Debtors 5,850 *less* Bad debts provision 170, Debtor for rent 25, Prepaid 50, Bank 680. Liabilities: Capital—15,000, *add* Net Profit 3,885 *less* Drawings 1,600, 17,285, Loan 1,200, Creditors 4,345, Wages owing 415, Loan interest owing 90. Totals: 23,335.

13.1 (a) Cash Book Balance after being written up 646.
(b) Balance per Cash Book 646+unpresented cheques (106+42) 148 = 794, *less* Bank Lodgments not entered on bank statement 116 = Balance per Bank Statement 678.

13.2 (a) Cash Book Balance after being written up 279.
(b) Balance per Cash Book 279+unpresented cheques (87+15) 102 = 381, *less* Bank Lodgements not entered on bank statement (83+109) 192 = Balance per Bank Statement 189.

13.3 (a) Cash Book Balance after being written up, overdraft of 360.
(b) Overdraft per Cash Book 360+Bank Lodgement not entered on bank statement 119 = 479 *less* unpresented cheque 77 = Overdraft per Bank Statement 402.

13.4 Cash Book balance 471+Credit transfer 114 *less* Bank charges 14, Trade subscription 12 = adjusted Cash Book balance 559.
BRS Balance per Cash Book 559+Unpresented cheques 268, *less* Lodgement not credited 28 = Balance per bank statement 799.

13.5 Cash at Bank 678+Unpresented cheques 256+Credit transfers 56 *less* Lodgement not recorded 115 = Balance per bank statement 875.

13.6 (i) Cash Book 273+rates overstated 9 *less* trade subscription 12 and banking overstated 4 = Adjusted Balance 266
(ii) BRS adjusted Cash Book balance 266+Unpresented cheques 245 *less* lodgements not credited 550 = Overdraft per bank statement 37.

13.7 (i) Cash Book: Dr Balance b/f 970, Credit transfer 64, Cr Discount in error 4, Trade subscription 18, Dishonoured cheque 120; Balance c/f 892
(ii) BRS Cash Book balance 892+Unpresented cheques 618 *less* Cheques not credited 386 = Balance per bank statement 1,124
(iii) as (ii).

14.1 *Trial Balance*—Drs: Discounts allowed 19, Cash 12, Bank 874, Bardsley 100, Duffy 48, Green 118, Pearson 67, Premises 2,000, Motor 750, Fixtures 600, Stock 1,289, Rent 15, Motor expenses 13, Drawings 20, Salaries 56, Rates 66, Purchases 344, Returns In 34. Crs: Discounts received 16, Hough 56, Gee 24, Johnson 89, Bamber 72, Capital 5,598, Sales 527, Returns out 43. Totals 6,425.

14.2 *Trial Balances*—Drs: Land 6,000, Plant 8,000, Stock 2,200, Motor 1,700, Wages 312, Stationery 26, Purchases 460, Insurance 30, Bad debts 30, Returns inwards 45, Morris 225, James 9, Discounts allowed 1, Cash 98, Bank 2,320. Crs: Sales 1,670, Goodall 2,100, F. Robbins 60, Capital 17,626. Totals: 21,456.

14.3 *Trial Balance*—Drs: Fixtures 550, Stocks vehicles 16,800, Petrol 115, Land 15,000, Cash 344, Bank 9,748, Farmer 82, Davies 720, Perrins 13, Adamson 42, Purchases 2,575, Discounts allowed 2, Breakdown lorry 1,600, Wages 250, National insurance 7, Crs: Sales 1,228, Exe Garages 40, Wye Petrol Co 495, Distributors 2,080, Brights 800, Capital 43,205. Totals: 47,848.

16.1 *Suspense*—Drs Appleton 30, Debtors 20, Cantrell 10, Crs Sales 10, original error Cr 50.

16.2 (*a*) (i) Advertisements Dr 27, Contractors Cr 27,

(ii) Purchases Dr 800, Motor Car Cr 800, Depreciation Dr 200, Profit and Loss Cr 200;
(iii) Sales Dr 25 Assets disposal Cr 25, Dr Asset 40 Cr Asset disposal 40 Profit and Loss Dr 15 Assets disposal Cr 15;

(*b*) Profit before adjustment 4,036+Depreciation excess 200 *less* loss on machine 15 = 4,221 *less* advertising 27 = 4,194. N.B. If Purchases needs increasing by 800 so also does Closing Stock, therefore no effect on Gross Profit.

16.3 (1) A. Smith Ltd Dr 150, A. Smith Cr 150
(2) L. Langford Dr 60, Suspense Cr 60
(3) Purchases Dr 100, Suspense Cr 100
(4) Suspense Dr 4, Sales Cr 4
(5) Machinery Dr 150, Purchases Cr 150. Original error was 156 entered on Dr side of Suspense Account.

16.4 (1) Dr Debtors
(2) Dr Carriage on Sales 4, Cr Carriage on purchases 4
(3) Dr Creditors 17
(4) Dr Drawings, Cr Sundry expenses
(5) Dr Postages and telephone 9
Altered items in Trial Balance: Debtors 1,829, Creditors 2,061; Carriage on purchases 105; Postages and telephone 100. Carriage on sales 188, Drawings 1,435, Sundry expenses 155. Trial Balance totals: 24,474.

16.5 (*a*) Profit per accounts 1,969+Rates prepaid 64+Packing materials overcharged 42 *less* Depreciation motors 280—Purchases omitted 175—bad debts 65—Provision for bad debts 40—Light and heat 45 = corrected Net profit 1,470

(*b*) Assets: Furniture 560, Motors 1,240 *less* Depreciation 280, Stock 2,275, Stock packing materials 42, Debtors 1,280 *less* Provision for Bad debts 40, Prepayments 64, Cash and bank 1,210; Liabilities: Capital 4,569+Net profit 1,470 *less* Drawings 2,038, 4,001, Creditors 2,305, Light and heat owing 45. Totals: 6,351.

16.6 (*a*) Bank Charges Dr 7, Suspense Cr 7; Suspense Dr 9, Depreciation Cr 9; Furniture Dr 20, Suspense Cr 20; Suspense Dr 18, Bell Cr 18; Suspense Dr 2, Tate Cr 2; Suspense Dr 10, Muir Cr 10.

(*b*) *Profit and Loss:* Cr Net profit as before 2,970, Overcharged depreciation 9, Dr Bank charges 7, corrected Net profit 2,972.

(*c*) *Corrected Balance Sheet*—Assets: Furniture 490, Motors 1,430, Stock 3,146, Debtors 2,114, Cash and bank 1,862; Capital: 6,093, *add* Net profit 2,972 *less* Drawings 2,500, 6,565, Creditors 2,477. Totals: 9,042.

16.7 (*a*) (i) 5,000
(ii) 6,840
(iii) 1,040.

(*b*) Assets: Premises 3,350, Furniture 1,800, Van 500, Stock 1,170, Debtors 260, Cash and bank 1,260; Capital: 7,250, Bank loan 400, Creditors 690. Totals: 8,340.

17.1 Dr Balances b/f 4,936, Sales 49,916, Cr Returns inwards 1,139, Cheques and cash 46,490, Discounts allowed 1,455, Bad debts 99, Set-offs 259, Balances c/f 5,410. Totals: 54,852.

17.2 Dr Returns outwards 1,098, Cheques 38,765, Discounts 887, Set-offs 77, Balances c/f 5,294, Cr Balances b/f 3,676, Purchases 42,257, Cash 188. Totals: 46,121.

17.3 Purchases Ledger Control: Drs Returns outwards 2,648, Cheques 146,100, Petty cash 78, Discounts received 2,134, Set-offs 1,036, Balances c/f 14,530—Total: 166,526. Crs Balances b/f 11,874, Purchases 154,562. Total: 166,436. Difference between two sides 90.
Sales Ledger Control: Drs Balances b/f 19,744, Sales 199,962, Dishonoured cheque 30; Crs Returns inwards 4,556, Cheques 185,960, Discounts allowed 5,830, Bad debts 396, Set-offs 1,036, Balances c/f 21,658. Both totals are 219,436.

17.4 Dr Balances b/d 5,082, Sales 61,228; Crs Discounts allowed 1,485, Receipts 58,946, Returns 16, Balances c/d 5,863.
Adjusted balances per list 5,502+209+132+36−16 = 5,863.

18.1 *Statement of Affairs*—Assets: Motor van 450; Stock 840; Debtors 189; Prepaid 25, Bank 275, Cash 10, Capital 800, *add* Profit (difference) 949, *less* Drawings 475, 1,274, Creditors 496, Electricity owing 19. Totals: 1,789.

18.2 Opening Capital (balance) 1,630.
Balance Sheet 31.3.19–3—Assets: Furniture 302, Motor 600 *less* Depreciation 150, Stock 1,470, Debtors 820, Bank 768, Cash 32. Capital: 1,630 *add* Net profit 1,234, *add* Cash introduced 600 *less* Drawings 900, 2,564; Liabilities: Creditors 1,278. Totals: 3,842.

18.3 *Trading Account:* Dr Decorating materials 224, Gross profit 386, Cr Work Done 610; *Profit and Loss:* Dr Rent 126, Business expenses 30, Depreciation 12, Net profit 218. *Balance Sheet*—Assets: Equipment 40, Debtors 26, Bank 59. Capital: 100, *add* Net profit 218 *less* Drawings 210, 108; Liabilities: Creditors 14, Expenses owing 3. Totals: 125.

18.4 Opening capital calculated Assets—Liabilities = 4,140.
Trading: Stock 2,430, Purchases 18,700, *less* Stock 3,150, Gross profit 9,020, Cr Sales 27,000. *Profit and Loss:* Dr Rent 768, General 1,750, Wages 1,280, Net profit 5,372; Cr Gross profit 9,020, Discounts received 150.
Balance Sheet: Capital 4,140, *add* Net profit 5,372 *less* Drawings 4,588, 4,924. Liabilities: Creditors 1,709, General expenses owing 134, Bank overdraft 118. Assets: Furniture 1,000, Stock 3,150, Debtors 2,690, Prepaid 45. Totals: 6,885.

18.5 *Trading:* Dr Stock 1,020, Purchases 12,535, *less* Stock 924, Gross profit 3,671; Cr Sales 16,302. *Profit and Loss:* Rent 100, General 1,602, Discounts allowed 300, Depreciation 20, Net Profit 1,649.
Balance Sheet—Capital 1,510, *add* Net profit 1,649, *less* Drawings 1,900, 1,259. Liabilities: Creditors 965, General Expenses owing 410, Rent owing 50. Assets: Furniture 200 *less* Depreciation 20, Stock 924, Debtors 1,172, Bank 408. Totals: 2,684.

18.6 *Trading:* Dr Stock 950, Purchases 4,304, *less* Stock 900, Gross profit 2,206, Sales: Cash 3,290, Credit 3,270. *Profit and Loss:* Dr Wages 560, Rent 295, General 260, Provision for bad debts 10, Depreciation 35, Underprovision for depreciation in past years 20, Net profit 1,078, Cr Gross profit 2,206, Rent received 52.
Balance Sheet—Capital 3,880, *add* Net profit 1,078, *add* Cash introduced 150, *less* Drawings (cash and goods 676, Income Tax 275), 4,157. Liabilities: Creditors 1,060. Assets: Fixtures 700 *less* depreciation 35, Stock 900, Debtors (net) 1,492, Bank 2,135, Cash 25.

18.7 (*a*) Rate of turnover 12 (*b*) 25 per cent
The rate of turnover must increase by 4 to 16.

18.8 (*a*) 33,604 (*c*) 25,972 (*e*) 24 per cent.
(*b*) 25,536 (*d*) 16
Trading Account: Stock 1,378 *add* Purchases 25,972, *less* Stock 1,814, Gross profit 8,068. Sales 33,984 *less* Returns 380.

18.9 *Trading:* Dr Stock 3,488 *add* Purchases 1,600, *less* Stock 3,300, Gross profit 596, Cr Sales 2,400 *less* Returns 16.

19.1 *I & E A/c*—Dr Prizes 22, Rent 93, Rates 30, Printing 20, Stationery 22, Postages 19, Secretary's expenses 14, Repairs 27, Wages 120, Refreshments 51, Surplus 95. Cr Subscriptions 240, Dance profits 148, Football match collections 25, Competition fees 18, Sale of refreshments 82. *Balance Sheet*—Capital 70 *add* Surplus 95, 165. Liabilities: Printing owing 4. Assets: Equipment 20, Rent prepaid 12, Bank 137. Totals: 169.

19.2 *I & E A/c*—Dr Catering 95, Band fees 25, Repairs (tennis nets) 19, Tennis balls 42, Match expenses 17, Repairs (to club house) 65, Depreciation (of equipment) 18, Surplus 48. Crs Profit on lawn mower 5, Sale tennis balls 15, Dances and socials 139, Locker rents 10, Subscriptions 160.
Balance Sheet Capital: 1,114 *add* Surplus 48, 1,162, Creditors (for tennis balls) 11. Assets: Club-house 1,000, Equipment 120 *less* Depreciation 18, Debtors 4, Bank 67. Totals: 1,173.

19.3 *I & E A/c*—Dr Rent 72, Wages 340, Secretary's expenses 59, Depreciation (equipment) 30, (furniture) 60, Surplus 257. Cr Refreshment profit 180, Dance profit 53, Subscriptions 560, Interest 25.
Balance Sheet—Capital: 4,160 *add* Surplus 257. Liabilities: Wages owing 15, Next year's subscription 22. Assets: Premises 3,000, Furniture 460 *less* Depreciation 60, Equipment 300, Investments 700, Bank 54. Totals: 4,454.

19.4 Dr Arrear b/f 87, I & E A/c, 1,143, In advance c/d 108, Crs in advance b/f 71, Cash 1,214, Arrears c/d 53.

19.5 *I & E A/c:* Dr Wages 669, Salary 156, Car allowance 25, Rent & Rates 370, Lighting 385, Printing 300, Depreciation 240, Surplus 288.
Cr Entrance fees 160, Subscriptions 1,781, Bar profits (Takings 2,840 *less* Cost of sales 2,520 *less* Steward's bonus 22) 298, Competition receipts 382, *less* Cost of prizes 200, B.S. Interest 12.
Balance Sheet—Capital: 2,517 *add* Surplus 288. Liabilities: Subscriptions in advance 20, Bar purchases owing 280, Car allowance 25, Loan 4, Steward's

commission 22. Assets: Furniture 2,400 *less* Depreciation 240, B.S. Deposit 400, Bar stocks 150, Stock prizes 25, Rent prepaid 65, Subscriptions due 50, B.S. Interest due 12, Bank 294. Balance sheet totals: 3,156.

20.1 *Manufacturing:* Dr Stock R.M. 6,300, Purchases 22,000, Carriage In 880, *less* Stock R.M. 5,080, Wages 22,000, Prime cost 46,100, O/H Expenses rent $\frac{3}{4}$ 750, Gas $\frac{3}{4}$ 1,350, Depreciation 1,800, +W. in P. 8,000, −W. in P. 18,000.
Cr Production cost c/d 40,000. *Trading:* Dr Stock F.G. 6,000, *add* Production cost 40,000, *less* Stock F.G. 5,000, Gross profit 32,600. Cr Sales 73,600, *Profit and Loss:* Dr Rent $\frac{1}{4}$ 250, Gas $\frac{1}{4}$ 450, Salaries 2,300, Net profit 29,600. Cr Gross profit b/d 32,600.

$$\text{Production cost 1 article} = \frac{40{,}000}{100{,}000} = \text{£}0{\cdot}40.$$

20.2 *Manufacturing:* Dr Stock 2,462, Purchases 31,318, *less* Stock 3,015, Wages 45,294, Prime cost 76,059, O/H Expenses factory 12,347, Power 2,825, Depreciation 4,200, *less* Increase in W. in P. 640. Cr Production cost c/d 94,791. *Trading:* Dr Production cost b/d 94,791 *add* Decrease in stock 1,716, Gross profit 31,143. Cr Sales 127,650. *Profit and Loss:* Dr Office 3,943, Advertisements 500, Salesmen 5,035, Delivery 1,268, Depreciation (delivery) 1,575, Net Profit 18,822.

20.3 *Manufacturing:* Stock R.M. 7,102, Purchases 49,944—Stock 7,064, Wages 10,054, Prime cost 60,036, O/H Expenses light 1,445, Sundry 530, Rent 150, Depreciation plant 500. Cr Production cost c/d 62,661. *Trading:* Dr Stock F.G. 7,278, Production cost b/d 62,661,—Stock F.G. 7,448, Gross profit 9,089. Cr Sales 71,580. *Profit and Loss:* Dr Light 138, Salaries 2,116, Advertisements 808, Sundry 399, Commission 880, Rent 69, B.D. Provision 303, Depreciation office machinery 100, Net profit 4,276.
Balance Sheet—Capital: 19,150 *add* Net profit 4,276 *less* Drawings 1,600, 21,826. Liabilities: Loan 5,600, Creditors 7,733, Wages owing 136. Assets: Premises 4,050, Plant 10,000 *less* Depreciation 3,000, Office machinery 1,000 *less* 600, Stocks F.G. 7,448, Raw materials 7,064, Debtors 7,575 *less* Provision 303, Prepaid 48, Cash and bank 2,013. Totals: 35,295.

20.8 Gross Pay 60; Income Tax 8; National Insurance 3; Net Pay 49.

20.9 Gross Pay 140; Income Tax 30; National Insurance 7; Net Pay 103.

20.10 Gross Pay 800; Income Tax 210; National Insurance 25; Net Pay 565.

20.11 Gross Pay 700; Super 70; National Insurance 30; Income Tax 225.

21.1 *Appropriation A/c:* Dr Salary High 800, Interest on capitals Low 375, High 350, Broad 325. Balance of profits Low 1,754, High 1,754, Broad 877. Cr Net profit 6,200, Int on drawings Low 15, High 10, Broad 10.
Capital A/cs: Low Dr Cash 1,000, Cr Balance b/f 8,000, High Cr Balance b/f 7,000, Broad Cr Bal b/f 6,000, Cash 1,000.
Current A/cs: Low, Dr Interest on drawings 15, Cash drawings 1,200, Balance c/d 1,554; Cr Bal b/f 640, Interest on Capital 375, Share profit 1,754: High; Dr Interest on drawings 10, Cash drawings 800, Bal c/d 2,654, Cr Bal b/f 560, Interest on Capital 350, Salary 800, Share profit 1,754:

Broad, Dr Interest on drawings 10, Cash drawings 800, Bal c/f 872, Cr Bal b/f 480, Interest on Capital 325, Share of profit 877.

21.2 *Appropriation A/c:* Dr Interest on Capital Ford 78, Morris 60, Profits shared Ford 700, Morris 700; Cr Net profit 1,538.
Balance Sheet: Capitals Ford 2,600, Morris 2,000, Current A/cs: Ford—Interest on Capital 78 *add* Profit 700 *less* Dr balance 750, 28. Morris—Interest on Capital 60 *add* Profit 700 *less* Dr balance 750, 10 *Liabilities* creditors 2,496, Expense creditors 40, *assets* Furniture 285, Motors 2,160, Stock 3,127, Debtors 510, Prepaid 16, Bank and cash 1,076. Totals: 7,174.

21.3 *Trading:* Dr Stock 3,600, Purchases 25,700, *less* Stock 4,100, Gross Profit 13,410; Cr Sales 38,610. *Profit and Loss:* Dr Wages 4,140, Motor expenses 1,480, Rates 964, General 1,994, Depreciation (motors) 315, Land 102, Net profit 4,440; Cr gross profit 13,410, reduction in Provision for bad debts 25. Appropriation Dr Profit J.C. 2,664, L.C. 1,776.
Balance Sheet: Capital J.C. 5,000 L.C. 3,000, Current a/c J.C. Profit 2,664 *less* Drawings 800, 1,864, L.C. Profit 1,776 *less* Drawings 600, 1,176. Current liabilities—creditors 3,670. Assets—Land 5,100 *less* 102, Motors 1,260 *less* 315, Stock 4,100, Debtors 3,960 *less* Provision 75, Cash and bank 782. Totals: 14,710.

21.4 *Trading:* Dr Stock 3,500, Purchases 16,000 *less* Returns 60, *less* Stock 2,800, Gross profit 11,220, Cr Sales 28,000 less Returns 80. *Profit and Loss:* Dr Wages 3,000, Salaries 1,400, Rates 400, Insurance 140, Bad debts 50, Provision 550, Carriage out 40, Discounts allowed 100, Office 110, Depreciation 450, Net profit 5,000. Cr Gross profit 11,220, Discounts received 20. Appropriation Dr Interest on Capital J. 300, W. 300, Salary J. 500, Profits J. 1,950, W. 1,950; Cr Net profit 5,000.
Balance Sheet—Capitals J. 6,000, W. 6,000, Current A/cs J. Share Profit 1,950, Interest on Capital 300, Salary 500, *less* Drawings 800, *less* Dr Balance 100, 1,850, W. Cr Balance 150 *add* Profit 1,950 *add* Interest on Capital 300, *less* Drawings 900, 1,500. Liabilities: Creditors 5,000, Expenses owing 400. Assets: Premises 6,000, Fixtures 4,500 *less* 450, Stock 2,800, Debtors 8,000 *less* Provision 800, Cash and bank 700. Totals: 20,750.

21.5 *Trading:* Dr Stock 2,395, *add* Purchases 19,463 *less* Returns out 286 *less* Goods own use 75, Carriage In 216, *less* Closing stock 5,623, Gross profit 12,597. Cr Sales 28,797 *less* Returns in 110. *Profit and Loss*: Dr Wages 4,389, Rent 542, Insurance 104, Delivery 309, Motor 635, General 204, Loan interest 140, Discounts 392, Depreciation (motors) 187, Bad debts provision 320, Net profit 5,779. Cr Gross profit 12,597, Discounts 404. Appropriation A/c Dr Salary H 300, Interest on Capital P 450, H 240, Balance of profits P 2,932, H 1,954. Cr Net profit 5,779, Interest on drawings P 58, H 39.
Balance Sheet—Capitals: P 9,000, H 4,800, Current A/cs P balance 880 *add* Profit 2,932 *add* Interest on Capital 450, *less* Interest on drawings 58 and drawings 1,825, 2,379, H Profit 1,954 *add* Interest on Capital 240, *less* Dr balance 120 and interest on drawings 39 and drawings 1,429, 606. Liabilities: Loan 2,000, Rates owing 57, Trade creditors 1,899, Loan interest owing 140. Assets: Premises 10,000, Motors 1,870 *less* 187, Stock 5,623, Debtors 3,462 *less* Provision 320, Prepaid 12, Bank 241, Cash 180. Totals: 20,881.

22.1 (*a*) Wright—Dr Sales 800, Bill dishonoured 800, Noting 1, Sundry receipts 5, Cr Bill receivable 800, Returns 40, Bill receivable 766.
Bills receivable—Dr Wright 800 and 766, Cr Cash 800 and 766.
Cash Book—Dr Bills receivable 800 and 766, Cr Discounting charges 10, Bill dishonoured 800, Noting 1.
Discounting charges—Dr 10.
Sundry receipts Cr 5.

(*b*) Acre—Dr Bill payable 800 and 766, Returns 40, Cr Purchases 800, Bill payable (dishonoured) 800, Noting 1, Sundry charges 5.
Bills payable—Dr Acre 800, Cash 766, Cr Acre 800 and 766.
Sundry expenses Dr 5.
Noting charges Dr 1.

22.2 T. Glue—Dr Cash 120, Bill payable 100, Bill receivable 30, Cash 60, Bill payable 40, Cr Goods 250, Bill payable withdrawn 100.
C. Smith—Dr Cash 40, Balance c/d 30, Cr Goods 70.
P. Bacon—Dr Goods 120, Bill dishonoured 120, Cr Bill receivable 120, Returns 40, Balance c/d 80.
F. Webb—Dr Goods 50, Balance c/d 15, Cr Cash 20, Bill received 30, Returns 15.
Bills receivable—Dr Bacon 120, Webb 30, Cr Cash 120, T. Glue 30.
Bills payable—Dr Glue 100, Balance c/d 40, Cr Glue 100 and 40.

22.3 A.B.—Dr Balance b/f 320, Bank 320, Cr Bill Received 320, Bank 120, Bad debts 200.
Bills receivable—Dr AB 320, Cr Bank 320.
Bank—Dr Bill receivable 320, AB 120, Cr Discounting charges 4, AB (discounted bill) 320.
Discounting Charges—Dr Bank 4.
Bad Debts—Dr AB 200.

22.4 *Creditors Control*—Dr Returns out 528, Allowances 89, Cash 9,325, Discount received 183, Contra 22, Balance c/d 2,524, Cr Balance b/f 3,282, Purchases 9,389.
Debtors Control—Dr Balance b/f 8,884, Sales 10,322, Bad debts recovered 18, Bill received, dishonoured 33, Interest 3, Dishonoured cheque 98, Discount cancelled 2, Balance c/d 27. Cr Returns In 280, Allowances 23, Bills received 392, Bad debts 254, Cash received 9,873, Discount allowed 89, Contra 22, Balance c/d 8,454.

22.5 *Sales Ledger Control*—Dr Balances c/f 3,276, Bad debts recouped 56, Sales 48,814, Balances c/d 83, Cr Cash 43,664, Returns in 627, Discount allowed 1,231, Bills accepted 1,875, Set-offs 124, Balances c/d 4,708. (Workings to calculate figure for Sales Control—Balance b/f 350+Bills accepted? = Cash 1,725+Balance c/d 500. Therefore difference is 1,875.)
Purchases Ledger Control—Dr Returns out 249, Discount received 942, Cash 34,480, Set-offs 124, Balances c/d (difference) 3,140, Cr Balances b/f 2,819, Purchases 36,116.

23.1 (*a*) Goodwill Dr 6,000, Capitals Cr X 3,000, Y 3,000. Cash Dr 7,000, Capital Z 7,000.

(*b*) *Balance Sheet*—Assets: Goodwill 6,000, Fixed and Current 15,000,

Cash 9,000. Balance Sheet totals 30,000. Capitals—X 11,000, Y 7,000, Z 7,000, Current Liabilities 5,000.

(*c*) Capitals Dr X 2,400, Y 1,800, Z 1,800, Goodwill Cr 6,000. Workings—Old goodwill X half 3,000, Y half 3,000, New goodwill X 2,400, Y 1,800, Z 1,800.

23.2 *Capital Account*—Wacks Cr Balance b/f 3,000, Adjustment for goodwill 4,500, Dr Balance c/d 7,500, Rouse Cr Balance b/f 5,000, Adjustment for goodwill 1,200, Dr Balance c/d 6,200. Patterson Cr Balance b/f 4,000, Dr Adjustment for goodwill 1,200, Balance c/d 2,800. Pickering Cr Cash 3,000, Dr Adjustment for goodwill 3,000. Tinker Cr Balance c/d 1,500, Dr Balance c/d 1,500.

24.1 *Revaluation*—Dr Plant 4,000, Equipment 600, Profit H one-half 13,800, V one-third 9,200, D one-sixth 4,600, Cr Premises 21,000, Goodwill 11,200. *Balance Sheet*—Capitals H 27,800, V 43,200, D 18,600, Creditors 6,400, Total 96,000, Goodwill 11,200, Premises 42,000, Plant 28,000, Equipment 3,600, Debtors 5,400, Bank 5,800, Total 96,000.

24.2 *Revaluation*—Dr Plant 1,500, Provision for bad debts 200, Staff pensions 2,000, Stock 600, Provision for professional charges 120, Capitals—B one-half 915, R one-third 610, L one-sixth 305, Cr Premises 6,000, Creditors 250.

Birch Loan—Dr Bank 2,500, Balance c/f to remain on loan 16,515, to be repaid 960, Cr Balance b/f 2,500, Capital—Balance transferred 16,515, Current account—Balance transferred 960.

Balance Sheet—Capitals R 4,210, L 2,105, Current Accounts R 840, L 560, Loan B 16,515, Provision for staff pensions 5,000, Creditors 4,670, B 960, Total 34,860. Premises 12,000, Plant 7,900, Stock 4,000. Debtors 6,200 *less* Provision 800, Bank 5,560.

Workings—Goodwill: 6,520+8,420+(7,210 *add* Provision written back 250 *less* Increase provision bad debts 200 also stock written off 600) 6,660 = 21,600. Average profits 7,200.

Capitals—Dr Goodwill contra ratio 2:1 R 4,800, L 2,400, Loan balance transferred B 16,515, Balances c/d R 4,210, L 2,105. Cr balances per draft Balance Sheet B 12,000, R 6,000, L 3,000, Revaluation B 915, R 610, L 305, Goodwill ratios 3:2:1, per contra B 3,600, R 2,400, L 1,200.

24.3 *Capitals:* B, W and G—Dr Goodwill contra W 2,667, G 1,333, Transfer to B Loan B 12,560, Balances transferred to new firm W 3,893, G 2,947, Cr Balances b/f B 8,000, W 6,000, G 4,000, Share goodwill contra B 4,000, Profit on revaluation B, 560, W 560, G 280.

Capitals: W, G and F—Dr Goodwill contra W 7,000, G 3,500, F 3,500, Transfers to Current Accounts G 280, F 1,060, Balances c/d W 5,000, G 2,500, F 2,500, Credits—Balances transferred old firm W 3,893, G 2,947, Net assets intro (see workings) F 3,060, Goodwill (contra) W 6,667, G 3,333, F 4,000, Transferred to Current W 1,440.

Balance Sheet—Capital W 5,000, G 2,500, F 2,500, Current Accounts W (debit) 1,440, G (credit) 280, F (credit) 1,060, leaving net deficit of 100 on Current Accounts, B Loan 12,560, Creditors 11,000, Total 33,460.

Premises 8,000, Plant 6,100, Stocks 8,500, Debtors 11,000 *less* Provision 1,040, Bank 900, Total 33,460.

Workings (*a*) Profit on revaluation—Increase premises 2,000 *less* Decrease plant 400 Provision bad debts 200 = 1,400; (*b*) Net assets intro by F 3,000 *add* Increase plant and motors 500, *less* Increase provision bad debts 440 = 3,060.

24.4 (*a*) *Trading:* Dr Stock 4,100, Purchases (15,800 *less* D drawings 100) 15,700, *less* Stock 4,200, Gross profit C and D (one-fifth) 1,280,C, D and E (four-fifths) 5,120, Cr Sales 22,000.

(*b*) *Profit and Loss*—C and D Dr General expenses 280, Depreciation 200, Net profit 800, Cr Gross profit b/d 1,280.
Profit and Loss—C, D and E Dr General expenses 840, Depreciation 600, Net profit 3,680, Cr Gross profit 5,120.
Appropriation C and D—Dr Salary D 300, Balance profits C 300, D 200, Cr Net Profit b/d 800.
C, D and E Dr Sales D 900, E 600, Interest on Capital C 225, D 150, E 75, Balance profits C 692, D 692, E 346, Cr Gross profit 3,680.

(*c*) *Current D*—Dr Goods own use 100, Drawings 1,900, Balance c/d 1,042, Cr Balance b/f 80, Salary period (1) 300, period (2) 900, Interest 150, Profits (1) 200, (2) 692, Omit last year's salary 720.

24.5 (*a*) *Realization*—Dr Buildings, etc., 8,400, Investments 3,200, Stock 4,000, Debtors/Discounts/Bad debts 200, Costs 150, Profit on realization F three-fifths 4,890, Y two-fifths 3,260.
Cr M Ltd Purchase consideration 20,000, Investments 2,800, Capitals—F Motor 850, Y Motor 350, Discounts on creditors 100.

(*b*) *Bank*—Dr M Ltd 11,000, Investments 2,800, Debtors 3,300, Cr Balance b/f (overdraft) 1,596, Creditors 2,400, Costs 150, Capitals F 8,636, Y 4,318.

(*c*) *Capitals*—Dr Realization—motors F 850, Y 350, Balances c/d F 14,636, Y 7,318, Cr Balances b/f F 7,516, Y 4,408, Loan F 3,080, Profit on realization F 4,890, Y 3,260.
Then after balanced off—
Dr M Ltd F (14,000 shares) 6,000, Y (7,000 shares) 3,000, Bank F 8,636, Y 4,318, Balances b/d F 14,636, Y 7,318.

24.6 *Realization*—Dr Debtors 2,440, Stock 3,000, Investments 3,164, Plant 5,704, Buildings 2,932, Cr Investments 1,720, Debtors 2,112, Saunders stock, etc., 10,200, Discounts received 100, Loss shared S three-sixths 1,554, T two-sixths 1,036, B one-sixth 518.
Capitals—Saunders: Dr Assets taken 10,200, Share of loss 1,554, Share of B's deficiency 112, Cr Balance b/f 9,200, Current 860, Cash paid in 1,806.
Thomas—Share of Loss 1,036, Share B's deficiency 56, Cash to settle 4,028, Cr Balance b/f 4,600, Current 520.
Baker—Dr Current 1,950, Share of loss 518, Cr Balance b/f 2,300, Deficiency shared (per Garner *v.* Murray) S two-thirds 112, T one-third 56.
Bank—Balance b/f 1,790, Investments 1,720, Debtors 2,112, Capital S 1,806, Cr Creditors 3,400, Capital T 4,028.

24.7 *Realization*—Dr Goodwill 3,000, Premises 10,000, Fixtures 1,500, Stock 3,240, Debtors (net) 2,200, Costs 360, Cr Cash—Premises 10,000, Fittings 250, Stock 2,400, Debtors 2,130, Loss A three-eighths 2,070, B three-eighths 2,070, Z one-quarter 1,380.
Capitals (A) Dr Loss on realization 2,070, Share Z deficiency 330, Bank to settle 3,800, Cr Balance b/f 6,000, Current 200.

(B) Dr Loss on realization 2,070, Share Z deficiency 220, Bank to clear 2,010, Cr Balance b/f 4,000, Current 300.
(Z) Dr Current 170, Loss on realization 1,380, Cr Balance b/f 1,000, Deficiency shared A six-tenths 330, B four-tenths 220.
Bank—Dr Premises 10,000, Fittings 250, Stock 2,400, Debtors 2,130, Cash banked 10, Cr Balance b/f 3,800, Costs 360, Creditors 4,820, Capitals (A) 3,800, (B) 2,010.
Cash—Dr Balance b/f 10, Cr Banked 10.

25.1 *Trading*—Sales A 15,000, B 10,000, C 25,000, *less* Cost of sales calculated stock 1 April 19–5. A 250, B 200, C 450, *add* Purchases A 11,800, B 8,200, C 20,000, *less* Stock 31 March 19–6 A 300, B 150, C 450 = A 11,750, B 8,250, C 20,000, Gross profits A 3,250, B 1,750, C 5,000. Wages (actual) A 1,000, B 750, C 1,750, News Del wages (actual) A 150, B —, C 150, General office salaries (Turnover) A 450, B 300, C 750, Rates (floor area) A 26, B 104, C 130, Fire insurance (area) A 10, B 40, C 50, Lighting (area) A 24, B 96, C 120, Repairs (area) A 5, B 20, C 25, Telephone (area) A 5, B 20, C 25, Cleaning (area) A 6, B 24, C 30, Accountancy (turnover) A 72, B 48, C 120, General office expenses (turnover) A 36, B 24, C 60, Net profits A 1,466, B 324, C 1,790.

25.2 *Trading*—Stocks 1 September 19–1. (5) 5,000, (8) 4,400, (9) 6,000. *Add* Purchases (5) 5,700, (8) 5,000, (9) 6,000, *less* estimated stock 31 December 19–1. (5) 4,200, (8) 5,800, (9) 3,900, Gross profits (5) 3,500, (8) 1,800, (9) 2,700, Sales (5) 10,000, (8) 5,400, (9) 10,800, Profit and Loss—Dr Direct expenses (turnover) (5), 1,710, (8) 850, (9) 1,280, Indirect expenses (5) 600, (8) 324, (9) 648, Stock reserves (5) 504, (8) 696, (9) 468, Net profit (5) 686, (9) 304, Cr Gross profit (5) 3,500, (8) 1,800, (9) 2,700, Net loss (8) 70 (assumed no stock reserves on opening stock).

26.1 *Charles Books*—J.V. Account: Dr Cash: 3 cars 900, Repairs 60, Profit 237, Balance c/d 403, Cr Sales 1,600, After balancing down Dr Cash 403, Cr Balance b/d 403.
Jones Books—J.V. Account: Dr Rent 20, Adverts 10, Licence 36, Vehicle 100, Profit 237, Cr Balance c/d 403, After balanced down Dr Balance b/d 403, Cr Cash 403.

26.2 (*a*) *J.V. Account*—Dr T. Purchases 2,000, T Repairs 248, T Drivers wages 24, T Insurance 36, T Discounts Allowed 56, Creditors—purchases 5,000, Bills receivable—Reduction in Book value 32, Profit—Own 690, Turner 414, Cr T Sales, 2,800, Bank—Sales 3,600, Bills receivable sale 1,350, T Vehicle taken over 750.
(*b*) *Turner*—Dr Sale 2,800, Vehicle taken over 750, Cr Purchases 2,000, Repairs 248, Wages 24, Insurance 36, Discounts allowed 56, Share profit 414, Bank 772.

26.3 *Plant Books—J.V. Account:* Dr Rent 156, Labour planting 105, Fertilizing 36, Sundries 10, Labour 18, Fertilizer 29, Profit 266, Cr Balance c/d 620, after balancing down Dr Balance b/d 620, Cr Cash 620.
Hoe Books—J.V. Account: Dr Seeds 48, Motor expenses 17, Share profit 114, Cr Balance c/d 179, after balancing down Dr Balance b/d 179, Cr Cash 179.
Reap Books—J.V. Account: Dr Lifting 73, Sale expenses 39, Share profit

76, Balance c/d 799, Cr Sale proceeds 987, after balancing down Dr Cash (Plant) 620, (Hoe) 179, Cr Balance b/d 799.

Memo J.V. Account—Cr Sale proceeds 987, Dr Rent 156, Labour—Planting 105, Fertilizing 36, Sundry 18, Lifting 73, Fertilizer 29, Motor 17, Seeds 48, Sale expenses 39, Sundries 10, Profit Hoe 114, Plant 266, Reap 76.

26.4 *Consignment*—Dr Goods 3,000, Carriage 147, Insurance 93, Freight 240, Port charges 186 (total 3,666) Commission M.B. 175, Profit 270, Cr Sales 3,500, Stock c/d $\frac{20}{120}$ of 3,666 = 611.
M.B. Dr Sales 3,500, Cr Freight 240, Port charges 186, Commission 175, Bank 2,899.

26.5 (*a*) *Consignment*—Dr Goods 3,000, Carriage 75, Landing 30, Commission 159, Net profit 628, Cr Sales 2,650, Stock (40 × £30 = 1,200+4/10ths of 105 = 42) 1,242.
Lintang & Co—Dr Consignment 2,650, Cr Bill receivable 2,000, Landing 30, Commission 159, Bank 461.
Bills Receivable—Dr 2,000, Cr Bank 2,000.
Bank—Dr Bill receivable 2,000, Lintang 461, Cr Discount charges 20, Carriage 75.
Discounting charges—Dr 20.

(*b*) Hope & Sons—Dr Bill pay 2,000, Landing 30, Commission 159, Bank 461, Cr Debtors 2,650.
Bills Payable—Dr Bank 2,000, Cr Hope 2,000.
Bank—Cr Bill payable 2,000, Hope and Sons 461.
Commission—Cr Hope 159.

27.1 *Balance Sheet*—Authorized Capital (as note only—not included in balance sheet totals) Preference 20,000, Ordinary 180,000, Issued: Preference 20,000, Ordinary 75,000, Revenue Reserves 30,000. Assets: Fixed 90,000 *less* 20,250, current 62,750 *less* current liabilities 7,500 to give net current assets 55,250. Totals: 125,000.

27.2 Authorized Capital (note only) 30,000, Issued 200,000 Revenue 15,000 *Profit and Loss:* 1,500: Current liabilities: 3,500, Assets: Fixed 185,000, *less* 79,000, Current 114,000. Totals: 220,000.

27.3 *Trading:* Dr Stock 9,500, Purchases (92,000−725), *less* Stock 9,000, Gross profit 39,950. Cr Sales (132,025 *less* 300). *Profit and Loss:* Dr Wages 15,312, Motor 1,481, Rates 527, General 6,984, Loss van 40, Depreciation van 990, Directors fees 4,500, Net profit 10,116, Appropriation A/c Dividend 4,000, Balance c/f 14,616. Cr Net profit 10,116, Balance b/f 8,500.
Balance Sheet—Capital: 40,000, Profit and Loss 14,616. *Liabilities:* Trade 13,970, Dividend 4,000. Assets: Land 37,000, Motors 4,950 *less* 3,315, Stock 9,000, Debtors 12,318, Insurance Co 725, Prepaid 112, Bank 11,750, Cash 46, Totals: 72,586.

27.4 Trading: Dr Stock 25,689; Add Purchases 201,698; *less* Stock 29,142; Gross Profit 118,565; Cr Sales 316,810; Profit and Loss Dr Wages 54,788; Rent and Rates 4,000; Lighting and Heating 1,549; Bad Debts 748+77 = 825; General 32,168; Depreciation 5,500; Net Profit 19,735; Cr Gross Profit 118,565; Appropriation A/c Dr b/d 19,735; Balance from last year 34,280.

Balance Sheet—Capital 100,000; Profit and Loss 44,015; Liabilities: Proposed dividend 10,000; Creditors 17,493; Expenses owing 28,074; Fixed Assets—Premises 65,000; Machinery 55,000 *less* depreciation 21,784; Current Assets; Stock 29,142; Debtors 21,784 *less* Provision 938; Prepayments 300; Bank 23,101. Totals 172,089.

Full Paper I

Kandy Stores

Balance Sheet as at 31 December 19–5

		£			£
Capital		£	*Fixed Assets*		£
Balance as at 1.1.19–5		20,000	Freehold Premises		12,000
Add Net Profit for the year		7,364	Furniture and Fittings		2,500
			Motor Vehicles		4,960
		27,364			
Less Drawings		3,000			19,460
		24,364			
Current Liabilities			*Current Assets*		
Trade Creditors	5,140		Stock-in-Trade	4,656	
Accrued Expenses	240		Trade Debtors	6,420	
Bank Overdraft	1,500	6,880	Prepaid Expenses	460	
			Cash	248	11,784
		31,244			31,244

2. (a) J. Coral: Cash Book (Bank Columns)

19–6		£	19–6		£
Apr 30	Balance b/f	390	Apr 30	Bank Charges	25
„ 30	S. King	48	„ 30	Balance c/f	413
		438			438

(b) **J. Coral**

Bank Reconciliation Statement as on 30 April 19–6

	£
Balance in hand per cash book	413
Add unpresented cheques (£21+£42)	63
	476
Less Bank Lodgement not entered on bank statement	62
Balance in hand as per bank statement	414

3. **S. Drive**

Trading & Profit & Loss Accounts for the year ended 31 December 19–5

	£	£		£	£
Purchases	15,750		Sales	20,500	
Less Returns Outwards	278	15,472	*Less* Returns Inwards	456	20,044
Carriage Inwards		84			
		15,556			
Less Closing Stock		4,750			
Cost of Goods Sold		10,806			
Gross Profit c/d		9,238			
		20,044			20,044
Wages		2,500	Gross Profit b/d		9,238
Rent and Rates (725−70)		655	Discount Received		140
Office Expenses		470			
Motor Van Expenses		320			
Advertising		240			
Insurance (125+20)		145			
Heat and Light		75			
Interest on Loan		60			
Discount Allowed		210			
Provision for Doubtful Debts		100			
Depreciation: Motor Van		300			
Net Profit for the year		4,303			
		9,378			9,378

4. **Petty Cash Book**

Receipts	*Date*	*Details*	*Total*	*Travelling*	*Office Expenses*	*Postages & Stationery*	*Ledger Accounts*
£	19–6		£	£	£	£	£
100	Feb. 2	Cash					
	,, 5	Document Folders	6			6	
	,, 6	S. Haines	15				15
	,, 6	Office Cleaner	5		5		
	,, 9	Petrol	5	5			
	,, 9	Postages	3			3	
	,, 10	Fares	1	1			
	,, 10	Desk Calendar	2		2		
	,, 13	Office Cleaner	5		5		
	,, 20	Postages	2			2	
	,, 20	Fares	3	3			
	,, 24	Biros and Pencils	3		3		

Receipts	Date	Details	Total	Travelling	Office Expenses	Postages & Stationery	Ledger Accounts
£	19–6		£	£	£	£	£
	„ 27	H. Carter	12				12
	„ 27	Office Cleaner	5		5		
67	„ 27	Cash					
	„ 27	Balance c/d	100				
167			167	9	20	11	27

5. (a) credit — Purchases Returns
   (b) debit — Discount Payable
   (c) credit — credit
   (d) debit — credit
   (e) working capital

6.

Item	Effect on Capital	Effect on Working Capital
(a)	No effect	No effect
(b)	+	+
(c)	–	No effect
(d)	–	–
(e)	–	+

7. **The Journal**

		Dr	Cr
		£	£
(a)	Drawings	800	
	Wages		560
	Materials		240
	Correction of error whereby business expense accounts were debited with private expenditure		
(b)	A. H. Clark	84	
	H. Clarkson		84
	Correction of error whereby payment was entered in wrong account		
(c)	Office Machinery	300	
	Purchases		300
	Correction of error whereby a fixed asset had been charged to an expense account		

Full Paper II

1. (a)

A Sole Trader

Calculation of correct Net Profit for the year ending 31 October 19–6

		£
Net Profit per balance sheet		1,380
Add Discount Received		80
		1,460
Less: Bad Debts	90	
Discounts Allowed	120	210
Correct Net Profit		1,250

(b) The balance sheet has been drafted, here in a vertical style, because the question stipulated that 'modern practice' be observed.

A Sole Trader

Balance Sheet as at 31 October 19–6

			£
Capital			
Balance as at 1.10.19–5			1,980
Add Net Profit for the year			1,250
			3,230
Less Drawings			1,160
			2,070
Represented by:			
Fixed Assets			
Office Furniture			300
Current Assets			
Stock		1,470	
Debtors		1,670	
Cash in Hand		40	
		3,180	
Less: Current liabilities			
Creditors	930		
Bank Overdraft	480	1,410	
Net Working Capital			1,770
			2,070

2. (a) Gross Profit as a percentage of sales

$$= \frac{2{,}200}{11{,}000} \times \frac{100}{1} = 20\%$$

(b) A Trading Account for the period 1.1.19–6 to 15.4.19–6 should be drafted. It is known that the gross profit as per cent of sales = 20 per cent. Therefore as the Sales for the period are £3,000, the gross profit will be £3,000 × 20 per cent = £600. After that the closing stock and the Cost of Goods sold will be the figures needed to make the Trading Account Balance.

Robert
Trading Account for the period 1.1.19–6 to 15.4.19–6

	£		£
Stock 1.1.19–6	1,490	Sales	3,000
Add Purchases	2,180		
	3,670		
Less Stock 15.4.19–6	1,270		
Cost of Goods Sold	2,400		
Gross Profit (20% of 3,000)	600		
	3,000		3,000

3. (a)

Sales Control

	£		£
19–5		19–6	
Nov 1 Debtors b/fwd	920	Oct 31 Cash	4,870
19–6			
Oct 31 Sales to Trading A/c	4,980	Oct 31 Debtors c/fwd	1,030
	5,900		5,900

Purchases Control

	£		£
19–6		19–5	
Oct 31 Cash	3,130	Nov 1 Creditors b/fwd	360
Oct 31 Creditors c/fwd	440	19–6	
		Oct 31 Purchases to Trading A/c	3,210
	3,570		3,570

(b)

A Sole Trader

Trading Account for the year ended 31 October 19–6

	£		£
Opening Stock	670	Sales	4,980
Add Purchases	3,210		
	3,880		
Less Closing Stock	720		
Cost of goods sold	3,160		
Gross Profit	1,820		
	4,980		4,980

4.

George Holt

Trading & Profit & Loss Accounts for the year ended 31 October 19–6

	£		£
Opening Stock	1,970	Sales	9,620
Add Purchases	5,930		
	7,900		
Less Closing Stock	1,980		
Cost of Goods Sold	7,900		
Gross Profit c/d	1,780		
	9,620		9,620
Wages & Salaries	1,520	Gross Profit b/d	3,500
Rent, Rates & Insurance	240	Discounts Received	90
Bad Debts	110		
Discounts Allowed	130		
General Office Expenses	190		
Depreciation:			
Fixtures & Fittings	100		
Net Profit	1,300		
	3,590		3,590

Balance Sheet as at 31 October 19–6

Capital		£	*Fixed Assets*		£
Balance as at 1.11.19–5		2,700	Fixtures & Fittings as at 1.11.19–5		400
Add Net Profit for the year		1,300	*Less* Depreciation for year		100
		4,000			300
Less Drawings		1,440			
		2,560			
Current Liabilities			*Current Assets*		
Creditors	1,680		Stock	1,780	
Bank Overdraft	260	1,940	Debtors	2,350	
			Expenses prepaid	40	
			Cash in hand	30	4,200
		4,500			4,500

Comparison of Question Numbers

Old edition (2nd)	*This edition (3rd)*	*Old edition (2nd)*	*This edition (3rd)*	*Old edition (2nd)*	*This edition (3rd)*
1.1	1.1	5.1	5.1	—	9.15A
1.2	1.2	5.2	5.2	—	—
1.3	1.3	5.3	5.3	—	—
—	1.4	—	5.4	10.1	10.1
—	1.5	5.4A	5.5A	10.2	10.2
—	1.6	5.5A	5.6A	10.3	10.3
1.4A	1.7A	—	5.7A	10.4	10.4
1.5A	1.8A	6.1	6.1	10.5	10.5
1.6A	1.9A	6.2	6.2	10.6	10.6
1.7A	1.10A	6.3	6.3	10.7A	10.7A
—	1.11A	6.4	6.4	10.8A	10.8A
—	1.12A	—	6.5	10.9A	10.9A
—	1.13A	6.5	6.6	10.10A	10.10A
2.1	2.1	6.6	6.7	10.11A	10.11A
2.2	2.2	—	6.8	—	11.1
2.3	2.3	6.7A	6.9A	—	
2.4	2.4	6.8A	6.10A	—	11.2
2.5	2.5	6.9A	6.11A	—	11.3
—	2.6	6.10A	6.12A	—	11.4
2.6A	2.7A	—	6.13A	—	11.5
2.7A	2.8A	—	6.14A	11.1	11.6
2.8A	2.9A	—	6.15A	11.2	11.7
—	2.10A	—	—	11.3	11.8
3.1	3.1	8.1	8.1	11.4	11.9
3.2	3.2	8.2	8.2	11.5A	11.10A
3.3	3.3	8.3	8.3	11.6A	11.11A
3.4	3.4	8.4	8.4	11.7A	11.12A
3.5	3.5	—	8.5A	11.8A	11.13A
—	3.6	—	8.6A	—	—
3.6A	3.7A	8.5A	8.7A	—	13.1
—	3.8A	8.6A	8.8A	—	13.2
3.7A	3.9A	—	8.9A	—	13.3
3.8A	3.10A	—	—	13.1	13.4
—	3.11A	9.1	9.1	13.2	13.5
—	—	9.2	9.2	13.3	13.6
—	—	9.3	9.3	13.4	13.7
4.1	4.1	9.4A	9.4A	13.5A	13.8A
4.2	4.2	9.5A	9.5A	—	13.9A
4.3	4.3	—	9.6A	13.6A	13.10A
4.4	4.4	—	9.7	13.7A	13.11A
4.5A	4.5A	—	9.8	13.8A	13.12A
4.6A	4.6A	—	9.9	—	—
4.7A	4.7A	—	9.10A	—	—
—	—	—	9.11A	14.1	14.1
—	4.8A	—	9.12A	14.2	14.2
—	4.9A	—	9.13	14.3	14.3
—	—	—	9.14	14.4A	14.4A

Old edition (2nd)	*This edition (3rd)*	*Old edition (2nd)*	*This edition (3rd)*	*Old edition (2nd)*	*This edition (3rd)*
14.5A	14.5A	—	18.19A	22.6A	22.6A
14.6A	14.6A	—	18.20A	22.7A	22.7A
—	14.7A	—	18.21A	22.8A	22.8A
—	—	—	—	—	—
15.1	15.1	19.1	19.1	23.1	23.1
15.2	15.2	19.2	19.2	23.2	23.2
15.3A	15.3A	19.3	19.3	23.3A	23.3A
—	15.4A	19.4	19.4	23.4A	23.4A
—	—	19.5	19.5	—	—
16.1	16.1	19.6A	19.6A	24.1	24.1
16.2	16.2	19.7A	19.7A	24.2	24.2
16.3	16.3	19.8A	19.8A	24.3	24.3
16.4	16.4	19.9A	19.9A	24.4	24.4
16.5	16.5	—	—	24.5	24.5
16.6	16.6	20.1	20.1	24.6	24.6
16.7	16.7	20.2	20.3	24.7	24.7
16.8A	16.8A	20.2	20.3	24.8A	24.8A
16.9A	16.9A	—	20.4A	24.9A	24.9A
16.10A	16.10A	—	—	24.10A	24.10A
16.11A	16.11A	20.4A	20.5A	—	—
17.1	17.1	20.5A	20.6A	24.11A	24.11A
17.2	17.2	20.6A	20.7A	25.1	25.1
17.3	17.3	—	20.8	25.2	25.2
17.4	17.4	—	20.9	25.3A	25.3A
17.5A	17.5A	—	20.10	25.4A	25.4A
17.6A	17.6A	—	20.11	—	25.5A
17.7A	17.7A	—	20.12A	26.1	26.1
—	17.8A	—	20.13A	26.2	26.2
18.1	18.1	—	20.14A	26.3	26.3
18.2	18.2	—	—	26.4	26.4
18.3	18.3	—	—	26.5	26.5
18.4	18.4	—	—	26.6A	26.6A
18.5	18.5	21.1	21.1	26.7A	26.7A
18.6	18.6	21.2	21.2	26.8A	26.8A
18.7	18.7	21.3	21.3	—	26.9A
18.8	18.8	21.4	21.4	—	—
18.9	18.9	21.5	21.5	27.1	27.1
18.10A	18.10A	21.6A	21.6A	27.2	27.2
18.11A	18.11A	21.7A	21.7A	27.3	27.3
18.12A	18.12A	21.8A	21.8A	—	27.4
18.13A	18.13A	21.9A	21.9A	27.4A	27.5A
18.14A	18.14A	22.1	22.1	27.5A	27.6A
18.15A	18.15A	22.2	22.2	27.6A	27.7A
18.16A	18.16A	22.3	22.3	27.7A	27.8A
18.17A	18.17A	22.4	22.4	27.8A	27.9A
18.18A	18.18A	22.5	22.5		

Index